# CAR CRAZY

# CAR CRAZY

THE BATTLE
FOR SUPREMACY
BETWEEN
FORD AND OLDS
AND THE DAWN OF
THE AUTOMOBILE AGE

---

## G. WAYNE MILLER

PUBLICAFFAIRS
New York

Published in the United States by PublicAffairs™, a Member of the Perseus Books Group

PublicAffairs books are available at special discounts for bulk purchases in the U.S. by corporations, institutions, and other organizations. For more information, please contact the Special Markets Department at the Perseus Books Group, 2300 Chestnut Street, Suite 200, Philadelphia, PA 19103, call (800) 810-4145, ext. 5000, or e-mail special.markets@perseusbooks.com.

Book Design by Trish Wilkinson
Set in 11 point Minion Pro

Library of Congress Cataloging-in-Publication Data

Miller, G. Wayne, author.
   Car crazy : the battle for supremacy between Ford and Olds and the dawn of the automobile age / G. Wayne Miller. — First edition.
      pages   cm
   Includes bibliographical references and index.
   ISBN 978-1-61039-551-9 (hardcover) — ISBN 978-1-61039-552-6 (e-book)  1. Ford, Henry, 1863–1947.  2. Ford Motor Company. 3. Ford Model T automobile—History.  4. Olds, Ransom Eli, 1864–1950. 5. General Motors Corporation. Oldsmobile Division—History. 6. Oldsmobile automobile—History.  7. Automobile industry and trade—United States—History.  8. Automobile industry and trade— United States—Management.  I. Title.
TL215.F7M53 2015
338.4'7629222097309041—dc23

                                                    2015024477

First Edition

10 9 8 7 6 5 4 3 2 1

*To my late mother-in-law, Daisy Gabrielle, a woman of great kindness, courage, and wisdom. Daisy was filled with humor and grace. Being with her was always magical.*

# Contents

# Cast of Characters

## THE CARMAKERS

**Karl Friedrich Benz**, German engineer, inventor, and manufacturer

**Roy D. Chapin**, Oldsmobile sales chief and test driver; founder of Hudson Motor Car Company

**James J. Couzens**, Ford Motor Company secretary

**William Crapo "Billy" Durant**, creator of General Motors

**Charles E. and J. Frank Duryea**, builders of the first US production car

**Henry Ford**, founder of Ford Motor Company

**Edward S. "Spider" Huff**, Ford's brilliant but bedeviled leading engineer

**Émile Levassor**, founder of French pioneer auto company Panhard et Levassor

**Alexander Y. Malcomson**, early partner of Henry Ford

**Ransom Eli Olds**, founder of Oldsmobile

**Frederic L. Smith**, secretary-treasurer of Oldsmobile

## THE DRIVERS

**Tom Cooper**, a winner on the track who died in a midnight race through Central Park

**Dwight B. Huss**, one of two men who competed in history's first race across the continent

**Webb Jay**, whose racing career ended when he crashed his steam car, "Whistling Billy"

**Ernest D. Keeler**, a young racing star who died in a crash three days after Cooper

**Percy F. Megargel**, a writer and romantic who raced Huss from Manhattan to Oregon, then made the first winter and double-continental crossing, from New York to the West Coast and back

**Barney Oldfield**, greatest race-car driver of the early era . . . and maybe ever

## THE MECHANICS

**David F. Fassett**, rode with Megargel on the winter crossing

**Barton Stanchfield**, rode with Megargel during the cross-continent race

**Milford Wigle**, rode with Huss during the cross-continent race

## THE PATENT PLAYERS

**Frederick P. Fish**, president of AT&T and lawyer for the anti-Ford side

**Charles M. Hough**, judge who decided the Selden suit

**Walter C. Noyes**, judge who decided the Selden suit on appeal

**George B. Selden**, who claimed in a US patent to have invented the automobile

**Ralzemond B. Parker**, battled-hardened lawyer hired to defend Ford in the Selden suit

## THE GOOD ROADS EVANGELISTS

**James W. Abbott**, official with the Federal Highway Administration's precursor agency

**Albert Augustus Pope**, bicycle- and carmaking magnate

**Isaac B. Potter**, editor, engineer, and lawyer

**Roy Stone**, first head of the US Office of Road Inquiry

## THE SCOUNDRELS

**Lone John,** a lunatic Wyoming shepherd

**Big Nose George Parrott,** an outlaw who met a most bizarre fate

**The Road Hog,** any of various anti-car farmers

**The ruffians,** lads, and men in New York who stoned "evil" motorists

**Edward R. Thomas,** wealthy Manhattan heir and murderous driver

# Introduction

SINCE MY FIRST CAR, an old black Ford sedan that I drove in high school, I have owned more than ten automobiles. That qualifies me as a motorist, but until this book, I was not alone in believing the US car industry essentially began with Henry Ford's Model T, introduced in 1908. I thought that iconic vehicle and a few others made by a handful of fellow manufacturers began the profound transformation of American society that has culminated in our way of life today.

The Model T indeed was revolutionary—but it wasn't first. Oldsmobile founder Ransom Eli Olds built his first car, a three-wheeled thing steered with a tiller and powered by a steam engine, in 1887. The first US vehicle intended for sale was demonstrated in 1893, in Springfield, Massachusetts. Ford drove the first automobile he made, a boxlike contraption on big bicycle tires, through the streets of Detroit in 1896. Many others in America and Europe, where the auto industry really began, were also building cars—or planning to. Then, between 1900 and 1908, more than five hundred domestic carmakers went into business. Competition was brutal. The vast majority of firms failed. And a colorful cast of characters abounded: heroes, villains, schemers, and visionaries—the people who imagined a wondrous future with the automobile. That future, as we know today, was both blessing and curse.

By the dawn of what would be called the American Century, the car was already causing unprecedented turmoil—and it intensified during that first decade of the 1900s, the period I primarily chronicle in this book. Car enthusiasts battled car-haters in courts, in legislatures, and on the roads. Farmers, spooked by the evil new machines, defended their terrified horses—sometimes with shotguns and threats of murder. Motorists ridiculed the horse as filthy and useless, and the old-fashioned farmer as ignorant. Rowdies stoned Gilded Age aristocrats as they flaunted their high-priced imports on the streets of Manhattan. The police chase, the hit-and-run, and the fatal accident became staples of a dramatic new journalistic genre.

The car wars—between one manufacturer and another; one driver and another; between pedestrian and horse and machine; between bucolic past and engine-powered future—played out in the trade journals and the general-circulation newspapers, in the countryside and in urban centers, in most states and in many cities, especially New York City, the early heart of the car market and the nation's media capital, then as now.

These battles were personified in one of the longest and most expensive lawsuits in the history of American business: the Selden patent case, which pitted Ford against the cutthroat executive Frederic L. Smith, who took over Oldsmobile in 1904. That story is a central narrative of this book.

And the car wars deeply involved the three main companies whose stories are told in *Car Crazy*: Oldsmobile, the most successful US car manufacturer of the early era; Buick, which became General Motors (GM), thanks to William C. Durant, one of the most creative and daring, if now largely forgotten, figures in automotive history; and Ford Motor Company, built by an obsessed genius who rose from humble beginnings to industry dominance and great personal wealth.

———

THE ROOTS OF *Car Crazy* lie in the season I spent following NASCAR's premiere racing series embedded in legendary Jack Roush's Ford racing team, now Roush Fenway Racing, for my 2002 book *Men and Speed*. At some point, I learned about a storied race between two automobiles from Manhattan to Portland, Oregon—in 1905.

The cars were two-seat Curved Dash vehicles, built without sides, roof, or windshield, and steered with a tiller, not a steering wheel. Their gas engines generated 7 horsepower, roughly equivalent to a lawn mower today. They had a top speed of about 20 miles per hour. Although many thoroughfares in major cities were paved, beyond them there were few hard-surfaced roads or streets in the vast American landscape these cars had traveled across, particularly in the West, and rain turned the trails and stagecoach routes to nearly impassable mud. Maps were scarce. So was gasoline.

Years later, as I began to contemplate writing this book, I wondered how this race—conducted years before I thought there even was an American car industry—had come to pass. Who were the drivers, and how did their primitive cars manage to make the distance? As I looked deeper into the competition, it became clear just how crazy the idea had been. But what also began to come into focus was a fascinating, largely untold story of the earliest years of the automobile industry, and the beginning of a technological, social, and cultural upheaval that would fundamentally change America and the lives of its people.

I hope you enjoy the ride!

*G. WAYNE MILLER*
Providence, Rhode Island

# 1

# FASTEST MAN ON EARTH

## THE 999 AND ARROW

It was a time when sane people did crazy things.

Henry Ford was one of those people.

On January 9, 1904, on the shore of frozen Anchor Bay, Lake St. Clair, some thirty miles northeast of Detroit, he vowed to be the first person to drive 100 miles per hour. The possibility that he might spin out of control and be killed as he roared across the ice did not deter him.

It did, however, attract a crowd.

Ford had deliberately scheduled his attempt for a Saturday, when kindly employers gave their workers the afternoon off. Then he'd created publicity that had filled the Detroit papers all week, mesmerizing a city that had already begun to thrum with the business of motors.

A brilliant inventor and engineer, Ford was also a skilled marketer. He knew that machine-powered speed excited many people unlike anything before—and that word of the latest spectacle sent consumers to dealers, where they could buy an automobile of their own. He knew also that cars angered and alienated other people—the horse-bound traditionalists—but with time, he believed, almost everyone would come around.

"Henry Ford of the Ford Motor Works of Detroit will attempt to lower the Worlds Record," read the handbills Ford had arranged to be posted. "The race will be over a four-mile straight track on the ice opposite The Hotel Chesterfield. The snow will be cleared from the ice and the track will be sanded. The races will start at 2 o'clock and continue until Mr. Ford lowers the world's record. He proposes to make a mile in 36 seconds."

That would greatly eclipse the existing auto record of 84.732 miles per hour, set in 1903. It conceivably would be faster than anyone had ever moved.

The claimed land speed record was 112.5 miles per hour by the crew of a locomotive on May 10, 1893, on a stretch of Cornelius Vanderbilt's mighty New York Central Railroad, but in this era so rife with tall tales, doubt existed that the train, the 999, had really traveled faster than about 90 miles per hour. Nonetheless, the train had generated international headlines—and Ford, hoping to capitalize on its enduring fame, named one of the two identical race cars that he built after it. Like that sixty-two-ton locomotive, Ford's 999 racer and its twin, Arrow—the machine that Ford had brought to frozen Lake St. Clair—were essentially monster motors on wheels, producing as much as 80 horsepower, ten or more times the power of many stock models—"built to speed, and speed alone," wrote the *Automobile and Motor Review*.

————

MANY IN THE CROWD knew about Ford, this slightly built forty-year-old man with the piercing gray eyes, prominent nose, and long, thin hands who seemed always to have a sly grin on his lips. He had been building and driving horseless carriages around Detroit since 1896, when American-built cars were little more than a dream, and had founded and then left two other companies before incorporating a third, the Ford Motor Company, on June 16, 1903.

Son of a farmer, raised on a farm outside Detroit, Ford should have been destined to till the land, like so many of his nineteenth-century peers. But even as a young child, his father's tools fascinated him more than horses or fields, and by the time he turned teenager, machines had become his obsession. At first it was unpowered machines, the watches and clocks he taught himself to take apart and repair. And then, not long after, he saw his first steam engine. The operator took the time to explain its mechanizations to the boy. And thus was Ford's true destiny revealed to him.

Many in the shivering crowd also already knew about Ford's race cars from the man who had steered several of them to national headlines: Barney Oldfield, the greatest American race car driver of the early era, a man even more daring than Ford. A champion bicyclist at age sixteen, Oldfield had never driven a motor vehicle of any kind until Ford, seeking publicity for his second attempt at an auto company, asked him to race the 999 in a competition. At the time, Ford himself was leery of driving it, except on the test track. Saying he would try anything once, Oldfield, twenty-four, agreed. Ford entered the 999 in the October 1902 Manufacturer's Challenge Cup at Detroit's Grosse Pointe Blue Ribbon Track, venerable home of harness racing, and set about acquainting Oldfield with the car's quirky features.

"It took us only a week to teach him to drive," Ford later recalled. "The man did not know what fear was. All that he had to learn was how to control the monster." Meaning specifically, how to gun it through corners without rolling over.

"The steering wheel had not yet been thought of," Ford recalled. "On this one, I put a two-handed tiller, for holding the car in line required all the strength of a strong man."

While Ford was cranking the 999 to life, Oldfield said: "Well, this chariot may kill me, but they will say afterward that I was going like hell when she took me over the bank."

He did go like hell, winning that October 1902 race against the already legendary automaker and racer Alexander Winton, who until then was thought to be invincible.

In the summer of 1903, Oldfield drove Ford's Arrow to world records at Midwest fairgrounds and then on July 25, at a track in Yonkers, New York. A few weeks later, he raced again at Grosse Pointe. He had just passed the leader when a tire exploded and Arrow plowed into a fence, killing a spectator from Ohio. Oldfield, a newspaper reported, "escaped by a miracle, as his machine was reduced to a mass of tangled iron and wood. That more people were not killed or maimed is a cause for wonder." Cocky and gifted, a man who loved women as much as machines, Oldfield would maim and kill many more before the end of his career.

As Oldfield recovered from his injuries, the repaired Arrow took the starting flag in Milwaukee a week after the luckless Ohio man's death. Promising young racer Frank Day was at the tiller. But the Arrow proved too much to manage, and he spun out. Ford's racer rolled end over end, landing "on the unfortunate chauffeur, grinding him into the ground, an unrecognizable mess," a paper reported.

For those who did not share autoists' enthusiasm—and there were many who did not, influential politicians, judges, and editorialists among them—Day's death was new cause for condemnation.

"We saw the young man who rode to his death on the day preceding the fatality," the *Wisconsin State Journal* opined. "A cleaner, fresher youth never delighted his parents' eyes. The wind tousled his abundant hair on his clear forehead as he whirled about the track; determination and en-thusiasm were in his eyes; the cheers of the impassioned mob impelled him as soldiers go to certain death under martial music."

And then, an unrecognizable mess.

"We are not wholesome enough to enjoy the triumphs of the soil and noble horses and royal-blooded cattle," the *State Journal* proclaimed. "The incident is a disgrace."

For Ford, it was a disquieting but momentary setback. Back in Michigan, he rebuilt Arrow once again. He had further use for its awesome power.

———

PURE SPEED WAS NOT the only lure for the spectators in their gloves and fur-trimmed coats at Lake St. Clair on that January day in 1904. In the first half-decade of what would be called the American Century, railroads, ships, bicycles, horses, and horse-drawn vehicles still transported most people and goods, but the country was witnessing an astonishing prolifer-ation of horseless carriage manufacturers and models. Every new entry

Barney Oldfield, left, and Ford with the 999.
From the Collections of The Henry Ford.

seemed to generate buzz. Whether you liked cars or hated them, lived in a city where they swarmed the streets or in the country where they were rarely, if ever, seen, you could hardly get through a day without talking about them.

Carmaking had started in earnest in America just a decade before, with bicycle maker Charles E. Duryea, thirty-one, in partnership with his twenty-four-year-old mechanic brother, J. Frank—the first Americans to publicly declare their intention of creating a commercial enterprise from building and selling cars, contraptions most folks at the time thought were cobbled together by men possessing more free time than common sense. In September 1893 in Springfield, Massachusetts, Frank completed construction of a vehicle that married a custom-built single-cylinder gasoline motor to a horse-drawn phaeton buggy purchased secondhand for $70.

Shortly before he road-tested the car, Frank granted an interview to the *Springfield Evening Union*, which published a story on September 16, 1893, under the headline:

## NO USE FOR HORSES
*Springfield Mechanics Devise a New Mode of Travel*
*Ingenious Wagon Being Made in This City*
*For Which the Makers Claim Great Things*

"A new motor carriage when, if the preliminary tests prove successful as expected, will revolutionize the mode of travel on highways, and do away with the horse as a means of transportation, is being made in this city," the reporter wrote. "It is quite probable that within a short period of time one may be able to see an ordinary carriage in almost every respect running along the streets or climbing country hills without visible means of propulsion."

Frank was more than a good pitchman. The car he had built with his brother's help and the support of lone financial backer Erwin F. Markham, a nurse who had invested $1,000 in the Duryeas, did indeed succeed its first time on the road. On the afternoon of September 20, the vehicle was hauled by horse from Frank's machine shop to a friend's yard on the outskirts of the city. The next morning, Frank took a streetcar out to the neighborhood. As he rode, he fantasized that "once well started on the open road, the machine would roll along sweetly for at least a mile or two. . . . With this pleasant thought in mind, I enthusiastically pushed the car from under the apple tree."

Frank started the engine and his car chugged onto Spruce Street. "America's first gasoline automobile had now appeared," he would recall. "It had done what it was designed and built to do, in that it carried the driver on the road and had been steered in the direction the driver wished to go."

The car only traveled about one hundred feet before stalling—but it restarted quickly, and each time again after successive stallings, providing sufficient encouragement for the Duryeas to continue. By March 1895, they had a smoother-operating machine that successfully completed an eighteen-mile round trip to Westfield, Massachusetts, along rough, steep, horse-ravaged roads—a feat that suggested the brothers really were onto something. On September 21, 1895, they incorporated the Duryea Motor Wagon Company.

————

"THOSE WHO HAVE TAKEN the pains to search below the surface for the great tendencies of the age know that a giant industry is struggling into being," wrote the editor of the *Horseless Age*, America's second automobile journal, in its inaugural issue, published in November 1895. "It is often said that a civilization may be measured by its facilities of Locomotion. If this is true, as seems abundantly proved by present facts and the testimony of History, the New Civilization that is rolling in with the Horseless Carriage will be Higher Civilization than the one that you enjoy."

Like the *Horseless Age*'s editor, the growing ranks of motorists saw the car as the future; along with the locomotive, the telegram, photography, and electricity, it was a technology that would move mankind valiantly forward. They envisioned a day when a motorist could comfortably drive from East Coast to West and all points between, when everyone could, and would, own a car.

This vision of the future seemed fairly delusional to the naysayers, whose numbers grew as the nineteenth century gave way to the twentieth. They viewed the gas- or steam-powered car, by whatever name, as a loud, dangerous, and polluting fiend that threatened the social fabric—an enemy of God-fearing people and noble horses. They dismissed the car, however propelled, as a fad soon to fade. Common sense alone told you it couldn't last.

In those early days, most cars were so finicky that repair kits were included as standard features and wealthy owners hired mechanics to ride with them. Many cars had no cabins, roofs, headlamps, or doors. They could explode or burst into flame for no apparent reason. "As gasoline tanks and leads sometimes leak and the fluid more rarely becomes ignited," the *Automobile*, a leading weekly, wrote, "it is a wise precaution on the part of the automobilist to carry a fire extinguisher in the car for such emergencies. Even though it may never be required, it will add something to the driver's feeling of security; and should it ever be wanted, it will, like a revolver in the West, be wanted badly."

And if the machine itself was at a primitive stage of development, the experience of motoring was cruder still. No training, registration, or licenses to drive were required in most jurisdictions. There were few stop signs and no traffic lights. Accidents that injured or killed motorists and pedestrians abounded. Only a tiny percentage of US roads were hard-surfaced. Service stations were scarce, gasoline rare in the outskirts and smaller cities, maps unreliable or nonexistent. Motorists venturing off the beaten path were advised to carry guns, for protection against wildlife, irate horse-loving citizens, and ornery constables determined to avenge the evil of the new machine.

Regardless, the car was a siren's call to inventors, entrepreneurs, and all manner of tinkerers. In America, as in Europe, a new sort of gold rush was underway.

Like the Duryeas, some of the new manufacturers had been building bicycles before falling under the spell of the self-propelled machine. Horse-drawn carriage builders also sensed opportunity, as did blacksmiths, ship builders, sewing-machine makers, and many others. Unlike the railroad, petroleum, coal, and steel industries, the cost of entry was minimal. Not even a technical background was required, at least to stake a claim: In March 1901, an industry publication reported that The Reverend H. A. Frantz of Cherryville, Pennsylvania, "believes he has received a call to the motor trade, and will henceforth make petrol cars in place of sermons."

This was an era when many car companies managed to build just a single vehicle or two a year and annual production of a few dozen was cause for hallelujah. The Duryea brothers' Duryea Motor Wagon Company, the first US firm to serially produce a car, built and sold just thirteen vehicles during its first full year of operation, 1896; sales were sporadic after that and in 1898, with Frank and Charles feuding, the company went out of business.

This was by far the most common story of the early era. According to calculations Charles Duryea made in 1909, in the years 1900 to 1908, 502

US carmakers went into business, an average of 55 a year, or more than one a week. Of that total, 273 failed, and another 29 went into some other field, a failure rate of greater than 60 percent.

————

GIVEN HIS OBSESSION WITH machines and his gift for building and improving them, Henry Ford seemed to have decent odds for enduring success. His business record, however, suggested he had much to learn. Two previous companies he'd started had failed, and rival firms—particularly industry leader Olds Motor Works, whose founder, Ransom Eli Olds, was also greatly mechanically gifted—were already building devoted followings. Ford needed more than just a good car to succeed. In this frenzied period, so intense with competition, he needed attention. Speed records and racing got attention.

————

THE WINTER SUN SHONE weakly, bringing no warmth to the people lining the shore near the front porch of the Hotel Chesterfield. Among them were Ford's wife, Clara, and the couple's only child, their ten-year-old son, Edsel.

The Chesterfield, since it first opened in 1900, was one of the finest establishments in the resort community of New Baltimore, known for its mineral baths, opera house, saloons, and bathing, fishing, and sailing on Anchor Bay, just an hour by rail from Detroit. It offered the best food and amenities, including electric lights and steam heat throughout. Here was a clientele that might buy a Ford car; possibly, a potential investor or two was lurking in the crowd that second Saturday of January 1904. A much larger audience would read about Ford's attempt in the newspapers, thanks to the reporters on hand.

The iceboat races Ford had arranged as a sort of opening act ended, and the Arrow race car was brought onto the ice. Ugly and weird, it looked as though it had been concocted by someone who had failed his mechanics apprenticeship and taken to whiskey, not by an engineering genius. How else to explain its steel-reinforced wood frame, spoke wheels, single seat, and bewildering arrangement of exposed wires, gears, levers, and controls—all in the service of an open motor that occupied nearly half the length of the vehicle and drenched the driver in oil and grease when it fired, for it had no oil pan or engine compartment.

Men hired by Ford had cleared a fifteen-foot-wide strip of ice four miles long on Anchor Bay, then coated it with cinders from the coal-fired power plant north of the Hotel Chesterfield. The first two miles would allow Arrow to come up to speed, the third mile would be timed, and the last was for deceleration. The event would have been easier (not to mention warmer) on the long, flat sands of Ormond Beach, Florida, just north of Daytona, future birthplace of NASCAR, where car racing was already enormously popular. But the auto show at New York's Madison Square Garden, America's largest, began the next weekend, before the start of the Daytona season. Ford hoped to arrive in Manhattan with a headline-making story of the incredible cars he could build.

Assuming no tragic accident occurred, that is. A thought that, when Ford walked onto the ice, left him uncharacteristically unnerved.

But it was too late to stop.

"If I had called off the trial," he later said, "we would have secured an immense amount of the wrong kind of advertising."

Starting any car in 1904 was never easy—but firing in subfreezing temperatures one of the largest automobile engines ever built was akin to raising the dead. Ford called on Edward S. "Spider" Huff, one of a small group of employees whose mechanical skills and ingenuity rivaled the boss's. So valuable was Huff to Ford that the boss not only forgave him his habit of chewing tobacco, which Ford loathed, but allowed him to install a spittoon in his car. He also overlooked Spider's disappearances for days inside houses of ill repute, where he sought relief from his recurring depression.

Spider warmed parts of Arrow with a blowtorch and poured hot water into the cooling system to help coax the beast to life. A spectator volunteered to hand crank the open engine, whose cast-iron heart was four massive seven-by-seven-inch cylinders.

The motor caught with a thunder that rattled the windows of the Hotel Chesterfield. Flame shot from Arrow's exhausts and oil sprayed everywhere.

"The roar of those cylinders alone was enough to half kill a man," Ford said of the first time they had been fired. More shock had awaited when he took Arrow and 999 onto the test track on their maiden runs. "We let them out at full speed," he said. "I cannot quite describe the sensation. Going over Niagara Falls would have been but a pastime after a ride in one of them."

Ford took his seat. A warm-up revealed something no test course or track had predicted: when the car hit fissures in the ice, the impact rattled the vehicle so violently that the driver could not keep a steady hand on the gas. Ford would never be able to bring Arrow full-throttle alone. Spider would have to ride with him, one hand controlling the gas and the other holding on, while hunkered down on the floorboards. There was no other place on the race car. "There was only one seat," Ford said.

The afternoon was advancing, the January sun weakening. The American Automobile Association, the AAA, had agreed to officially certify the race—but the organization's three timers were tardy and Ford decided to make a run without them. His speed would not be official, but at least he'd have a number. As the iceboats circled, Spider and Ford drove to the start of the four-mile course. Men with stopwatches stood ready.

Spider leaned on the gas and Arrow rocketed down the ice. This time, the fissures did more than rattle and shake—they launched the car repeatedly into the air. The laws of physics were being tested, but Ford and Spider miraculously maintained control.

Some four minutes later, they coasted to a stop.

A speed of 100 miles an hour had been clocked.

That indeed buried the existing mark of 84.732 miles per hour, set on solid ground two months before by Arthur Duray, a twenty-one-year-old who drove a French-built stock car that, its manufacturer claimed, could run not just on gasoline but also gin or brandy, presumably an enticement to the upper-class buyer in those twilight days of the Gilded Age. Duray's record was the latest in a series of officially sanctioned advances that dated back to 1898, when a wedge-shaped, battery-powered vehicle had reached 39.2 miles per hour, about as fast as a thoroughbred could gallop.

But Ford's mark was not official: the AAA timekeepers had not arrived.

When they finally did, Ford brought Arrow back to the start of the course. But the car's 225-pound flywheel whirred loose, nearly hitting him and Spider. "Ford narrowly escaped with his life," wrote the *Detroit Journal*, which called Ford "a mechanic who began to design automobiles several years ago, when the craze for them began."

Repairs could not be accomplished in the waning light, and the contest was postponed until Tuesday afternoon, January 12. With luck, Ford might still make it to New York a hero.

## A MICHIGAN WOLVERINE

There is no evidence that Frederic L. Smith was present at Anchor Bay on January 9, 1904. But he surely paid attention. He had Ford locked in his crosshairs.

Son of Samuel L. Smith, a Michigan magnate who had made his fortune in lumber, shipping, mining, and railroads, Fred Smith was a wiry man who tended to smirk rather than smile. A member of the Detroit Athletic Club and the city's Fellowcraft Club—elite places Ford would never frequent, even if he'd been invited—he was more comfortable in a boardroom than in a machine shop or on the factory floor. He did not dirty his hands, and he certainly could not have made a carburetor or a piston, yet he professed superior knowledge of an industry built with wrenches and sweat. He had been raised in privilege, the sort of background that Ford, son of a farmer, did not much appreciate, either. Smith was, in short, the classic suit.

After graduating in 1886 from Michigan Military Academy, an expensive institution in the tony Detroit suburb of Orchard Lake Village, Smith enrolled at the University of Michigan, where he joined the Xi Chapter of the Zeta Psi Fraternity and served on the Junior Hop committee. He played sports: winning the lightweight wrestling championship and quarterbacking the 1888 Wolverines, which began their season on a four-year

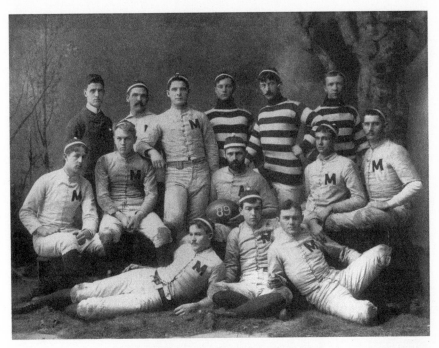

The 1888 Wolverines. Smith, front and center.
Bentley Historical Library, University of Michigan.

undefeated streak during which they'd outscored opponents 258 to 12. Michigan played only a handful of games each year during that period, but the Wolverines nonetheless were so celebrated that no less than future president Theodore Roosevelt praised the team in a speech in October 1888 in Ann Arbor. Smith achieved his first national prominence when, on November 29 of that year, the Wolverines competed in a football game against the Chicago University Club, played on the home field of the Chicago National League Ball Club, later the Chicago Cubs, that dazzled reporters. "Three thousand persons, largely drawn from the most fashionable people of Chicago, witnessed this afternoon what was undoubtedly the greatest football event that ever took place in the West," wrote the *New York Times*, one of several papers to cover the game. Smith was just eighteen years old.

Was the young man's ego swelled by the fanfare? Or was he humiliated when his team lost, 26 to 4, breaking Michigan's almost-five-year undefeated run?

Whatever the case, he did not play football for Michigan again. After he graduated in 1890, his father sent him overseas for two years' study at the University of Berlin. He returned home in 1892, to a job in Samuel's businesses.

In 1897, those businesses included Olds Motor Works, the company founded by the pioneering Ransom Olds in which Samuel had bought five hundred $10 shares. In 1899, Samuel, by now majority stockholder, was elected president; his son Fred, not yet thirty, was elected secretary-treasurer. The post seemed a stretch for a legacy child not long out of college, but the Smiths held the winning hand.

And Olds had a winning car: its Curved Dash model, far and away the best-selling automobile in America as 1904 began.

Named for the resemblance its nose bore to a sleigh, the 7-horsepower Curved Dash sold for an affordable $650, about $17,000 in today's dollars, approximately the cost of a subcompact, and was marketed as a dependable and technologically superior machine—"the highest achievement in mechanical genius and skill, *the best thing on wheels*," as one ad proclaimed. In what may have been the first use of sex appeal to sell automobiles, Olds also aimed for the hearts of young ladies and the wallets of young men by casting the Curved Dash as romantic. So effective was this marketing that the car was the subject of a hit song, "In My Merry Oldsmobile," which teased of more than horseless transportation: "Young Johnny Steele has an Oldsmobile; he loves his dear little girl; she is the queen of his gas machine; she has his heart in a whirl. . . . They love to 'spark' in the dark old park; as they go flying along."

The company seemed to have found the Midas touch. But nothing was forever or even very long in this volatile new industry, Fred Smith well understood. Ford, he had concluded, represented an unusually grave threat. He was tireless and obsessed, and he clearly had his eye on the popular market that the Curved Dash then dominated.

———

LIKE MANY CARS OF the time, the Model A, the first offering from Ford's third company, lacked the reliability that consumers wanted. But in other respects, it was more appealing than the Curved Dash. The Model A had a steering wheel, not a tiller. Its 8-horsepower engine—one more than the Olds—supported a top speed of about 30 miles per hour, a bit faster than the Curved Dash. It cost $200 more than Olds's staple car, but all in all, it could be presented as a better value. Painted a jaunty red, with black leather seats and brass trim all over, the Model A was also pretty. For the money, the car was a good value.

Ford's car had been on the market only a few days when, on July 26, 1903, Smith tossed a bomb. That day, the *Detroit News* published his two-column ad warning that "any person making, selling or using" automobiles that did not carry the Selden patent—US Patent No. 549,160, which claimed invention of the gas-powered automobile—"will be liable to prosecution for infringement." The patent holder, the New York–based Association of Licensed Automobile Manufacturers, maintained that no automobile with a gasoline engine—whether manufactured in the United States or abroad—could be sold domestically without paying royalties to the ALAM. As its first president, Fred Smith controlled the New York group.

Ford fired back almost immediately. In an advertisement two days later in the Detroit *Free Press*, he promised "dealers, importers, agents and users of our gasoline automobiles" that the Ford Motor Company would "protect you against any prosecution for alleged infringements of patents."

Ford continued with a taunt:

We are the pioneers of the GASOLINE AUTOMOBILE. Our Mr. Ford also built the famous "999" Gasoline Automobile, which was driven by Barney Oldfield in New York on July 25, 1903, a mile in 55 4/5 seconds, on a circular track, which is the world's record.

Mr. Ford, driving his own machine, beat Mr. Winton at Grosse Point track in 1901.

We have always been winners.

On October 22, 1903, Smith's group filed suit against Ford in a New York City federal court. On November 5, a company that had purchased

Ford cars was second to be sued, and on December 28, two French firms, Panhard et Levassor and André Massénat, were brought to court. Many more suits would follow.

Smith was determined to force Ford from business. He probably at that point did not understand what kind of enemy he had made.

———

THEIR APPETITE WHETTED BY the excitement of Ford's unofficial record-breaking performance the previous Saturday, a crowd of more than 1,000 assembled at Anchor Bay on the following Tuesday, January 12, 1904. By 3:00 p.m., the temperature had climbed to almost 30° F. Workers cleared the inch of fresh snow that had fallen. The AAA timekeepers took their posts.

Arrow idled at the starting line. The timers with their stopwatches and checkered flags signaled their readiness, and Spider leaned on the gas. The people lining the measured mile watched the car accelerate, "a speck in the distance" heading their way, the Chicago-based *Motor Age* weekly said.

As the car reached full throttle, it again repeatedly lifted into the air, forcing Ford to white-knuckle it back into control, which put Arrow on a zigzag trajectory, not the desired straight line. Twice, the "puffing machine," as one paper described it, swerved altogether from the cleared ice, plowing through snowbanks and momentarily disappearing in clouds of white. Ford had gone past the point of reason, but Spider kept his hand on the gas.

Arrow completed the measured mile. After nearly ramming a boat frozen into the ice, it overshot the final mile, plunging through a snow bank and spinning to a stop.

The AAA timekeepers checked their watches.

One mile in 39.4 seconds.

That was 91.37 miles per hour, an officially sanctioned new world record.

Ford and Spider parked their racer. One paper reported that the men "looked a bit pale," but when he spoke to the press, Ford was composed, albeit an oily mess.

"The beauty of the race is the fact that we were scarcely in danger, although we were literally flying through the air," he told the Detroit *Free Press*. Scarcely in danger, indeed.

A full-page ad Ford placed the next day in the *Horseless Age* detailed the "fastest time ever made with an automobile on any race track in the world," a record achieved in "A FORD MACHINE." Lest there be doubt as to authenticity, the ad noted that the AAA, the official sanctioning body, had clocked the run "with three watches at the start and three at the finish."

"FORD IS KING," the ad declared.

Inside Olds Motor Works, Fred Smith really was king. He had just pulled off the most stunning coup American motor making had ever witnessed.

# 2

## NATIVE SONS

### ENGINES

The Civil War was four years along when Ransom Eli Olds, the youngest of Sarah Whipple and Pliny Fisk Olds's five children, was born in Geneva, Illinois, on June 3, 1864. Pliny was a blacksmith, but he did not prosper early at his trade, and in 1870 he moved his family to Cleveland and took a job as superintendent of an ironworks that constructed bridges and buildings. That lasted four years. He farmed during the next four years on property outside Cleveland, returning to the city in 1878 to take a job as a pattern maker. Two years later, he brought his family to Lansing, Michigan, where he opened up a machine shop.

Pliny's mechanical talents influenced his youngest child, a shy boy who enjoyed visiting the ironworks and, later, watching his father in the small shop he built on the farm. But agriculture was not for Ransom: he hated especially the smell of horses and did not see his future in building or servicing vehicles that were powered by them or using them to work a farm. He wanted a role in his father's Lansing machine shop, P.F. Olds & Son, founded with his older brother, Wallace, as partner. Ransom worked part-time from the firm's beginning, the year he turned sixteen, and he was full-time by 1883, while he was still a teen. Two years later, he bought out his brother's interest.

By then, the company had achieved a reputation as "Practical Machinists," an ad from the period said—and also as a manufacturer of "steam yachts [and] vertical steam engines, of 3, 5 and 10 horsepower." Soon, P.F. Olds & Son was building steam engines that produced 12, 25, and 60 horsepower. Ransom, whose ambition and inventiveness had outstripped his father's, began to imagine connecting one of them to a carriage. He later recalled that he designed several such crude automobiles in his head before putting a plan on paper.

"I could almost see myself flying down the street," he remembered.

In 1887, Olds began to construct his first horseless carriage: a three-wheeled wood-and-steel vehicle that was steered with a tiller and powered by one of P.F. Olds & Son's 1-horsepower steam engines. Word spread through Lansing of the strange machine being built, and curious residents stopped by the shop to watch its progress—but Ransom, wishing to avoid embarrassment if he failed, wanted no witnesses to the first drive.

Before dawn one day in the summer of 1887, he fired up the engine and motored out of his shop.

"I had but little trouble reaching the road and running a block without a stop," he later recalled. "At this point, the efforts of the engine were exhausted, and an assistant was necessary, as it was getting quite light and there was no more time to be lost. I secured two pushers behind, and together with the engine, got it back without an accident, which ended my first trip in a horseless carriage."

Little discouraged, Olds built a second, more powerful steam-powered car. Completed by early 1892, this one had four wheels and ran more smoothly. Olds claimed ease of operation and a "usual" speed of 15 miles an hour for the 1,200-pound vehicle—and he managed to get coverage in *Scientific American*, the widely read and respected New York–based journal in which P.F. Olds & Son already advertised. The May 21, 1893, *Scientific American* story was reprinted in a carriage trade journal that came to the attention of an English company, which bought the car for $400 and shipped it to a branch office in India, apparently the first export of a US-built automobile.

The Young Ransom Eli Olds.
Michigan State University Archives and Historical Collections.

Here was a lesson in another kind of power: the power of the press to move product.

Olds might have continued down the steam-car path if not for his visit to the 1893 Chicago World's Fair, where he saw gasoline engines on display—as well as a gas-powered automobile built by Karl Friedrich Benz, a German engineer and inventor. The future, he concluded, did not lie with P.F. Olds & Son's signature steam engines.

NO ONE PERSON INVENTED the automobile or the engines that powered it: like every complex technology, it resulted from the evolutionary contributions of many individuals, some working together and others apart.

The earliest automobile pioneers were active during the first Industrial Revolution, which began in Great Britain in the 1700s and spread to the European continent and then America.

Steam, which replaced water power used in early factories, was the first energy form to move a horseless carriage. In about 1770, the French artillery office and engineer Nicolas-Joseph Cugnot built what is recognized as the first self-propelled vehicle: a three-wheel steam-powered tractor that he envisioned pulling military cannons. Scottish engineer William Murdoch built a similar steam-powered carriage, or "road locomotive," in 1784, and Cornish engineer Richard Trevithick followed Murdoch's lead in 1801 when he built "Puffing Dragon"—a large boiler mounted on wheels—and an improved model, the "London Steam Carriage," two years later.

Gas entered the picture for good in 1860, when the Belgian engineer Jean Joseph Étienne Lenoir, following experiments by others in Europe and America, patented a two-stroke, coal-gas fired engine, which he used to propel a carriage. After reading reports of Lenoir's engine, a young German named Nikolaus August Otto designed one of his own, and in partnership with the businessman Eugen Langen, made further improvements. Awarded the Gold Medal at the International Exposition of 1867, held in Paris, the Otto engine went into large-scale production in 1872 when Langen established his Deutz Gas-Engine Factory. For chief engineer, Langen hired fellow countryman Gottlieb Wilhelm Daimler. By 1875, the company was producing ninety engines a month. The engines were used to power equipment, not carriages, at the time, but their revolutionary nature—small size, compared to steam, and sturdy performance—made them appealing.

In America, meanwhile, George B. Brayton had been building a similar motor. An Englishman living in Boston, Brayton was apparently the first to use petroleum instead of coal gas or other fuel to fire an internal-combustion engine. With the discovery of oil near Titusville, Pennsylvania, in 1859, an industry that would become symbiotic with motor-vehicle manufacturing had been born.

Inevitably, inventors saw the new internal-combustion engine as suitable for powering a horseless carriage. The first apparently was the German Austrian Siegfried Marcus, who built an engine of his own and attached it to a four-wheel carriage in about 1864. Fearing the police, he drove it around the streets of Vienna under cloak of darkness—but the noise could not be hidden, and it attracted the authorities, who ordered Marcus to stop his experiments.

The next two decades saw greater progress, and it was Benz and Daimler who led the way. Daimler had begun to imagine a self-propelled vehicle during his early days working for Langen and Otto, and when he left the company in 1882, he began to develop his own engine, which he used to power a wooden motorcycle that he patented in 1885. The next year, Daimler tested a carriage—his first car. He received patents for the machine in Germany and in France. Working separately, Benz, who also had been inspired by the Otto engine, mounted an engine to a tricycle. He tested it in 1885 and perfected it the next year, whereupon his Benz Patent-Motorwagen was granted German patent number 37,435. The vehicle, wrote *Neue Badische Landeszeitung* on July 3, 1886, "should prove itself quite practical and useful to doctors, travelers, and lovers of sport."

Useful, perhaps—but these first automobiles from Daimler and Benz did not operate dependably and were not immediately popular. Steam carriages enjoyed greater favor, and electric vehicles, whose roots lay in the first half of the nineteenth century, were also being manufactured.

And then two French citizens stepped in, setting the stage for their country to become the early global leader in automaking.

Louise Sarazin was the widow of Edouard Sarazin, a lawyer for Deutz Gas-Engine Factory who had known Daimler and had been impressed by his brilliance. Edouard had been negotiating with Émile Levassor and René Panhard, owners of a carriage and woodworking factory in Paris, to sell Daimler's inventions in France when he became gravely ill. Before he died, he urged Louise to conclude the agreement. "You may have complete faith" in Daimler's genius, he is reported to have said. "It has a future beyond anything we can now imagine." Louise heeded her husband's wishes and signed with Panhard et Levassor, which exhibited two road carriages and a streetcar using Daimler engines at the 1889 Paris Exposition. Louise and Panhard were soon more than business partners: they married on May 17, 1890. Panhard et Levassor began commercial production, which it supported with clever marketing, including a catalog of its vehicles published in January 1892 and a leaflet with customer testimonials published that October.

Benz also discovered opportunity in France when, in early 1888, French engineer Émile Roger visited him at his Mannheim factory. Roger bought a Patent-Motorwagen and secured the rights to sell it outside Germany—in France, under the name Roger-Benz, which, he had decided, would not turn off potential customers who might be offended by a purely German name. France's defeat in the 1870 Franco-Prussian War still smarted. A Benz was exhibited at the 1889 Paris Exposition and four years later in Chicago.

By then, other French firms were making cars—most famously, Peugeot, which displayed a three-wheel steam-powered car at the 1889 Paris Exposition, and the next year abandoned steam in favor of a gas-powered four-wheel car. Imported German engineering was not the only factor in making France the epicenter of the new industry: Thanks to Napoleon Bonaparte's ambitious public-works projects, France boasted superior roads and bridges. Reports of French cars reached America, where native inventors were working on machines of their own. *Scientific American*, first published in 1845, was among those carrying stories of the wonders abroad.

But it would take two automobile races to truly ignite the industry, in Europe and across the Atlantic.

## TINKERING

Like Ransom Olds, Henry Ford hated farming. And like Olds, Ford, born July 30, 1863, to a farmer and his wife whose ninety-acre homestead was on the outskirts of Detroit, showed mechanical aptitude early in life. His interest in machinery displeased his father, William, an Irish immigrant married to Mary Litogot Ford, an orphaned carpenter's daughter who had been raised by neighbors.

"From the beginning, I never could work up much interest in the labour of farming," Ford later wrote. "I wanted to have something to do with machinery. My father was not entirely in sympathy with my bent toward mechanics. He thought I ought to be a farmer." Ford complained of "too much hard hand labour" in agriculture during that period after the Civil War. "It was life on the farm that drove me into devising ways and means to better transportation."

Ford's favorite childhood toys were not tops or marbles but tools and "odds and ends of metal" with which he played in a small workshop. "Every fragment of machinery was a treasure," he said. The young boy kept his pockets filled with washers and nuts and at the age of thirteen, he took a broken watch apart and successfully repaired it; soon, he claimed, he could repair any watch. He learned by tinkering, a habit that would serve him well when he began working on bigger devices.

"There is an immense amount to be learned simply by tinkering with things," Ford declared. "It is not possible to learn from books how every-thing is made—and a real mechanic ought to know how nearly everything is made."

One day around the time that he first fixed a watch, Ford encountered the first vehicle he had seen that was not powered by a horse. It was a road locomotive: a giant steam-powered machine, built by Nichols, Shepard and Company of Battle Creek, that crawled on steel wheels from farm to farm, providing portable power for threshing and other agricultural tasks. The driver had pulled the machine over to let Ford and his father in their horse-drawn wagon pass, but before William could stop him, Henry had hopped off and met the locomotive's engineer, a friendly sort who was delighted to explain how his machine worked. The encounter profoundly impressed the boy.

"It was that engine which took me into automotive transportation," Ford later wrote in his autobiography, *My Life and Work.*

At school, the boy experimented with building a steam turbine and a forge. In late 1879, his formal studies finished, the seventeen-year-old left for Detroit, where he apprenticed by day at a machine shop and repaired watches and clocks by night. His father did not endorse his choice—"I was all but given up for lost," Ford would recall—but William no longer had such a strong hold on him, and his beloved mother, who might have persuaded him to remain on the farm, had died three years before.

In the summer of 1880, Ford took a new apprenticeship at Detroit Drydock Company, largest of the city's shipbuilding firms. Working in

A "road locomotive" at The Henry Ford museum.
Courtesy of the author.

the engine works department, he completed his three-year apprenticeship and then took a job with Westinghouse Engine Company, which made road locomotives like the one that had fascinated him as a boy.

And then he married a young woman named Clara Ala Bryant. Lured by his father, who owned a tract of uncut timber near his farm, he settled with his new wife in a small house and operated a sawmill, which provided a modest income for the newlyweds.

But engines still called Ford. He built small gasoline ones in his home shop and read what he could about the emerging technology. In 1891, the offer of a position that paid well as an engineer with the Detroit Edison Illuminating Company brought him with Clara back to the city. Again, he worked days at his job and experimented at night and on weekends in the shop he built in a shed by his house. The papers and trade journals were carrying reports of the horseless carriage and Ford wanted in.

By late 1893, Ford had built a small experimental gasoline-powered engine that might be the progenitor of a larger motor that could propel a car. Following supper on that Christmas Eve, he brought it into the kitchen, secured it on the sink, and asked Clara for help in starting it. His wife dripped gasoline into a metal cup that served as a carburetor and followed his directions in adjusting the intake valve as he turned the flywheel. As house current delivered electricity to the engine's primitive spark plug, the kitchen lights flickered—but the motor started in a burst of flames and vibration. Ford let it run for several minutes, satisfied that he had the basics of a working design that he could incorporate into a larger version.

By 1895, Ford, with the assistance of Spider Huff and a few others, was building his first car from parts he made, scrounged, and bought. He did not have the benefit of blueprints for this vehicle, which he called the "Quadricycle," except for the plans he himself drew up.

"I had to work from the ground up," Ford said, "that is, although I knew that a number of people were working on horseless carriages, I could not know what they were doing." He was a man obsessed, and his obsession strained the finances of the family. But Clara supported her husband, and he kept going. As 1896 began, Ford knew the day would soon arrive when he would be able to test-drive the Quadricycle.

———

FRENCH ROADS WERE SUITED for speed, and the Parisian daily newspaper *Le Petit Journal* took advantage on July 19, 1894, when it sponsored the world's first automobile competition, a race from Paris to Rouen. More than one hundred vehicles were entered, but only twenty-one started. A steam-powered French De Dion-Bouton placed first, covering the nearly eighty miles in six hours and forty-eight minutes, an average speed of about 12 miles per hour. Two Panhards and two Peugeots rounded out the top five. A Benz placed fourteenth.

The contest and the four days of qualifying and exhibition surrounding it generated exciting headlines that proved a boon for the young industry, inspiring a committee of journalists and manufacturers to stage a more ambitious competition the next June: a true race, from Paris to Bordeaux and back, a distance of 732 miles. Driving one of his Panhards, Levassor placed first, covering the course in just under forty-eight hours. Peugeots took the second through fourth spots, with a Benz finishing fifth.

Lunching at his club in Chicago one day not long after, Herman H. Kohlsaat, publisher of the *Chicago Times-Herald*, happened upon a copy of the French weekly *L'Illustration* that featured photographs of the race. Imagine if the car really caught on in America just as it had in Europe, as some were predicting! The advertising revenues might rival the cash flow from ads for clothes, cosmetics, soaps, beverages, bicycles, restaurants, hotels, and the other consumer goods and services that were proliferating as the nineteenth century drew to a close. And how better to push things along than to sponsor a race in Chicago, where bicycle and horse competitions enjoyed great popularity and the sensation of the magnificent 1893 Chicago World's Fair still resonated?

Kohlsaat managed to get the attention of President Grover Cleveland, persuading him that the development of horseless carriages someday would benefit the army—and that a highly publicized race, modeled after the ones in France, would spur that development. Cleveland assigned a general to assist the publisher in planning the contest, the first on American soil. Kohlsaat offered a $5,000 purse—nearly $150,000 in 2014 dollars—and an equal amount to cover racers' expenses. A one-hundred-mile route in and around Chicago was advertised, although that was an exaggeration (the actual length was ninety-two miles). The race was scheduled for November 2, 1895.

Equal parts showman and journalist, Kohlsaat also sponsored a readers' contest, with a $500 prize, to suggest the best name for the motor vehicle. "Horseless carriage," "vehicle motor," "automobile carriage," "motocycle," and "automobile," borrowed from the French, were among the submitted names. The *Times-Herald* declared "motocycle" the winner, but it was not a word that would catch on. *Automobile* would, along with *car*, a derivative of *carre*, meaning "wheeled vehicle," which also had ancient French (and Latin) roots.

Of the more than seventy-five cars that had entered Kohlsaat's race, only two made it to the starting line on November 2: a new Duryea, the second made by Frank and his brother, and an imported Benz that had been modified by Hieronymus A. Mueller, a prodigious inventor who operated a shop with his sons in Decatur, Illinois. Kohlsaat postponed the official race until Thanksgiving Day, November 28, when he hoped more cars would make the effort, but he allowed the Duryea and the modified Benz to compete in a two-car "consolation" event. With Mueller's son Oscar driving, the Mueller-Benz beat the Duryea, driven by Frank with brother Charles his passenger.

On Thanksgiving morning, Chicagoans awoke to find several inches of snow. Just six cars assembled at the starting line, at the Midway Plaisance on the former World's Fair grounds: the Duryea, the Mueller-Benz, and two other gas vehicles; and two electric-powered cars, a Sturges, built in Chicago, and the Electroboat, built by a Philadelphia engineer and his chemist partner. With deteriorating road conditions, the route was shortened to fifty-four miles: from Chicago to Evanston and back. At 8:55 a.m., the race began.

With Frank driving again and an umpire riding along, the Duryea took an early lead, lost it, and then gained it again when a competitor smashed into a horse-drawn taxi that refused to let it by. Frank lost two miles when he took a wrong turn, and more time when a steering gear broke, but he managed to get back into the race and once more take the lead.

Dark was falling on a cold, wet night, sending the crowds home, just a sleigh or two on the snowy streets, when the Duryea neared the end. Only a local reporter was on hand to see the car as it motored through Douglas Park and down South California Avenue, the finish line within striking distance. "Lacking spectators, except here and there," the journal *Autocar* reported, "a solitary watchman at one of the ill-smelling soap factories of the district hastening to his odorous place of duty, the men on the motor gave vent to war-whoops, cheers, catcalls and other manifestations of joy over the victory they were winning."

After stopping for four minutes while a train crossed, the Duryea won the race at 7:18 p.m. An hour and thirty-five minutes later, the Mueller-Benz finished second.

Newspapers everywhere published accounts of the race, emphasizing the American triumph over the modified European import. The young industry generally benefited from the publicity, but second-place Mueller-Benz would not get much value. The company built just five vehicles before it folded, in the wake of a gasoline explosion that killed founder Mueller on March 1, 1900, in his shop.

---

BACK HOME IN LANSING after the 1893 Chicago World's Fair, Ransom Olds, in full control of the company now that his father had essentially retired, began development of a gas engine. In 1895, he applied for a patent, which was granted the following year. The engine was a commercial success, substantially increasing company revenues and supporting a 10,000-square-foot addition to the factory. Olds later recalled that sales for the engine itself were so robust that meeting demand hindered work on a vehicle, his own version of Benz's machine, to be powered by his own Olds gas engine.

He found time in 1896, when he constructed a two-seat, single-cylinder, 5-horsepower car with solid rubber tires, green body, red trim, and leather furnishings—a "beauty" of a vehicle, a local reporter wrote when Olds demonstrated the car for him that August.

"There is no doubt that the much mooted question of the horseless carriage has been successfully solved," the reporter declared. Word spread and soon other newspapers and magazines also were trumpeting the car. "Probably the most successful vehicle of its kind ever turned out," wrote the Detroit *Free Press*. "Said to work to perfection and [Olds's] friends predict that it will come into general use," declared the *Grand Rapids Democrat*.

An ad announcing that Olds's "Moto-Cycle" was available for sale appeared later in 1896. The car cost $1,000 and was offered with one or two seats. The manufacture of gas engines, not vehicles, remained the company's bread and butter—but Ransom remained fascinated with automobiles. Intuiting the marketing value of a real-life demonstration of a car, he continued to drive his Moto-Cycle through the streets of Lansing, so prominently that a newspaper claimed nearly every resident of the city was "doubtless familiar" with the machine. One of the residents was the wealthy Edward W. Sparrow, an Irish immigrant who had made his money as a landlord, developer, and timber speculator.

Sparrow had the means to gamble on the new machine, and he had faith in Ransom Olds, who had grown a small company into a big one—but who needed outside investment if he was to grow it bigger still and begin large-scale automobile production. On August 21, 1897, during a meeting in Sparrow's office, the Olds Motor Vehicle Company was organized. Capitalized at $50,000, the company issued 5,000 shares of stock valued at $10 apiece to investors. Ransom received half the shares; Sparrow and his friend Samuel L. Smith, a copper and lumber magnate, each received five hundred. Sparrow was named president, with Ransom Olds becoming manager.

————

IN ITS FIRST YEAR, Olds Motor Vehicle Company built just four "Motor Wagon" vehicles. The year also saw the first in a dizzying succession of divisions, acquisitions, expansions, restructurings, and recapitalizations that by the end of 1899 left Samuel Smith and his sons in command of Olds Motor Works, as the company was by then called. Of its 35,000 shares of stock, Ransom (and his father) controlled just 7,625 in 1899, fewer than one-fourth. In January 1900, Olds was elected president, Samuel Smith vice president, and Smith's son Fred secretary-treasurer. But titles meant less than large shares of stock. The Smith family owned a majority of the stock. Olds was no longer captain of his ship.

Ransom and his mechanics kept designing cars. They produced an electric vehicle, selling it for $600, the same price as one of Olds's gasoline models, but the limitations of batteries discouraged Ransom from doing more with electricity. Having become one of the few men to build cars with all three types of power, he had concluded that gas was the future. An engine promising efficient gas mileage that powered a vehicle that was easy to operate would help entice buyers, he believed.

For the moment, the Smiths were content to let Olds set overall direction. Certainly no respectable businessman could quibble with the numbers: from $17,859 in 1891, overall sales in 1900 had grown to $186,209, an impressive tenfold increase. Most of that, however, was through sales of engines, not motor vehicles.

That was about to change.

After what he described as "a long sleepless night" midway through 1900, Ransom sketched for one of his engineers the new car he wanted to build. The Curved Dash runabout, he said, should cost $300 to manufacture and retail for $650, yielding an enviable profit. Work began, and in early 1901, advertisements appeared. "The Oldsmobile is a marvel to most people," one declared. "It is only a simple fact, however. Runs 40 miles on one gallon of gas. Starts at will from seat. Perfectly safe for a child to operate. Fully guaranteed." The company began receiving orders. A fire destroyed the Detroit factory in early March, but it was rebuilt and a new one was constructed in Lansing. Just as production was revving up, in the summer and fall of 1901, a golden marketing opportunity materialized. Not surprisingly, it came from racing.

## "POETRY OF MOTION"

In a final burst of sleepless energy in the spring of 1896 that Clara feared would cause a nervous breakdown, Ford finished his Quadricycle. Before dawn on June 4, he readied it for its first street run. Incredibly, Ford had not figured the size of the shed door into his calculations and the car was too big to fit through. With an ax, he broke down part of the brick wall. The Quadricycle roared to life and Ford drove it down the cobblestone street, an assistant preceding him on bicycle to warn it was coming.

Back home, Clara served her husband breakfast. After bidding good-bye to her and their son, Edsel, who had just turned three, Ford got to work on time.

In the ensuing weeks, Ford drove the Quadricycle around Detroit. It was an odd contraption, weighing only about five hundred pounds and looking like some sort of boxy, half-baked buggy mounted on large pneumatic bicycle tires. It had two forward gears capable of propelling it at up to 20 miles per hour, Ford claimed, but no reverse gear; a two-cylinder, air-cooled gas engine fed by a three-gallon tank connected to a belt and chain to power the rear wheels. It seated two people—though two average-size people dwarfed it. But the tiny vehicle attracted attention, good and bad, wherever Ford went with it.

Henry Ford driving his 1896 Quadricycle.
From the Collections of The Henry Ford.

"It was considered something of a nuisance, for it made a racket and it scared horses," Ford later recalled. "Also, it blocked traffic. For if I stopped my machine anywhere in town, a crowd was around it before I could start up again. If I left it even for a minute some inquisitive person always tried to run it. Finally, I had to carry a chain and chain it to a lamp post whenever I left it anywhere. And then there was trouble with the police. . . . I had to get a special permit from the mayor and thus for a time enjoyed the distinction of being the only licensed chauffeur in America."

Ford's invention did not earn him his father's approval. On the day he drove it out to William's farm, the old man refused to take a ride. The son went back to Detroit.

FORD BUILT A BETTER car, attracted investors, and left his job at the Edison electric company to found the Detroit Automobile Company in August 1899. The company's first vehicle, a 1,200-pound delivery wagon that sold for $1,000, debuted that winter. In early February 1900, Ford took a reporter for the Detroit *News-Tribune* for a ride. No advertisement could surpass the value of the journalist's exuberant praise in an illustrated story that editors played on the front page of the second section, where few could miss it.

To the reporter's amazement, Ford started the engine without lighting a match. And then a frightening thought occurred to the scribe.

Gas was explosive.

Ford assured his passenger that though the vehicle carried three gallons of gas in its tank, it would not blow up. "It's perfectly safe," Ford said. "There's no fire about here."

Ford drove his car out of the factory and onto the snowy streets.

"It flew along with the very poetry of motion," the reporter wrote, moving with "a dream-like smoothness."

Ford told the journalist that anyone could learn to drive the vehicle in a few days or even a few hours, that no mechanical background was required. When he brought the car to full speed, about 25 miles per hour, the reporter experienced a sensation he described as startlingly new.

There has always been at each decisive period in this world's history some voice, some note, that represented for the time being the prevailing power.

There was a time when the supreme cry of authority was the lion's roar.

Then, came the voice of man.

After that, it was the crackle of fire.

By and by, it was the hammering of the stone ax.

Then, it was the slapping of oars in the Roman galleys.

Next it was the voice of the wind against sails.

It came at last to speak with a loud report, such as announced the reign of gunpowder.

The roar of dynamite was a long time later.

The shriek of the steam whistle for several generations has been the compelling power of civilization.

And now, finally, there was heard in the streets of Detroit the murmur of this newest and most perfect of forces, the automobile, rushing along at the rate of 25 miles an hour.

What kind of noise is it?

That is difficult to set down on paper.

It was not like any other sound ever heard in this world. It is not like the puff! puff! of the exhaust of gasoline in a river launch; neither is it like the cry! cry! of a working steam engine; but a long, quick, mellow gurgling sound, not harsh, not unmusical, not distressing; a note that falls with pleasure on the ear. It must be heard to be appreciated. And the sooner you hear the newest chuck! chuck! the sooner you will be in touch with civilization's latest lisp, its newest voice.

Praiseful press could enhance an automaker's reputation, but it could not remedy the situation inside the infant Detroit Automobile Company. Ford's majority stockholders prevented him from improving his vehicles, which would have cost money and taken time; they believed that only by selling inferior vehicles at an inflated price would they get the quick return on their investment they wanted. Shoddy workmanship was not how Ford, no longer a mere tinkerer, believed cars should be built.

"We continued making cars more or less on the model of my first car," he recalled. "We sold very few of them; I could get no support at all toward making better cars to be sold to the public at large. The whole thought was to make to order and to get the largest possible price for each order. The main idea seemed to be to get the money. And being without authority other than my engineering position gave me, I found that the new company was not a vehicle for realizing my ideas, but merely a money-making concern—that did not make much money."

In January 1901, the company was dissolved. Ford returned to his workshop, where he began to build his first race car, Sweepstakes, a precursor to Arrow and 999.

## A LEGEND GOES DOWN IN DISGRACE

Led by mounted police and a band that played in a tally-ho coach, more than a hundred steam-, electric-, and gas-powered vehicles paraded from downtown Detroit to Grosse Pointe Blue Ribbon Track on the afternoon of October 10, 1901, for what was billed as the World Championships of automobile racing. The newspapers had drummed up such a buzz that

The 1903 Oldsmobile catalog touted the Curved Dash's smooth performance.
Michigan State University Archives and Historical Collections.

court had been adjourned after lunch, so the judge and members of the bar might attend. Ransom Olds gave his employees the afternoon off, too. For Oldsmobile, which had survived the Detroit factory fire and was ramping up production of its Curved Dash vehicles, this was a welcome opportunity for free publicity.

Before a crowd of some 8,000 people, Olds drivers demonstrated the new car. In the spirit of a circus, the company had devised a number of stunts for its cars, including climbing a flight of wooden stairs specially constructed for the occasion; keeping three cars in motion on a forty-foot balancing beam; and having a trapeze artist walk a pole attached to the runabout above the driver while the vehicle was in motion, "a severe test to prove the absence of vibration," an Olds manual said. Vibration bedeviled manufacturers, who knew that consumers would not have much good to say about a car that rattled their bones.

The poor racehorses residing at Grosse Pointe Blue Ribbon Track were lost to the mob of people and machines.

"All around the horses were other things, large, small, white, black, red, yellow," a journalist observed. It was, he said, an "invasion of the temple."

A battle of steam cars began the contests, with the winner of the five-mile race clocking an average speed of 32 miles per hour. The electrics proved a quiet snore, with an average speed of just 15 miles per hour. Competing in the ten-mile race for cars that weighed less than half a ton, young Olds test driver and new hire Roy D. Chapin and another man in their Oldsmobiles lost to a steamer. But the presence of the many Olds vehicles was important brand-building.

The main attraction on that autumn 1901 day, a ten-mile competition of gas vehicles, featured Ford, driving Sweepstakes; another man the papers called "a Pittsburgh millionaire" who had more money than experience; and the accomplished Alexander Winton. Yet another of the bicycle makers turned car manufacturers, Winton had set the first US track record in 1897—and had since won nearly every American and foreign competition he'd entered. The cars he brought to market were prized for their reliability. He had personally demonstrated this in 1897, when he drove one from Cleveland to New York, a 500-mile trip that took a week and four days but in those early days of automobiles nonetheless amazed the masses. In a few short years, Winton had become legendary in the motoring world.

When the Pittsburgh millionaire's car busted a cylinder at the starting line, Ford faced only the legend. Propelled by an engine that put out 70 horsepower, nearly triple Ford's stated 26, Winton was soon a commanding one-fifth of a mile ahead. Ford was having trouble controlling Sweepstakes. Huff was riding tandem, serving as purveyor of oil to the car's thirsty motor and counterweight as Ford took the corners in the dirt.

"Ford's mechanic hung far out in his effort to ballast the car," one paper reported, "but she swung wide at every turn. That Mr. Ford was an amateur was plainly shown by the way he took the curves. At the turns, he was compelled to shut off the power entirely and two-fifths of the time, his machine was simply coasting."

But Ford began to gain on the straightaways. He was closing in when Winton's car sputtered to a crawl in a cloud of blue smoke. The engine bearings had overheated. His mechanic frantically poured oil on the dying motor, to no avail.

"Mr. Ford swept by them as though they were standing still," a reporter wrote. "Down the stretch he came like a demon and the crowd yelled itself

Ford drives Sweepstakes, with Spider Huff, at Grosse Pointe, 1901.
From the Collections of The Henry Ford.

hoarse. In the next three miles, Ford increased his lead to fully three-quarters of a mile and won amid great cheering."

Among those applauding were a lumber baron and other wealthy men who had invested in Ford's first firm, the Detroit Automobile Company. With their second round of investments, the Detroit Automobile Company was reorganized into the Henry Ford Company a month after Winton went down in smoke and disgrace. Literally and figuratively, Ford had won big.

But as the weeks passed, other financial backers of his new firm began to sour when it became clear that Ford intended to keep racing, not devote himself solely to building cars. They did not see racing's value to the bottom line—or share Ford's seeming addiction to the thrills of speed and competition, which had only intensified with the excitement of beating Winton.

The disagreement was bubbling over in January 1902, when Ford wrote to an acquaintance, expressing his hope of bringing the celebrated French driver Henri Fournier, winner of the 1901 Paris-to-Berlin and Paris-to-Bordeaux road races, into the firm. "If I can bring Mr. Fournier in line, there is a barrel of money in this business," he wrote. "My Company will kick about me following racing but they will get the Advertising and I expect to make $ where I can't make ¢s at Manufacturing."

In March 1902, Ford left the Henry Ford Company, which later that year was reorganized as Cadillac, named for the founder of Detroit, Antoine de la Mothe Cadillac. On August 20, Ford entered into partnership with Detroit-area coal dealer Alexander Y. Malcomson to build a new car: once it was designed and ready for production, they agreed, Ford & Malcomson, having raised the necessary capital, would be replaced by a corporation in which each man would have equal shares and majority control. Malcomson's smart young clerk, James Couzens, a fiery native of Canada who was destined to be mayor of Detroit and a US senator, came into the new business, joining Spider Huff and a few others. Ford continued to build race cars without the grumblings of investors who did not share his obsession with speed.

Oldfield's October 1902 win in the 999 over Winton in the Manufacturer's Challenge Cup at Grosse Pointe motivated the new partners, and the men got serious. Malcomson raised more money. Ford and his partner hired two more mechanics, a pattern maker, a draftsman, and a blacksmith. Dissatisfied with the new car he had been designing, Ford and his small crew began work on another—what would become the Model A. Operations were moved from the tiny Park Place shop to a former wagon shop on Mack Avenue, a larger space, where they installed tools and equipment that were powered by an Olds gasoline engine. They negotiated contracts for parts: chassis from John F. and Horace E. Dodge, carburetors from George Holley, bodies from C.R. Wilson Carriage Company, wheels from the Prudden Company, and tires from Hartford Rubber.

With a final infusion of capital from investors including Malcomson's banker uncle John S. Gray and Charles H. Bennett, an executive with Daisy Air Rifle, the Ford Motor Company was incorporated on June 16, 1903. A month later, Ford company sold its first car, the $850 Model A, to a Chicago dentist. By January 1904, Ford had sold many more and orders were coming in steadily, providing revenue to continue development, grow his labor force to more than one hundred, and make a small but encouraging profit.

## OUT, BUT NOT DOWN

Encouraged by the response to the Curved Dash at the October 10, 1901, Grosse Pointe championship won by Ford, Olds decided to stage a bold adventure that, if publicized properly, would dwarf the return from a car climbing wooden stairs. Olds had twenty-one-year-old test driver Chapin drive a Curved Dash from Detroit to New York City, a more than six-hundred-mile trip that no automobile had ever completed before.

Chapin, who was destined to found the Hudson Motor Car Company and be US secretary of commerce, had dropped out of the University of Michigan that spring of 1901 to take a job with Oldsmobile. He happily accepted the boss's assignment. Departing Detroit on October 27, he arrived in Manhattan on November 5, in time to wow the crowds at the second New York Auto Show.

Conveniently neglecting to mention that Chapin had endured a major breakdown along with problems with the car's steering, axles, transmission, tires, and cylinder gaskets, Olds featured the trip in advertising as evidence of the model's reliability. The publicity worked. Olds negotiated a contract with leading auto dealer Ray M. Owen to sell 1,000 Curved Dash vehicles, an unprecedented number for any automobile, in New York City and other large markets, and by January 1902 was reporting weekly sales of twenty runabouts in New York alone. (He would fail in his agreement to sell 1,000 of them, but he did move some 750 in New York that year, likely a record number for any car by any US dealer to that date.)

Despite the delays from the March 1901 fire, Olds still managed to make nearly 500 Curved Dash cars by the end of the year, an extraordinary output for the time. Olds recorded total sales in 1901 of $410,401, mostly from the runabout. Olds Motor Works's net worth was $531,529. The year 1902 was more impressive, with sales of about 2,500 vehicles that brought in $1.6 million. Net worth rose to $1.2 million.

By now, Olds, like other manufacturers, fully appreciated the marketing value of the proliferating number of races, endurance contests, hill

Roy Chapin in a Curved Dash Olds, 1901.
Bentley Historical Library, University of Michigan.

climbs, and other car competitions: they not only drew spectators who almost instantly could become new consumers but they also attracted reporters, who could send stories nationally and overseas by wire service. In March 1902, Chapin took the wheel again in Chicago, winning a one-mile contest. Oldsmobiles fared well the next month in a one-hundred-mile endurance run on Long Island, and a similar run that August in Chicago featured Chapin, mechanic Milford Wigle, and two others. In October, dealer Owen drove an Oldsmobile in a New York to Boston Reliability Run. He was the only driver in the under-1,000 pound class to finish without penalty.

Olds generated more headlines from competitions in 1903. Dwight B. Huss, another test driver, won gold and silver medals in the English Reliability Trials, a series of eight daily runs totaling 1,019 miles from London to coastal cities and back. Wigle won medals and trophies racing on dirt tracks, and an Olds engineer raced Pirate, a custom-built Olds race car, to an American record on the sands of Daytona. Further publicity came from Indianapolis, where Olds dealer Carl G. Fisher, who would build the Indianapolis Motor Speedway a few years later, took the $1,000 prize in a newspaper-sponsored one-hundred-mile run.

When the books closed for the year, 1903 had been an unqualified success, with total sales of $2.3 million from record sales of nearly 4,000 cars—more than one-third of all cars sold in the United States in 1903. Net worth passed $2 million, a fourfold increase in just two years. Olds had expanded its dealerships throughout much of the country and established sales agencies in Canada and abroad. It had broadened its advertising reach beyond trade publications and general-circulation newspapers, opening accounts with *Harper's* and *Saturday Evening Post*.

And it became only the second car company to advertise in *Ladies Home Journal*, which that year passed the 1 million circulation mark to continue its reign as the largest-circulation magazine in America. "The ideal vehicle for shopping and calling—equally suited for a pleasant afternoon drive or an extended tour," read one of Olds's ads. Women did not constitute a majority of buyers, but many men, Olds had discovered, needed their approval before writing the check. "The Oldsmobile has endeared itself to the feminine heart, just as it has established itself in the business world," read another *Ladies Home Journal* ad.

In his treasurer's report submitted on December 31, 1903, Fred Smith seemed optimistic. He noted that production capacity had again nearly doubled, and increased output was planned for 1904. He was certain Olds would continue to trounce its competitors.

"The prospect for the coming year seems good and the foreign market has opened up in a gratifying manner," Smith stated, "so that we can confidently hope for steady business and can feel justified in building up our organization to supply the world with Oldsmobiles promptly and with satisfactory results. Our automobile output, heretofore confined to one type of machine only, will from now on consist of three machines giving a considerable latitude of choice to the buying public. . . . In general, we expect to progress along new lines as rapidly and economically as possible in the effort to keep our lead in the automobile industry."

———

RANSOM E. OLDS         FREDERIC LATTA SMITH

The 1904 book *Men of Michigan* displayed Olds and Smith side-by-side.
By that year, they were bitter enemies.

As 1904 BEGAN, Olds Motor Works seemed a company to envy: for three straight years now, it had reigned supreme. But out of public view, Fred Smith and Ransom Olds had been locked in a deadly struggle. Smith wanted to rule. Olds would not hand over the throne.

The founder had sensed Smith's ambition to run the company as early as the spring of 1901, when Ransom was hospitalized for some unrecorded illness so severe that an acquaintance urged him to buy life insurance. When he finally returned to work, he found that Smith had assumed some of his duties. Ransom bristled. But Samuel Smith, who had been elected president that January, had given his son permission.

Tension between Olds and Fred Smith continued into 1902, when development of a larger alternative to the Curved Dash began. Smith was enthusiastic about the more expensive car, which could multiply profits— although he faced stiff competition from imported French and German cars, and American makers who were producing luxury automobiles. Smith urged Olds to have a model ready for exhibit at the January 1903 New York show. Ransom's men built the vehicle: a 10-horsepower tonneau that weighed 1,350 pounds, substantially larger than the runabout, and a step toward an even bigger and more costly machine.

The industry press applauded. *Cycle and Automobile Trade Journal* described the tonneau—a style of car that featured a rear passenger compartment—as practical and graceful, declaring that "it is the evident intention of the Olds people to meet all demands for a touring car, having the same practical features which have made the Oldsmobile so popular." Touring cars were intended for trips longer than the day-to-day travels of the smaller runabouts.

But Olds lacked enthusiasm for the bigger car, seeing the future not in luxury automobiles, which only the wealthy would ever be able to afford, but in the mass market. Likely to Smith's ire, Olds expressed his sentiments publicly. In an article he wrote for the *Detroit News* in early February, he criticized American carmakers who sought to copy the German and French companies that made big machines—who aimed to make "the automobile the child of luxury, instead of the child of necessity." Race cars would continue to have monstrous power, he predicted, but "the lighter and lesser horsepower vehicle will certainly be the future."

Cars like his Curved Dash, in other words.

"Within the next ten years the automobile most generally used will be one of 700 to 800 pounds in weight, small, compact, and always under instant control," Olds predicted. His comments hardly endeared him to Smith, for whom the larger vehicle was a pet project.

Whether Olds intentionally delayed production of the 1,350-pound tonneau or it was beset by legitimate manufacturing problems, none of the cars had been shipped by late April, when Smith expressed his frustration to him. Agents were clamoring for the vehicles they had been promised at the New York show, he said, and Olds Motor Works must deliver.

More tension arose when Smith promoted test driver Chapin to the sales department, where the twenty-three-year-old instituted standardized policies that clashed with Ransom's good-old-boy practices, in which a handshake was enough to finalize a sale. Ransom also believed that a

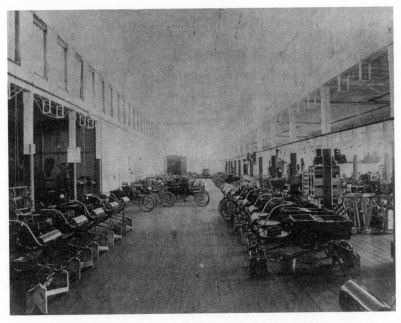

Olds Motor Works factory with Curved Dash cars being assembled, 1903.
Michigan State University Archives and Historical Collections.

sales executive needed a thorough knowledge of the machine he sold, which he thought Chapin lacked. Smith disagreed.

"The very best tobacco salesman in Detroit doesn't nor ever did smoke or chew and doesn't really know what he's talking about," Smith said, "but he's the best judge of human nature I ever ran across."

Smith's worry that Olds was minimizing customer complaints about the Curved Dash further worsened the bad feelings between the men. Dealers were reporting defects, but Olds was slow to correct them.

"The repair items are a fright and the black eye our runabout will get from breakage complaints will grow worse the deeper we get in," Smith had told Olds in 1902. Samuel now upped the pressure, ordering Olds: "Don't rest a day or put away work on anything new until you have planned & *perfected* [every] part of this machine as far as practical."

A joke began to spread that a question mark, not a period, should be placed at the end of the Olds slogan: "Built to run, and does it."

Ransom Olds believed his car had proved itself worthy—in competitions and the daily experiences of thousands of owners. Given the state of the art, he anticipated problems but believed they should be addressed after a sale, when owners could receive replacement parts for free. To an extent, he blamed ignorant owners and improperly trained repairmen for problems, and did not wholeheartedly endorse, as Smith did, a better effort to identify and correct defects before cars left the factory; in other words, quality control.

"The old model is too weak and flimsy and none of our agents want it," Smith said. "I can't see any point in puddling away with that old batch of stuff."

When Ransom learned—indirectly—of Smith's idea for a new experimental shop, he felt double-crossed. Adding insult to injury, Smith wanted to open the shop in Detroit, the Smiths' center of power, some eighty miles from Lansing, where Olds lived and worked.

On May 1, 1903, Olds wrote Smith a scathing letter. Relations between the men were nearing the breaking point.

"Dear sir," the letter began. "I learned this morning by a round about way that you were putting in an experimental room at Detroit. Now if this is your policy to do business underhanded and unbeknown to me, as you have several other things, I do not care to be associated with you. I am Vice President and Manager of this company and such things should not be taken up without my consent or the consent of the board. I have had all I want of this treatment."

Olds continued: "I have been sick with the LaGrippe [influenza] for the past three days or would have been down this week. I now see why you have been so anxious the last two weeks to have our meetings at Lansing so you could smuggle this through before I knew it. I do not care to have my interest handled in this way."

But both men understood where the real power within the company rested. It rested with the majority stockholders.

On the morning of January 5, 1904, readers of the *State Republican* in Lansing, Michigan, where Olds operated one of its factories, awoke to startling news:

GENERAL MANAGER OLDS RETIRES
*FROM ACTIVE DUTY AT MOTOR WORKS*
*Affairs of the Company Will Hereafter Be*
*Directed by Secy.-Treas. Smith*
*From Detroit*

The newspaper implied that Ransom had left voluntarily, with Olds telling a reporter that his departure was "due to his desire to relinquish some of his duties in the active management of the concern, and give more time to follow his own inclinations." The paper suggested that after building America's most successful car company, the founder was ready for a well-deserved life of leisure.

"Mr. Olds is planning to take his family to California soon, to spend at least a few months," the paper reported. "In the summer, he may take a European trip."

He would not be in Manhattan in mid-January for the fourth annual New York automobile show, which now rivaled its great Paris counterpart.

William C. "Billy" Durant, future creator of General Motors, would not be there, either. At the start of 1904, he ran one of the world's largest horse-drawn carriage businesses. He did not yet see what others did in the new machine.

# 3

## THE SELDEN PATENT

### "MOTOR CAR BEAUTY"

When the fourth annual New York automobile show opened on Saturday night, January 16, 1904, a raft of new technologies was already exciting the public imagination. Americans marveled at Guglielmo Marconi's radio transmissions and Thomas Edison's motion pictures. They recalled the events of the previous month at Kitty Hawk, North Carolina, when two brothers from Ohio had flown through the air in the first controlled, powered, heavier-than-air flight aboard a winged machine they'd built in their bicycle shop. On the streets of Manhattan, where electric lamps now lit the way, horseless carriages swept by horse-drawn vehicles, a real-time illustration of an intensifying revolution whose consequences could not yet be fully appreciated.

Several cities hosted car shows in 1904, but New York's, in the heart of the nation's largest city and biggest car and media markets, was America's grandest.

Held at Stanford White's magnificent Madison Square Garden, itself a monument to the age, the New York auto show rivaled the majestic Berlin, London, and Paris shows. It had created a splash with its inaugural event, staged from November 3 to November 10, 1900, when Gilded Age titans William K. Vanderbilt I, grandson of railroad magnate Cornelius Vanderbilt, and John Jacob Astor IV, destined to die on the *Titanic*, had shown off their pricy European imports amid the more modest offerings from some thirty domestic manufacturers of steam, electric, and gas vehicles. That first show had averaged an estimated 6,000 attendees daily until closing day, when a record crowd of some 12,000 packed the Garden. Autoists held banquets and packed Broadway theaters. The Tenderloin, Manhattan's notorious red-light district, was exceptionally busy. On this occasion, both the now-thriving trade publications and mainstream newspapers, which had begun to employ a new class of journalist, the "auto writer," trumpeted the opening of the 1904 edition.

"To one who has never visited an automobile show," wrote *Motor Age*, "this one in splendor will present the picture of a miniature world's fair. To those who have visited all of the Garden automobile shows, it will present a wonderful lesson of the industry's growth. . . . Spectacular, brilliant, crowded with motor car beauty—a picture in itself—the show is yet full of commercial and mechanical interest. It is not one-sided; not a show for any certain class. . . . It has value for buyer, curiosity seeker, tradesman, and mechanic, more so than the recent Paris show, for it shows a greater progress in a twelvemonth than did that show. It is typical, national, superb."

In its story the day after the show opened, the *New York Times* wrote that beneath the many electric lights and hundreds of flags hung from the galleries, the cars "fairly gleamed with dazzling brightness." The approving reporter, perhaps an autoist himself, summarized the cultural shift of the last decade, at least in America's most populous city:

The public no longer looks upon the automobile as freaks, although there are, of course, some freak machines. The old-time wonder at the sight of an automobile has passed away and there is an intelligent understanding of them. In the latter respect, the ladies last night showed, in a majority of cases, where small groups were discussing the peculiarities of fine-looking machines, that their understanding was fully equal to that of their male escorts. Even the children . . . revealed a surprising amount of automobile knowledge.

Nearly two hundred exhibitors entered. About half showcased the parts, accessories, and supplies they made; General Electric had a booth for its switches, meters, and battery chargers, and Firestone and Goodyear displayed their tires. The latest offerings from the burgeoning auto-fashion industry were featured: goggles, gloves, scarves, and touring caps for the gentlemen, and for the ladies, "serviceable" cloaks, "smart headgear in leather, cloth and fur," and a woolen "driving suit," wrote the *Automobile*. The weekly's correspondent especially enjoyed the suit, declaring:

"A hood shaped like a diver's helmet finishes off this costume, which we plead guilty to admiring, but which would certainly have startled our grandmothers if it had been given to them to meet on the streets women dressed like that! Well, well, time brings wonderful changes! Is this not the age of the automobile?"

The main attractions, of course, were the latest vehicles. Mercedes, American Motor, Locomobile, Buffalo Electric Carriage, and Rochester Steam Motor Works were there. So were Packard and Pierce, companies destined to last longer than most. The esteemed Winton Motor Carriage and Cadillac, the new name of the company Ford had left in 1902, among others, were displayed. Gasoline-powered cars were beginning to out-number, though not yet supplant, electrics and steamers. Vehicles ranged in price from a few hundred to many thousands of dollars. Prospective buyers could not only see them inside the Garden; they could take a test drive, which was becoming an essential part of the sales pitch.

"This is found to be an absolute necessity, for the purchasers are be-coming very particular about all the minor points, and one slight im-provement by a rival firm that charges practically the same price for a similar machine may make a world of difference in the number of sales," wrote the *Times*.

———

WITH ITS TOP-SELLING Curved Dash runabout, still just $650, and its new, upscale $950 Light Tonneau, which Frederic Smith had so strongly pushed, Olds Motor Works commanded attention. Confirming his firm's status as America's leader, Smith presided over three large booths in the center of Madison Square Garden's main floor.

Two aisles away, in a single small booth on the periphery, Ford displayed his new cars: the $2,000 Model B, which featured a formidable 24-horsepower engine and polished wood and brass trim; and the $900 Model C, a slightly longer and more powerful version of the Model A, which continued to sell for $850.

If not for his crazy dash across a frozen lake, Ford might have been lost—but there with his stock cars was the star of the show, Arrow, which he had shipped by rail to New York. Smith could not have missed it. He surely observed Ford himself, handsome in a suit, posing for the photographers and greeting the journalists and awestruck show-goers as he sat in the driver's seat of the world's most famous race car. Ford had arrived in New York on the tide of publicity he had sought.

Accounts of his record-setting run four days before, dispatched by wire, had appeared in publications around the industrialized world. The *New York Times* captured the drama of the finish, when "Ford rushed over the end of the course into a snow bank, and for fully a quarter of a mile went across the untracked ice, narrowly escaping injury." In all, the *Times* devoted a story and an editorial to Ford's exploit, mentioning it in four additional stories during a two-week period that January.

"Whether, under any conditions, an automobile will ever travel a faster mile than that of Ford on the Lake St. Clair ice, when he drove the straightaway in :39 2–5, remains a most interesting question," wrote the *Detroit Tribune*, controlled by newspaper magnate James E. Scripps. "It seems probable that the negative reply is about as likely to be fulfilled as the affirmative." And heaven forbid a driver should take Arrow or 999 onto a track again, the writer declared. "In all probability, the chauffeur would be thrown from his seat by the slightest inequality of the surface and a riderless automobile would take a sheer and capsize, tearing itself to pieces."

Friends and friendly manufacturers sent Ford congratulatory letters and telegrams. "Wishing you lots of success in the future," wrote a man with Detroit's Central Savings Bank, the sort of institution Ford hoped to please. Manufacturers of parts Ford used in building Arrow published ads, with G & J Tire Company of Indianapolis trumpeting "A Wild Mile by Henry Ford," and Kokomo, Indiana's Byrne-Kingston & Co. claiming that the record "proves that for producing Power and Speed, the Kingston Carburetor HAS NO EQUAL."

But a *Times* editorial on January 15, the day before the New York show opened, highlighted continuing opposition to automobiles. Not everyone at the paper shared the enthusiasm of the opening-night reporter, with his descriptions of dazzling brightness; like the nation itself, the *Times* remained divided on the merits of the machine.

Despite passage by the New York State Assembly in 1903 of an 8-mile-per-hour city speed limit—which Governor Benjamin B. Odell Jr. signed into law over the vigorous objections of the Vanderbilts, John Jacob Astor IV, and other prominent enthusiasts—cars racing through the streets of New York continued to imperil pedestrians. Children were especially vulnerable. Police on motorcycles and bicycles chased the auto outlaws, some of them inebriated, and justices were strict with their lectures, fines, and jail sentences. But the authorities could not stop the mayhem.

"Near Detroit, on the frozen surface of Lake St. Clair, a young speed maniac named FORD lately accomplished the remarkable feat of driving an automobile a measured mile in 39.4 seconds," the *Times* editorialist asserted, misstating the record by a fifth of a second. "The track was 'lumpy,' and neither quite safe nor comfortable—qualities which greatly added to the interest of the experiment." Which the editorialist did not on principle oppose: under controlled conditions such as Ford's run, "there is no objection, unless offered by the friends and relatives of the person who risks his neck to attain a perfectly useless result." The true harm of record-setting runs such as Ford's, the editorialist wrote, "is that it will lead a number of idiots to try similar exploits on public roads, in which case the least to be regretted of the resulting casualties will be the breaking of the chauffeur's neck."

Even when not running, the editorialist asserted, autos capable even of "a fraction of the speed" of Arrow should bring their owners criminal prosecution. He compared them to people who set mantraps and spring guns, with the potential to maim or kill, to thwart trespassers. Even if they had not yet done harm, their mere possession should be illegal, the paper said.

"An automobile which can be run at dangerous speed sooner or later will be so run," the editorial asserted. "If its owner has too much self-respect or respect for others to abuse it, some servant will do this the moment his back is turned. There is something in human nature which cannot resist the temptation to go fast when the means are at hand: and, curiously, those want to go fastest whose time is worth least."

The *Times* editorial department was no lone voice. Among the many other anti-car publications was *Harper's Weekly*, which had recently deplored "the characteristic diabolism of the motor cars. They run over folks, they run down wagons, they scare horses, they dispute with railroad trains and with trolley cars about the right of way. Sometimes, also, their steering breaks and they smash into something . . . the most shameful and outrageous propensity of the automobile is to run away after it has hurt someone."

———

AUTOISTS COUNTERED ANTI-CAR sentiments with advertisements, lobbying, and public-awareness campaigns sponsored by clubs and organizations. Manufacturers wined and dined journalists, treated them to all-expenses-paid factory junkets and test drives, and connected them to Barney Oldfield and other celebrity drivers. During their week in New York, the new class found strength in numbers—and the endorsements of influential enthusiasts.

Edison, Astor, airship pioneer Alberto Santos-Dumont, leading insurance broker Gage E. Tarbell, three members of Congress, and recently retired commanding general of the US Army Nelson A. Miles, a hero of the Civil, Indian, and Spanish-American Wars, were among the 350 people who attended the fifth annual meeting of the Automobile Club of America at the Waldorf-Astoria Hotel on January 23, 1904. Martin Dodge, director of the US Office of Public Road Inquiries, successor to the Office of Road Inquiry, was also there. Founded by wealthy advertising executive Homer W. Hedge and others during a meeting at the Waldorf in October 1899, the ACA shared the spirit of similarly effete clubs in Europe.

A quartet entertained at the fifth annual meeting, singing an ode to the previous October's nine-day endurance run from Manhattan to Pittsburgh, sponsored by the National Association of Automobile Manufacturers (NAAM) and immortalized in the press for its rain, mud, floods, and mishaps, including the total loss of a car—captured in a frightening photograph—when a spark ignited its leaking gas tank and it went up in flames. Some considered the Pittsburgh run a public-relations debacle, but others, emphasizing that twenty-four of the thirty-four starting vehicles had finished despite nightmarish conditions, cast it as a triumph.

Participating autoists had followed a route marked each morning by fresh confetti, a common navigational aid through unmapped territory, a fact incorporated into the song the quartet performed for the ACA banqueters:

*How the darkeys shouted when they heard the muffled sound!*
*How the turkeys gobbled when our confetti trail they found!*
*How the sweet school ma'ams goo-goo'd but bravely stood their ground*
*While you were driving to Pittsburgh.*

With the *Times* editorial perhaps in mind, speakers at the Waldorf warned of the consequences of poor driving, with corporate lawyer and soon-to-be New Jersey judge James B. Dill asserting that the growing numbers of laws, ordinances, and fines resulted from "the recklessness of the driver of the machine," not some fundamental flaw in the technology itself. Dill urged autoists to respect pedestrians and horse-drawn vehicles in order to avoid draconian sanctions. "To be sure," he said, "legislation has not gone so far as to put all motor vehicle users in distinctive garments, like those who are, for the good of society, relegated to Sing Sing." Still, he advised, best to "voluntarily remove any just cause for a public opinion hostile to automobiles rather than to attempt to meet the difficulty by appealing through our committees and clubs to the legislatures." In other words, don't be a stinker behind the wheel.

Other speakers lent support to the Good Roads movement, a national effort by leading motorists to build and maintain highways and streets that were suitable for travel by fast, wheeled machines—a movement that shared kinship with bicyclists' longer fight for the same. South Carolina senator Asbury C. Latimer spoke of the many millions of dollars the federal government spent on rivers and harbors, but precious little on highways. Tennessee representative Walter P. Brownlow added his voice, citing expenditure of "$750 million of the people's money in relieving the oppressed Cuban" during the Spanish-American War, eight years before. The $750-million figure was an exaggeration, but the point was made: automobiling needed more government support. Brownlow urged the assembled to send letters to Congress demanding more money to build and maintain more and better roads and bridges—an infrastructure—to serve the auto, which stockbroker and ACA president Winthrop E. Scarritt naively believed would solve a pressing urban problem.

"What is the self-propelled vehicle to do for us?" Scarritt asked. "It is to solve the problem of congested traffic in our city streets. If every horse-drawn vehicle in New York could be replaced by a motor car, what would that mean? First, that the space now occupied by horses would be saved; second, that the streets would be clean; third, that the motor car would carry twice the load at double the speed. . . . If ever there was a city under the sun with narrow, congested, up-torn streets that needed salvation from itself, surely it is our metropolis."

Jacob H. Gallinger, US senator from New Hampshire, agreed with Scarritt. What had swayed his commitment to better city and country roads was not personal experience with cars—but with horses, which not only ravaged roads but left droppings wherever they went.

"While I have not had the pleasure of automobiling," the senator said, "I have had the discomfort of riding behind a horse in thousands of miles of rough roads in the state of New Hampshire. I am for good roads."

But autoists could not ride into the glorious future on good roads without good machines to put on them. Automobiles had improved since those designed by the Duryea brothers, but even the costliest and best-built models were prone to flats, overheating, breakdowns, fires, and all manner of mechanical woes, which is why most models were sold with repair kits and aristocrats hired mechanics to ride along with them. Horses by contrast seemed virtually trouble free: properly fed and sheltered, they pretty much did what they were supposed to do until old age brought them down, long past the life expectancy of the average auto. At the start of 1904, reliability remained the carmakers' Holy Grail.

Noted hotelier and wit Simeon Ford (no relation to Henry) entertained the Waldorf crowd with a humorous speech laced with painful truth. He spoke of his own car, repaired so many times that the only original part remaining was the horn. He joked that he was so defeated that he wanted to be rid of his vehicle—but was unable to part with it, no matter what he did.

"I have tried in vain to dispose of it at private sale, by public auction, by trade, gift, raffle, grab-bag and fishpond," Simeon said. "I have left it by the roadside, unattended for long periods, hoping some fool would come and steal it. I have freely tendered it to friends, enemies, relatives, old ladies' homes, poorhouses, gold cures and lunatic asylums, and it has always been refused with scorn and vituperation."

And yet, the witty hotelier said, the allure of the auto still outweighed its drawbacks.

"There have been moments—rare moments—when I have experienced the keenest delight from its use," he said. "Sometimes, when it has been returned to me, fresh from the factory, having been entirely reconstructed, and I have succeeded in getting my wife to join me in putting another mortgage on our humble home, it has run smoothly and swiftly for several moments, before disintegrating. At such times, I have experienced an exhilaration such as the bird must feel, when, with motionless wing it drops with lightning speed from the far heights of the blue empyrean."

———

ELSEWHERE IN MANHATTAN, members of the American Automobile Association were meeting.

Founded on March 2, 1902, when nine motoring clubs from Chicago, Philadelphia, Utica, Rhode Island, New Jersey, Princeton University, and other places had combined, the AAA offered drivers of ordinary means an alternative to the upscale ACA. On the minds of AAA officers that January was a proposed merger with the American Motor League, the world's first auto organization, founded in November 1895 by, among others, the

Duryea brothers and the eccentric poet, mystic, and inventor Charles Brady King. The merger would be concluded later that year.

In New York, the AAA continued planning the speed competitions it would sanction at the end of January on Ormond-Daytona Beach, Florida. The organization hoped for new publicity-generating records, as did race-car drivers, including twenty-five-year-old William K. Vanderbilt II, great-grandson of Cornelius, a champion yachtsman who had forsaken sails for motors, and Barney Oldfield, the swaggering speed demon. Oldfield used an appearance at Madison Square Garden to criticize Ford, who had parted ways with the temperamental driver. Oldfield, perhaps envious, described Ford's Anchor Bay run as a "freak" that he did not believe would be allowed to officially stand.

"I don't want to appear boastful," Oldfield told the press, "but I was the one who suggested the possibility of making fast time on ice some time ago. Ford took it up and you see what he has done. It was a freak record, but I want to say right here that I can beat it. Yes, I fully believe that I can make a mile in 30 seconds." That would be 120 miles per hour, an outrageous speed that few except Oldfield really believed possible.

Oldfield dared Ford to travel to Florida so the two could compete man-to-man. He backed his challenge with a bet of up to $5,000 that he would win—and he offered to pay the expenses of shipping Arrow to Ormond-Daytona.

Ford did not take the bait.

"It is not my intention to make any further attempts at reducing this record until it is equaled or bettered by someone else," Ford said before leaving New York. Arrow had served its purpose. And its world record was officially certified.

———

THRILLING THOUGH RACES MIGHT be, they had no direct relevance to everyday autoists, who would never drive a race car. Hill climbs, tours, overnighters, and endurance runs, typically open to anyone—and conducted with stock models, which anyone could buy—were another matter. Even auto haters took interest, as the press coverage brought readers to places they might never visit. And there was something compelling about a car put to the test, even if you were rooting for it to fail.

So AAA officials could all but bank on international publicity for what the *New York Times* on February 6, 1904, reported would be "the largest and longest endurance run ever held in this country," an approximately 1,400-mile summer parade of automobiles from New York to St. Louis, where the Louisiana Purchase Exposition was expected to rival the 1893 Chicago World's Fair. Sponsor AAA hoped to demonstrate the pleasures of motoring on a grand scale, and also further the good roads and reliability causes, priorities it shared with the Automobile Club of America and other organizations.

By spring, plans were being finalized. Newspapers spread word, the trade publications contributed to the hype, and the AAA published a sixteen-page pamphlet drawn up by its National Touring Committee. Anyone willing to pay the $10 entry fee was welcome.

"Main Line" motorists would depart from Fifth Avenue in Manhattan on Monday, July 25, with the goal of reaching St. Louis on Wednesday, August 10, after traveling through Albany; Rochester; Buffalo; Erie; Cleveland; Toledo; South Bend; Chicago; Springfield, Missouri; and other cities. Separate divisions from Boston; Philadelphia; Baltimore; and Washington, DC, also hoped to reach St. Louis on August 10, joining the Main Line vehicles for a grand entrance onto the fair grounds. The AAA hoped for a Denver division, but it never materialized. The distance was too daunting.

The AAA and journalists made much of the timing: the dry summer season, when, with a bit of luck, motorists would not encounter the drenching rains that had turned roads to quagmires during the autumn 1903 Pittsburgh run. Nonetheless, the AAA advised motorists to carry spare parts and tires and lengths of sturdy rope, in case of "slippery" weather.

The organization emphasized that each day's travel would average only about one hundred miles, confetti would help mark the routes, and restaurant and hotel accommodations would be the finest, with fun the first order of business throughout the long trip: this was no contest, the AAA decreed, but a movable party.

"At almost every night stop, some form of entertainment is being planned by the local clubs and the social side of the tour will be most pronounced," the *Automobile* wrote on April 2. "The opportunity of getting together in the evening at a smoker or informal dinner or talking over with other tourists the events of the day will be without doubt one of the most enjoyable features of the tour and one which is not offered to the tourist who takes a trip by himself."

Although it was expected that men would drive, as they mostly did in daily life, women were invited to be passengers.

"A special effort is being made to provide comfortable quarters for ladies participating in the tour," the *Automobile* wrote. "The management desires it to be understood that they are especially welcome and that no fair motorist need decide not to enter for fear that other ladies will not be in the cavalcade."

## TAKING THE STAND

George B. Selden, the man whose patent was roiling the automobile industry in 1904, had long been a familiar figure in Rochester, New York, where he lived much of his life.

Some people there knew him as a lawyer who had once counted Eastman Kodak founder George Eastman, another city resident, among his clients. Some knew of his US Patent No. 549,160, issued in 1895—and some of those may have believed his unwavering claim that he and he alone, of anyone in America or the world, was the father of the automobile. Others may have dismissed him as an eccentric whose strange experiments more than a quarter of a century before had not given birth to the automobile, but only revealed him to be a grandiose fool.

Son of Henry R. Selden, a former New York lieutenant governor, state assemblyman, and judge who had once defended women's suffrage activist Susan B. Anthony, also a Rochester resident, Selden had become fascinated with the idea of a self-propelled vehicle as a teenager in the early 1860s, when reports of such contraptions in Europe reached America. His overbearing father thought the idea ridiculous and discouraged his son's interest; Henry wanted George to be a lawyer. Selden enrolled at Yale but cut short his classical studies to spend two years at the university's scientific school, greatly displeasing Henry. George returned to Rochester and was admitted to the bar. He specialized in patent law, which at least offered peripheral involvement in invention.

Selden frequently complained that he never had the time or money to truly indulge his passion, so his free hours became precious. As a young man, he withdrew to a basement workshop in his father's house, where he conducted experiments related—and unrelated—to his horseless carriage dream. He designed a typewriter and created machines that made barrel hoops, for which he received patents. He visited libraries, learning what he could about mechanized power, including steam carriages and road locomotives. He became acquainted with local draftsmen and others with a mechanical bent and formed a partnership with a Rochester machinist, William Gomm, who had a talent for constructing three-dimensional models.

In the spring and early summer of 1876, Selden spent nearly two months in Philadelphia at the Centennial Exhibition. He had come to display his barrel-hoop-making machines, but the stationary steam-powered, crude-petroleum, and other engines from the United States and abroad that were exhibited in the massive Machinery Hall mesmerized him. Manufactured by a company in Providence, Rhode Island, where its inventor—George Henry Corliss—lived, the Corliss steam engine, forty feet tall and weighing 680 tons, was king of the show. A much smaller machine built by the Boston-based George Brayton inspired Selden. The Brayton engine was still too big to be adapted to a horseless carriage, but its design principles might be incorporated into a feasible means of power for one, Selden concluded. Back in Rochester, he and machinist Gomm experimented.

Working in a shop near the Genesee River, which powered the city's mills, the men ignited kerosene, benzene, and gasoline, assessing their suitability as a fuel: gasoline, which exploded in a forceful flash that might be harnessed, seemed best. They bored out one of the cylinders of a three-cylinder internal-combustion engine, equipped it with a crank and other parts, and on a day in May 1878, they fired it up. It caught briefly, then coughed to a stop in a cloud of exhaust. Nonetheless, it had run, and further modifications improved its performance.

It never did run for more than a few minutes—and always falteringly, at that—and it never was connected to a carriage, nor did it ever propel one. (After its final trials, Selden brought the motor home, where it remained in storage until 1904, when he used it to power a lathe.)

Still, Selden was elated.

"Billy, we have struck a new power," he said to Gomm.

Others, including his father, thought them both nonsensical, if not insane. Selden would later recall how he had been "sneered at and otherwise discouraged."

Well, let them sneer. The last laugh would be his.

In the spring of 1879, Selden filed for a patent with an inefficient, disorganized US Patent Office whose poorly paid workers, many of them inexperienced and badly trained, were overwhelmed by the flood of inventions from the Second Industrial Revolution—factors that Selden understood intimately from his law practice, and which he intended to exploit. In his filing, Selden submitted only words, numbers, and drawings: against the advice of Gomm, he had not built an operational prototype, only described a concept. This, too, he believed would work to his advantage.

In the ensuing years, Selden followed closely the endless advances in power and transportation technology—advances that soon overtook the crude design of his own sputtering creation. By constantly filing amendments and revisions to his patent application, the patent attorney was able to buy time until a real automobile industry was taking root and he could require others to pay him royalties. He was scheming.

In 1895, the year the Duryeas began commercial production of their cars, and seven years after Karl Benz first produced his for sale, Selden decided the time was finally right. After approximately one hundred changes to his application of sixteen years before, his patent was granted.

As Ford's lawyers would seek to prove, Selden's true genius lay not in invention, but in clever trickery.

———

IRONICALLY, SELDEN HAD ASSIGNED his patent in 1899 for an initial fee of $10,000 to the Electric Vehicle Company, a manufacturer of battery-powered taxis. Former US Navy secretary and wealthy financier William

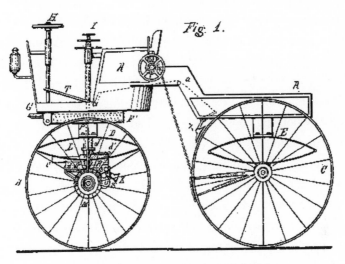

G. B. SELDEN.
ROAD ENGINE.

No. 549,160. Patented Nov. 5, 1895.

Fig. 1.

Drawing included in Selden patent application.
United States Patent and Trademark Office.

Collins Whitney owned a majority share of the company, which had banked on electric automobiles becoming the dominant mode of taxi transportation in America. By the end of 1902, with internal-combustion engines having greatly improved and gasoline becoming more plentiful— and with internal labor troubles and maintenance issues plaguing the company—that ambition was proving folly. The company was burdened with staggering debt. But the Selden patent, Frederic Smith recognized, might still be worth something.

Smith, still secretary-treasurer of Olds Motor Works at the time, met secretly with representatives of Peerless, Pierce, Locomobile, and a handful of other gas-powered-car makers on January 2, 1903, in the Detroit offices of Packard Motor Company head Henry B. Joy to form an organization to approach Electric Vehicle. Whitney's company had already tried, mostly unsuccessfully, to enforce the patent by filing suits against individual companies, but Smith, Joy, and the others believed that a new and stronger organization could succeed where Electric Vehicle had failed—extracting royalties from companies that complied, and forcing resistant companies out of business.

At another secret meeting a month later in Chicago, Smith was elected president of their newly formed Manufacturers' Mutual Association. They created a $2,500 "fighting fund," as Smith called it, and scheduled a meeting with Electric Vehicle Company representatives to be held at Whitney's Fifth Avenue mansion in New York City. Whitney, who had not become a millionaire by pouring good money after bad, accepted Smith's offer on the spot. In return for a tiny percentage—three-fourths of a cent—of royalties to his company, the financier granted all rights in the patent to Smith's group, which during a four-day meeting in early March drew up articles of agreement establishing the Association of Licensed Automobile Manufacturers, the more formal group that replaced the MMA. Smith was again executive president, Henry Joy secretary-treasurer. George H. Day, who had worked for bicycle- and car-manufacturing titan Albert Augustus Pope, was named general manager.

An executive committee that included Smith would oversee ALAM. Member companies would pay a royalty of 1.25 percent of the retail price of every gas-powered car sold, plus a $2,500 membership fee. Electric Vehicle would keep three-fifths of the royalties, paying one-third of that to Selden; two-fifths would go to the ALAM treasury, which would pay lawyers' fees and other expenses. ALAM members would receive rebates from anything left over and Electric Vehicle would live to see another day. Henceforth, Smith and Joy declared, only gasoline-vehicle manufacturers who obtained a license and paid royalties could legally conduct business. All others, including those who sold and bought gas cars—dealers and consumers—would be subject to suit.

Henry Ford initially thought it best to pay royalties, and he applied for membership in ALAM soon after its incorporation. But Smith and Joy denied him, ridiculing his enterprise as nothing but another of the many "fly-by-night" car companies that had sprung up everywhere—not a true manufacturer, but an "assemblage" firm that used parts made by others to build its models. Of course virtually every company of the era, including Smith's Olds and Joy's Packard, did the same, but never mind. The "assemblage" label was an insult to Ford's mechanical prowess. He did not appreciate the slight, but he had the opinions of others—and business realities—to consider.

As Ford raised capital for the Ford Motor Company in the spring of 1903, some investors worried that the Selden situation would imperil his latest enterprise. With his cash reserves being depleted by development of the Model A, soon to enter production—and hoping to avoid the high costs of defending a suit—Ford approached Smith again at about the time the Ford Motor Company was incorporated on June 16. Meanwhile, Detroit lawyer John W. Anderson, who had invested $5,000 in the new company, arranged a luncheon meeting with Smith. Ford, Anderson, and company secretary James J. Couzens were among those who attended.

According to one account of the meeting, Smith explained the Selden patent and ALAM's intention of suing anyone who did not surrender. So what was Ford's decision?

"Selden can take his patent and go to hell with it!" Couzens said.

"You men are foolish," Smith said. "The Selden crowd can put you out of business—and will."

Ford stood and pointed a finger at Smith. "Let them try it," he said.

———

THE STOCKHOLDERS OF FORD'S new company who met on September 18 faced a fateful decision. Smith's ad published on July 26, 1903, was no hollow threat, the stockholders concluded: ALAM would unquestionably file lawsuits against infringers, they believed. And Ford would likely be the first hauled into court. They needed a great lawyer, and they found one in Ralzemond B. Parker.

Parker had been toughened in battle, literally. Born on February 17, 1843, into a family whose ancestors had fought in the Revolutionary War and the War of 1812, Parker was nineteen years old when he enlisted in the Michigan Infantry, 17th Regiment, Company E. A month later, he fought in the Civil War at Antietam, the bloodiest one-day battle in US history. He may have been injured there: records show he was discharged from a Baltimore army hospital "for disability" in February 1863.

Nine years later, Parker graduated from the University of Michigan Law School. He thrived, becoming senior member of his law firm and admitted to practice before the US Supreme Court. He served as a judge, and "Judge" is how many addressed him thereafter. Patent law became his specialty, and by the summer of 1903, he was said to be the leading patent attorney in Detroit, city of invention. He was said never to have lost a case.

Principle mattered to Parker: the man who as a teenager had enlisted to serve a cause he believed righteous had no tolerance for things he considered unjust. Such was his assessment of George Selden's claim that he was the father of the automobile. Along with disputing the ridiculous notion that any one person alone could have conceived such a complicated machine, Parker agreed with Ford that the patent suits were an affront to free enterprise and competition, bedrock principles of the American economic system.

"He believed in justice for the little fellow," his son later said. He believed, too, in the future of the automobile.

With his burly build, beard, and gray eyes, Parker resembled the poet and diplomat James Russell Lowell. But he was no poet, and in court, he was often undiplomatic: as witnesses he cross-examined would learn, he was intense, unflappable, mechanically knowledgeable, and possessed of an iron intellect and a prodigious memory. He set traps, in which witnesses unwittingly revealed embarrassing contradictions and concealed falsehoods.

"They are putty in the hands of Parker and when he has finished with one of them, there is a gleam in his eye which indicates he is satisfied he had made the opponent's witness his own best advocate," wrote a New York *Sunday American* reporter who watched him in action.

At the September 18 meeting, Parker informed the stockholders of his estimate of the costs should litigation go all the way to the US Supreme Court, the worst-case scenario: $40,000, which was $4,000 more than the company's gross profits to date.

But he was convinced that Ford would ultimately win—if the little company could stay in business long enough. After discussion, the stockholders decided to "throw down the gauntlet," as the person keeping the minutes wrote.

In an open letter written by Parker and Couzens and published shortly after the meeting in trade publications including *Motor Age* and *Horseless Age*, Ford's iron resolve was revealed. The letter described the "monopoly" of the Selden patent as "unwarranted and without foundation in fact." It reiterated the vow already spelled out in ads that Ford would not only defend itself, but "our agents and customers to the fullest extent."

Regarding George Selden himself, Parker and Couzens punched with bare knuckles.

"We cannot conscientiously feel that Mr. Selden ever added anything to the art in which we are engaged," they wrote. "We believe that the art would have been just as far advanced today if Mr. Selden had never been born. That he made no discovery and gave none to the world."

Smith responded swiftly.

On October 23, 1903, ALAM, acting through George Selden and the Electric Vehicle Company, filed suit in the US Circuit Court for the Southern District of New York against Ford and C. A. Duerr & Co., Ford's New York City dealer.

"The Selden lightning has finally descended," wrote *Motor World*. "It is aimed to strike the Ford Motor Company, of Detroit, who have so boldly defied it."

The lightning had followed the car industry to the fourth annual auto show, where John Wanamaker had succeeded C. A. Duerr & Co. as Ford's agent. Sixty-five years old, the Philadelphia native had founded a thriving department-store chain and was known for his marketing and advertising prowess. He had served as postmaster general. He could not be bullied. When ALAM sued Ford and then him as successor to Duerr, he responded with a blistering counterattack.

Under the headline "Don't Give $600 to the Bogey Man," Wanamaker's oversized ad published in the *New York Times* on January 28, 1904, noted Arrow's speed record and said Ford "put the same extraordinary mechanical ability into building the best Motors Cars yet produced for popular use. And he has the facilities to produce them in great numbers." Ford's new four-passenger Model C, Wanamaker stated, cost $900—compared to $1,500 for similar vehicles offered by "the Trust," ALAM members. Smith's own 1904 offering in this category, his light tonneau, cost $50 more than Ford's. For some customers, that savings was substantial.

"The Ford Motor Car cannot be beaten by the Trust in competition, so they have erected a scarecrow, to frighten the buying public," Wanamaker's ad continued. "The smart crow knows that there is always corn where the scarecrow is, and the man who wants to get his money's worth when buying an automobile can depend on it that all these suits instigated against the Ford Motor Company are brought only because the Trust believes it can't compete with Henry Ford and his splendid $800 and $900 cars. . . . *When you buy a Ford Motor Car from John Wanamaker, you are guaranteed against any trouble with the Trust.*"

Dealers could be forgiven if they doubted that, for ALAM had hired some of America's best lawyers: Betts, Betts, Sheffield & Betts, as well as Redding, Kiddle & Greeley, both of Manhattan. As the war went on, ALAM also would bring Attorney Frederick P. Fish onto the field. A Harvard graduate whose knowledge of patent law rivaled or surpassed Parker's—he counted the Wright brothers among his clients—Fish also was president of American Telephone and Telegraph from 1901 to 1907. Fish knew, and meant, business. He was a man Smith could admire.

————

THE FRONT PAGE OF the July 20, 1904, Detroit *Free Press* carried news of the Russo-Japanese War, a bricklayers' strike in Washington, DC, and the injury sustained by prominent Michigander David C. Whitney when his auto went over an embankment near Saginaw after a long drive from the big city. An inside ad announced another Mark Twain short story due to be published in the August issue of *Harper's Magazine*. Moneylenders advertised their services and a downtown merchant was selling ladies' shoes as cheaply as $1.48. Another retailer sold electric fans for $10 and also offered them for rent. The business pages had the latest developments from the copper, grain, wool, livestock, coffee, railroad, and other industries.

But there was no mention that day or in the days that followed of the first witness called in the Selden patent suit, which had shaken the young auto industry. At 11:00 a.m. on that summer day, Parker began to depose Ford in the attorney's downtown Detroit offices.

Parker began by asking Ford to recount his experiences with engines of any kind. Ford said his interest dated to his boyhood. He recalled the first gasoline engines that he built, in the early 1890s, and his first automobile, the Quadricycle, which he first drove in 1896. The Quadricycle was entered as Exhibit No. 1.

"Where was it run?" Parker asked.

"In Detroit," Ford said.

"Whereabouts in Detroit did it run?"

"Central part."

"Was it on the highway, streets?"

"Yes, on the streets."

"What can you say as to whether or not, the general public during that time, had an opportunity of seeing it?"

"Well, there were thousands who saw it."

"Did anyone ride with you on it that you remember?"

"Yes, Mr. Huff, Mr. Bishop and others." James W. Bishop was another of Ford's assistants in the early days.

Ford spoke rapidly but easily, without raising his voice: an engineer fond of engineering language who was not given to exaggeration, emotion, or verbosity. He seemed happiest when describing his completed designs—and the valves, cylinders, pistons, carburetors, countershafts, chains, crankshafts, belts, axles, tanks, water jackets, exhaust pipes, and other parts of the many machines he had built.

Parker had made discrediting Selden a cornerstone of his defense against Smith's ALAM.

"Have you examined the letters patent issued to George B. Selden, 549,160?" Parker asked.

"Yes," Ford said.

"When did you first know of it?"

"About 1898. . . . "

"Prior to that time, you may state whether you ever heard of Mr. Selden or anything he has ever done, said or claimed in this line?"

"I never heard of him."

"You may state whether or not, directly or indirectly, you ever obtained any ideas from Mr. Selden in regard to the construction of automobiles driven by internal combustion engines?"

"I never did."

Parker then asked Ford to "please state in relation to the construction of any racing machines driven by internal combustions engines and what have you done in that relation?"

"I have built several fast racing machines; one known as '999' which has held several world records, including the world's record of last winter on the ice."

"What was its speed and who drove it on that occasion?"

"I drove it myself and the speed was 39 2–5 seconds to the measured mile."

In his cross-examination, ALAM lawyer Samuel R. Betts sought to discredit Ford's seemingly photographic memory for machines. One concerned the road locomotive that Ford had seen as a boy. This was the wondrous thing that had revealed Ford's destiny.

"You speak of knowing of certain self-propelled steams engines in 1875 or 1876 at Battle Creek and out of Detroit," Betts said. "Now, you were only 12 or 13 years old at the time; what observation did you have of this engines at that age which enables you to state their construction and operation at the present time?"

"I knew that they propelled themselves on the road," Ford said.

"You saw them running on the road?"

"Yes."

"You made no careful examination of their mechanism, did you?"

"Yes, I did."

"I should like to know what examination you made of these engines as a boy of 12 or 13 years old, which would enable you 29 or 30 years afterwards, to come in and testify as to exactly what those engines did beyond perhaps remembering that you saw them run without horses?" Betts said.

"That they put them in and out of gear the same as a mowing machine."

"You mean to say that you have carried that recollection with you from then to the present time in connection with these particular Battle Creek engines?"

"Yes, better than I remember things that happened last year."

Openly skeptical, Betts drilled down on how Ford possibly could remember details of something so long ago—in particular a "disconnecting device" that allowed the road locomotive to transfer from propulsion to providing power to run equipment.

"Do you mean to say that as a boy of 12 or 13 you noticed that specific mechanical device and have carried it in your mind ever since so that now after 29 or 30 years you can testify as to that fact in regard to those engines?" Betts asked.

"Yes," Ford said.

"Now you mean to say that in regard to those Nichols, Shepard & Co. Battle Creek engines which you say you observed in 1875 or 1876, you have carried with you since the age of 12 or 13 and to the present time a recollection which you can swear to as to relative speeds of the driving shafts and traction wheels?"

"Yes, sir."

"How many times a minute did these Nichols, Shepard & Co. engines run?"

"I suppose about 200."

"Why do you suppose; why don't you remember?"

"Because I never counted them."

"Why do you guess 200?"

"Because I asked the man who was running it how fast the engine ran and he told me 200 turns per minute and I have never forgotten it."

"And you remember that ever since you were a boy of 12?"

"Yes, sir, as distinctly as I can remember yesterday."

When Smith was briefed on the deposition he must have wondered if Ford might be unbeatable. And as Parker continued on with his defense—moving from Detroit to take testimony in Reading, Pennsylvania; Boston; Providence, Rhode Island; Pittsburgh; New York City; and Ithaca, New York—Smith also must have wondered if Parker was the equal, if not the better, of ALAM's own attorneys.

# 4

## MEET ME IN ST. LOUIS

### MEGARGEL, HUSS, AND AN EXPOSITION

When twenty-nine-year-old Percy F. Megargel learned of plans for the AAA's St. Louis tour, he knew he must participate. A restless young man who thirsted for adventure, Megargel had fallen for automobiling after an earlier love of bicycling, which had attracted so many of his peers before they, too, gravitated to the new speed.

Oldest of three sons of a well-to-do Scranton, Pennsylvania, banker and businessman, Megargel attended Cayuga Lake Military Academy in Aurora, New York, where he played football and tennis, captained the bicycle club, and was president of the Athletic Association. With a diploma in English, math, and science, Megargel, eighteen at the time, moved in 1895 to New York City and joined the Central Wheelmen, a bicycling club in Brooklyn. A two-day ride from New York to Philadelphia and back that June put Megargel in the news. The next year, he was elected first lieutenant of the Wheelmen and given charge of the club's press relations. His appearance at the January 1896 bicycle manufacturers' show at Madison Square Garden, which drew tens of thousands, put him in the news yet again when he was included in a list of noteworthy attendees.

The bicycle show, two months after the first New York auto show, earned rave reviews from the press, with a *New York Times* reporter implying that the newer machine would never eclipse the two-wheeled one. "In the face of the tremendous crowd that packed Madison Square Garden last night," he wrote in a January 21 story, "talk of abandoning cycle shows seems nonsensical. It would have been impossible to have packed more people in the Garden than were there last evening. As it was, one got a good idea of how a sardine must feel when packed in his little box of oil, if he is capable of feeling at that time."

Megargel's affection for cycling continued through 1896, and by 1897, he had moved to Rochester, a center of American bicycling manufacture. He found employment at Novelty Bicycle Works, a retailer that advertised itself as carrying the "largest and most up to date line in Western New York. Sold for cash or on easy terms. A handsome souvenir to every lady purchaser." Beginning in 1898, Megargel copublished and wrote for *Sidepaths*, a sixteen-page bicycle biweekly that claimed a circulation of a few thousand able to "reach the wealthiest and most enlightened class of bicycle riders." Writing had become another of Megargel's serious interests, and he also had a sideline as a journalist, writing for the small Rochester News Bureau, which supplied local copy to area newspapers. It was not spellbinding work, and it seemed unlikely to propel Megargel to national literary success, but it did give him opportunity to improve his craft:

"Patrick Collins, 30 years of age, of 120 Seneca Street, Oswego, came to Rochester yesterday afternoon to have his artificial arm fitted and brought the money with him to pay for it," Megargel wrote in a Rochester News Bureau dispatch published in the *Oswego Daily Times* on November 20, 1900. "He met friendly strangers on Front Street, Rochester's Bowery, and while drinking with them was relieved of his entire roll." Poor Collins, employed at a yarn mill where he perhaps lost his limb, was not only robbed; he was arrested at his hotel for drunkenness, the dispatch noted. The thieves remained at large. The story was a standard crime brief, nothing more. It did not foretell glory for Megargel.

By 1904, Megargel had become intrigued by the horseless carriage—and his writing had improved sufficiently that the *Automobile* retained him to take a preview drive of AAA's New York–to–St. Louis parade.

It was a plum assignment: the *Automobile*, published weekly from the Flatiron Building in Manhattan, with bureaus in Chicago, London, Paris, and Berlin, and illustrated with high-quality photographs and drawings, was an authoritative voice of American automobiling. It printed some 14,000 copies every issue, a robust circulation.

With his brother Ralph and *Sidepaths* copublisher William S. Harrison riding as passengers, Megargel in late spring set off for St. Louis in an $850 Pathfinder, "a beautiful and luxurious car," as its manufacturer, Elmore, advertised it. Elmore, a member of Smith's ALAM, promoted the trip in ads, claiming Megargel chose the Pathfinder after "careful investigation of many styles of motor cars" and urging readers to follow its journey in Megargel's dispatches from the road.

Perhaps inspired by Jack London, whose novel *The Call of the Wild* had been a sensation the previous year, Megargel opened his first installment as he might have a popular novel: with interesting characters, a compelling challenge, and a hint of danger.

"While it is probably unnecessary to go armed," he wrote, on the sixty-pound typewriter with which he traveled, "our trio carried a revolver of large caliber apiece, fearing that tramps, certain to be met along some of the roads, would try a hold-up, under the general supposition that all automobilists are men of wealth."

The men were not even seventy miles from Manhattan en route to Albany when they experienced their first mishap; rain turned the roads "fierce," and Megargel and his companions had to unload the car and push it through the mud, ruining their French leather suits. Further on, an engine malfunction sent a cloud of blue smoke into the air. Kindly folk rushed to the rescue of something that needed no rescue. "Several inhabitants of a nearby farmhouse rushed out with buckets of water and other fire extinguishing apparatus, courteously ready to give assistance," Megargel wrote.

Horses often reacted differently. Some were strangers to the machine, and it could terrify them. Cursing the "red devil," owners demanded that Megargel stop, which he did.

"Great care should be exercised by tourists when passing rigs driven by women or children," he advised, "and if the horse shows signs of fright, one of the passengers in the automobile should get out and lead the horses by."

But no respectful touch could appease the fearsome Road Hog, a term originally used to describe ornery folk who tangled with bicyclists. With the advent of the car, the Road Hog had made a comeback—and Megargel and his passengers encountered one east of Buffalo as they were ascending a steep grade, "a difficult feat," as Megargel described it, as they risked tipping over if they did not keep speed and the center of the narrow road.

Megargel sounded his horn.

The Road Hog looked behind him but did not move his horse-drawn rig aside.

As Megargel was slowing, the man suddenly pulled on the reins and the Elmore rear-ended the wagon. Neither vehicle was damaged, but the man erupted.

Megargel wrote that he "showered such abuse upon us and automobilists in general as one seldom hears, even in counties traversed by the [Erie] canal. We asked him to pull aside and allow us to pass, but not he. Finally, after a delay of fifteen minutes, during all of which time he was threatening us with everything from murder on down, one of our party jumped out of the tonneau, grasped his horse by the bridle and led the animal and vehicle to one side of the road, despite a fierce resistance from the driver, and we proceeded on the way toward Buffalo."

Other country people reacted with peaceful befuddlement at the sight of an automobile.

"In several of the little towns," Megargel wrote, "the inhabitants gathered around us and looked over the machine with a great deal of curiosity, telling us that it was the first automobile that had ever stopped at that place. . . . The inhabitants were very ignorant regarding an automobile and its equipment. The suggestion by one village sage that the extra tire in the black tire case strapped on in front was a life preserver and that the goggle strapped across the visors of our caps were lamps to be used at night were generally accepted as facts by the rural populace, while it seemed to be the general verdict that our tires were solid rubber, our speedometer a patent clock and that our car or any other automobile was capable of traveling sixty miles an hour easily."

Having overcome rain, mud, sand, dust, holes, breakdowns, bad roads, washed-out and weak bridges, unmarked routes, one Road Hog, several angry farmers, belligerent police, skittish horses, kicking mules, snapping hounds, and lazy cows, Megargel ended his journey in early July when he paid the 35-cent toll, crossed a bridge over the Mississippi River, and arrived safely in St. Louis. His seven-part travelogue had displayed an eye for detail, a command of narrative, and a style that was a cut above ordinary auto journalism.

Megargel had found his voice. This was a writer with talent for the road-trip story, a narrative form practiced by James Fenimore Cooper and Mark Twain.

Having pleased the *Automobile*'s editors with coverage of the preview drive, Megargel was hired to write in-depth coverage of the parade itself, set to begin shortly after his return to New York.

———

DWIGHT B. HUSS, THIRTY, the Olds employee Smith would assign to officially represent the company in the 1904 run to St. Louis, had not craved adventure in automobiling, though it found him. He did not aspire to write. He only wanted a job.

The younger of two children of a woman who loved poetry and a fruit farmer who also operated a carriage and harness business, Huss was raised in Clyde, Ohio, the small town later fictionalized as *Winesburg, Ohio*, in the short story collection by Sherwood Anderson, who passed much of his childhood in Clyde at the same time as Huss. As a youth, Huss played baseball and he rode bicycles. He raced bikes for a while, too, the first time in a competition from his hometown to Green Springs, six miles distant.

"The prize was a grand piano," Huss later recalled. "I was ahead when a chicken flew into my chain and got wrapped around the sprocket. Lost the race."

Influenced by his father, a clever man who had patented a thumb-mounted corn-husking device that helped him capture the title of area corn-husking champ, Huss showed an aptitude for mechanics at an early age. After working as a machine-shop pattern maker, he was hired by

Ransom Olds in 1899 to work in Olds Motor Works' experimental shop, a privileged position that brought him into the heart of design and development.

If anyone knew an Oldsmobile bolt-by-bolt, it was Huss.

Confident that he could keep an Olds running under any circumstance, the company gave him a new role as ambassador, sending him east from Michigan with a Curved Dash in 1902. He made headlines for his appearances, including in Rhode Island, where automobiling was gaining popularity, in part because wealthy Newport summer colonists—Astors and Vanderbilts and other Gilded Age titans—flaunted their brass-trimmed machines before commoners and reporters who lined Bellevue Avenue to watch them pass.

In 1903, Olds sent Huss overseas, and that September, he steered a Curved Dash to fame in the Reliability Trials. "Far beyond my expectations, and we got the gold and silver medals, the highest awards in our class, beating twenty-three cars," Huss wrote to a friend back home in Michigan. "We have done a very good business over here and have sent many orders to the Olds Motor for 1904."

From England, Huss left for the continent, where he visited Sweden, Germany, and Poland. Autumn found him in Russia, which he entered only after taking an oath that he was Christian, because, in an era renowned for anti-Semitic pogroms, "as you well know the Russians don't want any Jews over there," he wrote to his friend. From Odessa, Huss ventured to St. Petersburg and Moscow. Olds claimed he was the first person to drive an automobile into the Kremlin—an exotic milestone the company exploited in its marketing, and which became ingrained in company lore. During the Christmas season, Huss represented Olds at the Paris Salon, a show that had grown in popularity every year since its 1898 debut.

Here, too, he proved a good salesman. "I sold three cars in about one hour Saturday afternoon," he wrote home. "The auto exhibits are very good, by far the finest ever seen up to date. The French cars are beautiful but very expensive."

But he thought little of the hosts.

"The French have just begun to wake up to the fact they are not the only people that can build cars," he wrote. "I hate the French as a people. I think they are very vulgar and disgusting. You have only to spend a few days here to see for yourself."

Publicly, Huss was more diplomatic, and, having impressed Europeans with American ingenuity, he returned home, more valuable to Olds than ever. Smith was running the company by then, but Huss remained in management's good graces. When Smith learned of the AAA's 1904 trip to St. Louis, he knew Huss would be his man.

————

SIXTEEN AUTOMOBILES IDLED THEIR engines at Fifth Avenue and Fifty-Eighth Street, outside the Manhattan offices of the Automobile Club of America, on the morning of Monday, July 25, 1904. The Main Line was about to depart for St. Louis.

"Certainly the scene was a bright one," Megargel wrote in the first installment of his account for the *Automobile.* "It was evident that most of the cars had been cleaned and polished with special care, and presented a most attractive appearance for the word that would start them on their 1,350-mile journey."

Cars manufactured in New York, Indiana, Michigan, Ohio, Germany, and France waited to depart. AAA president Harlan Whipple, who had notified participants the previous week by letter that "the eyes of the entire public are on us in this tour," was driving car No. 1, a German Mercedes. The French Darracq belonged to F. A. La Roche, a prominent autoist who had lost against Oldfield in the recording-breaking July 1903 Yonkers competition. La Roche had declared his intention of running the Darracq's engine around the clock, even while he slept, for the entire trip—and straight through on his return to Manhattan, a feat that, if accomplished, would stand as a record of reliability that would have been inconceivable just a year or two before. Another New Yorker was ready to drive a Cadillac, built by the company that had been created from the remnants of the Henry Ford Company. There was no Ford automobile, nor would one join the parade along the route, but Ford would display cars at the St. Louis fair.

No electric vehicles were departing New York: a battery could not hold a charge that long, and the uncertainties of recharging along the route, especially in rural areas that lacked electricity altogether, made the trip impossible. But four of the sixteen Main Line vehicles were steam-powered autos built by the White Sewing Machine Company of Cleveland, Ohio, which boasted in advertisements that its vehicles were "absolutely non-explosive . . . in touring, will make 100 miles without adding a drop of water or fuel to the original supply." White sought to reassure prospective buyers who had heard of the scary things steam could do.

Traveling with Megargel was his other brother, Roy G., a young Wall Street financier who would later be remembered for resurrecting Pepsi-Cola Company from bankruptcy in 1923. Megargel took particular note of Huss's car: not a Curved Dash, but the upscale Light Tonneau Olds that had debuted at Madison Square Garden.

"The new Oldsmobile tonneau looked bright and clean, innocent of knowledge of what lay before it," Megargel wrote. "Its progress will be watched with interest, as this is its first public performance of the kind." Smith also would watch with interest. The $950 Light Tonneau was a step toward the more expensive market he coveted.

At 9:30 a.m., Augustus Post, chairman of AAA's touring committee, whose greatest fame would be as a pioneering aviator, headed north on Fifth Avenue in his red-colored White steamer. The three other Whites fell in line, and behind them, the other cars.

―――――――

AFTER OVERNIGHTING IN POUGHKEEPSIE, the Main Line division reached Albany on the afternoon of Tuesday, July 26. The Boston–New England division, headed by the swashbuckling Charles Jasper Glidden, who drove a British Napier, joined them there. Glidden had used the fortune he'd made in the telephone industry to indulge in automobiling and had already completed part of an unprecedented, self-proclaimed "world tour" that would continue in fits and starts for several years and total, by his measure, nearly 50,000 miles. Glidden, who courted the press, made news practically everywhere he went.

Like Huss, Glidden seemed to take offense at the French auto industry's high opinion of itself. During a stop at Albany's grand Ten Eyck Hotel, he joined a conversation about an attempt to rid the English language of French-derived motor-vehicle terms.

"The general sentiment" of the drivers at the Ten Eyck, Megargel wrote, "appeared to be in favor of the adoption of plain English terms, and Charles J. Glidden said that during the recent Climb to the Clouds, a proclamation had been issued from the summit of Mount Washington which called for the complete abolition of the French word 'chauffeur' and the use of 'engineer' for 'mechanician,' 'motor car' for 'automobile,' 'motorist' for 'automobilist,' and 'motor-house' for 'garage.' This pleased the majority, and later the word 'engineer' was heard everywhere and 'motor-house' was the direction given to the arrivals." But resentments did not decide the language. The Mount Washington proclamation was but a whisper in the New Hampshire pines.

From Albany, the motorists went west, spending nights in Utica, Syracuse, and Rochester. They reached Buffalo on Saturday, July 30.

Megargel reported on road conditions, little changed since his preview run—although a relative absence of rain left dust, more annoying than it was a hindrance. By Buffalo, though, several cars had suffered breakdowns and accidents. "Trouble with ignition, spark plugs, coils, tires and springs has bothered almost everyone of the tourists," Megargel wrote. The constant jolting and vibration damaged Megargel's typewriter.

Glidden had the misfortune of meeting a close cousin of the Road Hog.

He was driving in Erie County, Pennsylvania, when he happened upon an irate farmer whose prize Plymouth Rock chicken lay writhing, its legs broken by a car that had preceded Glidden. Armed with a double-barreled shotgun, the farmer barked a demand.

"I want one dollar from you to pay for that chicken which someone in your party killed," he said. "I don't care who killed it, you belong to the gang and you have got to pay for it."

Glidden handed him a dollar.

"Well, I will let you go this time," the farmer said, "but if you or any of your friends ever kill another of my chickens there will be some other bloodshed, and don't you forget it."

————

MEGARGEL CHRONICLED THE EVENING spent in Rattlesnake Pete's, a club in Rochester, where an "exhibition of Pete's fearless handling of the dreaded rattler that caused these men, who fear nothing while traveling behind the steering wheels at a forty-mile clip, to draw back until yards separated them from the den of live and squirming snakes. Webb Jay hasn't gotten the sound of that rattling out of his ears yet, he says." Jay, who ranked with Oldfield as one of America's best racers, was driving a White steamer to St. Louis.

Megargel wrote also of the hoteliers and local auto clubs that hosted nightly feasts, memorably the one in Syracuse attended by some 150 drivers, passengers, and "a dozen or more prominent Syracuse society women" who partook from a menu of such playfully named dishes as "four-cylinder clams on the half shell," "broiled chicken differential style," "float feed sorbet," and "automobile ice cream," all accompanied by "gasoline cocktails" and "roller bearing burgundy." That evening ended with the pleasure of "spark plug cigarettes" and "open exhaust cigars"—for the men only. Tobacco in 1904 remained a forbidden pleasure for ladies.

And Megargel wrote of the open secret of the tour: despite the AAA's insistence it was noncompetitive, men of a certain type could not resist the temptation to race. They hungered to beat each other and make the front page for arriving first in communities along the way.

"Everyone declares most emphatically that this is a pleasure tour, not a race or endurance run, and they are sincere in their declarations," Megargel wrote. "Yet these same individuals, when a car comes rushing up behind them, shove their throttle wide open, advance their spark until their engine, whether it be one, two or four cylinder, is working to its fullest capacity. . . . No, there is no racing on this trip, yet why do owners of machines capable of traveling forty miles an hour get up at 3:30 a.m. and without a bite to eat drive their cars at the limit toward the night control only 100 miles away, an easy five-hour trip?"

Megargel was but one of many writers covering the tour. Beginning with "AN ARMY OF AUTOS TO CROSS HALF THE CONTINENT," a lengthy story published in the *New York Times* the day before the Main Line departed chronicled the event, as did numerous other national, local, and trade publications. Wire services sent accounts overseas. A writer with a reputation greater than Megargel's filed daily reports as he rode with Huss in his Oldsmobile: the hard-drinking F. Ed Spooner, photographer and correspondent for the New York *Globe and Commercial Advertiser*.

"Greatest newspaperman who ever lived," Huss later recalled. "Every night I'd lie in bed trying to get some sleep and Spooner would be pounding the typewriter beside my ear. Every 20 minutes, regular as clockwork, there would be a knock on the door and there would be a waiter with another highball for Ed."

———

MEGARGEL WAS SELECTED TO lead the cars out of Chicago on the last leg south to Missouri. The *New York Times* noted the honor in a story datelined August 7.

"The automobile tourists will start on the last stage of their long journey from New York to St. Louis early tomorrow morning," the story began. "The Pathfinder, driven by Percy Megargel of Rochester, N.Y., will lead the way, starting from the Michigan Ave. clubhouse of the Chicago Automobile Club at 6 o'clock and throwing confetti along the course."

Navigating by confetti could be tricky.

Megargel had already described the confusion created on the trip from Erie, Pennsylvania, to Cleveland, when the pilot vehicle, driven by a local autoist, had left a proper trail—only to have a speeding French Panhard kick up a whirlwind that scattered it everywhere. Another sort of complication arose in Painesville, Ohio, outside Cleveland, when a street sweeper swept up the confetti. Drivers who brought up the rear always had trouble. "On most occasions," Megargel wrote, "those in the pilot cars strew so much paper along the roadway for the first ten or twenty miles that by the time seventy-five or one hundred miles has been covered there is no confetti left and the tourists have to decide for themselves which roads to take."

But the departure from Chicago went smoothly and two days later, at about 2:30 p.m. on August 10, the tourists began to roll into St. Louis. Crowds cheered and threw flowers as the cars headed to the Hotel Jefferson, named for the president who negotiated the Louisiana Purchase. Of the seventy-seven vehicles that officially started from the various points, sixty-nine completed their journeys. Huss and Spooner made it, though Spooner's typewriter suffered damage, like Megargel's. Among the losers were two cars disabled by broken crankshafts, a car destroyed by an express train, and a Chicago man's Oldsmobile that caught fire.

The St. Louis exposition commemorated the centennial of the Louisiana Purchase. Outdoing even Chicago's 1893 fair, it occupied some 1,200 acres and featured a twenty-six-story-high Ferris wheel and nearly 1,500 buildings, including the Festival Hall and twelve "palaces" devoted to agriculture, education, electricity, fine arts, liberal arts, horticulture, mines, machinery, manufacturing, miscellaneous industries, transportation, and fish, game, and forestry. Fifty foreign nations sponsored exhibits, as did all but three of the then forty-five states. The 1904 Summer Olympic Games, the first Olympic competition to be held in America, was held at the fair.

Marvels were plentiful. There was the radiophone, an apparatus that "enables one to talk over a beam of light . . . a form of wireless telephony," said its exhibitors, General Electric and American Telephone and Telegraph. There were sewing machines from the Singer Manufacturing Company, weighing devices from American Talking Scales, cash registers from National Cash Register, music machines made by the Regina Music Box Company, and Blickensderfer electric typewriters. The Gillette Safety Razor Company offered a free trial of its new shaving-friendly product—it cut and nicked far less than a straight-edge—for which inventor King C. Gillette received a patent that year. And there were electric stoves and deluxe tubs, showers, and sinks requiring indoor plumbing. The Standard Sanitary Manufacturing Company's bathroom products prompted the *World's Work*, a monthly founded by noted publisher Walter Hines Page, to declare: "If we are not the cleanest people in the world, as we are apt to pride ourselves on being, it is not because we have not been provided with every facility for cleanliness." Fortunately, there was Standard Sanitary. "Here is all the luxury of cleanliness, such as Roman nobles never dreamed of," the *World's Work* wrote.

From its opening on April 30, when some 200,000 visitors turned out, until its last day on December 1, almost 20 million people—about one-fourth of all US residents—attended the fair. President Theodore Roosevelt telegraphed greetings on the first day, then paid a visit late in the year. Helen Keller, Scott Joplin, John Philip Sousa, Geronimo, T. S. Eliot, and distiller Jack Daniel, whose Tennessee sour mash took gold medal for best whiskey, were among the others who visited, spoke, or performed. America had taken its place in the forefront of Great Nations, or so the Americans who journeyed to St. Louis in 1904 had to believe.

Automobiles had also moved front and center, if their presence on the grounds and inside the nearly sixteen-acre, one-fourth of a mile long Palace of Transportation was the measure.

Locomotives and railcars were the giants inside the palace, but some 160 foreign and domestic automobiles shared space, a showing that the *World's Work* declared was a barometer of the overall technology revolution. "The longest stretch of progress between the World's Fair at Chicago and this one at St. Louis is unquestionably that covered by the automobile," the magazine wrote. "Comparisons here are so startling that they become contrasts."

With its display of a Curved Dash, the new Light Tonneau, and other vehicles, Olds enjoyed a prominent role.

"It was by no mere chance that the managers of the St Louis Fair selected the Oldsmobile as the ideal of transportation progress," the *World's Work* wrote, "for the Olds Motor Works are not only the pioneer builders of automobiles in America but they have the largest factory in the world, the product of which is greater and perhaps more widely distributed than that of any other automobile concern in the world."

But Ford was no bit player. "The Ford Motor Company, who exhibit several cars, have produced a machine that in running qualities, appearance and particularly in price is typically American. Built to stand the strain of uneven American roads—and with an appreciation of the national dislike for fussy complications, the Ford easily earns its subtitle, the car of satisfaction," wrote the *World's Work*.

"To sum up, the Ford is a thoroughly tested car, ready to run at a moment's notice, or no notice at all, over any reasonable road and to climb any reasonable hill, without giving the least anxiety to the driver."

———

The magnificent Palace of Transportation, St. Louis World's Fair, 1904.
Missouri History Museum, St. Louis.

WHEN THEY WEREN'T PARTYING, the AAA tourists joined other autoists in parades through the fairgrounds and along the streets of St. Louis.

On August 12, Megargel wrote:

The picture in front of the Jefferson Hotel at 1:30 this afternoon was worthy of the brush of some impressionistic artist who wishes to paint American life at its fullest. . . . Under a Western breadth of sky and the high sun was the Jefferson as a background for the scene: a modern, light grey brick hotel distinctly American in its skyscraper outline.

And in front of this building on Twelfth Street, one of the broadest cross-town thoroughfares in the United States, were gathered automobiles of every size, and nearly all of the machines were chic in gay decorations. Bunting in green and red, the American Automobile Association colors, was festooned in a hundred artistic ways through wheel spokes and over canopies. . . . Seated in these gaily decorated cars were women from the East, West, North and South. All were attired in fetching holiday gowns.

Parade of automobiles at the 1904 St. Louis World's Fair. Women ride but don't drive.
Missouri History Museum, St. Louis.

Delicately tinted chiffon veils, white hats, and dainty dresses were completed by bewilderingly pretty parasols. The tilting of these sunshades was so evanescent that the line of color moved up and down and around like a Florodora chorus [written by two Englishmen, the musical comedy *Florodora* began its long run on Broadway in 1900].

What a glorious spectacle Megargel painted. But the writer did not shy from describing motoring's dark side.

Drivers frightened horses but rarely killed them. Smaller creatures were a different matter. Cars provoked certain dogs into snarling attacks, and cats and other animals often reacted with terrified confusion.

"One of the most unpleasant recollections of the World's Fair Tour was the slaughter of domestic fowl and animals along the road," Megargel wrote. "Few automobilists drive more carefully than we do, and if you multiply our record of four dogs and a half dozen chickens by the total number of cars entered in the run, plus the machines used as escorts from different cities and towns en route, the grand total would be in the neighborhood of 400 dogs and 600 chickens, plus an unknown number of cats, turkeys, geese, ducks, rabbits and even pigs. A trail of feathers marked each day's run, and the dead dogs, pigs and poultry lined the course in increasing numbers as the number of machines passing over the route grew."

The carnage to dogs troubled Megargel especially.

"These never seemed to miss an opportunity of running out in front of our car and barking," he wrote. "That in itself would not amount to very much, but dogs have not learned yet to accurately gauge the speed of an automobile and one out of every three that runs in front of a machine to bark gets caught by the front wheel or takes a trip through the machinery and sometimes both."

For them, horns were futile—but a rubber slingshot, "the kind used when a boy," loaded with fine bird shot, proved effective, Megargel said. "I shall never take another trip of any length without taking my sling."

A motoring friend and Humane Society member tried a softer approach. He bought an ammonia gun to scare off a dog while his car passed. He was riding along at some 25 miles per hour when he encountered one and fired.

"A strong wind blew the ammonia, which was nearly pure, into his face and that of his chauffeur," Megargel recounted. "The latter lost control of the machine for a second, ran over the dog, went over an embankment and eventually carried away three sections of a rail fence. . . . Now he thinks that possibly there may be some merits in the sling-shot. It's strange how some people change their minds."

---

Barney Oldfield generated more press than dead chickens or spooked horses.

After taunting Ford at Madison Square Garden, Oldfield had gone south to Ormond-Daytona where, on January 27, William K. Vanderbilt II, driving a 90-horsepower German Mercedes, shaved two-fifths of a second off Ford's Anchor Bay run to set a new world record. Oldfield did not compete—but the next day, he met Vanderbilt in a race the *New York Times* described as "a battle royal." The men ran neck and neck at the start, but "at the quarter-mile point," the *Times* reported, "Oldfield began to gain slowly by inches, and gradually he crawled ahead, going at a frightful pace." Oldfield won.

As spring approached, Oldfield kept winning—but increasingly, the headlines concerned his off-track shenanigans. Even the company he kept made for great copy.

In a March 15 story from New Orleans headlined "STEAL AUTO FOR A LARK: Barney Oldfield's Manager Arrested for Entertaining Show Girls," a *Times* correspondent captured Oldfield's raucous off-track world.

"As the result of a sensational chase by the police for violating the speed laws, J. E. Doorhoefer, son of a Louisville tobacco manufacturer and bookmaker at the Fair Grounds, and Col. "Billy" Thompson, manager for Barney Oldfield, formerly holder of the mile automobile record of America, were arrested here to-day," the correspondent wrote.

"They also answered to the charge of stealing an auto belonging to Dominick O'Malley, owner of *The New Orleans Item*. The Kentuckian and Thompson wanted a second machine to take a crowd of actresses out for a morning lark, and took O'Malley's car. The police were notified, and a squad started in pursuit, but the automobilists would not stop. After a thrilling chase, Doorhoefer and Oldfield's manager were arrested in the Tenderloin as they alighted from O'Malley's auto. The women escaped."

Oldfield himself was arrested for speeding, in Cleveland on June 13, when he was caught driving 35 miles per hour in a 16-mile-per-hour zone. He had faced bigger trouble in April, when the AAA's Racing Committee barred him from competing in association-sanctioned races. Meeting at AAA headquarters in Manhattan's Fifth Avenue headquarters, the committee ruled that Oldfield had disqualified himself by competing at events—in Savannah, Georgia, on February 25, and at Birmingham, Alabama, on March 8—that the Racing Committee had not approved. Oldfield claimed the events were "exhibitions," not races, but after paying a $100 fine, he was reinstated. Oldfield's reputation followed him on the tour to St. Louis, when he made the papers for driving the Buffalo-to-Cleveland leg, telling the *Times* on August 1 during a stop in Erie, Pennsylvania, that he "had not attempted any speeding on the way," a claim that only the most gullible would have believed. Oldfield's reputation was so well known that soon cops stopping ordinary speeders would often say: "Who do you think you are, Barney Oldfield?"

————

AND THEN CAME THE late-August races at the Louisiana Purchase Exposition fairgrounds, which Megargel declared "the first automobile speed contests of importance that have yet taken place in St. Louis."

Some 20,000 spectators were in attendance the afternoon of August 28 when Oldfield and A. C. Webb of Joplin, Missouri, met in a ten-mile heat for the Louisiana Purchase Trophy, which carried a $500 prize. With his signature cigar in mouth—to protect his teeth from violent vibration, not to smoke—Oldfield took the wheel of his Peerless Green Dragon II, an eight-cylinder, 120-horsepower machine that made Ford's Arrow and 999 seem frivolous by comparison. Oldfield was dressed in a green driving suit and helmet, to match the color of his car.

The track was dusty and dry in the summer heat, but the drivers refused to allow the organizers to spray water, which could turn the track into slippery mud. On the second corner of the second lap, Oldfield tried to pass Webb—but lost in a cloud of dust, he crashed into a fence. The Green Dragon mowed down one hundred or more feet of rails—and two men—before it shot partway up a maple tree, overturned, and fell back to earth, demolished. Witnesses found Oldfield, dazed and bleeding, in shrubs. His right leg was limp. The men were dead.

"The two men were killed leaning over the fence watching the races," Megargel wrote. "One was a watchman at the track, another a negro. John Scott, the watchman, had both legs cut off by the racing machine and was killed instantly. The negro, whose body was torn and horribly cut, lived for an hour but died while being carried to the hospital. The policemen picked up the legs of [Scott] and laid them beside his body, covering the corpse with newspapers until the coroner arrived. It is only just to say that the police had repeatedly warned spectators away from the fence, the line having been patrolled less than twelve minutes before the accident."

Barney Oldfield, greatest race-car driver of the early era.
Library of Congress, LC-DIG-ggbain-16397.

Speaking from Missouri Baptist Hospital, where he was treated for broken ribs and a fractured right ankle, Oldfield called the accident "deplorable and lamentable" and vowed never to race again. He could not keep such a vow, of course.

## THE REAL COMPETITION INTENSIFIES

Ransom E. Olds returned to auto manufacturing on August 16, 1904, six days after Megargel and the AAA tourists reached St. Louis. The press received word of his incorporation of the R. E. Olds Company, which would build a factory employing hundreds in Lansing, Michigan, enthusiastically. "Lucky Lansing," declared the Detroit *Free Press*.

Fred Smith did not join in the applause. Since forcing Ransom from Oldsmobile, he had gone out of his way to harass the founder.

In a letter he sent on May 28, Smith asked Olds if he might be interested in a new car.

"There still is in stock at Lansing the large coupe which was made up some time last year," Smith wrote. "Is there some possibility that you might wish this carriage yourself? Would be glad to hear from you if you could use it at a very reasonable price."

Smith also peevishly sued Ransom for return of three Oldsmobiles that he said were company property (Ransom ultimately paid Smith $1,800 for the cars).

More substantially, Smith had tried to keep Olds from returning to carmaking.

"My friend, F.L., I am told, has now written to all my new stockholders with a view of discouraging them by talking litigation, etc.," Ransom wrote to a doctor friend.

"All our banks here have received letters, I suppose, in hopes to affect our credit, but he might as well talk to a stone. While he will no doubt do something by way of the Selden patent, the world will know its workings. It cost the old company last year nearly $30,000.00 for no protection, only the honor of F.L. being its president. Nothing can prosper, in my estimation, that buys people off . . . and is not founded on good and just principles."

In the letter, Olds painted Smith as a scheming villain in almost Shakespearean terms.

"The desire of another to be its manager and get the credit was so great that he completely converted the other directors, his own family," Olds wrote. "I could then see how trifling things were made into mountains."

On August 18, a day after the news of the incorporation of R. E. Olds Company, a letter to Ransom threatened litigation over his use of his own name in his own new company.

Signed "Olds Motor Works" but apparently authored by Smith, the letter said that "the use of the name 'Olds' by you in an automobile company, or in the automobile business, is clearly an infringement of our rights. We are sending you this notice at an early date so that you may know our position in the matter and so that if your disposition is to avoid litigation and conflict between the two companies because of the similarity of the names, you can without any loss in prestige and advertising make a change which will eliminate the name Olds and save the trouble and annoyance and expense of litigation that necessarily must follow in case you do not change."

Smith was not done. On August 29, Ransom received a letter from ALAM attorneys warning that if he manufactured cars without the group's permission, "you will render yourself liable to a suit for an injunction and accounting of the said Selden Patent." Like Ford, Ransom believed the patent was phooey—and here, he stood his ground, declining to apply for a license and preparing for an eventual suit (which came, belatedly, in 1907). In September, Ransom reached out to Ford to lend his support, and the next month, suggested that they form the nucleus of a new group representing unlicensed manufacturers. The idea would come to fruition in February 1905 with the establishment of the American Motor Car Manufacturers' Association (AMCMA).

On September 27, Ransom and fellow stockholders voted to drop his name but incorporate his initials into "Reo Car Company," later changed to "Reo Motor Car Company." Olds returned to the business of making cars, and on October 14, in Lansing, the new firm test drove its first model: a tonneau that produced 16 horsepower, seated five passengers, weighed three-fourths of a ton, and could reach 40 miles per hour. The ads would highlight its creator, while taking a swipe at Smith.

"This splendid, roomy, speedy, up-to-date car was invented and built by Mr. R. E. Olds, inventor and builder of the first practical runabout and recognized everywhere as foremost among the world's motor engineers and builders," one read. "The secret of its great speed and power is the lightness and compactness of its wonderful engine; worked out on principles originally discovered and demonstrated by Mr. Olds but now for the first time brought to their fullest perfection." At $1,250, the car would compete with Smith's own tonneau. A two-passenger Reo also was available—for $650, the exact cost of an Olds Curved Dash. The public would get its first look at the cars at the 1905 New York Auto Show.

———

THE SUMMER HEAT STILL smothered St. Louis when, on August 13, 1904, a doctor bought the first production car from the Buick Motor Company of Flint, Michigan. Incorporated on May 19, 1903, the firm was the latest incarnation of the small manufacturing enterprise founded in Detroit in 1899 by Scottish immigrant David Dunbar Buick.

The $950, two-cylinder, 12-horsepower Model B that Dr. Herbert H. Hills purchased gave an uncomfortable ride, but it was a sturdy vehicle that had demonstrated its worth the month before, when a test vehicle completed a round trip from the Flint plant to Detroit, a total distance of nearly 150 miles.

"The machine ran without a skip," Buick engineer Walter L. Marr, who traveled with David Buick's son, Thomas, told the *Flint Journal* in a July 13 page-one story. "We took hills handily with our high-speed gear and the machine sounded like a locomotive. It simply climbed. In one place, we raced with an electric car and showed them the way. We went so fast at another time that we could not see the village 'six-mile-an-hour' sign." The publicity helped bring seventeen orders before Hills took delivery of the first Model B.

To the public, Buick seemed poised to take off. But inside the company, anxiety ran high.

Buick's investors and managers knew how Smith's ALAM consortium had crushed the dream of Alexander Brownell Cullen Hardy, another once-promising local carmaker. With local banks at the time leery of investing in the new industry, Hardy in 1901 had used $5,000 of his own money to found the Flint Automobile Company, and by the end of the next year, he was building Flint Roadsters—snappy two-seat runabouts with red leather and paint, polished brass, and a single-cylinder engine that cost $750 to $850. By the end of 1903, Hardy had sold fifty-two cars, a respectable number. Such a handsome vehicle might help Hardy break out of the pack.

But Smith's group had been watching. ALAM demanded a $50 Selden patent royalty for each of Hardy's cars, and it obtained federal court orders to force payment on all fifty-two. The cost was prohibitive. Hardy folded his company and moved to Iowa, where he took a job as manager of an old-fashioned carriage company.

If ALAM came after Buick, the cost in royalties—or in defending lawsuits—would be substantial. Compounding the situation was Buick's debt to local banks, which had shut off credit. President and majority stockholder James H. Whiting turned to William C. "Billy" Durant, an old acquaintance, fellow Flint resident, and millionaire at age forty-two. A soft-spoken, slightly built man of average height whose gleaming brown eyes and charming manner suggested confidence but not cockiness, Durant was so gifted with salesmanship that his friend Walter P. Chrysler once declared that "he could coax a bird right down out of a tree."

## LATE TO THE GAME

Born December 8, 1861, in Boston, William Crapo Durant was the second child of a bank clerk and Rebecca Crapo, a daughter of Henry Howland Crapo, who began his rise to wealth and political power in New Bedford, Massachusetts. Henry invested in whaling and was the city's treasurer, clerk, and tax collector—but when he became interested in Michigan timber, he moved to the village of Flint to better manage his investments. By 1860, he was mayor. He was elected state senator and twice governor of Michigan, in 1864 and 1866. And he made money, a lot of money, from investments similar to Samuel Smith's.

Crapo took interest in the grandson who bore his name, even though Billy and his mother, Rebecca, did not move to Michigan until after his death. For the boy's third birthday, Crapo made Billy an honorary major in the Michigan Cavalry and "promoted" him to colonel four years later. In a letter from his deathbed in 1869, he praised Billy, back in Boston, for acknowledging a gift.

"My dear little grandson, 'Willie' C. Durant," he wrote. "Grandpa has received both of his very good letters and is very proud of them as he is of his noble boy. . . . I am very glad indeed that you like your Michigan sled and wagon, and hope you will have a great deal of pleasure playing with them."

But Crapo had no use for the boy's father, William Clark Durant. Durant drank and squandered money on what the father-in-law described as "reckless ventures" and "wild speculations." Crapo wrote his will so that Durant could not get the money he left to Rebecca. He explained his rationale in a letter to his only son, William, Billy's uncle.

Of William Clark Durant, he wrote: "Soon he will be an old man with a son to be provided for and settle with some kind of business, and this last is not anything that can be done by simply saying, 'Willie go here' or 'Willie go there.' The habits of the boy are to be formed, both by parental training and parental example, in order to give him proper notions of business."

Durant abandoned his wife and children after Crapo's funeral, and in 1872, the family of three relocated to Flint. With her inheritance, Rebecca purchased a large home that she furnished with hand-carved furniture and crystal chandeliers. Billy's father visited occasionally and was last heard from when his younger son was about sixteen. A letter he sent at that time indicated he worked in Detroit for a lumber company and lived at the YMCA.

Billy attended the Flint Conservatory of Music and drummed in a marching band. He played baseball, though not very well—but his charm was already in evidence when his peers voted him manager of the Flint Athletics, an amateur baseball team. At Flint High School, Durant followed a classical course of instruction: Latin, French, rhetoric, physiology, geography, and algebra. Relatives thought he might become a Presbyterian preacher or lawyer, so they must have been surprised when in early 1876, just months before graduating, he told his mother he was not returning to school. He wanted to roll up his sleeves and go to work.

Durant took a job at Crapo Lumber Company, founded by his late grandfather and run by his uncle William; at night, he clerked at a drugstore that sold patent medicines. Soon, he was pedaling snake oil to farmers on the outskirts of Flint. He was still living with his mother when he began selling cigars. He returned from his maiden outing with orders for 22,000 cigars—in just two days, a phenomenal accomplishment. The story held that Durant was so talented that his boss got from him the work of three ordinary salesmen. "They finally gave me a salary of $100 a month—$1,200 a year—and I had been working in a lumber yard at 75 cents a day," Durant would recall.

A handsome young man, Durant spoke softly but rapidly. He slept but four or five hours a night and seemed incapable of sitting still. He adored his mother, who had suffered through life with an alcoholic husband, a disappointment in every regard.

From selling cigars, Durant moved to the position of secretary with a private waterworks in Flint. The job included responsibility for collecting overdue bills—no easy task ever, but more difficult in this case, given the waterworks' notoriously inferior service. But Durant succeeded, helping to improve overall service in the process.

Fire insurance next intrigued him. A skilled negotiator now, after his bill-collecting experience, Durant merged several insurance companies into one. Now he was becoming a master of consolidation, too.

His restlessness kept Durant on the hunt for new opportunities. He dipped into real estate and construction and became one of three proprietors of a roller skating rink. But a random ride an acquaintance offered him in a new type of horse-drawn, two-wheel road cart in September 1886, when he was twenty-four, would be a decisive turning point.

Thanks to its ingenious design, the cart, made in a small shop in Coldwater, 120 miles away, did not sway or bounce like similar vehicles—a feature Durant believed he could sell in quantity to the masses. Seeking to buy a percentage of the business, Durant took a train to Coldwater and found the inventor, a middle-aged carriage maker, in his shop.

"Why not buy it all?" the man said—the wood used in manufacture, wheels and axles and springs, unfinished and completed vehicles, everything but the tools. The carriage maker and his partner wanted $1,500, with future royalties from the patent they held.

Durant did not have the money, nor did he want to share royalties. Talking the partners out of a royalty clause, he promised them their $1,500, even though he did not have it.

"If you will go down to the office of your attorney with me and execute a bill of sale and assign the patent and deposit all of the papers in your bank," he said, "I will go to Flint this afternoon and see if I can obtain the money, which must be in your hands within five days or no deal." The partners agreed.

Back home, Durant sold his proposition to the president of a local bank, who issued a loan for $2,000, the cost of the cart maker's assets, plus money to transfer operations to Flint. Durant brought his friend J. Dallas Dort into the business, and on September 28, the Flint Road Cart Company was organized. In 1895, their firm was reorganized as the Durant-Dort Carriage Company.

Billy Durant, sales and financial genius.
Library of Congress, LC-DIG-ggbain-21075.

Thus was confirmed the Durant modus operandi: make the pitch, promise results, shake on the deal, and hustle for the financial backing, counting on charm and confidence to win in the end.

The same nervous energy helped Durant build Durant-Dort into a giant that at its peak, 1906, employed some 1,000 factory workers who produced nearly five hundred vehicles a day. The company owned mills and forests in several states, and had interests in other carriage companies in Atlanta, Toronto, Kansas City, and elsewhere.

DURANT POSSESSED RARE TALENT for opening financiers' wallets and making complicated deals, but until the late summer of 1904, he had no interest in automobiles.

"I thought it was terrible the way these noisy contraptions, especially the old steam engines, shocked people and frightened horses," he later recalled. "My cousin, W.C. Orrell, had one and I was mighty provoked with anyone who would drive around, annoying people that way. I was not in the least bit interested in managing an automobile concern."

On September 4, Buick president and stockholder Whiting nevertheless arranged for his friend to take a ride with Dr. Hill in his Buick. Whiting also drove him around, and Durant later took the wheel himself. He was impressed—not only with the car's performance but with the attention it attracted, as if its mere presence was a persuasive advertisement in itself.

Durant's ambition overrode his annoyance. He was in.

On November 1, Durant assumed control of the company when Buick's board elected him a member. He left the presidency to Charles M. Begole, son of a former governor of Michigan (and later president of Chevrolet Motor Company), but he owned a majority share of Buick's stock. Durant began to appease angry Buick creditors, promising them an eventual return if they backed off from their claims, which they did, and he shifted production of Buick automobiles to an empty Durant-Dort Carriage Company factory in Jackson, Michigan. Deciding that appeasing ALAM would be less costly than fighting, he acquired the license held by Pope-Robinson Company, a Hyde Park, Massachusetts, manufacturer of luxury cars that ceased operations in 1904 after four years in business.

On November 3, the master salesman put on a grand show, arranging for several Buicks "with tooting bugles," the Flint *Daily News* wrote, to assemble at an intersection in downtown Flint—where, the paper reported, the cars attracted "a great deal of attention and much favorable comment." A review in the December 10 *Automobile Review* heightened the hype, calling the car "one of the new machines put on the market during the past summer and which gives promise of enjoying wide sales in the 1905 trade because of numerous good features in its design. . . . The advantages claimed for this machine are ease of control, one-hand lever, and foot pedals being used . . . easy riding resulting."

———

TRUSTING HIS LAWYERS TO handle litigation during that autumn of 1904, Ford concentrated on building cars. In the company fiscal year that ended on September 30, 1904, his new firm had sold 1,700 vehicles. Far from crushing Ford, the Selden patent suit seemed to have further energized him.

Ford completed transfer of production to a new three-story plant on Piquette Avenue that was ten times larger than the cramped old carriage shop on Mack Avenue in which the company had been operating. He spent much of his time in the experimental room, where new designs were born—a room to which only he and a handful of engineers and close associates had keys. He spent time on the assembly floor, where he was welcomed by workers who appreciated his backslapping and practical jokes while understanding he expected obedience and honest work. He arrived for work by 7:00 a.m. and frequently was at the shop until 11:00 p.m. He was a man possessed.

Company secretary James Couzens toiled similarly, but not with the boss's good humor. Pugnacious and prone to outbursts of temper, he frightened employees. "He was a manhandler," one employee recalled. "We went in enthusiastically and he opened up the hydrant on us and chilled us off."

But Ford needed him. During that autumn of 1904, Couzens was building a national network of dealers and handling the customers' complaints. He dispatched mechanics to dealerships to help with repairs and reported back to Ford deficiencies that could be avoided during design of future models. He paid the bills and kept the proverbial trains running on time.

Couzens was indispensable to Ford—but nominal company treasurer Alexander Y. Malcomson, who had helped grow his coal business with the slogan "Hotter Than Sunshine" painted on his horse-drawn delivery wagons, was not. Malcomson had helped arrange much of the investment in Ford Motor Company in return for 255 founding shares worth $51,000, the same as Ford (Couzens received 25 shares and brothers John F. and Horace E. Dodge, who supplied Ford with many of his parts, 50 shares apiece); and he and Ford had started out controlling the company together; but their visions of the future soon diverged.

Ford wanted to focus on inexpensive cars. Like Smith, Malcomson wanted to build costlier models. For the moment, their disagreement simmered but did not boil over.

# 5

## SENSATION

### HEAVY TOURING

Fred Smith really needed some good press for his new lineup when the fifth annual New York Auto Show opened on January 14, 1905. The year just ended, the first under his full control, had been a disappointment: Olds Motor Works had sold only about 3,400 vehicles, down from the company's record 1903 performance of nearly 4,000 sales. Smith's upscale $950 Light Tonneau, introduced at the 1904 show, had been a dud.

Still, Olds remained the industry leader, its Curved Dash still the gold standard for low-priced cars. Unchastened by the Light Tonneau's failure, Smith had rolled the dice for 1905 on a more luxurious machine: the four-seat, 2,350-pound, 20-horsepower Heavy Touring, advertised as capable of reaching 40 miles per hour, an impressive number for those into speed. The Heavy Touring was Olds's first two-cylinder car, and at $1,400, it was the company's most expensive car ever, but it promised profit if it sold in volume. Smith was also offering a small bus: the ten-passenger, $2,200 Wagonette, "an attractive investment for street service in small towns, for stage line work, for depot services and for report service," as one ad declared. Also in the 1905 line was a longer and more powerful version of the Light Delivery Wagon, a truck often called the "pie wagon." Only a handful had been sold in 1904, but Smith believed the vehicle would gain traction. Obsessed with luxury automobiles, Smith also wanted a piece of the growing commercial motor-vehicle market.

Smith was backing his new bets with money and purpose. He was expanding factory capacity, and his seasoned sales force was ready to go; new advertising was planned, and Olds would be a major presence at trade shows in America and abroad. For New York, he had arranged a 640-square-foot space in the center of Madison Square Garden's main floor. Only Peerless, with 656 square feet; Studebaker, with 750 square feet; and Pope, Locomobile, and Electric Vehicle, which each had a 1,312-square-foot presence, were more commanding.

But space alone did not guarantee Smith the excited interest that he sought, for the competition had intensified in the past year.

More than one hundred carmakers were showing their models in New York—along with nearly twice that many manufacturers of tires, tools, jacks, pumps, chains, ball bearings, joints, radiators, gas tanks, batteries, spark plugs, carburetors, distributors, gears, springs, lubricants, locks, horns, lamps, clothing, hampers, baskets, field glasses, speed recording instruments, and other parts and accessories. Motorcycle makers displayed their vehicles. Many companies had been turned away, for even by further expanding into the Garden's balconies, concert hall, basement, and restaurant, there was insufficient room to meet demand.

"Never before in the history of American industrial exhibits has so large a number of automobiles and motor car accessories been assembled under one roof," the *New York Times* wrote. "With barely two or three exceptions, the show represents the highest triumphs of American ingenuity, originality and perfection in automobiles." Gasoline-powered vehicles predominated, the *Automobile* observed, "yet steam has not by any means disappeared, as is shown by the exhibits of four makers of steam vehicles exclusively; while electricity as a motive power is strongly, though not largely, represented."

Overall, the year just ended had been the most remarkable yet for the industry. According to the January 21 edition of Chicago-based *Automobile Review,* more than $26 million worth of automobiles had been manufactured in the United States in 1904, compared to only "a few thousand

Madison Square Garden, circa 1905.
Library of Congress, LC-DIG-det-4a08182.

dollars" a decade before—with approximately $40 million in cars pro-jected to be built in 1905, based on materials already ordered. "At present, 150 firms are engaged in the manufacture of cars alone, some of the larger of which employ over 1,000 workmen," the publication wrote.

Motor vehicles continued to assimilate into more sectors of the American economy.

"Our express companies are now delivering and collecting merchandise with gasoline and electric cars," *Automobile Review* observed. "Our post office departments are having their mails brought to and delivered from central stations in the horseless car. Our big departmental stores depend upon it for the rapid delivery of their goods. It is used by our large manu-facturers for conveying their products from the warehouses to the railroad depot. Fire departments in large cities are substituting it for the horse, and in almost every avenue of commercial life, we see daily evidence of this irresistible invasion of the motor car."

The heart of the market remained the individual consumer. Visitors to the New York show saw cars for a wide range of budgets, "from the runabout type, as low as $450 in price," the *New York Times* reported, "to the richly upholstered Limousine top touring cars, from 24 to 40 horsepower, which sell from $5,000 to $8,000 and find no lack of purchasers."

Journalists wrote of record-breaking attendance inside the Garden and traffic congestion outside as people took test drives. "Over 100 puffing automobiles of all descriptions and sizes could be seen there at any hour of the day yesterday," the *Times* reported on January 19. "A constant stream of prospective buyers was being led out from the Garden by hopeful agents from early in the morning until late at night."

The agents courted customers with leisurely trips along Fifth Avenue and around Madison Square Park—but in their sales pitches, they lauded the joy of the full throttle, agreeing with an *Automobile Review* editorial published on the eve of the New York show, which asserted that the desire to move fast had permeated the culture.

"The great American nation loves speed, whether it is on a train, a steamboat, or in an automobile," the magazine wrote. "To supply this demand, horsepowers have increased, and where formerly a forty-horsepower car was considered a racer, it is now looked upon as an ordinary touring car."

Power elicited the worst behaviors in some drivers, as events in Manhattan demonstrated again during that 1905 show week: visiting French race-car driver Henri Fournier, for example, made headlines for speeding up Fifth Avenue with three women on Monday, January 16, in what the *Times* described as a "big car." Bicycle policeman William A. Sherry caught sight of him at Fifty-Ninth Street, the paper reported, and had chased furiously for twenty-six blocks before finally catching him. Fournier paid a $10 fine but insisted he did not realize Sherry meant to arrest him until the cop pulled alongside.

"If I had known he was after me," Fournier said, "he would never have caught me."

A tougher sanction awaited Maurice Frederick Maximilian Bruen, a former chauffeur for William K. Vanderbilt, for his reckless driving through midtown Manhattan the same day as Fournier's dash up Fifth Avenue. As astonished onlookers watched, Bruen sped through the streets, dodging a trolley, taking corners on two wheels, and spinning his machine in a 360-degree circle as police pursued him. Bruen knocked one officer and his motorcycle into the air and was arrested after he tackled another officer and was finally subdued. No one sustained serious injuries, but the incident made the front page of the January 17 *Times*.

"He acted like a wild man last night," Jefferson Market Court magistrate Alfred E. Ommen said when Bruen and his lawyer appeared before him the next day. "He literally plowed his auto through the streets, and over crosswalks, in sections of the city where the night crowds are always greatest. That he didn't kill someone seems to me miraculous."

Ommen cut Bruen's lawyer no slack.

"A man who will deliberately do what this man did ought to be confined in some institution for the rest of his life," the magistrate said.

"He was chauffeur for William K. Vanderbilt," the lawyer said.

"The fact that this prisoner was once in the employ of William K. Vanderbilt should be the greater reason for this particular chauffeur to abide by the law," Ommen replied. "He knows right from wrong, as far as driving an auto is concerned. This is to me a clear case against this prisoner. I shall hold you, Bruen, in $500 bail on the charge of violating the speed law and in $1,500 bail on the charge of felonious assault."

"I consider that bail far too heavy," the lawyer said.

"It ought to be greater," Ommen replied. "The bail will not be reduced."

———

RUSSIAN ENAMEL AUTOMOBILE HAT pins were among the favors handed out to lady guests at Mrs. John Jacob Astor's annual ball at her Fifth Avenue townhouse the evening of January 16. Another sign of the times was seen on the same night, when George B. McClellan Jr. became the first mayor of New York to attend, in official capacity, a dinner of an automobile organization.

The occasion was AAA's annual dinner, held at the Waldorf-Astoria. When McClellan rose to speak, members applauded.

"The motor car has surely come to stay," the mayor said, "and no longer is the once familiar cry of 'get a horse' heard when one travels in the eastern part of the city. Indeed, it is possible to go almost anywhere now, and only be stoned occasionally." As New Yorkers well knew, rowdies regularly expressed their hatred for the machine by hurling rocks and stones at passing motorists.

This touch of dark humor was followed by "sallies of laugher," the *New York Times* reported, when McClellan lampooned the complaints against motor vehicles voiced by the West Side Association, a tony civic group. "You still have your oppressors," the mayor said, "and as a bit of interesting information let me say right here that a few days ago I received a petition from a very respectable body of taxpayers begging that they might have better police service as a protection against burglars and motor cars."

Turning serious, McClellan all but spoke for Ford.

"What the motor car industry really needs is an engine that is cheap, simple and strong," he said. "By hard experience, I know the difficulty of achieving all of these attributes, but I know that American ingenuity will eventually succeed in giving us the ideal motor car."

Five days later, when the Automobile Club of America held its annual banquet, also at the Waldorf Astoria, club president D. H. Morris echoed McClellan's themes.

"At first we were looked upon merely as sporting enthusiasts—children with a toy," Morris said. "Legislators, though still attacking the great industry, do it timidly, for they are beginning to feel the power of the new force, the thousands of voters who own and are yet to own automobiles. We strive for the development of the automobile into a low-priced and perfected machine for the rapid and efficient transportation of man and merchandise, for the building and maintenance of good roads, for the enactment and enforcement of salutary and reasonable laws, for the carrying out of the Golden Rule of the road, and for the punishment of those offending the written and unwritten laws."

Former ACA president Scarritt predicted success: "Four years ago, there was in this country one automobile to every 1,500,000 inhabitants," he said, exaggerating the numbers somewhat. "Two years ago, there was one to every 6,500 inhabitants. Today there is one to every 1,200 inhabitants. Give us another five years, and they will be as thick in this country as mosquitoes on the Hackensack Meadows."

———

Away from the banquets and the ballrooms, a nastier business was conducted in New York that January 1905. ALAM was ramping up its war with Ford and others who continued to defy the Selden patent.

The organization deployed patent sleuths who scoured the streets for imported automobiles that did not display the brass Selden license tag, threatening to sue owners who did not pay royalties. It attempted to scare agents of nonlicensed vehicles in what a Ford director said was an effort designed "to create such a feeling of distrust and fear on the part of dealers, which would so intimidate them, that they would not sign a contract for sale of Ford cars." And it engineered a coup that Smith must have found wickedly satisfying.

In news that *Automobile Review* called "the sensation of automobile week in New York," Smith's group announced that it had secured an exclusive two-year lease of the Garden for the 1906 and 1907 shows, with an option for 1908 and 1909. "What this change of management will mean is not yet evident, but many unlicensed makers exhibiting this year will doubtless be barred in 1906," the magazine said. That meant Ford and others on his side.

Smith gave no statement on the matter, but in his remarks, ALAM president Colonel Charles Clifton, secretary and treasurer of Buffalo-based George N. Pierce Co., forerunner of Pierce-Arrow, portrayed the lease as a logical response to counterproductive overcrowding—and a kindly gesture to the supposedly overwhelmed owners of the arena.

"The shows are growing too congested. . . . The garden company is suffering from the present state of affairs," he told *Motor Age* in its massive show edition. More magnanimously still, Clifton asserted, the lease was another protection that the good-hearted members of ALAM offered consumers.

"All of our members are responsible makers [and] will be able to give a representative American show and offer the public cars worth buying with guarantees that amount to something. There are, though, small and irresponsible makers who take this chance to offer to the public cars that have not been properly tested or proven reliable. In this way, the public is placed in danger to its peril and the injury of the American industry. Such a restricted show as ours [will be] the logical solution of the present situation."

But *Motor Age* didn't buy it. The weekly's editors surely intended tongue-in-cheek with their headline to their story: "A.L.A.M. WOULD BE BOSS: It Has Corralled Madison Square Garden for Future Automobile Shows and Will Restrict the Number of Exhibitors, the Object Being to Protect the Dear, Innocent Public."

But Ford and his allies did not use tongue-in-cheek to debunk Clifton. They called it hogwash.

"This ALAM show advertising is a bluff," said W. D. Gash, who worked for John Wanamaker. "If they think to compel us to come into their ranks on the threat of shutting us out of the show, they are mistaken. They cannot keep us from showing and selling our cars to New Yorkers or letting them know all about them."

Another leading figure in the car business who asked that his name not be used "had a lot of warmly embellished comments to make," *Motor Age* wrote. "He said, in part, 'This move of the licensed people is un-American. The ALAM is merely a trust to boost the price of its cars. Licensed cars are listed at from $300 to $400 above unlicensed cars of equal merit.'"

Rambler founder Thomas B. Jeffery, whose sales rivaled those of Olds Motor Works, predicted that Smith's exclusionary policy would backfire. "We can sell all the cars we want without exhibiting here," he said. "It is a foolish move to shut us out. It will tend to concentrate and solidify opposition and make friends for the independents." Should the non-ALAM makers wish, Jeffery said, "we could easily find a place wherein to hold it."

Couzens agreed, declaring that "an opposition show would be a hardship on the American public. The independents, though, have as much capital behind them as the trust and could run a show of their own if they cared to do so."

And that, and more, is what soon happened.

On February 24, 1905, leaders of several unlicensed automakers who had quietly begun discussions during the Chicago auto show, held two weeks before, met secretly at Ford's Detroit plant to found the American Motor Car Manufacturers' Association. Couzens was elected chairman of the group, which included Ford, Duryea Power Co., Maxwell-Briscoe Company, and sixteen other carmakers. Ransom Olds was not among the founders, although eventually he would join.

Establishing its headquarters in Chicago, the AMCMA adopted seven articles of organization relating to advertising, racing, dealerships, engineering standards, and increasing citizen support for the machine that was transforming the country, as stated in Articles 2 and 5: "To increase the interest of the public in the purchase and use of motor cars. . . . To promote public interest in good roads and to arouse public opinion to oppose legislation which discriminates against the proper use of motor cars."

In comments to the *Motor World,* general counsel Job E. Hedges spoke unambiguously of AMCMA's first purpose: marshaling the collective strength of nineteen manufacturers to combat ALAM. Come early 1906, that meant staging a show to compete with Smith's Madison Square Garden event. "The show will be held in New York," said Hedges, a former New York deputy attorney general and secretary to late New York mayor William L. Strong. "It will be promoted by men whose standing in the social, financial and automobile worlds will be recognized the moment their names are made public."

The *Motor World* took Hedges at his word, writing: "That the association is meant to stiffen the backbone of the independent agents is patent on its face, and that it will serve its purpose cannot well be doubted."

Never accused of subtlety, Couzens drove the point home.

"We are in this fight for blood, and we mean to draw it," he said.

Two months later, AMCMA signed a lease for a show at the new Sixty-Ninth Regiment Armory, on Lexington Avenue between Twenty-Fifth and Twenty-Sixth Streets—just a half block from an entrance to Madison Square Garden. A jewel of a building designed by Hunt & Hunt, "its enormous floor space, giving over 152,000 square feet," the *New York Times* would report, "is admirably adapted to the placing of machines so that their good points and mechanical feature may be inspected with the minutest care."

Not only would the Ford group's show be almost literally on top of Smith's—it would open on Saturday evening, January 13, 1906, precisely when the ALAM event would begin. And it would be staged under the banner of the Automobile Club of America, which banqueted at the Waldorf-Astoria.

## "SHOW US HOW TO FLY TO THE MOON"

Unaware of the impetus he'd given independent manufacturers to organize, Smith left New York after the January show satisfied with ALAM's coup. And if Olds's hype was to be believed, his 1905 line had generated the buzz he needed.

A full-page ad the company had run during auto week trumpeted Olds trucks as "the prime favorites of their class" and the standard Curved Dash as "the leading car in its class." The ad maintained that the Olds Light Tonneau and its Touring Runabout, a more expensive version of the Curved Dash that featured a steering wheel instead of a tiller, enjoyed "increased popularity from their success of last year." Smith's top-of-the-line Heavy Touring was "the sensation of the show."

The ad declared: "If you have followed the crowd at Madison Square Garden, and who hasn't, you have seen our exhibit. You have examined the most complete line of light cars ever put on the market. . . . Altogether you have found convincing evidence that the Oldsmobile line will continue to be, as in the past, the most thoroughly successful."

Reality, however, differed. The Light Tonneau had generated no more excitement than it had the year before, and the Heavy Touring was anything but a sensation. Journalists did not exactly bubble over with excitement at anything Olds offered. *Automobile Review* published photographs of the two cars and the Olds exhibit in its two editions with reports from the show, but the magazine's general reporter and engineering columnist did not mention the company or its cars in their accounts. They did cover Ford, and they reserved their highest praise for Ransom Olds's new

Durant made this Buick a winner.
Courtesy of the AACA Library and
Research Center, Hershey, PA.

company: "The Reo is a new star in the auto firmament and promises to glow with increasing brightness," the magazine wrote. The *Automobile* devoted just thirty-six lines to the Olds line—but more than double that for Reo and for Ford, whose Model C runabout and new $2,000 Model B and $1,000 Model F touring cars attracted attention.

But the most remarkable development from Manhattan was one that went virtually unnoticed by the press. Buick was still so small that Durant had managed only to get one car shown—not on the main floor but in the restaurant, with another display, of a chassis only, in the basement, a barely whispered presence that led the *Automobile* to publish just twelve lines of basic description and *Automobile Review* to note merely that "Buick Motor Car Co., Jackson, Mich." was among the hundreds of exhibitors.

Against this backdrop, Durant worked his sales magic. Buick had sold only thirty-seven cars before the show, but he returned home with orders for more than 1,100.

———————

STILL, SMITH HAD NO need to be overly pessimistic, for the year was young; the prime selling season, spring and summer, lay ahead. He ran a company in which strong marketing ran deep in the veins. He still sold the basic Curved Dash runabout, mainstream America's all-time favorite model—holding the price at just $650, a bargain few competitors could match. And he lived at a time when the nation craved sensation, which could serve an automaker well, as Ford's Arrow had amply demonstrated.

This was an era when audiences packed circuses and fairs, and stunts thrilled the masses, most memorably the great staged Texas train wreck of 1896, in which two thirty-five-ton locomotives had hurtled head-on into each other in a town named Crush for the occasion. Proliferating human cannonballs risked their lives with every launch; the circus daredevil Volo the Volitant performed "bird-like bicycle flight through space"; and sixty-three-year-old schoolteacher Annie Edson Taylor went over Niagara Falls in a barrel.

"I would rather face a cannon, knowing that I would be blown to pieces, than go over the falls again," Taylor told the press. Her assessment failed to discourage others. The very day her stunt was reported, the *Boston Globe* ran a story about "George J. Palmer, the East Upton farmer, who has plans underway to tumble over Niagara Falls in a rubber ball."

Inevitably, the new machine made it to center ring. No sooner had the 1905 New York auto show ended than Mademoiselle Mauricia de Tiers of Paris, the "aerial automobilist," was booked into Madison Square Garden. She was such a sensation overseas that the *New York Times* heralded her arrival, on the liner *La Touraine*, as she came to America to "loop the gap," a hair-raising stunt that seemed to defy the laws of physics.

"Before you can realize it," de Tiers's advertisement proclaimed, "the car has descended the incline, turned upside down and, still inverted, has shot into space. Twenty feet away, across a veritable chasm of death, is a

Mlle. Mauricia de Tiers in her car.
Library of Congress, LC-USZC4–5229.

moonshaped incline. Your breath comes fast. You gasp. Your heart seems to stop pulsating. Will the auto strike the incline? Will it be upright?"

Mademoiselle de Tiers herself spoke to the zeitgeist when she told the *New York World* that she had only approached a frontier, not conquered it.

"I am courting death each day in le Tourbillon De La Mort, the supposed limit of human daring," she said. "But this act of plunging down the steep incline in an automobile that turns a back somersault in midair and lands on a runway is not really the limit of human daring. It is only the most perilous act that human imagination has so far devised for human daring. But it is only the limit for the moment. Hundreds of inventors are hard at work trying to perfect a machine that will make a double turn. . . . So get your minds fermenting; give your imagination free play; and invent the real limit of human daring. Show us how to fly to the moon."

Smith's most ambitious marketing effort in 1905 would be the motoring equivalent of a trip to the moon. He would send two Curved Dash Olds on a race from Manhattan to Portland, Oregon.

Such an event would overshadow any of the other contests that had multiplied in America since the first official race, in 1895. The year 1904 had seen more than two hundred contests on tracks, roads, and beaches in Rhode Island, New York, New Jersey, Nebraska, Michigan, Florida, California, Colorado, Pennsylvania, Georgia, South Carolina, Illinois, Indiana, Missouri, Minnesota, and Ohio. Stock cars and race cars had competed in handicaps, free-for-alls, special heats, and other events. Henry Ford had set a speed record on ice. But no one had ever suggested, let alone attempted, a race across the continent.

Only four cars, noncompeting, had even made the passage since the initial attempt in 1899.

The first success was by Dr. Horatio Nelson Jackson of Vermont and mechanic Sewall K. Crocker, who drove a Winton from San Francisco to New York, a trip lasting sixty-three days: from May 23 to July 26, 1903. Second was mechanic E. Thomas Fetch, who drove a Packard from San Francisco to New York in sixty-two days: June 30 to August 21, 1903. Third was mechanic Lester L. Whitman, who drove a Curved Dash with mechanic Eugene I. Hammond from San Francisco to New York in seventy-two days: July 6 to September 17, 1903. Fourth was Whitman again, with mechanic Clayton S. Carris, who drove a Franklin from San Francisco to New York in an incredible thirty-two days: from August 1 to September 3, 1904.

Whitman's 1903 trip had proved a marketing bonanza for Olds Motor Works, which sponsored the adventure with the support of Ransom Olds and the assistance of Chapin, whose stamp was evident from the start of the trip, when Whitman and Hammond posed in their Curved Dash at San Francisco City Hall as Mayor Eugene E. Schmitz handed them a letter to carry to New York mayor Seth Low—the first US mail, it was claimed, to be delivered by motor vehicle across the continent. In photographs published in many places, the words "Oldsmobile: Enroute from San Francisco to New York," painted on three sides of the chassis, were plainly visible.

"As the clock struck the hour of 11 this morning, E. I. Hammond and L. L. Whitman, two enthusiastic automobilists, began what they hope will prove a successful attempt to cross the United States in an automobile," read the July 6, 1903, *San Francisco Bulletin*, one of many newspapers and magazines to chronicle the trip.

Wearing pith helmets as protection against the sun, the men drove east. They shipped gasoline ahead by stagecoach and rail, and at one stop, filled their tank with liquid provided by a friendly saloon keeper, fuel they described as smelling more like whiskey than motor fuel. They carried only the clothes they wore, buying new outfits as they progressed.

The drivers reached Manhattan the afternoon of September 17. The next morning, they drove up City Hall steps—a crowd-pleasing stunt—to deliver Schmitz's letter to Low, who read it aloud in a ceremony that drew reporters.

"San Francisco sends her greetings to the great metropolis of New York," Schmitz wrote. The next day, Whitman and Hammond continued on toward Portland, Maine, arriving there on September 23, having averaged 2.41 miles per hour along a route of 4,225 miles.

Olds trumpeted the crossing in its ads.

"The Oldsmobile trans-continental trip is the most wonderful automobile journey ever made," one proclaimed. "From San Francisco to New York, over mountains, across deserts, through sand and mud, the Oldsmobile won its way, surmounting every difficulty and proving to the world it is 'built to run *and does it.*' By this remarkable trip, the Oldsmobile demonstrates its equality with the high-priced touring car."

———

A TRANSCONTINENTAL CROSSING WAS a phenomenal achievement and marketing boon, but a transcontinental race, first in history? What a sensation it would be! Adding competitive drama to the intrinsic dangers of the trip would intensify interest among the press and everyday people, Smith believed, for who could resist tuning in as the days passed, the drivers battling nature and each other, all the while praying that their machines not give out?

Smith went to work, bringing Chapin, now Olds sales manager, into the planning. They were joined by James W. Abbott of the US Department of Agriculture's Office of Public Roads, a precursor to the Federal Highway Administration. A leader in the growing Good Roads movement, Abbott envisioned a future when motor highways connected the coasts and the smallest points between. Like Olds, he understood the power of publicity.

Smith chose New York as the starting point of the race and Portland, Oregon, as the finish. A New York start promised press coverage before the race even began, and Portland was hosting America's grandest fair in 1905: the Lewis and Clark Centennial Exposition, commemorating Lewis and Clark's historic expedition, commissioned by President Thomas Jefferson a century before to explore land acquired with the Louisiana Purchase.

More fortuitously still, the National Good Roads Association was holding its annual meeting at the exposition on June 21, the first day of the summer of 1905.

———

SPRING ARRIVED, AND SMITH, Chapin, and Abbott finalized their plans.

They mapped out a route that would bring the drivers through Albany, Utica, Syracuse, Rochester, and Buffalo, New York; Erie, Pennsylvania; Cleveland and Toledo, Ohio; South Bend, Indiana; Chicago, Illinois; Davenport and Des Moines, Iowa; Omaha, Nebraska; Julesburg, Colorado; Cheyenne and Laramie, Wyoming; Boise, Idaho; and across Oregon to Portland. They named the competing Curved Dash cars Old Scout and Old Steady and arranged for gasoline and repair parts to be shipped by rail to distant points. They produced maps of the route for exhibit in Olds dealerships, and dealers were instructed to give the racers a hearty welcome when they reached town—and to alert town fathers and local reporters in advance of their arrival. Olds would wire daily bulletins to newspapers once the race began and Abbott arranged to travel by train ahead of the drivers to help smooth the way. In total, Smith would invest about $14,000—more than $363,000 in 2014 dollars—in the race, but the value from the free publicity would be exponentially higher.

Smith was set to select the two drivers when a story in the March 30 *Motor World* caught his attention.

The magazine disclosed Ford's intent to build a new factory in Detroit for the eventual large-scale production of a new, low-price car, as yet not formally announced. *Motor World* wrote that Ford, "which in the twenty months of existence has convinced the trade that it believes in doing things and knows how to do them, and, because of the fact, has made itself one of the very best known automobile concerns in the universe, is hatching another surprise. It has to do with a new Ford car, the price of which will supply the sensation."

No figure had been made public, *Motor World* wrote, "but it is known that it will be of a popular price in the fullest significance of that term."

How popular, exactly? The question was posed to an unnamed Ford officer.

"So popular that everyone can own an automobile," said the officer, likely Couzens or Ford himself.

"Despite the fact that the Ford people only this year erected a huge new factory," *Motor World* wrote, "for their new creation, they have secured an option on a large tract of land close by the present plant, and arrangements are under way for the erection of a still larger factory which will have a capacity of at least 10,000 of the popular priced machines."

## "THAT THOUSAND DOLLARS IN COLD CASH"

Readers of the April 20, 1905, edition of the *Motor World* found a double-page ad of unusual interest. The headline read: "$1000.00: Oldsmobile Volunteers Wanted."

The ad explained that "On May 8th, we will start two OLDSMOBILE STANDARD RUNABOUT stock cars from New York City overland to the Lewis & Clark Exposition, Portland, Oregon. Two drivers will be selected from those who volunteer. We will pay all their expenses on the trip and will give the driver bringing his machine first into Portland a cash prize of $1000.00. The second man will receive the machine he drives."

The ad noted Whitman and Hammond's historic 1903 crossing, calling that vehicle "the first light car to cross the American Continent under its own power" and proclaiming the 1905 race "in the interests of Good Roads." Olds chose the Curved Dash for the race, the ad asserted, for its motor, "fully adequate to meet the most exacting emergencies"; its generous water and gasoline capacities, which could support a drive of more than one hundred miles before refilling; easy control, with just "one lever and two brakes, nothing to confuse"; and its overall durability. "It is immensely strong and breakages are rare." Candidates were instructed to cable or write Olds Department 53, Detroit.

But the excitement would not be limited to two lucky drivers: Enterprising citizens who photographed them along the way would also be rewarded, with a $25 first prize; two second prizes, for $15 and $10; twenty-five prizes of $2; and fifty prizes of $1 each for the best photographs.

Soon, stories about the race—with its prize of "that thousand dollars in cold cash," as a Washington state newspaper called it—were proliferating. "The race will be an exciting one and the capacity of the cars will be tested to the utmost limit," wrote the *Omaha Daily Bee*.

"One, or rather two, of those chances of a lifetime which are often heard about but rarely encountered are being literally dangled by the Olds Motor Works within easy reach of all men able to drive an automobile," the *Motor World* wrote a week after the ad. "Applications from all comers will be considered and each will be judged on his merits. On the face of things, it would seem that there should be enough to keep hot the wires to Detroit and to largely increase the receipt of mail matter at that point during the next few days."

The competition had yet to start, and already it was the sensation Smith wanted. Another move from the playbook successfully executed.

Olds never publicly revealed the actual number of people who hoped to drive Old Scout and Old Steady, but press accounts suggested the *Motor World's* prediction came true. The *Automobile* stated that Olds heard from "several hundred applicants." The *New York Mail Express* estimated higher, reporting that "fully a thousand applicants" wrote or cabled Detroit.

"As was to have been expected, a deluge of applications have poured in," the *Motor World* reported on May 4. "The applications represent all classes and conditions: professional drivers, amateur drivers, those having experience, and those who are evidently beginners, and from women as well as men. One man and wife have volunteered to make the trip together while another application comes from a woman journalist of note. The drivers have not yet been selected but will undoubtedly be men of more or less national reputation as tourists, which will add zest to the contest."

The *Motor World* was right. Olds selected Dwight Huss, the hard-working Everyman, and Percy Megargel, the writer with a romantic image.

## OLD SCOUT AND OLD STEADY

In the lead-up to the contest, Abbott traveled to New York to preach the Good Roads gospel at Coney Island's Brighton Beach Race Course, a thoroughbred track that, like Michigan's Grosse Pointe, was being co-opted by the new machine.

The popular Brighton track made the news when Paul Sartori, driver of Alfred G. Vanderbilt's 90-horsepower Italian car, rolled over during a Friday, May 5, practice run, "turning two or three somersaults before it landed, clear off the track, with its wheels up in the air," the *New York Times* reported. "The horrified spectators rushed to the spot, expecting to see Vanderbilt's chauffeur badly hurt," the paper wrote, but Sartori was uninjured. "His escape was little short of miraculous, for the running gear of the racer was totally smashed. Two wheels were ripped off and the machine looked as if it were eligible for the scrap-iron heap."

But Abbott had no interest in discussing wrecks when he spoke with a *Times* reporter at Brighton Beach for a story to be published on Monday, start of the transcontinental race.

"The automobile interest is only beginning in the far West," Abbott said. "In California, there are many active automobile centers, but in the far Northwest, the number of machines is yet very few. The Good Roads Movement is absolutely necessary to make the automobile popular, and if the two cars now starting succeed in making the trip on time, which will be within forty-four days, I think it will pave the way for future trips across the continent by many private motor car owners who will undertake the journey, perhaps more leisurely, for pleasure."

IN NEW YORK ON Monday morning, May 8, 1905, Abbott joined Chapin and others outside the Oldsmobile dealership at Columbus Circle. Journalists with their notebooks and cameras stood ready.

Megargel and Huss would not be traveling alone.

To provide relief at the tiller during the long hours and for assistance in maintaining the machines, Smith had assigned two mechanics to accompany them: Barton Stanchfield with Megargel, and Milford Wigle, who had won several dirt-track races, with Huss.

Even here, Olds had created drama.

"Stanchfield and Wigle are respectively from the Lansing and Detroit factories of the Olds Motor Works, between which there is said to be the keenest rivalry, so that each party can be relied on to do everything that is fair to finish the tour first," asserted the *Automobile*. The Detroit *Free Press* claimed the factory rivalry was so intense that the race would be "for blood."

As the start of the race approached, the midtown crowd milled about the Curved Dash cars, which had been painted with the slogan: "OLDS-MOBILE, EN ROUTE, NEW YORK–PORTLAND, OREGON, $1,000 RACE." Tools, spare parts, foul-weather gear, blankets, revolvers, and ropes and pulleys were packed inside the steamer trunks strapped to the rear of each car. Old Steady and Old Scout each carried a spare tire, with the expectation that their crews would need to buy more along the way. The men carried compasses, cameras, and cigars. Megargel had his typewriter. He would chronicle the race in regular installments in the *Automobile*.

With the aid of headlights—what the *New York Mail* described as two "exceptionally powerful acetylene lamps," each powered by "enough gas compressed into its tank to burn for 72 hours"—the racers intended to drive as much as sixteen to twenty hours a day. Mindful of the anti-car folk, they had pledged to obey traffic laws, where they existed.

"One of the restrictions imposed on the drivers will be the observation of the road laws of the state through which they are passing," reported the New York *Sun*. "Under no circumstances are they to exceed the speed limit." That decision, of course, was between the drivers and their consciences.

Huss, Wigle, Megargel, and Stanchfield, at race start in Manhattan.
GM Media Archive.

"When the Cascade Mountains are reached," the *New York Times* wrote, "the hardships of the trip will come, for besides crossing the mountains, an arid desert must be passed over." The reporter's geography was off— Oregon's Cascades were a long way from the Wyoming desert—but no matter. The paper, like so many others, was giving Smith coverage.

"The transcontinental tourists are to remain with their cars throughout the trip," the *Times* further observed. "One man will not go on ahead by rail, picking up the car at some future point. If the men wish to sleep in a more comfortable bed than can be afforded by the light runabouts, they must do so at their own loss of time."

AT 9:30 A.M., AN official with the New York Athletic Club gave the word to go. Megargel and Huss threw their cars into gear. With a dozen other cars following, they disappeared up Central Park West.

Twenty-five minutes later, they paused at Central Bridge, over the Harlem River, for a photograph.

"There the newspaper men and well-wishers who accompanied the tourists assumed attitudes about the two cars, held their hats aloft, and kept their mouths open long enough for the photographers to snap the scene of the 'cheering multitude,'" reported the *Motor World*. "At 9:58, Huss and Megargel said their final goodbyes and were fairly off on their long journey."

With the race underway, Chapin sent an encouraging telegram to Smith: "Cars started at nine thirty. Large enthusiastic crowd. Both drivers hope to reach Albany tonight."

———

THE SPORTS SECTION OF the May 10, 1905, Detroit *Free Press* carried news of Cincinnati beating Brooklyn and Pittsburgh defeating Philadelphia in National League baseball action. Three stories concerned horse racing, including the upcoming Kentucky Derby and action at Grosse Pointe track. The lead photograph showed Megargel and Huss with their mechanics and cars in New York: "Olds cars and crews that are making the transcontinental race," the caption read.

The *Free Press* gave less space that day to another local automaker.

There, in the Michigan pages, next to a story about a large sturgeon caught in Lake St. Clair and above an advertisement for Lydia Pinkham's patent medicine—"Young Girls: Avoid the Dangers and Suffering of Womanhood"—was a fifty-nine-word story headlined, "FORD MOTOR CO. TO PUT OUT $400 AUTOS." The story read: "It is proposed by the Ford Motor Co. to put on the market next year a $400 runabout, which will be the lowest priced automobile turned out by a famous house. This is one of the steps that will suit the pocketbooks of the masses, and the factory is planning an annual output of 10,000 machines at the start."

Although the *Free Press* did not reveal its name, the runabout in question was Ford's Model N, precursor to the car that would change everything, the Model T.

# 6

## BAD BEHAVIORS, BAD ROADS

### CAPITAL ISSUES

Megargel and Huss crossed the Harlem River into the Bronx and headed north, their route paralleling the eastern shore of the Hudson River. Albany was nearly 150 miles distant, a full day's travel even on the comparatively decent roads that connected Manhattan with the state capital. The men leaned on the gas.

In Yonkers, just a few miles into the journey, police ordered them to slow down but did not detain them; perhaps the lawmen knew about the race and were rooting for the drivers. The slogans on Old Steady and Old Scout certainly identified the cars.

Leaving the cops behind, the drivers picked up speed again, but they did not keep full throttle: before leaving Manhattan, Megargel and Huss had agreed they would "not race in earnest," as Megargel put it. Rather, they would focus on reaching Albany intact and savoring the attention of the spectators who cheered and photographed them. Megargel let Huss lead, in order to better assess his competition. "We were content to let Old Steady run in second all day," he wrote, "taking care, however, to keep Old Scout in sight most of the time in order to gauge as nearly as possible the comparative speeds of the two cars."

Megargel's Old Steady suffered the race's first mishap near Peekskill, about one-third of the way to Albany: A nail punctured a rear tire casing, and by the time Megargel stopped the car, the inner tube had been destroyed. A fifteen-minute repair got them going again. Some while later, vibration broke a headlamp bracket. Meanwhile, the bottom of Huss's trunk broke, spilling its contents on the road. During the afternoon, a drizzle dampened the men, but it was insufficient to turn the roads to muck.

All in all, the first day was a success, Megargel concluded when he filed his first dispatch after reaching Albany at about 8:30 p.m., eleven hours after starting. "The roads, with the exception of several short stretches, were in excellent condition," he wrote, "and the two little runabouts, although only possessing seven horsepower, fairly flew along, easily making in one day the distance it took the large cars on last summer's St. Louis tour to accomplish."

The cars were cleaned and garaged for the night, which the men spent at the luxurious nine-story Ten Eyck Hotel, at the corner of State and North Pearl Streets, two blocks from the New York State Capitol. The Ten Eyck was a favorite watering hole for legislators and officials and the many reporters who covered the state Senate and Assembly.

———

NEW YORK WAS THE most populous state in the country in 1905, with 7.26 million people, nearly 10 percent of all Americans. More than 9,000 automobiles were registered there, also topping the nation. Not every state required registration, and not every owner required to register did, but the number was another measure of New York's prominence in the developing automobile age. What happened in the Empire State was watched throughout the nation and sometimes emulated.

Albany, with 94,151 residents, was only the Empire State's fifth-largest city, after New York (population 3.43 million), and the heavily industrialized Buffalo (352,387), Rochester (162,608), and Syracuse (108,374). But what transpired in Albany typified the many confrontations involving residents, legislators, jurists, law-enforcement personnel, and municipal officials wherever the automobile appeared, in whatever state.

Danger topped the concerns—and it was danger seemingly without escape. Unlike other potentially harmful technologies such as the railroad, the foundry, and the factory, no machine with such propensity for hurting and killing innocents had ever been capable of appearing in every city, town, and neighborhood.

Irishwoman Mary Ward became history's first recorded motor vehicle fatality on August 31, 1869, when she was thrown from an experimental steam car in Parsontown, Ireland, and died from a broken neck and fractured skull. The accident prompted a coroner's inquest, in which the driver, Ward's husband, was cleared of responsibility. A story in the September 1, 1869, *King's County Chronicle* newspaper captured her end.

"The vehicle had steam up, and was going at an easy pace," the *Chronicle* reported, "when on turning the sharp corner at the church, unfortunately the Hon. Mrs. Ward was thrown from the seat and fearfully injured, causing her almost immediate death. The unfortunate lady was taken into the house of Dr. Woods, which is nearly opposite the scene of the unhappy occurrence, and as that gentleman was on the spot, everything that could be done was done, but it was impossible to save her life. The utmost gloom pervades the town, and on every hand, sympathy is expressed with the husband and family of the accomplished and talented lady who has been so prematurely hurried into eternity."

America's first documented car accident occurred twenty-seven years later, on May 30, 1896, and it, too, made the papers, including the *New York Times*, although the *Times* and other papers missed the true circumstances of the mishap. The truth was, the responsible party—the driver of a powered "wagon," a Duryea—was competing in a race from Manhattan to Irvington-on-the-Hudson and back sponsored by *Cosmopolitan Magazine*, which offered a $3,000 prize to the winner, when he struck a bicyclist on Broadway.

"The wagon operated by Henry Wells of Springfield, Mass., wobbled furiously, going in a zigzag fashion, until it seemed that the driver had lost control of it," the *New-York Daily Tribune* wrote. "Evylyn Thomas, of No. 459 West 90th Street, was approaching on her bicycle, when suddenly the wheel and horseless carriage met, and there was a crash. A crowd gathered, and the woman was picked up unconscious, her leg fractured. An ambulance took her to the Manhattan Hospital, where last night it was reported that she would recover soon. Wells was taken to the West 125th Street station and held pending the results of the injuries to Miss Thomas. The wagon went on in charge of another operator."

In Manhattan three years later, real estate agent Henry H. Bliss became the first American to die in a motor-vehicle accident. Bliss was unlucky in other ways, too. Almost seventy, he had fallen on hard financial times after losing his second wife. His stepdaughter, Mary Alice Almont Livingston Fleming, was charged with killing her using arsenic mixed into her clam chowder—a scheme, the authorities claimed, to inherit $82,000 from her mother. The investigation and 1896 trial, in which Fleming was acquitted, made front-page news.

On September 13, 1899, the widower's sad fate turned crueler.

"Bliss, accompanied by a woman named Lee, was alighting from a southbound Eighth Avenue trolley car, when he was knocked down and run over by an automobile in charge of Arthur Smith of 151 West Sixty-Second Street," the New York Times wrote the next day. The automobile, an electric-powered taxi, "passed over his head and body," crushing Bliss's chest and skull. Cabbie Arthur Smith, who had been transporting Dr. David Orr Edson, the psychiatrist son of former Mayor Franklin Edson, was arrested and held on $1,000 bail.

Sensing a dramatic new narrative, journalists began inquiring about motor-vehicle accidents as they made their police rounds. They were amply rewarded. Twenty-six motor-vehicle fatalities were officially recorded in America in 1899, the first year for which the federal government today has data, and from that year on, the toll steadily increased: 36 deaths in 1900, 54 in 1901, 79 in 1902, 117 in 1903, 172 in 1904, and 252 in 1905, an increase of 700 percent in six years. The fatal car accident became a front-page staple.

———

THE BAD BEHAVIORS OF certain wealthy individuals and their chauffeurs inflamed emotions. These were the millionaires who flaunted their high-powered luxury cars, much as they did their mansions and yachts, and often drove them recklessly. The toiling classes were not amused. Nor were the good-driving advocates, those members of the AAA, the ACA, and other clubs and organizations that urged safe, courteous, and lawful motoring.

New Yorkers would long remember one of the most notorious offenders: the arrogant Edward R. Thomas, banker and heir to his Civil War general father's $20-million fortune, who had married a Kentucky heiress said to be one of America's most beautiful women in a Newport, Rhode Island, wedding that breathed a moment of freshness into the fading Gilded Age. Thomas owned thoroughbred racehorses before he developed a new obsession: fast cars.

In February 1902, Thomas was racing through Manhattan in "White Ghost," a German Daimler race car he had bought from William K. Vanderbilt, when he ran over a seven-year-old boy, leaving the child to die as he roared off. A mob trapped Thomas three blocks away. They were beating him when a policeman came to his rescue.

"I'll never ride in an automobile again as long as I live," Thomas said at the police station, where the boy's corpse was brought.

He was lying.

Three months later, on May 24, 1902, Thomas, his wife, and their chauffeur were showboating in another of his vehicles, a different German Daimler—an "immense red automobile," the *Times* called it—when they were spotted heading west on horse-clogged Forty-Fourth Street, between Second and Third Avenues. Residents bent on revenge had been waiting. A big red Daimler could not hide forever.

A thirteen-year-old boy rushed Thomas's car and hurled a can, striking the chauffeur in the head. The chauffeur sped off, a gang of strong-armed lads in furious pursuit. One pitched a kettle—a "boiler"—into the drive mechanism of the car, stopping it.

"Tin cans, boilers, pails, stones and sticks were hurled at the occupants of the vehicle," the *Times* wrote, "while the boys yelled themselves hoarse as they surrounded the machine . . . Mrs. Thomas was struck in the head with the lid of a boiler and rendered unconscious."

Even then, however, the gang did not stop.

"Mr. Thomas called to the lads to desist, but his voice was drowned by their jeers and cries, and they kept up the fusillade. Several hundred persons had been attracted to the scene, and they watched the fashionable vehicle being showered with all kinds of missiles."

Thomas's chauffeur managed to dislodge the kettle and the car sped off again, the mob on its tail. Further violence was prevented only by the appearance of a policeman. "Mr. Thomas was highly indignant at the treatment he and his party had received and promised to push the matter in the courts," the *Times* said.

The man could not be shamed. On the Saturday in January 1904 that Ford powered up Arrow on frozen Anchor Bay, the papers brought news from Rome, where Thomas, on an automobile tour of Europe, had struck and killed "a peasant woman, the mother of four children," the *New York Times* said. "Mr. Thomas, according to the story told by the local authorities, stopped his car to learn the extent of the woman's injuries, but the threatening attitude of a number of shepherds who witnessed the accident caused him to re-enter the vehicle and drive away. Mr. Thomas subsequently embarked with his car for Marseilles."

Nor could he break his addiction to speed. On February 10, 1905, Thomas set off in a supercharged Mercedes on a practice run for a one-hundred-mile road race near Havana, Cuba. Thomas suspected the brakes didn't work properly, but he nonetheless went full-throttle. He was racing at an estimated 60 miles per hour when a one-horse buggy turned into the road. The car's brakes failed and the Mercedes smashed into it, then into a tree; it then ran up and down a ditch and spun back into the road, crossed the road, and ricocheted off another ditch before finally stopping. In the process, a passenger was thrown from the Mercedes and hit by it, severely injuring him. Thomas was rendered unconscious. The buggy operator was unhurt.

Another car found Thomas and his passenger two minutes later, and sped off with them to a hospital—only to wreck when it crashed into an ox cart. A third vehicle, a touring car, succeeded in getting the men to medical attention.

"Mr. Thomas says he will never drive at speed again, except on [the sands of] Ormond Beach," the *Times* said, as if anyone could believe him.

———

Inspector Schmittberger, NYPD.
Library of Congress, LC-DIG-ggbain-12796.

STONINGS HAD EMERGED AS a form of blood sport, typically in protest of the new machine but also sometimes as entertainment for combative young lads and men—"hoodlums" and "ruffians," as the newspapermen called them. The fact that many cars lacked roofs, side windows, and even doors made motorists sitting ducks.

New York and Port Chester Railway Company president William C. Gotshall and his wife learned that the hard way. They were driving through Harlem on May 22, 1904, when someone hurled a rock weighing several pounds at Mrs. Gotshall's head, seriously injuring her. The suspect escaped. Police Commissioner William McAdoo assigned crack Inspector Max F. Schmittberger and his team to the case.

Schmittberger failed to find the Gotshall suspect or anyone else involved in stonings, leading McAdoo to conclude that the sight of their police uniforms kept the perpetrators in hiding. But dressing his cops in civilian clothes and adding a patrician-looking lady as a passenger, he decided, might lure the ruffians out. Schmittberger's wife agreed to wear a fashionable motoring coat and veil and ride along. She advised the cops to wear goggles, "just as the real millionaires do," she told a reporter.

On June 5, the Schmittbergers and three detectives, all attired as wealthy motorists and driven by a chauffeur, began to drive the streets of Manhattan in a fancy red automobile. They drew a response on Grand Street in the city's Lower East Side, where a crowd of boys opened fire with bricks, stones, and sticks. No one was hurt, but one stick "whizzed by and took a feather out of Mrs. Schmittberger's hat," the *Times* reported. An eleven-year-old boy was arrested and the car continued on as onlookers jeered. Soon, there was another stoning, and two more arrests. The inspector ordered the chauffeur to drive to Harlem.

When the car reached the vicinity of the Gotshall incident, a cursing mob of boys surrounded them. Mrs. Schmittberger dodged their stones while the officers grabbed two of the children, eleven and thirteen, threw them in the car, and sped off. They had traveled barely a block on First Avenue when a larger mob of women, children, and men—apparently believing the boys had been kidnapped—trapped them.

"The situation became so menacing at last that the Inspector and Lemon and Simerlein got out of the machine and drew their small 'billies,'" the *Times* reported. Then, "the Inspector threw back his coat and showed his badge, and the detective did likewise."

Things quieted and the prisoners were brought to jail. The next day, their parents paid fines of $3 and $5. Mrs. Schmittberger told reporters she was unsure if she would serve as bait again.

―――――

But hoodlums had their defenders, including citizens who in letters to the editor portrayed stonings as a justified response to the danger automobiles posed to innocent people, especially children playing. A clergyman quoted in the *Automobile* went further, declaring any reckless motorists got what they deserved when they were pelted with "stones, bricks, dead animals, decayed vegetables and dilapidated washboilers."

"What more natural, then," the preacher asked, "that the hoodlum of the street should blindly strike at the hoodlum of the automobile?"

A *Times* editorialist sided with the preacher.

"The news columns of the daily journals are full of distressing stories of wrecks and casualties due to the running down of carriages, pedestrians and children," the paper wrote in a June 16, 1902, editorial. "This explains why so many people who are normally orderly and law-abiding find pleasure in throwing things at vehicles of this description."

The editorial closed with a blast at the Vanderbilt set.

"The millionaire who finds his racing machine dented and scarred may think he has a grievance, but considering what people of his class or their imitators have done and are daily doing to make the automobile terrible, he would do well to give thanks that the dents and scars are not on his own head, where, to tell the plain truth, they would usually do the most good."

The unrepentant Thomas was but one of the aristocratic autoists whose bad driving drew ire.

There was department store owner Howard Gibb, who appeared in court after his driver sped over the Brooklyn Bridge on December 29, 1904. When the driver ignored a warning to stop, a policeman "telephoned to the officer at the 'runaway gate' at the other end of the bridge and thus stopped the machine," the *Times* reported. The driver was arrested. When Gibb came for him, the department-store owner unleashed a torrent of "threatening and abusive language" on the arresting Bridge Squad cop, "telling him, among other things, to 'go to blazes,' or words to that effect," the paper reported. After chastising Gibbs, a magistrate held the chauffeur on $300 bail.

There was the story out of Baltimore in early 1905 about the wife of Captain Isaac Emerson, millionaire yachtsman and creator of Bromo-Seltzer, and her indignant reaction to her driver's arrest for speeding. The arresting officer sued her for slander for calling him and other officers "puppies, liars and thieves," the *Times* reported on January 22, and the case went to jury trial—much to the public's delight.

"Hundreds of people, among them many women, contended to gain admission to the courtroom," the paper wrote. "Hats were torn off, satchels were lost, faces scratched, and gowns torn in the scrambles. Nearly a thousand people jammed the courthouse to suffocation every day."

When the jury found Mrs. Emerson guilty and fined her $4,000, she threatened to sell the Emerson mansion and move to New York.

"Mr. Emerson has spent $10,000 on the Naval Militia, and thousands on the poor, and this is the kind of treatment we get in return," she said. "I expected a verdict against me, because in a jury, there is always prejudice against people who have money."

And there was the tragic story of sixty-year-old Kate McGowan, of West Fifty-Third Street, who was struck and killed by an automobile carrying men and women who had left the Hotel Astor for a performance of the smash hit operetta *Babes in Toyland* at the Majestic Theatre on the evening of January 11, 1905. The car hit Mrs. McGowan as she was crossing Broadway at Fifty-Seventh Street.

"She was thrown a distance of ten feet and rolled into the gutter, unconscious," eyewitnesses told police, according to the *Times*. "When the machine struck Mrs. McGowan, the women became hysterical and clambered out of the machine, but soon called on the chauffeur to drive on before the reporters got hold of the affair. This instruction the chauffeur obeyed, and the party whirled on toward the theatre." The chauffeur was later arrested. At his arraignment, the paper reported, "he said that he would not have struck the woman had she not jumped in front of his machine." Like Thomas, he had no shame.

---

OTHER PRIVILEGED PEOPLE ALSO held themselves above the law where cars were concerned.

Spotting a large automobile speeding on Eighth Avenue one evening in late May 1904, a bicycle patrolman took chase. He caught the car after one-third of a mile. At the wheel was Mayor George B. McClellan Jr.'s driver, Martin Seiler.

Brought to the station house, Seiler tried to use clout to get himself off.

"Well, you see, it was like this," he said. "The Mayor is dining at Delmonico's tonight and he told me to be on hand for him at 9:30 sharp. I was a little late, so I speeded to get to Delmonico's on time. I knew I was exceeding the speed limit, but I was going after the Mayor."

The sergeant on duty locked him up.

Some two hours later, as it was nearing midnight, a member of the mayor's administration showed up. Commissioner of Street Cleaning John McGaw Woodbury, who would resign two years later in a political corruption scandal, stated that he had not come by to bail Seiler out.

"I am simply making a round of the district and dropped in here," he said. But then his tone turned threatening.

"Now, boys, let the Mayor down easy. I was arrested myself once for violating the speed limit and the newspapers ran a column about it next day. Don't do that with the Mayor."

During the trial of a young man arrested by the Bicycle Police for speeding on Manhattan Avenue, District Attorney William T. Jerome, a politically powerful figure who had made bad driving a crusade, expressed the frustration and fear many citizens felt in the face of those who drove without regard for others. "This town is getting dangerous through the recklessness of these chauffeurs, and it is time a halt was called," he said.

The young man was unable to pay a $50 fine, and Jerome sentenced him to twenty days in City Prison, the Tombs, a harsh punishment he hoped would prove to be a deterrent.

"It has been bad enough for old people to attempt to cross the street," Jerome said, "but now young persons take their lives in their hands in attempting to do so, owing to the recklessness of some of the inexperienced drivers of machines. There is no doubt in my mind that all autos exceed the speed limit."

———

RICH OR NOT, SOME motorists believed their horn indemnified them. They believed its sound was a command, and those who refused it must suffer the consequences, however unfortunate they might be.

One who suffered extremely was a young woman on November 10, 1904, when she attempted to cross Fifth Avenue near Twenty-Ninth Street in Manhattan.

She stopped to let a horse-drawn vehicle pass, but when she started out again, a cab carrying a couple who lived at the Waldorf-Astoria bore down on her. The driver sounded his horn, but the woman did not respond. The cab ran over her, leaving her to die as an angry crowd assembled. The cabbie ran away.

A cop caught him and dragged him back to the scene, where the crowd, numbering several hundred, called for his head. Police with nightsticks backed them off and arrested the man, charging him with homicide—but the couple, meanwhile, boarded a trolley and slunk away. According to the *New York Times*, which played the story on the front page, the woman, dead on arrival at Roosevelt Hospital, had not been identified when she was sent to the morgue. "She was about twenty-eight years old, dark hair and dark complexion. Her clothes were of good material. . . . She wore a dark skirt, a white waist and a brown hat."

The fact that some people might be deaf or hard of hearing, or too elderly or frail to respond quickly, did not seem to concern some motorists. Poor retired army captain Treadwell Seaman of Flushing, New York, was apparently both frail and hard of hearing when a driver who used his horn got him. Coming to Manhattan in the spring of 1905 for treatment of neuralgia, Seaman was hit when he stepped off a trolley at Columbus Circle. The driver told police that he tooted his horn, but Seaman, whose right foot was crushed, did not hear it.

"I am determined if possible to put a stop to the recklessness of chauffeurs and other automobilists," said Manhattan Magistrate Leroy B. Crane when he decided to raise the fines he imposed in Yorkville Court for bad driving in 1904. "Automobilists must learn that pedestrians have some rights, and they must learn to stop when a pedestrian is in danger, instead of simply blowing and tooting the horn."

———

ON THE VERY EVENING that Megargel and Huss began their race, New York City's journalists scored again when a motorcycle cop identified as Officer Casey spotted one of William K. Vanderbilt II's cars roaring up Seventh Avenue. It was the 90-horsepower Mercedes race car in which

Vanderbilt the year before at Ormond-Daytona had reached 92.3 miles per hour, shaving two-fifths of a second off Ford's record Anchor Bay run. A French-speaking employee of Vanderbilt was at the wheel.

Up Seventh Avenue the car and the motorcycle sped, the driver of Vanderbilt's car ignoring commands to stop, the people on the street craning their necks at "the pursued and pursuer," the *Times* reported. Casey was clocking the Mercedes at the rate of one block in four seconds, or approximately 45 miles an hour.

He was gaining on the car when it crossed trolley tracks at Fiftieth Street. Casey's patience was gone.

"Stop!" he shouted "I'll shoot!"

"This word worked like magic," the *Times* wrote. "The chug chug stopped, the brakes were put on, and the big car came to a halt."

"Why ees eet you stop me?" is how the paper recounted what Henri de Dailloux said. "I have ze engagement with Meester Vanderbilt."

"I stopped you because you're racing up the streets at about three times the legal rate," Casey said. "Now come to the station with me."

"Non, non," Dailloux said. "I have ze engagement at 10 o'clock. I cannot go wiz you!"

Casey blew his whistle. A second policeman came to his assistance, along with a crowd that cornered the Frenchman.

At the station, Dailloux described how difficult it was to drive a 90-horsepower car on a city street. Perhaps he wanted praise for not having injured or killed someone. The Mercedes, he said, was incapable of moving slower than 25 miles per hour when the engine was running. "To go slower," Dailloux told police, according to the *Times,* he had to "turn on the power a moment and then turn it off quickly. One cough sends the machine about a block."

---

REGULATING SPEED SEEMED THE answer to many problems. Some counties and municipalities enacted local restrictions, but this piecemeal approach was half a loaf at best. In New York, the movement to enact statewide limits and punishments for disregarding them began seriously in early 1902, when a Quaker senator offended by drivers like Thomas proposed legislation.

"I can see the Vanderbilts, the Whitneys, the Goulds and the rest speeding past my house at a rate of sixty miles an hour, more or less, and they take the centre of the road, complaining of the farmers who do not hurriedly get out of their way and give them full and sufficient space," said William Willets Cocks of Old Westbury, Long Island, some twenty miles east of Manhattan in an area renowned for its polo and fox hunting, and now, fast automobiling. Old Westbury had been a quiet Quaker community until titans of the Gilded Age discovered it.

"The automobile evil has become a menace to the general public," the senator said. "Woe be to the unpretentious farmer or lumberman who happens to be in their way."

Cocks proposed legislation establishing a speed limit of 7 miles an hour, with a $25 fine for a first offense and $50 for the second, and imprisonment in the county jail for failure to pay. He raised the limit to 8 miles an hour when the bill was submitted in mid-January 1902, and further modification at the Assembly resulted in a limit of 8 miles per hour within city and village limits, and 15 miles an hour outside. The measure found support with some members of the public. Others, including "An Anxious Mother" who wrote to the *Times* of watching a girl struck by a car that fled on Fifth Avenue without stopping, wanted harsher punishments.

"Not a day passes that I do not observe these outrageous vehicles rushing along in parks or streets," the woman wrote. "Fines mean absolutely nothing to automobilists. We must have imprisonment."

Such sentiments riled the Vanderbilt set. Led by the Automobile Club of America, opponents of Cocks's bill lobbied successfully to weaken it. The legislation that Governor Benjamin B. Odell Jr. signed into law in late March put the country speed limit at 20 miles per hour and gave law enforcement leeway in punishing violators: a fine not exceeding $50 for first offense and the same for a second, with the option also of a jail sentence.

In 1903, the speeding war resumed with an effort championed by Senator Edwin Bailey Jr., who represented Staten Island and eastern Long Island. The "Bailey Bill," as it came to be known, called for speed restrictions near post offices, public schools while in session, houses of worship on the

Sabbath while services were being conducted, and whenever passing a pedestrian or person on horseback or driving a horse-drawn vehicle. The Bailey Bill also required motorists to obtain licenses and register their vehicles with the state.

The bill's provisions seemed reasonable, but the aristocrats did not like restrictions on their sport. Once again, they protested.

"We have a strong feeling against the Bailey Automobile Bill. Please delay if possible," John Jacob Astor IV telegraphed to Albany County assemblyman George B. Clark on April 22, when representatives overwhelmingly approved a version of the senator's legislation. Clark brought the telegram to the attention of Governor Odell, who set a May 6 hearing.

Before a packed room that day, prominent lawyer and former district attorney De Lancey Nicoll, himself wealthy, argued against the Bailey Bill on behalf of the automobile industry. Were it to become law, he said, a $100-million manufacturing industry that employed 150,000 American workers—10,000 in New York state alone—would be seriously jeopardized.

"It is not conceivable," Nicoll said, "that any person in the state of New York would want to buy an automobile if this measure should go into effect."

Nicoll noted that horses could travel faster than the 8-mile-an-hour limit established by certain provisions of the proposed law—but no carriage operator was ever arrested for traveling 9 miles an hour or faster. He argued that another provision requiring revocation of a driver's license after a third violation "amounts to a virtual confiscation of his property. He is obliged to sell his automobile for whatever he can get for it." Another manufacturing lobbyist said his industry was "just as legitimate as the carriage business or the dry goods business and ought not to be singled out for oppressive legislation," wrote the *Times*.

But the bill had its supporters. One man presented evidence supporting a claim that Long Island averaged about three automobile accidents a day. Another suggested the bill would empower police—some of whom in New York City, it was alleged, declined to arrest wealthy drivers for fear of retaliation.

Two weeks later, Odell signed the Bailey Bill into law.

Autoists were outraged.

They returned to Albany with fresh fury when the 127th Legislature convened in January 1904, and this time they were joined by another lobby: the New York State Automobile Association, organized in late November with the union of smaller clubs from Buffalo, Rochester, Syracuse, Utica, and Albany. Members of the association, which affiliated with the AAA, had met at the Ten Eyck Hotel six days before Christmas to draft legislation to replace the law they hated—and which was widely ignored. *Motor Age* spoke for many motorists when it declared: "The occasion for the introduction of such a bill is the common dislike of the present Bailey law, which was enacted under strenuous protest and which has been almost wholly disregarded since its enactment on account of its manifold absurdities, conflicting provisions, and unconstitutional features."

Buffalo senator Henry W. Hill introduced the state automobile association's bill on January 18 to a favorable reception. "There seems at the present time no disposition on the part of the Legislature to oppose the passage of the Hill bill to provide a new automobile law for the state which shall be simple and compact and not foolishly restrictive," wrote the *Automobile* in a February 2 dispatch from Albany.

Hill's legislation required motorists to always drive at a speed that was "reasonable and proper," given traffic conditions, and it set limits of 10 miles per hour for any "built-up portion" of a village, city or town; 15 miles per hour in other sections of villages, towns and cities; and 20 miles per hour outside city, town, and village limits. The bill established rules of the road aimed at reducing confusion and accidents: Motorists henceforth would be required to keep to the right, except when passing, when they were to turn left, and then back to the right when they had completed the pass.

The law also set procedures for registering cars with the state (cost: $2) and displaying the registration number on the back of the vehicle, "the numbers to be in Arabic numerals, black on white ground, each not less than three inches in height, and each stroke to be of width not less than 1/2 inch and also as part of such number the initial letters of state in black on white ground, such letters be not less than 1 inch in height." Out-of-state drivers were not required to apply for registration, however, if they were in compliance with the laws of their state.

Every motor vehicle operated on a public road was required to have "good and efficient brakes"; a horn, bell, or other audible warning device; white headlamps "visible within a reasonable distance" in the direction the vehicle was traveling; and "a red light visible in the reverse direction." Drivers were required to sound the horn on approaching a pedestrian or a person riding a horse or operating a horse-drawn vehicle, and to stop at the hand signal of any such person. They were required to reduce speed when approaching "horses or other draft animals to prevent frightening the same." If asked, motorists involved in accidents were required to give their name and address to anyone they had injured.

With its seven main sections and twenty-four subsections, the bill was not simple or compact, as the *Automobile* implied. But it was clear, and except in the view of strident "motorphobes," as car enthusiasts disparaged their critics, it was reasonable and wise. Even Cocks, now an assemblyman, supported it. Many of its essential concepts would endure until today, in state laws across America.

After objection by the automobile lobby, the provision requiring motorists to sound their horns was stripped from the bill. Meeting in New York City, these automobilists with influence found a horn to be "an insufferable nuisance," the *Times* reported on January 22, 1904. As amended, "the bill will simply require chauffeurs to use every reasonable warning."

In the following weeks, the legislature raised possible penalties for speeding and other infractions but otherwise made few modifications. On April 7, the Assembly approved the bill without discussion and on May 3, Governor Odell signed it into law.

———

THE UNKNOWN DRIVER WHO nearly ran over popular writer Eugene Wood and state senators Patrick H. McCarren and John C. Fitzgerald while they were crossing Fifth Avenue one night in January 1905 may not have recognized the three men. But that near brush with death helped motivate Fitzpatrick to add his voice to others calling once again for harsher laws as the 128th New York State Legislature began its work that month.

Senator Martin Saxe and Assemblyman Theodore P. Wilsnack, both of New York City, were leading the campaign this time. Among other measures, their similar bills would have allowed magistrates greater liberty in sending violators to jail.

But some autoists believed that motorphobia seemed to be diminishing. Winthrop E. Scarritt made the point in a contentious hearing in Albany on February 28, while also repeating his somewhat inflated claim that in 1900, there had been but one car for every 1.5 million Americans, but that now the figure was one for every 1,200 inhabitants. Earlier in the month, speaking to members of the ACA, Scarritt had said that the sins of the few should not warrant harsh treatment of the many who drove responsibly, and that laws like the ones Bailey had proposed were supported "by hypocrites and bigots."

"The motorphobe requires you to put yourselves in the criminal class when you drive your cars in excess of the legal limit," Scarritt now told fellow legislators. "Accurate records taken in Central Park, Riverside Drive and Fifth Avenue showed that every one of 437 horse-drawn vehicles exceeded the speed limit and not a single arrest was made. Why should the law be enforced against one class of citizens and the same law be entirely ignored as to another class?"

After a final legislative hearing on March 21, the Saxe and Wilsnack bills were declared dead. The Committee on Internal Affairs did not report them for a floor vote.

The *Motor Way* was among the publications to celebrate the victory against "loud-mouthed cranks [who] get up and spiel motorphobia." The magazine wrote: "It is too early yet to claim complete victory, but in what has already been accomplished there is cause for automobilists all over the country to rejoice. It shows that not only are organized automobilists a power in themselves, but that by judicious agitation a great deal of general public support can be worked up for the automobile."

## MUD AND MIRE

The drizzle that Megargel and Huss had experienced on the road from Manhattan to Albany developed into a hard rain overnight, and when they left the Ten Eyck Hotel at 7:00 a.m. on Tuesday, May 9, bound for Utica and their second overnight stop in Syracuse, they drove on roads that Megargel described as "full of mud and water."

The Curved Dashed Olds cars met the challenge.

"The way these two little 7-horsepower runabouts ploughed through on high speed surprised us all," Megargel observed, even if spinning wheels were unforgiving: "We were soon covered from head to foot in mire, while our baggage and supplies, strapped on the rear deck, were almost unrecognizable."

The clouds cleared, and by the time the men had lunched at Utica, some ninety-five miles west of Albany, the sun was burning the racers, turning their necks and hands a painful red. But it was cold, prompting the racers to buy warm clothing. The battery on Megargel's car short-circuited, but Stanchfield was able to make the repair.

The second day brought interesting diversions. Megargel and Stanch-field encountered a drunk driving a team of horses and witnessed what Megargel described in his chronicle for the *Automobile* as "two very fine exhibitions of horsemanship." In one, a girl driving a milk wagon expertly commanded her horses when they froze at Old Steady's approach: "The way she laid on the whip left the horses no room to doubt that they were handled by a master. The result was that they passed our runabout without further misbehaving." In the other instance, a man whipped a colt into submission when it tried to run from the car.

Night fell, and the cars continued to Syracuse with their headlamps burning. Huss beat Megargel into the city, where a large turnout of spectators and journalists welcomed the crews. The cars were cleaned and the men went to bed at about midnight in rooms at the grand Yates Hotel. The next day, Wednesday, May 10, Huss got on the road again at 5:30 a.m. Megargel followed about a half hour later.

Huss would later describe the drive up Camillus Hill, a few miles west of Syracuse, as the first major triumph of the race.

"Some frankly doubting Thomases," the spectators who gathered at the base and top of the hill, did not believe Old Scout could conquer it: "The road up the hill was hard and medium dry and in fair condition," Huss recalled. "We had to resort to low gear but that type of car was an exceptionally good hill climber and we did the hill fairly easily . . . much to the crowd's disappointment."

The racers' encounter with the Montezuma Swamp, at the head of Cayuga Lake some thirty miles farther west, was no triumph, however. This was territory that Megargel knew well, from his days at Cayuga Lake Military Academy in nearby Aurora, and later during the years he lived in Rochester and wrote for *Sidepaths*. But the previous day's rain had flooded the main road through the swamp, and Megargel and Huss both got lost as they tried side roads in an effort to continue west.

They finally reached Rochester, ninety miles from Syracuse, in time for lunch at the Whitcomb Hotel. George B. Selden was among those to greet them.

The details of Selden's conversation with the racers are lost in time, but it can be assumed that they talked cars, Oldsmobiles especially. They may have talked about Huss's boss, Fred Smith—and also patent No. 549,160. Selden had yet to testify in ALAM's lawsuits, but Ralzemond Parker had him on the witness list. Already, Parker felt contempt for Selden. So did Ford, who, two weeks after Megargel and Huss met with Selden, said in an advertisement in the New York *Herald*, "It is perfectly safe to say that Mr. Selden has never advanced the automobile in a single particular."

Statements later published in Detroit's *News-Tribune* and the *Automobile* would be more scathing still: Selden, said Ford, did not possess even "one little grain of good faith or a glimmer of inventive genius . . . [he] did not and could not invent any part of an automobile." He was, Ford said, "not an inventor at all, but merely a patent attorney who was willing to prostitute his profession and avail himself of the blind alleys of the law to gain an end." Nothing but money had motivated him, in other words. Patent No. 549,160, Ford maintained, was but "a huge joke."

## MOVEMENT

Back in late November 1900, the cover of the biweekly publication *Sidepaths* had featured an image of the Locosurrey, "one of the prides of the Locomobile Company of America"—a car, it was claimed, that had twice ascended and descended New Hampshire's Mount Washington. The issue included a report from the first New York automobile show, held earlier that month in Madison Square Garden. The story, apparently written by Megargel, gushed with excitement for the new machine. The test drive on an indoor track that the writer had taken made an instant convert:

"The *Sidepaths* representative was favored with a spin in one of these 'horseless mobiles,' a racer, at a rapid clip, and [not] until one has actually 'had a ride' under the expert's management does he get the fever. Many sales were made by this means and it was a pretty sight to see them all on the track, and one would like to think that he was out on the road and that the sight that met his eyes was an everyday occurrence and not an exhibition. It was a sight . . . that would make the poor horse turn green with forty kinds of envy."

Although the *Sidepaths* masthead declared its devotion "to Constructing and Maintaining Bicycle Pathways throughout the United States and Canada"—good roads for bikes, in other words—the magazine during its four years of existence had increasingly incorporated coverage of automobiles. Cow paths, country lanes, and old Indian trails may have been tolerated by those driving horse-drawn vehicles, but they were anathema to bicyclists and now, automobilists. Except for hard-surfaced thoroughfares in certain cities and towns, American roads were mostly dry and dusty in summer, mucky in rain, often flooded, and almost always cratered, bumpy, and rutted. They could not support sustained speed or comfortable and safe travel in a bicycle or car. The first US Survey of American Roads, conducted in 1904, claimed the existence of 2 million miles of rural public roads—but only 154,000 miles were paved with stone, gravel, or other materials.

Members of the Good Roads movement were working to reshuffle that equation.

They could claim the legacy of Thomas Jefferson, who on March 29, 1806, signed legislation authorizing the building of a highway from a site on the Potomac River in Cumberland, Maryland, to the Ohio River in Wheeling, West Virginia, then a part of Virginia. Construction of the Cumberland Road had begun five years later and was completed in 1818.

Congress in 1820 approved extension of the National Road, as it came to be called, to St. Louis, but the road never reached there: the advent of the railroad, among other factors, had weakened federal support. Congress made its last appropriation for the National Road in 1838 and voted two years later not to complete the unfinished stretch. With some exceptions, states, counties, and local municipalities were not up to the task of constructing and caring for a national or any other road on a large scale. By the Civil War, the future of ground transportation seemed to belong to the train.

The two-wheeled, pedal-powered machine was the force behind the next substantial movement for good public roads. Made practical by European inventors in the first half of the nineteenth century, the bicycle became a commercial success in America after the Civil War, in part due to the entrepreneurial Albert Augustus Pope, a decorated Civil War veteran who had experienced the horrors of the Battle of Antietam. During a visit to the Centennial International Exhibition in Philadelphia in 1876, the Boston-born Pope, on the lookout for a moneymaking opportunity, saw an exhibit of British bicycles and was sold. He arranged to import a few bicycles and then began manufacturing his own, under the Columbia brand, in 1878. Demand soon outstripped supply. Pope became rich and powerful.

The explosive popularity of bicycles sold by Pope and others prompted some local officials to place bans or restrictions on their use—a sort of harbinger of the battles to come with automobiles. Pope punched back, founding the Wheeling Association, an advocacy group, and helping to build the League of American Wheelmen, organized in Newport, Rhode Island, on May 31, 1880, when more than one hundred bicyclists from smaller organizations paraded through city streets and attended a banquet. "Twenty-nine clubs from Washington, Baltimore, Philadelphia, Chicago, Trenton, New York, Saratoga, Brooklyn, Hartford, New Haven, Providence, Boston and elsewhere were represented," wrote the *New York Times*.

———

DURING THE NEXT DECADE, the League of American Wheelmen's influence grew. By 1891, it had a principal office in Manhattan; a claimed membership of 25,000, and divisions in Washington, DC, thirty (of forty-four) states, and London. It also deliberately extended its constituency to include farmers, who no more enjoyed bad roads than did bicyclists—and who had a greater economic interest in betterment than a cyclist out for a leisurely ride.

In his sixty-eight-page *The Gospel of Good Roads: A Letter to the American Farmer*, published in 1891, Isaac B. Potter, a civil engineer, lawyer, and member of the league's Committee on Improvement of Highways, argued for farmers to join bicyclists in demanding that the federal government improve, build, and maintain good roads. America's railroads were the finest in the world, Potter asserted, but its highways were inferior to every other industrially advanced nation. Quoting a US Department of Agriculture official, Potter argued that good roads would save farmers and the public millions of dollars, lower the price of goods at market, and decrease "the number of horses necessary as a motive of power." Smaller numbers of the animals would be injured, he also maintained, though his motivation was economic, not humane: fewer broken necks or legs, which required a horse to be put down, would bring savings, and a farmer could afford to invest in "better stock," he said.

Potter urged farmers to join bicyclists in pressuring Washington.

"Yes, my loyal friend," he wrote, "every year or two the election excitement gets into your borough and you are invited once or twice a week to shoulder a torch and chase the village band through miles of sludge to the tune of 'Kemo Kimo' [minstrel song] till election day comes, when, if your rheumatism lets up and the mud isn't too deep, you drive the patient old mare through miles of mangled soil to help elect somebody who is apt to serve your interests last and least of all."

In closing, Potter turned grandiloquent. Good roads, he said, would be "a reform that benefits all and injures none; makes you broader and better in your person and in your possessions; helps and hastens the happiness of your family; shields and saves the patient friend that drags your wagon so many miles from year to year; puts you on better terms with yourself and all mankind; and leaves you wondering what sort of farmer that was who lived and labored in a sea of mire."

In January 1892, the League of American Wheelmen began publishing its monthly *Good Roads* magazine, edited by Potter, which declared on the front cover that the state of a nation's highways characterized the very soul of the nation itself: "The road is that physical sign or symbol by which you will understand any age or people. If they have no roads, they are savages, for the road is the creation of man and a type of civilized society."

Later in 1892, Pope published "An Open Letter to the People of the United States," addressed to Congress and President Benjamin Harrison, in which he affirmed Potter's beliefs, saying "the construction of the public road is eminently a matter of the first and highest importance to any people." Pope founded a new advocacy group, the National League for Good Roads, which brought farmers deeper into the cause. He helped plan the October 1892 first meeting of the National League, in Chicago, which attracted more than 1,000 supporters of good roads, including representatives of trade and agriculture boards, farmers' organizations, and agricultural schools. Pope spoke at the convention, along with Potter and others prominent in the movement. Fellow Civil War veteran and civil engineer Roy Stone of New York City was named the National League's vice president and secretary.

———

STONE HAD EMERGED AS another disciple for renewed federal involvement in roads. Working with the League of American Wheelmen, he wrote legislation in the spring of 1892 that would establish a fifteen-member, fact-finding National Highway Commission, to be composed of US senators and representatives, the interior and war secretaries, the postmaster general, and five citizens named by the president. Senate and House versions of his bill were introduced in early summer, but the legislation died when the House adjourned without voting.

The Chicago convention charged Stone with a new lobbying effort for a federal study of the nation's roads needs—and this time, he succeeded. On March 3, 1893, Congress authorized and President Harrison approved the US Office of Road Inquiry, under the umbrella of the federal Department of Agriculture. Stone was named head of the office, and he got down to business with a $10,000 annual budget and, initially, a staff of one. A tireless analyst and prolific writer, Stone became the new face of the national Good Roads movement. In his many speeches, he summoned the spirit of the Founding Fathers to win converts and rally the faithful.

Speaking in 1895 at a convention in Tennessee, Stone described a glowing vision of an interstate highway system:

> A great national highway might be constructed called perhaps The Great Road of America, which should first join together the States along the Atlantic seaboard; then strike across the country on a central line, say from Washington to San Francisco joining there another line which connects the States on the Pacific coast; this road to be built not by the general government alone but by the States under such arrangements as they may make. . . .
>
> Such a scheme would arouse great interest among the whole people of the United States. It would be something worthy of the Nation, something worthy of the beginning of the twentieth century. The mere location of such a road would have great historic value and importance. The line along the Atlantic coast would be the old Post Road in the time of the Revolution. The route across the Alleghenies might be the line that the early settlers of this region followed when Daniel Boone and his comrades came over the mountains to settle these beautiful plains. The line across the Rocky Mountains might be the line of Lewis and Clark and Fremont, and when we struck the Pacific coast, we would strike the oldest road in all our history, the Camilla Real, the great Spanish Royal Highway, which joined together the Catholic Missions of the Pacific coast.
>
> The whole scheme would carry with it something that would inspire the entire Nation. It is not any new scheme; it is not any new idea. It was the idea of Jefferson and Madison and Gallatin and many other great men who helped to start the National Road.

---

BY 1897, THE YEAR Ransom Olds incorporated his car company, new allies in the Good Roads movement had taken up arms. Ford had built his first car, the Duryeas were selling production vehicles, and magnate Pope had diversified into automobiles. Manufacturers and motorists wanted street signs and maps that could be trusted. They wanted hard-surfaced roads with drainage that were built to last, and provisions for their maintenance and repair. They wanted weight-bearing bridges that did not wash away when rivers flooded. They wanted an infrastructure.

Stone found a new way to build support: the demonstration road, half a mile to a mile and a half in length, paved and equipped with drainage, that traveling teams of engineers and laborers built in communities around the country and the public was invited to drive. The first of many demonstration roads was constructed in June 1897 at the entrance to an agricultural school in New Brunswick, New Jersey. The federal share of the cost was $321.

"The lecturer on good roads, therefore, is listened to like one who tells fairy stories or travelers' tales of distant lands," Stone said, "but put down a piece of well-made macadam road as an illustration and let the people try it in all weathers and no lecturer is needed. The road speaks for itself, all doubts disappear, and the only question raised is how fast can it be extended and how soon can the improvement be general."

After returning from service in the Spanish-American War with a disabling disease, Stone resigned in October 1899 and was succeeded by Martin Dodge, an Ohio lawyer, state assemblyman, and first chairman of the Ohio Good Roads Commission. Dodge was Stone's evangelical equal, and during his five-year tenure as head of what was renamed the Office of Public Road Inquiries, the agency's budget tripled, a road-building testing laboratory was established, and an engineering program opened, among other accomplishments. Although significant federal funding of highways remained in the future, the future was closer.

In a 1903 opinion piece in *Munsey's Magazine*, Pope endorsed the new attention Congress and the states were paying to the movement. He wrote of the vital self-interest the car industry had in better roads—without which, manufacturers would eventually be stymied.

"In building up such an industry as the automobile represents in America, an enormous capital must necessarily be sunk before the business can be regarded as on a substantial basis," Pope wrote. "Few people outside the trade realize the amount already invested. Two or three million dollars might be the popular idea of the maximum, but this would fall far below the actual figure. Twenty millions would be nearer the mark. This immense sum has been sunk in plant and experiment, with the result that the automobile industry is to-day one of the most promising in the country."

Pope concluded: "To build automobiles is one thing, to sell them another. There are plenty of buyers in the market, as was abundantly proved at New York and Chicago during the recent shows. But the American who buys an automobile finds himself with this great difficulty: He has nowhere to use it. He must pick and choose between bad roads and worse. He finds his route so circumscribed that he can never realize the definition given to an automobile as a 'go-where-you-please.'"

In 1905, the federal agency again was renamed, to become the Office of Public Roads. A new director, Logan Page, took over from Dodge with a congressionally approved annual budget of $50,000. The staff now numbered ten people.

James W. Abbott was one of them. A civil and mining engineer from Denver, Abbott was appointed a special agent and road expert in August 1900. He, too, became an evangelist for the Good Roads movement.

## MISSING EXPLOSIONS

Their midday stop at Rochester's Whitcomb Hotel concluded, Megargel and Huss cranked their cars and continued west. Megargel trailed Huss until Huss stopped to let a long freight train go by, and Old Steady caught up. Huss got lost after that, and Megargel beat him into Buffalo by about half an hour. Yet another crowd awaited them at the Oldsmobile dealership, operated by W. C. Jaynes, who also sold Wintons, Popes, and Buicks. Jaynes had recently opened a 10,000-square foot garage with twenty-eight-foot-high ceilings, which attracted the attention of *Motor Age*. "An expensive new brick building," the publication hailed it.

Megargel told the *Buffalo Express* that the trip thus far had been a breeze.

"Three days from New York to Buffalo is good traveling for a car of 30 horsepower, to say nothing of seven," he said. "We're having no trouble at all. Take today's run, for instance. We were on the road not more than ten hours, hardly that, yet we made 150 miles without the slightest difficulty. This runabout can travel more than 25 miles an hour, but we don't let it out because we have many more miles to go."

His jaunty voice and minimization of challenges and frustrations seemed calculated. Megargel was not only competing, he was creating a persona; cultivating an image of himself as heroic and romantic adventurer—the dashing Johnny Steele, from the hit song "In My Merry Oldsmobile." The real Percy Megargel had a wife and young child. In 1901, he had married the former Olive A. Anderson, daughter of a New York City doctor. Their child, Gertrude, was born a year later. But Megargel never mentioned these circumstances in his own writing. Journalists who wrote about him and his automobile adventures never did, either.

————

AFTER AN OVERNIGHT AT the Genesee Hotel, the last grand establishment at which the racers would stay, Huss beat Megargel out of Buffalo by about ten minutes on Thursday, May 11. The men drove through country where automobiles had never been seen.

"A small boy on his way to school, whom we stopped to ask about the road, was frightened and commenced to cry violently," Megargel wrote. "Soon after, a girl, after taking one look at the begoggled, mud-covered tourists gave a yell and started down the road at top speed. When she saw we were overtaking her, she made for the side fields, falling several times before she finally convinced herself we were not really after her. The next youth we met dived bodily through a barbed wire fence and streaked it across the fields at top speed."

During lunch in Erie, Pennsylvania, a heavy rainstorm rolled in, forcing the racers to mount chains on their tires for traction through the muck. The rain short-circuited Megargel's battery, a tire went flat, and the men got thoroughly drenched.

On this fourth day of the race, Huss outpaced Megargel, reaching Painesville, Ohio, thirty miles east of Cleveland, for his overnight stop. Megargel only made it as far as Conneaut, forty-five miles behind his competitor—but he left early the next morning and caught up with Huss in

Cleveland. Passage out of the city was treacherous, with what Megargel described as "numerous mud puddles of uncertain depth to ford" and hundreds of acres of farmlands flooded in several feet of water. "At one point," he reported, "we ran for a quarter of a mile without seeing the road at all, the water in some places coming above our axles."

Seventy-five miles west of Cleveland, the cars stopped for the night at Clyde, Huss's hometown.

"Covered with mud from head to foot, travel-stained and bronzed by exposure, but in high spirits, with their auto, dubbed 'Old Scout,' looking as if it had been struck by a mud volcano, Dwight Huss, the Clyde boy, and his companion, Milford Wigle, whizzed into Clyde about 8 p.m. on their race across the continent," a Clyde weekly wrote. Both cars were garaged overnight at Huss's father's farm-equipment and carriage business, M. L. Huss & Co., where the men spent much of the night cleaning their machines.

Setting off together at 4:30 a.m. on Saturday, May 13, the racers drove into a worse mess than on Friday but were undeterred as they passed through Toledo. "We pushed our little car to its limit," Megargel wrote, "sending it charging again and again into some waterway that had us in doubt whether it possessed a bottom or not."

During this battering, Megargel punctured another tire. Old Steady's motor began to misfire, and he and Stanchfield lost hours checking the carburetor, batteries, spark plugs, "and the hundred and one other things that might cause a missing of any gasoline car," Megargel said. The rain returned as the crews ate a late supper in Kendallville, Indiana, and at nearly 10:00 p.m., they called it a night.

On Sunday, May 14, with Huss ahead, they crossed from Indiana into Illinois. They finally found the cause of the misfiring: a badly connected ground wire.

Megargel sent Smith a telegram: "Roads almost impassable. Water two feet deep in road and bridges down. Chicago probably Monday morning. Working hard." In a separate report, Megargel reassured Smith that interest in the race remained keen: "Escorted into each city by autoists. Reporters and cameras awaiting us everywhere."

Having averaged only about four hours of sleep a night since leaving New York, both crews were suffering from exhaustion—and taking chances they should not have, as Megargel related from his May 15 dispatch from Chicago: "The crews of both cars are in excellent spirits, although all four men have a faculty of falling asleep while at the wheel."

When the cross-continentalists had arrived, Abbott had immediately sent Smith a comforting telegram: "Megargel arrived noon. Huss still here. Both leaving this afternoon."

———

THE RAIN RESUMED AFTER Megargel and Huss left Chicago and it continued through Tuesday, May 16, as they passaged the Illinois plains. After a night in Mendota, they arrived in Geneseo shortly before midnight on the next day—the worst progress thus far, despite "the hardest work," Megargel observed.

"Illinois mud," he said, "even when taken at a racing gait, brought our mileage down to 64 miles for the day, and we worked tooth and nail ever since 5 a.m." The writer had particular disdain for what he described as "that sticky, thick, black mud that only Illinois and Missouri can boast of. To get through it, we were obliged on several occasions to use block and tackle. The water in our tank boiled, but the engine never faltered, although every one of the four wheels was so stuck up with mud as to render the spokes invisible."

On May 18, they would reach Davenport, Iowa, on the shore of the Mississippi River, some 860 miles from Manhattan as the crow flies. Leaving the heartland, they would venture into an America most Americans had never seen.

# 7

## THE HORSE LOSES POWER

### PASSING THE "IMPASSABLE"

The three-hundred-mile passage across Iowa from the Mississippi to the Missouri Rivers—from Davenport to Council Bluffs, east of Omaha, Nebraska—sorely tested Megargel and Huss. Five long days they traveled, on roads that with few exceptions were as bad or worse than those they had encountered during the miserable week before. The rain had stopped, momentarily, but the flood waters kept rising, washing out bridges and grounding ferries.

"In one place in Iowa it required three and a half hours to cover a distance of one half mile," the *New York World* wrote in a dispatch from Omaha. "The fact that they got through at all and in good running shape was the wonder of all spectators," wrote the *Davenport Democrat*.

Megargel outdid himself describing the nightmare of the South Skunk River watershed, about twenty-five miles east of Des Moines.

One of the worst mudholes thus far encountered was the Skunk River bottoms, several miles east of Altoona. Huss and I agreed to help each other across, or neither of us would have reached the other side. First, one car would plunge into the water and mud until stuck, then we would rig our

153

Endless mud and flooding stymied Megargel and Huss.
GM Media Archive.

blocks and tackle, attach it to the car axle and bring the other end back to the car still on dry land. By all of us pushing, and the free car towing, we managed to work our way across a swamp that everyone told us was impassable.

All of us worked in water and mud nearly waist deep. My rubber boots were not nearly high enough to escape wet feet, as the water simply poured in over the tops, and when I reached Des Moines I was able to pour several quarts out of each boot after nearly an hour's work in pulling the boots off. . . . The water was so deep that at one time all of the four wheels were out of sight and a stream flowed freely through the flooring of the wagon, soaking everything, filling the carbureter with water and short-circuiting the battery.

But the racers' determination through such deplorable conditions— really, their success was against all odds—made them seem almost godlike to the citizens and journalists who turned out to meet them. With US Office of Public Roads official Abbott amplifying the hype, newspapers had heralded their arrival and in some communities, the racers' progress was tracked on bulletin boards. On a sales trip to San Francisco, Chapin did his part, too. "Have arranged Evening Bulletin run daily accurate accounts continental race," Chapin wired Smith. The California market was large and growing, and Olds wanted its share.

"Wherever we stop our car," Megargel wrote from Brooklyn, Iowa, population about 1,200, "it is at once surrounded by an enthusiastic crowd of spectators who continue to stare at the mud-stained, battered Oldsmobile, until we eventually haul out of town. One motherly old woman who passed us as we were working on our car by the roadside exclaimed: 'You poor fellows, I'm awful sorry for you.'" But pity was the minority view. Villagers and townspeople at every stop shook their hands, inquired about their cars, fed them, and photographed them and their amazing vehicles.

Megargel experienced his own kind of awe, marveling at the size of Iowa farms and the large numbers of animals on them. City slickers back east could marvel, too.

"Each farmer raises from twenty to a hundred horses a year and several times that many head of cattle, while pigs are too numerous to mention," Megargel wrote. "There are hundreds—yes, thousands—of pigs on every farm, I believe. These droves of ham and pork chops occasionally block the road so that we are obliged to blow the horn for a long distance before we can get a clear road."

But grazing horses recoiled at the cars—and Megargel made a new farmer enemy.

"The horses all through Iowa cut up badly upon the approach of an automobile," he wrote. "One old farmer with long whiskers of the Populist variety, for whom we had stopped our car to get his horse and mule combination past, was highly indignant at 'an automobile from New York being on his road,' as he termed it."

"'Do you know the law in this state compels you fellows to run your machine in the field until we can drive by?' said Whiskers."

"When we informed him that we knew of no such law, and that our automobile was not afraid of his team, even if they were scarecrows, he wanted to 'lick the two of us,' as he put it."

But Whiskers's attitude ran contrary to other Iowans'.

"The ill feeling against automobilists that one encounters so frequently among the farmers in the east is lacking here, and every farmer met with is your friend, no matter how badly you scare his horses or how much damage his nag does before you finally get past him on the road," Megargel wrote. "There is no difference, however, in the nature of the horses. Some do not even prick up their ears at the approach of our machine, while others go through a series of rearing, kicking and bucking that would do credit to a wild west show. In passing horses on the road we have to be extremely careful, as several have kicked most viciously at our car and our occupants."

The horses could be forgiven. They had served mankind for millennia, and now they were under attack.

––––––––

THE WAR AGAINST THE noble steed was foreshadowed on September 16, 1893, when the Massachusetts *Springfield Evening Union* published its story about the Duryeas' first car under the headline:

### NO USE FOR HORSES

It accelerated with help from Ransom Olds, whose years on a farm seemed to have traumatized him.

As early as 1892, when he completed his second steam-powered car, Ransom made demeaning comparisons to the horse that contained the seeds of a mainstay of Oldsmobile marketing.

A motor vehicle, he told a reporter, "never kicks or bites, never tires out on long runs, and during hot weather [a motorist] can ride fast enough to make a breeze without sweating the horse. It does not require care in the stable, and only eats when it is on the road, which is no more than at the rate of one cent a mile."

When he built his first gas-powered car in 1896, Olds was delighted to tell the new magazine *Horseless Age*: "The time will come when the horse will be relegated to comparative discard. Men will travel from town to town in a vehicle driven by power machinery at a speed of at least thirty miles per hour. Soon every house will add an automobile room to shield their horseless carriage. Barns with their odors from horses will disappear from the city."

The next year, at a meeting of the Michigan Engineering Society, Olds again praised the practical advantages of the car over the animal.

A car, he said, "is always ready on a moment's notice; instead of hitching up a horse in the ordinary way, all one has to do is turn the motor over to draw in a mixture of gasoline and air, which is ignited inside the cylinder by an electric spark, and the engine at once starts and runs continuously, so that the operator has only to throw the lever to different points to back, stop, or start the carriage without any reference to the motor or mercy on the horse; especially when it is ninety in the shade, when flies and dust are unbearable, you have only to turn on a little more speed to secure a breeze and leave the dust behind. When through using, you have only to throw out the electric switch and the horse is taken care of until needed again."

Olds asked the engineers to imagine the city of the future, when cars had replaced horses. That urban tomorrow would hardly be the peaceful place that Olds depicted, but he was not alone in his sunny vision.

"Did you ever stop to think," he said, "what a grand thing it would be to dispense with the clanking of horses' hooves on the city pavements, how much cleaner our streets would be, and that with rubber tires, a city may become a veritable beehive of activity without the deafening noise of today, as well as the cracking of the whip, in order to force the poor horse over the pavements?"

Asked by someone in the audience if a multitude of cars would not inevitably cause a multitude of accidents, Olds answered no, "as the [horseless] carriage is under perfect control, not like a horse that might get frightened or shy at some passing object." Similarly, he said pedestrians would be safer, as "the horse obstructs the view in front of the driver to a certain extent."

Some of this was nonsense, and it is doubtful that Ransom really believed it. But he had cars to sell.

———

AT ONE POINT DURING his drive in his first Detroit Automobile Company vehicle with the Detroit *News-Tribune* reporter, in February 1900, Ford came upon a horse-drawn milk wagon.

"The horse pricked up his ears," the reporter wrote, "his eye gleamed ominously; he shivered as though about to run away. His driver applied the whip."

"'Ever frighten horses?'" the reporter asked.

"'Depends on the horse,'" Ford said. "'A low-bred, ignorant horse, yes; a high-born fellow, no. There's as much difference between horses as between dogs.'"

Further into the article, Ford minced no words.

"'The horse is doomed,' said the passenger."

"At that moment the auto whizzed past a poor team attached to a truck."

"'That's the kind,' said Ford. 'Those horses will be driven from the land. Their troubles will soon be over.'"

But Ford, along with many other manufacturers, focused more on the merits of his machines than the inadequacies of horses. Olds stressed his cars' virtues, too, but he saw the living creature as his direct, perhaps most formidable, competitor in those early days. He showed no mercy in his ads, pummeling the poor animal while exaggerating his cars' capabilities.

"Nature made a mistake in giving the horse brain; science did better and made the Oldsmobile," read one Curved Dash ad. Read another: "No accident with the Oldsmobile. Mechanical skill and mathematical exactness eliminate the danger of the horse's uncertain temper, sudden fright and unruly disposition—no 'Runaways' with *The Best Thing on Wheels.*'"

Oldsmobiles, the company proclaimed, could outrun horses—and were always ready to go, unlike a sleeping, lazy, or sick horse. A driver need only pay attention to the controls and the road ahead, not the reactions of an animal that might get spooked or require the whip. And motor vehicles were cheaper, Olds claimed. In an ad that depicted a feeding horse and a Curved Dash next to a small can of gas, the company claimed, without proof, that the cost of boarding a horse annually was $180, compared to just $35 in gasoline to run an Olds 10,000 miles.

Curved Dash Olds ad, circa 1905.
Courtesy of the AACA Library and Research Center, Hershey, PA.

"This graceful and practical automobile will do the work of six horses," the company asserted. Under the banner "The Passing of the Horse," another ad said "the silent horse power of this runabout is measureable, dependable and spontaneous—the horse-power generated by supplies of hay and oats is variable, uncertain and irresponsive. There is *'Nothing to watch but the road'* when you drive."

With their need to quickly make house calls, sometimes in the middle of the night, doctors would unquestionably want a car instead of a horse, Olds believed.

"The Oldsmobile has proved itself by long, hard service to be the ideal Motor Vehicle for Physicians," an ad declared. "It outwears a dozen horses, is always harnessed and fed—is built to run and does it." Even its *Ladies Home Journal* ads lambasted the horse. One depicted a stylish woman driving the pretty countryside, waving her handkerchief at a stallion with the caption: "Good Bye, Horse."

But a truth about the machine went unadvertised: in some respects, it was more finicky than its flesh-and-blood counterpart.

Under the headline, "HUMORING THE MOTOR: How Kindness Improves its Behavior and Lengthens its Term of Life," the *Motor World* on May 18, 1905, wrote:

> Probably few motorists realize to how great an extent kind treatment of the motor contributes to successful results in its action and in satisfactory operation of the car, for it is no exaggeration to say that the gasolene motor is as sensitive as a child and quickly resents any overtaxation of its powers, any abuse of its functions. . . . The proper understanding of a motor's action involves the almost unconscious reading of a great number of symptoms such as the sounds of the inlet, the whistling of the air in the carbureter, the sharp puff of the exhaust, and all the little metallic clicks and rattles of the various mechanisms.

A horse, by contrast, plugged along nicely on its own until reined in. Nothing much to monitor.

In terms that could have described a loving owner's feelings toward a horse, the magazine urged owners to always treat their vehicles with tenderness and respect: "It is really nothing more nor less than a matter of sympathy between man and motor, the perfect handling of the machine, and it is possible in the highest degree only with one who so loves the inanimate mechanism that it really pains him, 'goes against his grain' is a more conventional way of putting it, to see the thing abused."

———

OLDS'S MESSAGE RESONATED WITH the motoring press and some motorists. On May 5, 1905, an elite group of them demonstrated ridicule of the horse during an "observation run"—a race, really—through New York City streets. Durant participated in one of his Buicks. An Olds engineer drove an Oldsmobile. ALAM general manager George H. Day participated, as did M. J. Budlong, president of Electric Vehicle Company, and Packard general manager Henry B. Joy. Officials from Studebaker, Franklin, Locomobile, and other companies also drove. Journalists were invited to ride along.

"Up Central Park West, Seventh Avenue and later Jerome Avenue they tore," wrote the *Motor World*, rivals cutting one another out at every turn and passing and repassing one another." Lunch at the New York Athletic Club's Travers Island facility was provided by the New York Yacht Club, holder of the America's Cup. The magazine printed the menu: Muffled Clams, Clam gasolene on the side; Hot butter lubricant; Lock nut olives and Spark plug radishes; Crank case chowder; Throttled Fish with ball bearing potatoes; Rich mixture salad; Runover chicken on asbestos packing; Grease cup cheese; Beer a la Tonneau; Circulating water; and Exhaust crackers.

A highlight of the day, the magazine wrote, occurred during a reception at the Larchmont Yacht Club, where the parked cars blocked a horse-drawn phaeton. The animal panicked.

"The poor horse was completely surrounded by more automobiles than he had ever at one time regarded in his existence," the magazine reported, "and to his mind, in much closer proximity than was comfortable, as he exhibited a tendency to stand on his hind legs to get away from them. But there was no escape, for he was walled in on all sides. Mr. Day, realizing the predicament, of both horse and master, led the former to safety, much to the amusement of the gathering."

Day, the magazine wrote, had been a "star."

———

THE US CENSUS BUREAU counted 8.6 million horses in America in 1870, a number that had nearly tripled, to 21.2 million, in 1900. Slightly more than 1.5 million horses lived in urban areas in 1870—with almost double that number in 1900. New York City that year had 130,000 horses; Chicago, 74,000; and Philadelphia, 51,000. The streets were clogged with them, their urine and excrement everywhere, raising an odor impossible to escape. Sanitation departments struggled against the mess. Their job was compounded by the detestable owners who left their animals to rot when they died. Summer heat made the whole situation insufferable.

Apparently using Census Bureau numbers, the *Motor World* in 1910 stated that 200,000 mules and 4.5 million horses lived in American cities. Most in New York powered carriages and wagons.

"The 130,000 horses hitched to vehicles in the Empire City add a long and unnecessary line to the traffic parade," the magazine wrote. "Counting eight feet from the dashboard to each horse's head, the animals take up 200 miles of the streets. And if, for example, these horses were all harnessed to the wagons tandem fashion, 190 miles of horseflesh would pass before the first wagon appeared in sight. In other words, the first horse would be entering the city of Scranton, Pa., or Worcester, Mass., before the leading wagon pulled out of New York City."

Such a horde of perpetually defecating animals undeniably created a public health hazard.

"With all possible and reasonable precautions intended to keep the cities sanitary, little progress can be made so long as such an army of quadrupeds parade in endless procession up and down the thoroughfares," the magazine concluded. "The clouds of dust which sift above the pavements are not the wholesome earth of the fields but are filled with germs and lingering death. . . . The exit of the horse would mean the disappearance of the house fly, for it would remove its chief breeding source."

---

BEYOND BETTER PUBLIC HEALTH was the economic argument. As the quality and reliability of the automobile improved, manufacturers could convincingly argue that the machine was superior to the horse for transportation and labor.

In an article published on May 18, 1905, the day Megargel and Huss started through Iowa, the *Motor World* reported the experience of the New York–based Adams Express Company, a national conglomerate that had risen to prominence during the California Gold Rush of 1849 and the Civil War. The company relied on horses to pull its wagons around New York City—but also counted three gasoline and twelve electric vehicles in its fleet. The firm still held reservations about the costs of maintaining a car, but Adams's traffic manager was impressed by the performance of its motor vehicles. He could foresee phasing out horses.

"Mr. Wright said that roughly speaking, they had found the motor wagon capable of doing one and a half or two times as much work as could be done by horses in the same length of time," the *Motor World* wrote. "The use of machines in exacting work of this sort is of great value from an experimental standpoint not only in its specific application but as a lesson as to the requirements of the work, the relative fitness of the various types of machine, and as a proof of their ability to replace that troublesome and expensive proposition, the horse."

A month before, the magazine had catalogued the eleven automobiles owned by New York City municipal departments: the Department of Street Cleaning had six; the Department of Docks and Ferries, two; the Fire Department, two; and the Bureau of Public Works, one.

The Department of Street Cleaning, led by the flashy John McGaw Woodbury, was among the first to use cars.

"For two years and more," the magazine reported, Woodbury "and his deputies have been using automobiles in this work almost constantly. At first, cars were rented from time to time when unusually long trips were found necessary. At such times, the possibility of taking two or three officials with him to visit and inspect the dumping system of Brooklyn, for instance, including the vast land fill at Coney Island, and of being back in his office within four hours, having held a conference en route and entirely disposed of the matter which called him forth without having left the machine for more than ten or fifteen minutes, all told soon opened the commissioner's eyes to the advantage to be gained from its constant use."

Automobiles so impressed Woodbury that his department purchased one—a large touring car, unsurprisingly—for his own use. He posed in it for a photograph that ran in the magazine.

A year earlier, in February 1904, the *Automobile* published a page of stories comparing how horses and motor vehicles had fared in the city during a recent period of heavy snowfalls followed by thawing and then refreezing, which had resulted in disaster. "Ordinary vehicle traffic of all kinds has been much impeded," the magazine wrote.

The publication surveyed representatives of Adams Express, Saks & Co., a Broadway carpet company, a sightseeing firm, a brewery, and Roosevelt Hospital, which operated an electric ambulance. In every instance, the motor vehicle won.

"Manager Horn" of Saks told the magazine that of his fleet of twelve electric trucks and five horse-drawn wagons, the motor vehicles in general had proved better: "On slippery pavement the automobiles are harder to get going than the horses, but of course when they are once underway, they keep going far better than the horses." A manager with the brewery, owned by Jacob Ruppert, now a congressman and future owner of the Yankees, agreed with Horn that except for very deep snow, which horses negotiated more easily, motor wagons excelled. "In icy and slippery streets, they go better," he said.

Six days of regulated trials conducted in New York that April seemed to lay all doubt to rest. Sponsored by the Automobile Club of America, the trials divided motor wagons into five classes: small trucks that could carry loads of under half a ton; larger trucks sustaining loads between 1,000 and 2,000 pounds; medium-size trucks that could carry from a ton to a ton and a half; large trucks sustaining loads of two tons; and the largest trucks, capable of hauling two and a half tons or more. Olds, Knox, Pope-Waverly, and Electric Vehicle Company were among the manufacturers represented. The trucks, owned by companies around the city, made their rounds under the watch of ACA inspectors.

"Even before the official data of the individual performances had been collected," wrote the *Automobile,* which published five illustrated pages of coverage, the trials proved "that the business automobiles can make transfers and deliveries quicker than horse-drawn vehicles; that they can make more deliveries or transfers in a day; that they can cover a greater number of miles; that they are easier to handle in congested districts; that they are superior to horses on long runs, and that they occupy but half the ground space required by a team and wagon while loading."

A spokesman for department store R. H. Macy & Co., which owned fifteen electric wagons, was among those who preferred the truck. He noted the greater distances the electrics could cover, and the fact that they always were done their day's work by 6:00 p.m., whereas horse-drawn rigs didn't return until 10:00 or 11:00 p.m.

Unsurprisingly, manufacturers of commercial vehicles and parts also claimed the horse was a loser in business. "The marked economy of power wagons for delivery express and truck service and their superior reliability when in reasonably intelligent hands is so well established that those who are conversant with the facts cannot fail to see that power wagons are rapidly beginning to supersede horse service," the Garford Company of Elyria, Ohio, suppliers of gears, brakes, axles, and other parts, declared in a 1905 advertisement.

Packard made a similar point in advertising a truck it sold for $2,500: "The Packard 1-1/2 ton Motor Truck will do more work than two two-horse trucks and at one half the expense. Some who have used it say that it will do the work of three two-horse trucks and at less the cost of one. Neither the hottest days of summer nor the severest cold of winter affect its efficiency, and after a long hard day's work, it is just as fresh and ready to go again as before it started."

———

THE FACT THAT A critical measure of an automobile engine's capabilities was derived from the animal's own name—horsepower—intrinsically worked to the horse's disadvantage. Coined by the late-eighteenth-century Scottish inventor James Watt, who wanted an easily understood measure of the energy that his steam engines produced, the term "horsepower" was everywhere in advertisements and stories about cars. Manufacturers, journalists, and owners rarely described an automobile without stating—or bragging about—how many "horses" it had under the hood.

Carmakers emphasized that point.

In a June 1, 1905, advertisement for its $900 runabout, Autocar, a Detroit firm, depicted the vehicle appearing to pull a hitched team of horses against their will. The car, the ad declared, "has a motor of 10 mechanical horse-power, which is about equivalent to 15 animal horse-power. The horses, however, could furnish this power for only about 8 hours a day. As the Autocar Runabout can be run for 24 hours a day, it will be seen that if both power and endurance are considered, this car is equal to 45 horses." It was unlikely the runabout could not have run many—or even one— twenty-four-hour days without breaking down or overheating, but this was an ad, not a sworn statement.

In the matter of braking, the horse lost, too. Autoists spoke of everyday experiences in which, they said, cars could stop faster and more safely than horse-drawn vehicles. Manufacturers and journalists cited demonstrations pitting machine against animal. One of them, a series of "tests of braking power" conducted in spring 1905 at London's Crystal Palace, made headlines on both sides of the Atlantic. Six vehicles twice competed against six varieties of horse-powered vehicle: in each meet, the pairs started at the same time and, after a certain unannounced distance, were ordered to suddenly stop.

Not once did the horse-drawn vehicle win: The "motor van" beat a two-horse wagon; a "six-cylinder car" and an 18-horsepower Mercedes each beat a one-horse brougham; a 15-horsepower French De Dion outperformed a Hansom cab; and a "racing car" trounced a trotting sulky. Most impressive, the *Motor World* wrote, was the De Dion against a Hansom cab at the trials' fastest speed: 18.4 miles per hour. "The latter stopped in a distance of twenty four and a half feet, while the machine was rounded up in just one foot and six tenths," the magazine reported.

On May 25, the magazine reprinted the results of tests in France that might settle "all the discussion that has been raging over the speed question."

Conducted by the Toulon Automobile Club, the tests confirmed, in the opinion of the *Motor World,* at least, that "the horse is even further out classed: his ability as a back pedaller is not even fourth rate as compared with the modern automobile."

Against a traditional wagon, the magazine reported, "one of these ancient vehicles drawn by a team of horses" moving at "the extremely high rate of speed of eleven miles an hour," a car came to stop in roughly its own length, about nine feet—while the wagon required twenty yards. In a second test, at 13 miles per hour, the car won again. "All further tests where the horses were concerned were out of the question because they could not go any faster," the *Motor World* wrote.

"The moral is obvious and may be verified by any observing individual who will keep his eyes open on the city streets. The rapidity with which the motor car pulls up short is amazing but when a horse usually attached to an ambulance or fire engine attains to the same speed and the necessity for a stop abruptly presents itself in the form of another wagon or a dazed pedestrian, disaster results."

The magazine did not mention the consequences when reckless drivers moved at far greater speeds. Even the best brakes could not prevent accidents, as the daily headlines attested.

---

SOMETIME AFTER THE TURN of the century, word began to spread of the demands made by the Farmers Anti-Automobile Association of Pennsylvania.

The first item in the association's code of ethics required a motorist approaching a horse-drawn vehicle to pull over and cover the car with "a tarpaulin painted to correspond with the scenery"—to camouflage it, in other words, so that a horse would not sense its presence. Similarly, cars traveling the countryside were to be painted in the color of the season "so they will merge with pastoral ensemble and not be startling": green in spring, gold in summer, red in fall, and white in winter. After dark, motorists were to send up "red rockets" and roman candles to warn of their coming; by day, when approaching a blind corner, they were to toot a horn, ring a bell, fire a revolver, "halloo and send up three bombs at intervals of 5 mins."

Another item was yet more outrageous: "In case a horse will not pass an automobile, notwithstanding the scenic tarpaulin, the automobilist will take the machine apart as rapidly as possible and conceal the parts in the grass."

The Farmers Anti-Automobile Association of Pennsylvania almost certainly was fictitious, likely created by some car lover with a wicked wit. But this was real: far from urban areas, farmers generally had less inclination or opportunity to evaluate the motor vehicle. And as Megargel and many others had chronicled, ignorance could breed fear and anger.

Members of the Houston Automobile Club experienced the fury on May 19, 1905, when, on a moonlight run into the country, they encountered "an obstreperous farmer" who stubbornly blocked the road with his four-horse wagon, wrote the *Houston Post*. When one motorist tried to get around the team and ran into a ditch, club members "lined up back of that farmer and each one turned his auto horn loose full-blast in long, drawn toots. Such a chorus a pair of workhorses have, perhaps, never heard," the paper reported.

Although the horses had "long since lost their coltishness," the paper wrote, "they were not built to stand such a row." The horses tore down the road. The farmer, wrote the paper, "contented himself with hurling some warm remarks at the autoists, who gave him back some smiles for his heated words."

A worse reception awaited a St. Louis businessman on a trip through northern Missouri in the summer of 1905.

When a drenching rainstorm rolled through, the man—James E. Morse, "one of the liberty loving citizens of this free country," wrote the *Motor World*—asked a farmer sitting on his piazza if he and his mechanic could take shelter. But the "horny handed bucolic" ordered them off his property with "fierce invective" and by "denouncing them as individuals and as members of a hated class." Morse and his mechanic traveled on, stopping at a hostelry for lunch. The men enjoyed the meal until the proprietor, "a burly giant over 6 feet high," asked if Morse had a county motor vehicle license. Morse said he did not, but intended to get one.

"You're a d—-liar," the proprietor said, grabbing the businessman by the throat and punching him in the face several times.

"By this time," the *Motor World* reported, "there was quite a gathering of villagers and farmers from the surrounding country looking on in unsympathetic delight at the argument and encouraging the oppressor with shouts and jeers at the motorists."

The proprietor went to lock the men up. "Here, a citizen more rational than his fellows interfered and advised Morse to pay the $3.50," a dollar more than the actual license price—extortion, as the magazine called it.

Morse paid the $3.50 and was released, but his troubles were not over.

"At High Ridge, Jefferson County," the magazine wrote, "the automobile was surrounded by a curious throng who were out picnicking, farmer lads and their sweethearts mostly. Morse was approached by a deputy who was also the elder of a church giving the outing. Asked if he was provided with a county license, he replied that he was not, not being aware that he was in a new county. He was charged $2.50 for a license."

———

BUT FARMERS ULTIMATELY WOULD be persuaded: the new gas-powered technology made economic sense that would be impossible to ignore. Already by 1905, inventors on both sides of the Atlantic had built and were selling gas-powered tractors: Dan Albone in England and Iowa's John Froelich, whose Waterloo Gasoline Engine Company would be bought in 1918 by John Deere, founded in 1838 as a maker of horse-drawn plows. Ford, who foresaw the end of horses as farm labor, would contribute to the shift when he began selling tractors, in 1917.

In his 1891 *Gospel of Good Roads,* Potter wrote of farmers' stubborn opposition to any new technology—opposition that gave way to acceptance once knowledge replaced ignorance, the League of American Wheelmen leader maintained.

You do not forget that when the first railroads were projected, you appeared before the legislature of your State and opposed the granting of franchises to all such iniquitous schemes. You said that locomotives would burn your crops and set fire to the wool on the backs of your sheep; that the gases from the smoke stack would poison your family and your farm stock, and that travel in a railroad car at the frightful speed of twenty miles an hour would be fatal to many passengers and dangerous to all.

You opposed the telegraph and ridiculed the mowing machine, You took the sewing machine on sufferance and regarded the patent thresher with a suspicious eye; and I might almost say there is no great invention of commercial or agricultural value which was cheered by the warmth of your approval. . . . We don't always recognize a good thing at first sight.

You have changed your opinions about many things because you did not
at first understand their value.

————————

OCCASIONALLY, A HORSE fought back.

"Probably one of the most unusual accidents that have occurred in recent happened on Long Island one day last week," the *Motor World* wrote
on May 25, 1905. "An automobile which had halted was run into from the
rear by a carriage drawn by a frisky horse. The shafts penetrated the rear of
the tonneau and the struggles of the frantic horse resulted in the overturn-
ing of the automobile. Both of its occupants were thrown out and injured."

Judges hoped for a truce between motorist and animal, and most did
what they could to control the motorist.

In what was said to be "the first damage suit to be tried in Tennessee
over an automobile," brought by a man whose horse galloped away from
the machine that had frightened it, "the court held that in runaways, all
parties concerned should do all in their power to prevent the same," according to a story in the June 15, 1905, *Motor World*.

In another case in 1905, the New York Supreme Court acknowledged
motorists' frustration with horses—but also their responsibility. "It is not
pleasant to be obliged to slow down these rapid running machines to ac-
commodate persons driving or riding slow country horses that do not
readily become accustomed to the innovation," the court wrote. "It is
more agreeable to send the machine along and let the horse get on as best
he may. But it is well to understand if this course is adopted and accidents
and injury result that the automobile owner may be called upon to respond in damages for such injuries."

In the end, the court wrote, the onus was on the driver: "Some horses
are frightened when they meet these machines and it is the duty of persons running the machines to exercise reasonable care to avoid accident
when horses become frightened."

Other judges agreed. The *Horseless Age* reported the indictment of
an Illinois motorist for frightening a farmer's team of horses, an action
brought under the state's automobile law. The Supreme Court of Indiana

in 1905 upheld a lower court decision awarding $925 in damages to a man who was injured when a car startled his horse, which then ran away. The Indiana judges ruled:

> When the defendant saw that the plaintiff's horse had become frightened at the rapid approach of the strange, noisy carriage and that the plaintiff was in danger, which was reasonably certain to increase by the nearer approach of the motor, and from which it was plain that he could not extricate himself except by defendant stopping or slowing down until plaintiff could reach the cross street, it was the highest moral as well as legal duty of the defendant to stop and remove the plaintiff's peril rather than to increase it by rushing onward.
>
> Will anyone seriously say that the driver of such an automobile, recently brought to the vicinity, may speed it at twenty miles an hour along the highway toward approaching harnessed horses, puffing and whirring so as to be heard several hundred yards away, and seeing a horse in front of him hitched to a buggy, rearing, plunging, and trying to bolt back the road without any other apparent cause, is justified in maintaining his speed because he does not know what it is that causes the horse's fright? The law of the road does not tolerate any such inconsiderate and reckless disregard of the rights of other travelers on the highway.

———

HORSES WERE LIVING CREATURES, not soulless iron and steel, a reality that some autoists acknowledged; they did not deserve the fate that Ransom Olds predicted. Nor did they deserve the life many led in cities, where they suffered in extreme hot or cold and endured punishing whippings.

In its stories about the severe weather of February 1904 in New York, the *Automobile* chronicled the plight of horses in the snow and ice. In some instances, teamsters doubled the number of horses to their wagons—and still, the animals were overwhelmed.

"Large numbers of horses were crippled by falls and had to be killed, or sustained sprains by slipping on the icy pavements that necessitated their temporary retirement from use," the magazine wrote. Public safety was jeopardized as well: on Upper Broadway, the magazine reported, the Fire Department struggled to beat back a blaze:

"No less than three pieces of apparatus with fallen horses were seen within a single block. One of them was so badly stalled that it was not until a passing automobile truck went to its assistance and gave it a boost that it was able to get started again."

A charitable view was expressed by the Duluth Automobile Club, which circulated a letter to all Minnesota clubs urging a gentle touch with the horse.

"Whenever you see a horse or team that is showing fear of your machine, slow right down, or better still, come to a dead stop and let it pass you," the club wrote. "We want to make friends of horses and their drivers—not enemies."

## OMAHA

As Megargel and Huss continued west, Smith celebrated their progress in a series of weekly full-page ads that began when the racers were just three days out of Manhattan. The one published after they reached Chicago hailed the race as already an unprecedented triumph:

"New York to Chicago, the first stretch of the race, which is the only transcontinental trip ever undertaken from the Atlantic to the Pacific, seven days were required, or five days less than the St. Louis tourists of last summer, and this in spite of heavy rains and mud. A machine that stands up under the exacting requirements of such a contest is a pretty safe proposition for everyday use. Thousands of purchasers have demonstrated the truth of this assertion. Watch the race. Write us for full information regarding this or any other of our line. Send for catalog 53."

When the racers reached Omaha, Nebraska, Smith ran another of his ads, more laudatory still.

"Are you watching the Transcontinental Race between the two 7 HP Oldsmobile Runabouts Old Scout and Old Steady, from New York City to Portland, Oregon, for a prize of $1000? 1700 miles in 14 days is the record to Omaha, through mud every day but two. This is the most remarkable endurance contest ever attempted."

In truth, both drivers had become desperate in Iowa. Far from the indestructible machines that Smith depicted, the cars were falling apart.

"Must have new tires new steering spring and good new carburetor at Omaha ship immediately," Megargel wired to Smith on May 19 from the small city of Brooklyn, Iowa. Two days later, he telegraphed from Des Moines: "Both cars badly off for tires. need money at Omaha."

When they got there, a time-out was urgently needed. Huss broke the news in a May 22 telegram to Detroit: "Both cars arrived Omaha seven this evening two days repairing necessary."

The urgency of the situation was lost on the multitude that welcomed the motorists to Omaha, with a population of more than 100,000, Nebraska's largest city. The *Omaha Daily Bee* had been following the race religiously, with its latest update published the day before, in its Sunday, May 21, edition. An Olds ad in that edition noted, "the wonderful records of the two Oldsmobile Runabouts now racing from New York to Portland, Oregon."

"It is doubtful if any transcontinental wagon outfit since the earliest forties ever attracted as much attention on the streets of this city," Megargel declared.

The racers spent two full days in Omaha cleaning and repairing their vehicles and laying in supplies. Ahead lay vast expanses of nothingness that left Megargel apprehensive.

"Both crews have provided themselves with firearms," he wrote, "but should we encounter any hostile foe, whether he be wild animal or bad man, the others will have to be able to shoot straighter than I can with the big .38-caliber revolver I purchased for the trip. I tried for half an hour to hit a telegraph pole across the road, but couldn't do it on the one box of cartridges I carried. I'm going to buy another box and try again some day, but shooting with a revolver was never my forte, although I do possess a National Guardsman medal for marksmanship won during the Spanish-American War days."

The Honolulu *Evening Bulletin* was among the papers to report on Megargel and Huss as they prepared to leave Omaha, the morning of May 25.

"Everything is now ready for the real race, which begins in Omaha and ends 1,802 miles to the northwest," the paper said. According to the story,

Megargel and Huss were ten days behind schedule, an exaggerated figure, but the newspaper correctly outlined the arrangements that had been made, as did Abbott in a long piece in the *Automobile*.

Wrote the Hawaiian paper: "Supplies and other necessaries have been shipped to different points on the Union Pacific road through which the racers will pass and these will be taken up when the machines pass the towns. The racers will follow the old overland trail up the Platte valley to Cheyenne and will go over the mountains via the Fremont pass, which is used by the Union Pacific." The rails would be their North Star.

Having traveled more or less together since Manhattan, helping each other when needed, Huss and Megargel agreed that their chivalry was over: from Omaha to Portland, Oregon, they would really race. Megargel was optimistic that he would win.

"I feel that our chances for piloting Old Steady into Portland in first place are exceedingly good," he said.

But the next night, in Fremont, Nebraska, would be the last time the racers would be together. Beset by new woes he could not have imagined, Megargel would steadily fall behind.

# 8

## THE WEST, STILL WILD

### "REMARKABLY LUSTEROUS"

During much of their passage across Nebraska, the racers followed Union Pacific rail lines, miles of which paralleled the old Pony Express and Mormon Trails. But Nebraska showed the transcontinentalists no more mercy than Iowa. The spring downpours returned, hitting the drivers again with raging rivers, soupy roads, and monstrous holes.

"High water and bridges out," Megargel telegraphed Smith on May 25, when he and Huss reached Fremont, on the now-angry Platte River.

"Roads bad no postal," Huss telegraphed as he and Wigle passed through Overton on May 27, a day ahead of his competitors. "Arrived Cozad five-thirty roads almost impassable raining hard," Huss wired on May 29.

That same day, Megargel, falling farther behind, wired his worst news so far: "Old Steady goes through bridge both axles bent springs broken." He did not disclose what the *Motor World* reported: that the men "had a narrow escape from drowning." Stanchfield labored for hours to get the car moving again and it limped into Grand Island, where he made more substantial repairs. But there was only so much he could do: outside of Omaha, there was nothing resembling a motoring infrastructure.

With an area of 77,421 square miles, Nebraska was one-third larger than Iowa—but was home to 1.1 million residents, just half the population of its neighbor. And though early registration figures were not an accurate count of all motor vehicles, here, too, the disparity was pronounced: only 560 cars and ten trucks were then registered in the state, compared to 730 and seventy in Iowa. By contrast, New York state, smaller in size than Nebraska, had a population of 8 million—and 9,230 registered motor vehicles, the most of any state (Pennsylvania, with 9,130, was a close second). On their run across New York—through the bustling cities of Albany, Utica, Syracuse, Rochester, and Buffalo—Megargel and Huss had the benefit of garages, service stations, and dealerships, a budding infrastructure.

But this was not New York. Megargel and Stanchfield would not be able to completely fix their car until Boise, Idaho, more than 1,000 miles west. Until then, Megargel later said, Old Steady "was mended, but would break again at the slightest provocation, and that meant the delay of half a day every time."

Still, Megargel found a silver lining.

The motorists were now traveling through the part of America that the *Automobile* called "the terra incognita of the American automobilist"— the territory, west of the Missouri River, that was unfamiliar to most Easterners and to many others, motorist or not. But not for lack of interest, Megargel understood. Since their premiere in Omaha in 1883, Buffalo Bill's Wild West shows had remained greatly popular with audiences east of the Mississippi, tapping into a seemingly unquenchable desire by residents of long-settled parts of the country to see cowboys, Indians, and displays of horsemanship. Easterners had helped make celebrities of Sitting Bull, Annie Oakley, and other stars of William F. Cody's extravaganzas.

And so, Megargel had a rare opportunity to build his reputation as a writer. He could discover details that would later help in completing a novel.

Wildlife fascinated him—snakes, jackrabbits, prairie chickens, wolves, and coyotes, whose barking, "a distinctly new sound to me," kept him and Stanchfield from sleep. Prairie dogs greeted them everywhere. "We repeatedly ran through prairie dog towns. In fact, about every five miles, we would strike one of these dog villages, comprised of from two to five

Sitting Bull and Buffalo Bill.
Library of Congress, LC-USZ62–21207.

hundred mounds. The dogs would congregate on the tops of their houses until Old Steady would be almost upon them, when they would scamper down to the regions below."

Megargel pondered the Great Plains' stark emptiness—notably the 140 miles from Lodgepole, Nebraska, into Wyoming, during which he drove through three towns with populations of fewer than twenty-five. The rains had stopped and water was scarce. Gas, used to power farm equipment and other machines, was expensive and of poor quality: "Gasolene has commenced to come pretty high, while the quality goes in the opposite direction. There was a time in Ohio when we could get fuel at 15 to 18 cents a gallon. Now it is 30 to 35 cents a gallon, and every hundred miles farther west it is reported as being a few cents more."

And cowboys intrigued him. West of Cozad, Nebraska, Megargel wrote, "we encountered vast tracts of original prairie land without fencing of any kind, and every few miles we found herds of cattle, usually looked after by one or two cowboys mounted on fiery little ponies. The riders, as a rule, rather enjoy the antics of their animals as they buck and pitch at the sight of the automobile, and wave to us gaily as we pass them. The ranchmen treat us well, and when a stop is made for adjustment or oiling, they flock around us. . . . " Most people rode horseback, in contrast to the East, where they rode in carriages behind the horse.

Innocuous though the strangers were, the racers remained wary. They holstered their revolvers conspicuously, "our belts bristling with cartridges, as do many riders we meet along the road," wrote Megargel. But he used a gun just once: to kill a rattlesnake that measured more than six feet and had seven buttons to its rattle. He cut off the tail and photographed it for publication. It was another titillating detail for his Eastern readers.

———————

AFTER DIPPING INTO THE border town of Julesburg, Colorado, a short detour that gave the racers bragging rights to one more western state, Huss and Wigle reached Cheyenne, Wyoming, late on Wednesday, May 31. They were now a day ahead of Megargel and Stanchfield. Old Scout's arrival had been greatly anticipated, thanks again to Abbott and the still-breathless press, and cheering citizens greeted them outside the Depot Cafe.

"Coughing like a cigarette fiend, 'Old Scout,' one of the New York to Portland automobile race contestants, pulled into Cheyenne at 10:30 o'clock last night," the *Cheyenne Daily Leader* wrote. Huss and Wigle, the paper declared, "show the effects of their long and rough overland journey from New York, but are in the best of spirits."

Abbott had anticipated a grander entrance than puttering to a stop outside a cafe, but his plans were foiled when the city notables he'd arranged to welcome Huss in the outlying village of Archer experienced car trouble.

"Accompanying 'Old Scout' under its own power was one lone Oldsmobile driven by Thomas Myotte, the only one of the five machines which started for Archer yesterday afternoon to meet the racer to reach that destination," the *Daily Leader* wrote. "Trailing forlornly in the rear of Myotte's machine was a second Oldsmobile, attached to the leader by a cable of bailing [*sic*] wire. This machine was that of Dr. Crook, which became stalled while en route to Archer, and had to be hauled back to town. George Nagle's and Samuel Corson's Autocars and Dr. J.H. Conway's Oldsmobile, comprising the remainder of the reception parade, turned back before Archer was reached because of poor roads."

That any cars had been available to greet the racers was something of a wonder. Just fifty automobiles and no trucks were registered in 1905 in all of Wyoming, and until the transcontinental race, the state had rarely been mentioned in the trade press. One of the few stories, "Automobile Stage Line for Wyoming," appeared in the May 4 *Motor World*. A single paragraph long, the piece reported a local company's purchase of a twelve-passenger, 45-horsepower bus that would make one round trip daily between Walcott, east of Rawlins, and Encampment, near the Colorado border.

"It is thought that the operation of the automobile stage line will do much to build up the country, as the long and tiresome forty-five mile stage trip deters many from seeing it," the magazine wrote. "If the car is a success, two more will be put in operation."

———

BYPASSED BY LEWIS AND Clark in favor of a more northerly passage, the territory that became the state of Wyoming in July 1890, less than fifteen years before Megargel and Huss drove through, was the ancestral home of Native Americans, including the Shoshone people. On one stop, Huss gave two Shoshones a ride in Old Scout, then posed with them in a photograph that was captioned with the assurance that the Indians were "friendly."

Trappers and traders were the first Europeans to visit the region, about the time of Lewis and Clark's expedition. Beavers filled its waters, but with its constant wind, short growing season, and arid soil, Wyoming was ill-suited to farming, though cattle and sheep could graze. To the white settler, Wyoming was mostly a vast, empty place between more hospitable places. Mormons crossed it on their way to Utah. The California Gold Rush of 1848 brought prospectors through. By the early 1860s, there was enough traffic that stagecoach service began along the Overland Trail. But it seemed Wyoming was destined to remain a wasteland—more a place for people of European stock to transit than to settle.

And then something upended the equation. As the Industrial Revolution advanced, what ancient geology had bequeathed in abundance to Wyoming became coveted by Eastern and Midwestern industrialists. Coal was needed to power steamships and locomotives, to produce electricity, to feed the furnaces that made iron and steel, the guts of railways, bridges, and buildings—and, now, automobiles.

Trappers in the early nineteenth century had noted the presence of coal in Wyoming, though they had little use for it. It seemed to be everywhere—in massive outcroppings and "rich beds," as a pioneer wrote in 1835—so much bituminous coal that a surveyor for the US Army's Corps of Topographical Engineers in 1850 labeled the Overland Trail region the "Coal Basin." It was unusually shiny, seemingly of special quality—"remarkably lusterous" as the explorer John C. Frémont, later one of California's first two senators and Republican presidential candidate, described it.

The first commercial coal mines opened in the 1860s as two railroads joined the coasts. The Union Pacific was laying track west to Utah to meet the Central Pacific, which was building east from California, and southern Wyoming featured valleys with gentle grades—and coal to feed locomotives and sell to booming markets back east. Through an act of Congress, the Union Pacific had been given mineral rights with the land grants it received for the transcontinental railroad. The rights were an incentive to national unity, and they would prove as valuable as California gold.

The Union Pacific and the many coal companies that sprang up required men with pick and shovel who could endure twelve-hour days, and they required them in great number. Immigrants from England, Italy, China, Finland, and Poland answered the call, joining native-born

Americans. Coal towns sprang up along the Union Pacific main line and the branches built from it. Their names spoke to the hard nature of the land and the enterprise: Rock River, Rock Springs, Point of Rocks, Carbon.

Coal towns, though they varied in population from dozens to thousands of residents, were universally dirty, noisy, and bawdy. For every dry goods store there were saloons aplenty, where men drank a good percentage of their wages in the open and spent some of the rest on prostitutes in the back rooms. Most towns had a bank, a butcher shop, a bakery, a newspaper, a boarding house or two, and a hotel, for well-to-do visiting businessmen. Mormon and Methodist churches competed with the saloons for salvation. Miners mostly lived in poverty, their souls owed to the company store, as the song would later put it. Wood for houses was scarce, even for those who could afford to build them; cold, damp dugouts excavated into creek banks were home for many miners and their families.

"In case of sickness," one woman later recalled, "someone had to hold an umbrella over the patient in bed."

Coal country was enough to drive folk mad, and it regularly did.

———

MET BY THE SAME party that had greeted Huss the day before, Megargel and Stanchfield limped into Cheyenne, the state capital, on Thursday night, June 1. The *Cheyenne Daily Leader* gave the men the same colorful treatment it had afforded their competitors.

"Sorely injured, but puffing gamely," the paper wrote the next day, "'Old Steady,' the second of the Oldsmobile cross-continent contestants, rolled into Cheyenne at 9:15 o'clock last night, having covered the 120 miles from Lodgepole, Neb., since 9 o'clock a.m. Despite their hard drive, Percy Megargel and Bart Stanchfield, the crew of 'Old Steady,' appeared fresh and were not discouraged by the fact that their competitor, 'Old Scout,' driven by Huss and Wigle, reached Cheyenne 22 hours and 45 minutes in the lead. 'Old Scout' departed for Laramie yesterday afternoon but had not reached that place at 10 o'clock last night."

The paper noted that Megargel and Stanchfield would spend a day repairing their car, which was "almost a wreck." It said that the racers were expected to reach Portland, 1,200 miles distant, in ten days at most. Another paper, the *Wyoming Tribune*, reported that Megargel "confidently" expected to catch Huss.

Cheyenne was not a coal town, but its fortunes were similarly tied to the Union Pacific. It had grown from about 1,000 residents in 1867, when the railroad arrived, to more than 10,000 by the time the transcontinental racers arrived that spring. In 1905, it was Wyoming's largest city. Residents still talked of the glorious day two years before, when President Theodore Roosevelt rode in on horseback, perched on "a beautiful gold-mounted saddle," a gift from the citizens of Laramie, some fifty miles west, the *New York Times* reported. A crowd of "20,000 enthusiastic and cheering people," as the *Times* put it, greeted Roosevelt in the capital city. "In slouch hat, riding boots, spurs and gauntlets, the president rode direct to the speakers' stand in the city square," the paper wrote. The good citizens of Wyoming offered to let Roosevelt keep the handsome horse he'd borrowed for the occasion.

Although William McKinley was the first American president to ride in an automobile, in November 1899 when he was a passenger aboard a Stanley Steamer, Roosevelt became the first to ride publicly in one. Thousands had applauded him on a drive through Connecticut on August 22, 1902, that culminated in an appearance at Hartford's Pope Park, a public space that had been donated to the city by Albert Pope, the bicycle-maker-turned-automobile-magnate.

But the Rough Rider president still preferred horse-powered transportation. In an October 8, 1905, letter to an English author friend, Charles Hughes, B.A., he expressed his feelings.

"Motor cars are a trial, aren't they?" he wrote. "I suppose that ultimately we will get them into their proper place in the scheme of nature, and when by law and custom their use is regulated in proper fashion their objectionable features will probably be eliminated; but just at present I regard them as distinct additions to the discomfort of living."

————

Repairs completed, Megargel set off on Saturday morning, June 3, for Laramie. The view coming into the city, at the edge of the Continental Divide, thrilled him, even if the icy blasts of wind reminded him of the long Buffalo winter.

He and Stanchfield overnighted on a ranch west of Laramie and left the next day, when they saw prairie schooners, one of the iconoclastic symbols of the Old West. "Schooners, usually a single wagon," Megargel wrote, "drawn by two or four horses, or mules, with one or two saddle ponies and a cow tied behind, are visible for miles, their big white canvas bow tops glistening in the sunshine."

Over the next two days, Megargel would miscalculate the depth of a creek they had attempted to ford and lose hours freeing their car from the cold waters. He and Stanchfield would lose more time repairing their radiator, damaged by sagebrush. They would drive through weather that Megargel described as the equal to any he had experienced in New York. "We were not prepared for snowstorms," he wrote, "and with the wind whistling around our heads and the snow blowing in flurries around us, we felt the cold keenly."

———

When he passed through Hanna, some 180 miles west of Laramie, Megargel could be forgiven for believing that the land of coal was cursed. Two years before, Hanna had witnessed the worst disaster in Wyoming history. The accounts of June 30, 1903, when an explosion killed 169 miners, made headlines around the world.

"MANY MEN BURIED ALIVE: Explosion Blocks Exits and Entombs All Not Instantly Killed," the *New York Times* headline declared. "Some of the miners who escaped say they saw twenty dead bodies in entry No. 17," the paper wrote. "They reported that many of the men were crazed by the explosion and ran hither and thither in the mine. Many of these could have escaped, but they lay down, buried their faces in their hands, and gave up the fight."

Coal's cruel side could also be seen in Carbon, another town between Laramie and Rawlins. Founded by the Union Pacific in 1868, Carbon had once thrived, boasting two churches, an opera house, a school, a hotel, a miners' hall, eight saloons, and nearly 3,000 residents at its peak. Seven mines fed the frenzy. And then, in 1899, the coal began to run out. It was mostly gone by 1902, when the railroad moved its line north, to a gentler grade. By the time Megargel passed by, nothing was left but empty buildings and a cemetery.

But greater Carbon County still boasted one of the strangest stories of the West—of anywhere, really. Megargel may well have heard it during his days in Wyoming.

It was the story of Big Nose George Parrott, who with a gang of cattle rustlers decided by 1878 that gold bullion carried by the Union Pacific offered better opportunity than cows. Parrott, whose nose indeed was distinctively large, was no smooth operator: after bungling a robbery near Medicine Bow, between Laramie and Rawlins, he and his crew fled into the mountains, where a Union Pacific detective and a deputy sheriff found them. The gang opened fire, killing both lawmen. After stealing their weapons and one of their horses, Big Nose George fled again. A $20,000 bounty was placed on his head.

In Montana the next year, Big Nose George ambushed an army convoy, making off with thousands of dollars in soldiers' payroll. He began to boast of his exploits and the bounty on his head when he got drunk, which was regularly. Braggadocio got him arrested, and he was brought to Rawlins to be hanged, without the formality of a trial.

Days before he was scheduled to die, April 2, 1881, Parrott tried to escape jail—but he bungled the attempt, succeeding only in fracturing the skull of the jailer, which further infuriated the citizens of Rawlins, who dragged him from his cell, tied a rope around his neck, strung the rope from a telegraph pole, and stood him on a barrel. The rope broke when the barrel was kicked away, and Big Nose George fell to the ground, begging to be shot.

The mob did not oblige him. They sent him up a ladder to hanging height—where, begging again to be shot, he slowly choked to death.

Parrott's body hung for hours and when no one claimed it, Doctors Thomas Maghee and John Eugene Osborne, a Union Pacific Railroad surgeon, cut it down and took it—to study his brain, in hope of finding insight into his criminal behavior, or so they stated. First, though, the doctors made a plaster of Paris death mask of Parrott's head, which was earless, his ears having been chafed off in his struggles with the rope.

The strangeness was just starting.

Lillian Heath, a fifteen-year-old girl destined to be Wyoming's first female doctor, joined Maghee and Osborne at the autopsy—and as a souvenir, she was given the top half of Parrott's skull, which she later used variously as a doorstop, a pen holder, and an ash tray, apparently in that order. This sounded like the kind of tale Parrott himself might have told while on a bender, but Heath later verified it as true. Also verified was the destiny of other pieces of George: skin from his thighs and chest was sent to a Denver tannery and processed into a medical bag and a pair of shoes, which Dr. John W. Hoyt, third governor of Wyoming Territory, wore to his inauguration, or so legend held.

————

MEGARGEL WAS PLEASED WHEN he reached Rawlins on Monday, June 5, and found the Ferris Hotel, "a modern building, well equipped, and supplying an excellent table"—and running water. "Once more we are occupying a room with connecting bath," he wrote, "and having removed the alkali dust, both Stanchfield and I feel civilized again." This was the son of a wealthy family, not the rugged adventurer, momentarily speaking.

The men lost the next day to repairs, but the landscape lifted Megargel's spirits. Leaving Rawlins the morning of Wednesday, June 7, he was struck anew by the desolate beauty of southern Wyoming. He would re-create the feeling in *The Car and the Lady*, his 1908 novel.

Jerry Fleming, his alter ego in the novel, talks of

this silent following of a deserted trail up and down, up and down, meeting no living soul, seeing no living thing except a little cottontail whisking into its burrow. . . . The miraculous clearness of the atmosphere, the burning white sunlight, have a sharpness of outline which was as unreal to

Eastern eyes as a painted forest on the stage. To Fleming, the bigness and loneliness were like a stimulant. As mile after mile the trail unwound before him, he felt the exhilaration of the mariner steering through strange seas; the unquenchable spirit of youth rose within him to meet the demands of the adventure; he felt once more sure of himself and his victory.

But transcendence was fleeting: Megargel was five miles out of Rawlins when Old Steady's motor sputtered to a stop. After removing the crankcase, he and Stanchfield found "a paint-like solution that the heat of the cylinder had transformed into a hardened, sticky gum" that had cemented the piston. It was his own fault. Since leaving New York, he had been using Rockefeller's Mobiloil, some of it shipped ahead by rail, but he had neglected to pick up any in Laramie. With his motor running dry, Megargel had filled the crankcase with a substance advertised as "gas-engine oil" that he bought at a store. Whatever it was, it was not motor oil.

Megargel walked the five miles across cactus plains back to Rawlins, where he hired a team of horses to haul Old Steady into town. Oldsmobile railed against the beasts of burden, but in this instance, the horse had proved a savior to one of its automobiles.

"We worked most of Tuesday night, and until 10 o'clock Wednesday morning, cleaning out the engine," he recounted. "Gasoline, kerosene and lye had no effect, and it was not until we resorted to muriatic acid that the gum would dissolve. It was necessary to remove the body from the car to take the engine out. The tedious job was not rendered any more pleasant by the knowledge that Huss and Wigle were three and a half days ahead in Old Scout. . . . "

---

IN FACT, THEY WERE six days and nearly four hundred miles ahead: in Boise, Idaho. But they had not kept the lead without pain.

A wire report published in the Bridgeport, Connecticut, *Post*, described one of their days that began with a two-hour crossing of a stream, where "the water being waist deep, it was found necessary to bring their block and tackle into use." The crews of both cars were carrying these

The West punished Huss and Megargel severely.
GM Media Archive.

pulley-and-rope aids, which amplify human strength. As the day wore on, Huss and his mechanic crossed two more streams and a swamp without incident—but a third stream stymied them again.

"The block and tackle came into use for another hour before they were on their way again," the *Post* said. "From that time on, mudholes became worse and trouble came thick and fast. The roads were stony and the sage brush was two feet high between the tracks, making it impossible to drive faster than a walk." Huss advanced just thirty miles in seven hours—an average speed of 4 miles an hour, about the pace of a brisk walk.

Amazingly, the Curved Dash still ran. That any stock-model vehicle could was a testament to its design and construction.

"I cannot understand how the machine stood up under such hard usage," Huss told a reporter. "After leaving Rawlins, we had the worst piece of luck we have struck yet. We were spinning along at about 18 miles an hour when I saw a deep hole and in trying to dodge it, ran into a bigger hole and set my front axle back about eight inches. There we were, about 90 miles from the nearest blacksmith shop and things looked pretty dark. It still hangs together, however, and we will push ahead. . . . "

But not immediately. Suffering from an unspecified malaise that began early in their six days in Idaho, Huss had finally been persuaded to take bed rest in Boise.

"Huss had been loath to do so," *Motor World* reported, "and it was only at the earnest solicitation of friends that he consented to do anything of the sort. The plucky fellow is really in bad shape, and for the last four days has been going on nerve alone." Huss would later reveal that he and Wigle had gone nearly a week without sufficient water, which had left them dizzy.

"When we walked, we wobbled," he said.

Whether it was the altitude or something worse, Huss was in bad shape. He risked losing some or all of his lead over Megargel while he recuperated, but he had to take a break.

## MORE TROUBLE IN THE EMPIRE

Back in Detroit, Smith was keeping the copywriters busy with his weekly ads. The first, published three days after Megargel and Huss left Manhattan, launched a dose of publicity that would continue into summer—a double dose, when press coverage was factored in.

"Everyone interested in automobiles and thousands who are not are watching with daily increasing interest the plucky race between two Oldsmobile Standard Runabouts now in progress between New York City and Portland, Ore., a distance of over 3,000 miles," the first ad proclaimed. "It is a fight to the finish with a prize of $1,000 to the winner. Such a contest is only possible to cars of sterling quality."

The following week's ad mentioned Whitman and Hammond's historic 1903 crossing from San Francisco to Manhattan in a Curved Dash, declaring that the same machine was "the unquestioned choice" for Megargel and Huss's competition. Already, the ad declared, the cars had exceeded expectations.

Megargel was in Wyoming when an ad ran trumpeting the Curved Dash's superior performance in recent reliability trials between Paris and Toulon, citing a "well-known authority on automobile affairs" who called the runabout about the only American car that held its own against "the famous French makes." The ad concluded: "In the transcontinental race from New York City to Portland, Oregon, just drawing to its close, two Oldsmobile 7 h.p. runabouts, stock cars of the same type as mentioned above, are demonstrating the same characteristics of reliability and endurance as made them easy winners against all foreign competitors."

But in the privacy of his office, Smith was concerned. Manufacturers had learned that sales rose monthly from January until the peak season in May and June, when the weather was fair—then began to decline as the hot summer wore on, fall set in, and the dead of winter, when almost no one bought cars, approached. In late spring 1905, Olds sales were tracking nowhere near the record year of 1903. They even lagged behind 1904.

And though Smith didn't know it, there was another ominous cloud on Oldsmobile's horizon: a new rebellion was brewing inside the company. Chapin, like Ransom Olds before him, was beginning to disagree with the direction his boss was taking the company. Smith continued to seek the higher end of the market, which Chapin considered a mistake. Like Ransom Olds and Ford, he believed the future belonged to the low- to mid-price automobile—cars for the multitudes, not the elite.

As 1905 wore on, Chapin secretly investigated other opportunities. A New York financier who wanted him to become general manager of his automobile manufacturing company wooed him over dinner aboard his yacht, anchored off Staten Island, but in the end, Chapin declined. Instead, back in Detroit, he began to scheme with a small circle of friends at Olds who shared his displeasure with Smith. They had mastered the new industry while at Oldsmobile, and it was time now to strike out on their own.

Smith continued with his high-price plans. And in an expensive marketing endeavor likely inspired more by vanity than common sense, he invested resources in building a six-cylinder, 60-horsepower speedboat, *Six Shooter*, which he entered in the first National Motor Boat Carnival

races, held in late summer on the Hudson River off the West Side of New
York before a crowd of thousands.

The boat was an embarrassing flop. Smith's baby could not even complete the course, let alone compete for a win. This was not the sort of publicity that would persuade prospective buyers that an Oldsmobile was the
car for them.

"The Six Shooter started so late that she did not try to finish," the *New
York Times* reported. One winner was the loathsome Edward R. Thomas,
who steered his eight-cylinder, 150-horsepower *Dixie*, second most powerful of the two dozen boats entered, to a speed of 22 miles per hour. He
cut quite the figure, a skipper "clad in oil skins and wearing a big life preserver," the *Times* reported. Ironic, given the lives he had taken.

———

HENRY FORD ANSWERED SMITH'S weekly ads with full-page ones of his
own.

"THE FORD was the first practical car with a double opposed motor
to sell at a moderate price," read one that ran while Megargel and Huss
were in Iowa. "THE FORD was the first American made Automobile to
clip seconds off the mile record. THE FORD was the first car built with a
view to low cost of maintenance and is today the cheapest car of its class to
maintain. THE FORD was the first Automobile to be shipped in train lots
to one dealer. THE FORD was the first Automobile popular enough to
warrant the establishment of a factory in Canada. . . . Write for our book on
Maintenance and get in touch with us. FORD MOTOR COMPANY, Detroit, Mich., Member American Motor Car Manufacturers' Association."

During the spring and summer of 1905, Ford offered three cars: the
$800 Model C, successor to the popular Model A; the $1,000 Model F, a
touring car; and the speedy four-cylinder Model B, which retailed for
$2,000.

In the company's new plant on Piquette Avenue, work had already
started on the 1906 line. Ford was throwing all he had into one of the new
cars: the inexpensive four-cylinder Model N. But he was proceeding

under protest with another: the six-cylinder Model K, which would cost five times as much.

Investor and nominal treasurer Malcomson favored the Model K: like Smith, he wanted big cars with wide profit margins. Even an owner of a cheap runabout, he argued, would surely want to move up to a classier car with his next purchase.

The tension was magnified by Malcomson's desire to be more deeply involved in automobiles. To free up more time, he suggested that company secretary Couzens leave Ford and manage his coal business. Malcomson had hired Couzens, then a lowly railroad car checker, to be clerk of his coal company back in 1897, a job he'd held until he left for Ford, in 1903. Evidently, Malcomson thought he was still Couzens's boss.

Ford would have none of it.

At a director's meeting, Malcomson, apparently out of spite, moved to get rid of Couzens altogether—but the board voted to double Couzens's salary, to $8,000 a year. Outgunned, Malcomson retreated, but not for good.

Attorney Parker, meanwhile, reached a milestone in another matter of vital interest to Ford's long-term prospects. In July, he concluded his initial defense in the Selden patent case. He was ready to call Ransom Olds to the stand—and re-call Henry Ford.

## LONE JOHN

After a breakfast of ham and eggs, Megargel and Stanchfield left Rawlins at 10:30 a.m. on Thursday, June 7. They had equipped their car with soft, wide tires, to improve traction across the parched terrain.

"We struck into what is known as the Great American desert," Megargel wrote, "a stretch of sandy country in which absolutely nothing can grow except sagebrush, greasewood and cactus. There were no ranches, cattle or horses for many miles westward, and, in fact, hardly a living thing but jackrabbits, prairie dogs and rattlesnakes. Water is very scarce here, and long lines of tank cars stand on the sidings of the Union Pacific. When the water supply of one of the infrequent small towns along the railroad gives out, these cars are sent to a neighboring town to borrow."

Megargel required eleven hours to travel the eighty miles to Point of Rocks—an average speed of 7 miles per hour, a torturous pace that would not cut into Huss's lead. He was not rewarded with a hotel or fine meal when he reached the tiny outpost. Point of Rocks was home to but a few dozen people, who all lived in shacks. Megargel and Stanchfield ate another meal of ham and eggs, then slept in a Union Pacific freight house, their revolvers loaded.

Bound for Granger the next day, they passed through Rock Springs, where the mines continued to produce and the town remained burdened by the memory of a horrific atrocity.

Twenty years before, on September 2, 1885, a mob of white immigrants had massacred at least twenty-eight Chinese immigrant miners. The mob resented the Chinese because they agreed to lower railroad wages, which ostensibly deprived whites of jobs. The *Wyoming Tribune* was one of the newspapers that had stoked the hysteria, urging "white men" to "throw back the tide of heathen paupers from our shores." To do otherwise, the paper editorialized, would be traitorous.

"Every day a suicide, some poor devil of a white man out of money, too proud to beg, too honest to steal, too noble to starve, blows his brains out," the paper wrote. "All right white blood is at a discount and coffins are cheap."

On September 5, 1885, the *New York Times* described the massacre scene: "A glance over the battle ground of Wednesday reveals the fact that many of the bullets fired at the fleeing Chinamen found their mark. Lying in the smoldering embers where Chinatown stood were found 10 charred and shapeless trunks, sending up a noisome stench, while another, which had evidently been dragged from the ashes by boys, was found in the sage brush nearby. A search resulted in the finding of five more Chinamen, killed by rifle shots while fleeing from their pursuers. All were placed in pine coffins and buried yesterday afternoon."

The massacre prompted President Grover Cleveland to send army troops to Rock Springs, and he decried the killings in his State of the Union address. Clerics and newspapers back east judged the town harshly.

"The appropriate fate for a community of this kind would be that of Sodom and Gomorrah," wrote the *New York Times*.

---

ARRIVING IN GRANGER THE night of Friday, June 9, Megargel observed that the racers had left New York exactly one month before "on a trip we expected to accomplish in thirty days." But nearly 1,000 miles remained, if they were to make it to Portland.

The next day cast further doubt that he and Stanchfield would. They were outside Opal, yet another hardscrabble place, albeit one with an elegant name, when the sky turned black, the thunder and lightning came, and they were caught in a wicked hailstorm. "Both of us crawled under the car in the mud to save ourselves from the chunks of ice nearly two inches in diameter that descended in torrents," Megargel wrote.

Torrential rain followed and flash floods soon roiled the desert, trapping them. "We did the best we could with rope," Megargel reported, "but every little rivulet had been transformed into a raging mountain stream, and the first one we attempted to run engulfed Old Steady and pretty nearly swallowed up the crew. We half waded and half swam to shore, leaving the car with just the seat above water."

For hours, they waited for the flood to subside.

But the waters rose higher, swamping their car and threatening to sweep it away.

And then, the men saw a sheep ranch in the distance. They walked toward it.

They may have wished they hadn't. Pigs, chickens, and lambs shared the main house with its sole human occupant, Lone John, as Megargel called him, making the building "one of the foulest smelling places I have ever been in. Everything about the place was filthy to an extent that one could hardly conceive." Megargel knew the meaning of foulness from Omaha, with the overwhelming stink from its infamous Union Stockyards, so Lone John's dwelling must have been truly fetid.

They found Lone John in the barn with more livestock and a team of broncos. He was, Megargel wrote, "glad to see us, as company is scarce in this part of the world." He apparently was so glad that he unburdened himself with a rant about how dreadfully life had treated him.

"He was at war with several of his neighbors, and kept a loaded gun at hand at all times," Megargel wrote. "He had just been released for cutting open the head of one of his neighbors with an axe, and he regretted the fact that he had not killed the man. Despite his grievances, he willingly threw the harness on his horses, and telling us where we would find the wagon, and to use his team as we saw fit, went out to round up his flock of about 500 sheep and half that number of lambs."

With Lone John's team, Megargel and Stanchfield pulled their car from the water. Once again, the machine was miraculously resurrected: the men were able to start it and get moving again.

But Stanchfield was not so resilient. He had started to sweat and shiver uncontrollably, the victim, perhaps, of the same malady that had struck Huss. He needed a doctor, but there was none to be found. Opal had a glittering name, and little else.

Megargel drove through the night and into the next day, Stanchfield wrapped in a rubber coat and lying limp atop the trunk. When they finally reached the coal town of Diamondville the evening of Saturday, June 10, he was barely able to move. Megargel parked outside the Daly Hotel and helped him into the lobby and then up to a room. "Aches in every bone and muscle . . . a burning fever with intermittent cold chills . . . most miserable," Megargel later recounted to a newspaperman.

"After getting him to bed," Megargel wrote, "I spent the rest of the day hunting up a doctor. I finally managed to catch one at Kemmerer, ten miles distant, and brought him to Diamondville in Old Steady."

The doctor—"one of those nervous little men filled with his own importance and knowing it all at a glance"—judged the men to be fools.

The doctor had diagnosed mountain fever, "looked Bart over, prescribed a hot bath, hot lemonade, plenty of blankets and no air in the room," Megargel wrote. "Then he said his bill was $10, and wanted to know who was going to pay it. An automobilist is looked upon as an easy mark in the Far West, just as he is in other places." Megargel paid the physician, left his companion in bed, and went to the dining room, which served a respectable meal.

With its fifty rooms, barbershop, and saloon, one of a dozen in town, the three-story Daly Hotel—named for Anaconda Copper Co. co-founder Marcus Daly—was the grandest place in Diamondville. Which was not saying much. Diamondville's Mormon and Methodist churches were modest, the main street was lined with the usual coal-town establishments, and its miners' residences were typically shabby. Workers and their families found fraternity in ethnic clubs: the Italian Lodge, the Slavenski Dome for Slavic immigrants, the Finn Hall for Finns. The Finn Temperance Society competed with the saloons and a boarding house run by the infamous Joseph Kandelhofer. Two stories tall, with a bar, a wine room, a dining room, and bedrooms, Kandelhofer's establishment specialized in pretty young women—"good-lookers," they were called—who danced, played cards, and took men into the bedrooms, for a fee. They were on duty daily, 7:00 at night until 8:00 the next morning.

———————

DIAMONDVILLE CAME ON THE map in 1868, when a settler discovered black coal alongside the crystal waters of the Hams Fork River, where rainbow trout swam. It was superior grade. It resembled sparkling black diamonds, some who saw it said.

The Union Pacific and the Diamondville Coal & Coke Co., which had the financial backing of Anaconda, got busy. They lured men and their families from Almy, in southwest Wyoming, where the mines had finally closed after explosions in 1881, 1886, and 1896 that killed a total of 113, including at least two boys. The new miners of Diamondville were desperate for work—but they were beginning to listen to the United Mine Workers, which had gained strength in the East as it fought for fair wages and safe working conditions.

Like those in Hanna and Almy, Diamondville's unsafe mines were ripe for disaster. The first to occur was small, relatively speaking: two miners killed on February 12, 1899, inhaling "black damp," a mixture of lethal gases released by a fire. The dead were buried. The mining continued.

But now, Diamondville's miners were doing more than listening to the unionists. they were heeding the call of Mary Harris Jones—Mother Jones, the United Mine Workers of America organizer a US attorney dubbed "the most dangerous woman in America." In December 1899, six hundred miners struck Diamondville Coal & Coke Co. to demand higher wages and improved safety. The company hired scab workers to reopen the mine, and that was when the men and women of Diamondville showed their true colors.

"After a short shut-down," the *New York Times* reported on December 5, 1899, "operations were resumed with a small force of non-union men. Yesterday, a mob of 300 women and girls, armed with guns, knives, clubs and stones, marched on the mines and compelled the operators to leave. The miners at work were dragged and driven away. Several were injured by being struck with clubs and one man was shot at. The small group of deputies guarding the property of the company was powerless."

Diamondville was quiet in 1900. Then came February 25, 1901.

At the start of the night shift that day, a miner's lamp ignited a fire on Level 6 of Mine No. 1. The mine was sealed to extinguish the flames— while men and horses were still inside. Only one miner on the shift got out alive.

"Thirty-five miners perished, and their charred bodies are still in the mine," the Davenport, Iowa, *Daily Republican* reported on February 27. Wrote the *New York Times*: "It was just fourteen months ago today since a fire occurred in this same mine. It was desperately fought and overcome by brave men. . . . This one has cost a great many more lives. The scenes at the mouth of the mine during the night and today were heart-rending. Relatives and friends of the entombed miners rushed to the mine, frantically waving their hands and crying to the mine officials and miners to save their dear ones. Many of the women and children were slightly injured in the crowd and by falling over obstacles in the darkness."

Little wonder coal country seemed to drive some folk like Crazy John crazy.

Prominent Salt Lake City attorney Wiley L. Brown, who represented Diamondville miners during a 1898 strike and was charged with perjury in the resulting court cases, was another of them. Arrested in 1904 for strange behavior, including strolling around in public naked, Brown was brought before a judge and officially decreed insane, then released after he promised to behave. In 1905, he disappeared for good. Hunters found his body in the woods.

"For three years, Mr. Brown has been demented," reported the *Wyoming Press*. "Frequently he wandered about in the hills for days. The corpse was stripped, save for an undershirt, and lay not far from a trail leading over the ridge. The flesh was drawn and pinched, which made it evident that he had died from exposure."

Even the Daly Hotel seemed unable to escape the cloud that hung—at times, literally—over Wyoming coal towns. Completed in 1899, the hotel was bankrupt just three years later. "The hostelry and furniture was bought by the Diamond Coal & Coke Co. for $16,400," the *Wyoming Press* reported, "and Judge Holden purchased the piano."

Reopened under new ownership, the Daly soon witnessed more trouble. Four days before Christmas 1904, Harvey Rogers, engineer for the hotel's heating plant, nearly died attempting to control a buildup of hot water threatening to burst radiators.

"He turned his exhaust, so as to allow the hot water to escape, and after a reasonable time had elapsed, undertook to close the exhaust again," Cheyenne's *Wyoming Tribune* recounted. "About that time, the water getting low, an immense volume of hot steam was thrown out, knocking Mr. Rogers into the boiling water that had already run off. Mr. Rogers was unable to get out, and was found and removed from his precarious position. He was so seriously scalded and burned that he was removed to the Rock Springs hospital."

———

STANCHFIELD WAS STILL DEATHLY ill the morning of Sunday, June 11, when Megargel wanted to set off for Soda Springs, Idaho. But the mechanic could not endure another day in the blistering sun, draped over the trunk of Old Steady. Megargel telegraphed Smith with his plan: "Diamondville Wyo June 11th, 1905. Olds Motor Wks. Stanchfield has got Mountain Fever takes train for Lower Altitude don't tell his wife I am driving alone Percy F. Megargel."

The second location of the first J.C. Penney store, Kemmerer, WY.
DeGolyer Library, Southern Methodist University, JCPenney Collection.

Megargel brought his mechanic to the passenger station in adjacent Kemmerer, a town of about 1,000 where three years before, a young entrepreneur by the name of James Cash Penney had opened his first store, the Golden Rule, a dry goods store sandwiched between two saloons. Kemmerer, too, was cursed: on August 14, 1923, ninety-nine miners would die there in an explosion.

Megargel put his mechanic on a train bound for Soda Springs, one hundred miles away.

He prayed that when he reached the city—with luck by the next day—Stanchfield would be sufficiently recovered to be able to rejoin him.

# 9

## VICTORIES AND DEFEATS

### A LETTER FROM NEW YORK

Crossing Wyoming, Huss and Wigle had encountered many of the same difficulties as Megargel and Stanchfield: constant delays to clear sagebrush that became tangled in Old Scout's radiator and chain drive, often killing the motor; stops to cut ranchers' barbed wire so the car could get through; and other problems that added up to days that began before dawn but saw little progress by afternoon. Worst was the night when, traveling after dark, Huss crashed into a badger hole, destroying an axle. He plodded along on the twisted part, until, at midnight, they found a blacksmith shop. Huss and Wigle roused the owner from his sleep—but he said he could do nothing until morning. A $10 bill persuaded him to fire up his forge and help Huss and his mechanic repair the damage.

"These homemade repairs," Huss later recalled, "carried us through to Portland."

Despite the headaches, Huss, like Megargel, experienced moments of wonder. On one memorable occasion, cowboys rode out to greet him and Wigle, shooting their guns in the air in excitement and cheering them on with a wave of their hats and a shout of "Good luck, boys, give her hell!" Wild horses by the hundreds welcomed them, too: curious about Old

Scout, unlike some domesticated animals, they surrounded the car and galloped along with it, leading the way. "Often they ran until ready to drop from exhaustion," Huss wrote. "Then they would stagger to the side of the road and sway there as we went by."

But Idaho brought more mishap: a full day lost, in Boise, as Huss recovered from what apparently was pneumonia; bridges out and rivers to ford during heavy rain; a tumble down a twelve-foot embankment into a ditch; slow, narrow roads with "two ruts, perhaps gulleys would be a better word, cut by wagon wheels." Stuck at one point in sand, Huss paid Native Americans a few pennies to help Old Scout out. And then he replaced the car's regular tires with sand tires, made in Detroit of canvas, hair, board, straps, and buckles that gave a ten-inch tread, eight more than the ordinary tire. Huss marveled at their design and utility.

His car's engine also impressed him, for its performance despite the beating it took. He and Wigle deserved much of the credit, for their loving care. To save their motor when fording a stream, for example, they removed the car's batteries, shielding them from moisture; after they were across, they had to drain the motor of the dirty water that had seeped in by opening the petcock and cranking the engine.

"These became just ordinary things in our lives," Huss later wrote, "but they ate into our time, energy and patience."

Huss reached the small city of Ontario, Oregon—on the Snake River fifty-six miles west of Boise—on Thursday, June 15, five days ahead of Megargel and Stanchfield. Rare was the car in that city, and in all of Oregon: just nine hundred vehicles were registered in the state.

On Sunday afternoon, June 18, they passed through Prineville, where a reporter for the *Crook County Journal* described the car as "mud splattered, battered, worn, patched and wired together." Huss told the paper: "We've lost everything but the front wheels and our nerve," which was barely hyperbole. They lost money, too: the next day, at the hamlet of Sisters, they paid the highest price of the trip for gasoline: 90 cents a gallon, about $23 in 2014 dollars. The hamlet was unserved by railroad, and the fuel had to be brought in by stagecoach.

The next day's passage over the Cascades' Santiam Pass was especially harrowing. Built for horse-drawn vehicles, which themselves struggled mightily to get through, the trail was anathema to an auto, as Huss, who probably was the first to drive it, discovered.

"While stage coaches with large wheels could get through," Huss recalled, "we found it almost impossible." The men improvised for the ascent of Sevenmile Hill: Huss drove the car until the motor seemed about to die, then he stopped; Wigle, walking behind, placed his leather bag of heavy tools behind a rear wheel to brake Old Scout "for a breathing spell"; then they repeated the routine, again and again until they reached the summit.

The descent unnerved Huss and Wigle more than the climb.

"It was impossible to hold the car," Huss recalled. "All brakes were set, the rear wheels were sliding, and Wigle, who was holding to the rear, was dragged nearly seven miles. I held my breath as well as the steering lever, and expected every minute to be dashed down into the canyon several hundred feet below."

Huss and Wigle reached Salem, Oregon, after dark on Tuesday, June 20. The next morning, they set off on the last fifty miles of the race, reaching the outskirts of Portland at noon, on the forty-fifth day of the crossing. Abbott, Chapin, the Portland Oldsmobile dealer, and representatives of the *Evening Telegram* welcomed the men, and thousands of spectators cheered as they drove through the city to the grounds of the Lewis and Clark Centennial Exposition, with minutes to spare for the 1:00 p.m. start of the National Good Roads Association's 1905 convention. Huss delivered to the exposition president the letter he had carried from New York written by Melville E. Stone, founder of the *Chicago Daily News* and now general manager of the Associated Press.

"Dear Sir," Melville had written on May 5, three days before the racers left Manhattan, "I have a peculiar pleasure in complying with a request that I send you a greeting, to be conveyed by automobile across the continent. The century which has just passed was chiefly notable as the century which developed inter-communication. It was the century out of which came the ocean steamship, the railway, the telegraph, the cable, the telephone, wireless telegraphy, rotary and perfecting printing presses, news gathering associations and the newspapers.

"But nothing could better illustrate the progress of 100 years than a comparison of this new expedition by a twentieth-century motor car from the Atlantic seaboard to the land 'where rolls the Oregon,' with that other expedition of Lewis and Clark, which meant so much for our common country and the world's civilization."

Melville's wire service sent out an account of Huss's triumph to member papers.

"The race across the continent was a remarkable one," the AP wrote. "The machines and the drivers endured great hardships, meeting with accidents and obstacles without number. Roads constructed under the direction of engineers were skimmed over at a wonderful speed in some sections of the country, while in other sections it took entire days to go over a few miles of uncared for and poorly constructed highways. The delegates to the good roads convention believe that the race between 'Old Scout' and 'Old Steady' will have a great effect on the missionary work necessary to put the roads in all sections of the country in passable condition."

———————

MEGARGEL AND STANCHFIELD WERE in Vale, Oregon, just across the Idaho border, when they learned of Huss's decisive win. They were hardly surprised; they had been recalculating their sinking odds as they passed through towns where Old Scout had already been. By Boise, at the latest, they knew the race was over.

"Until the very last, they raced day and night with hope of catching the lead men," Portland's *Evening Telegram* reported, "but once the result reached them, they concluded to take some rest en route."

Megargel's final accounts for the *Automobile*, about the Idaho and Oregon legs, included descriptions of saloons and all-night card games at Boise; another bridge out; a ferry crossing conducted by a ferryman's wife; a night at a two-bed stage station; a flock of 3,000 sheep; and stories of cougars, bears, scorpions, elk, mule deer, wildcats, mountain lions, and more rattlesnakes. He chronicled an encounter with Paiute Native Americans.

"The Indians showed much surprise at our little car, the old one immediately concluding it was the work of the 'bad spirit,' and would have nothing to do with it," he wrote. "I tried to get a photograph of him sitting in the machine, but he would not have it, and covered his face with his hands when I attempted to take a snapshot of him."

Megargel and Stanchfield's journey through the Santiam Pass was much like Huss and Wigle's. To slow their descent of Sevenmile Hill, they cut a tree—with chisel and monkey wrench, for they had forgotten an ax—and chained it to the rear axle. With the tree providing drag, Old Steady's brakes forcefully applied, and repeated use of reverse gear, they proceeded downhill. Believing at one point that they finally were down, they cast the tree aside—only to come upon another steep slope. Skidding uncontrollably, the car hit a rock, throwing the men.

"The car, suspended by one rear wheel and the right step, which had caught in some bushes, hung over a 200-foot cliff," Megargel wrote, "and Stanchfield and myself, rubbing the mud out of our eyes, sat on the side of the road wondering why it did not go all the way over." With the help of a passing prairie schooner's crew, they rescued the car.

On the final miles into Salem, residents who had learned of Huss's victory and the impending arrival of Old Steady handed Megargel and Stanchfield bouquets of flowers. Like the winners, they received a rousing welcome when they reached Portland on Wednesday, June 28, one week after Huss and Wigle, and fifty-two days from Manhattan. Reporters estimated that Old Scout and Old Steady had logged as many as 4,000 miles on their trip.

"I am commencing to believe that possibly I do belong to the freak family," Megargel wrote, "a belief strengthened by the numerous mailing cards sent me, usually containing in bright letters of scarlet, 'It's great to be crazy and ride around in an automobile.'"

————

SMITH CAPITALIZED IMMEDIATELY ON Huss and Wigle's triumph. The day after their arrival in Portland, a full-page ad on the race was published detailing Huss's long journey "under the most trying weather and roads conditions," an accurate assessment, and quoting Huss, who gave no hint of the multitude of mechanical and other problems since leaving Manhattan.

"Our machine has made every mile of the distance without the aid of any power except its own engine and the strength of its drivers," Huss said. "We had to pull it out of the mud a few times. But for the bad roads in Illinois, Iowa, and Nebraska, we would have been here a week sooner and with the experience we have had, I believe we could make the trip in 30 days. . . . You would be astonished at what an automobile will stand and still be in working order."

Smith kept up the drumbeat with more ads into the summer, and publication, later in the year, of a forty-six-page booklet illustrated with dozens of photographs taken along the route. Abbott, Huss, and Megargel contributed commentary. The foreword declared the importance of the race to the Good Roads movement and said it had "made Huss and Wigle not only the heroes of the Good Roads Convention, but of Portland and her visiting thousands."

## AUGUST WRECKS

Megargel and Huss had kept a turtle's pace, their adventures, not their speed, drawing the public in. But many Americans did want to move fast.

"King Speed is up and running these days," *Motor Age* declared in its issue of June 15, 1905. "He is making Father Time look like a plugged nickel."

The magazine seemed overjoyed that people now could move at the most extreme speed—not in a car, but on the passenger train that was claimed to have reached 129 miles an hour recently on a line between New York and Chicago. You did not need to own a 120-horsepower Mercedes, like the one that had reached 110 miles per hour earlier that year at Daytona, to personally experience the sensation. All you needed was a train ticket.

"Those who cannot afford to own 120-horsepower automobiles that can travel at 110 miles an hour can step on a train and have a taste of fast going with all the comforts of home thrown in," the magazine said. "There may not be so much excitement in this as there would be in an automobile going at the same speed, but some people would rather have the comfort than the excitement."

Many, of course, did want the excitement—and they could have it in a fast car of their own, or vicariously by watching any of the continued proliferation of contests that manufacturers endorsed or entered. Smith with his Oldsmobiles, Durant with his Buicks, Ford with his cars, and Ransom Olds with his Reos were among the many manufacturers competing in the spring of 1905.

During one meet of a well-publicized hill race in Cincinnati on May 17, a Reo stock car took first place and a Ford took third. A week later, a distinguished crowd turned out for the hill climbs at Worcester, Massachusetts. "The road was lined with people and machines, Bostonians of course predominating, though all of New England was liberally represented," wrote *Automobile Review*. Ford cars took first and second, beating an Oldsmobile, in the competition among gasoline-powered cars selling for less than $850. In the meet for gas-powered cars costing less than $1,250, a Buick took second, a Reo fourth, and two Fords, fifth and sixth.

On June 10, Ransom Olds brought his 32-horsepower Reo Bird race car—"a new hummer," *Automobile Review* hailed it—to the Bronx's Morris Park Racecourse, home of the Belmont Stakes thoroughbred races for many years and now another temple of the new speed. The main race of the day was the opening round in the AAA-sanctioned National Motor Car Championship of America, the first US league established to select a national champion. Reo Bird finished second, behind a Fiat driven by Louis Chevrolet, a Swiss-born former bicycle racer, now a race-car driver living in New York.

"Chevrolet was clad in a long white duster and made a pretty picture," while the engine of his car, slowing for turns, sounded like the big guns on Admiral Tgō Heihachirō's battleship during Japan's defeat of the Russian fleet in the Battle of Tsushima the month before, *Automobile Review* wrote. The Morris Park spectators adored the Swiss racer. "When Chevrolet ran up to the stand, there was a rush for the rail to get a closer view at the speed wizard and the police had to force the crowd back."

Manufacturers kept on as the hot weather set in, entering stock cars in hill climbs and other events, and race cars in professional contests. The premiere series of the year, the AAA's national championship schedule, brought races to West Hartford, Yonkers, Pittsburgh, back to Morris Park, Detroit, Cleveland, Buffalo, Rhode Island, Massachusetts, and Poughkeep-sie for the series finale, on September 29. Based on accumulated points—first use of a system that would become widespread—the inaugural champion would be crowned there.

Grosse Pointe was a midsummer stop. Oldfield—who had ridiculously vowed never to race again after the 1904 tragedy in St. Louis—was com-peting on August 9 when a racer from Lansing hit his car, sending it into the infield in a cloud of dust. Thrown from his car, Oldfield was uncon-scious on the ground "when a dozen horrified spectators reached his side," the *New York Times* reported in a story headlined: "Oldfield Faces Death Again in Auto Race." Oldfield suffered a broken shoulder and a head injury.

The championship chase moved on to Cleveland, where popular racer Earl Kiser, driving a Winton named Bullet, lost control on a practice run on August 12. A record gathering watched as his car crashed through nearly a hundred feet of fence and exploded.

"Hundreds of persons hurried to his rescue," the *Automobile* wrote, "while others turned their efforts to extinguishing the flames in the burn-ing car. A runabout brought two physicians to the scene and ambulances were called. Earl's left leg was found to be crushed to a pulp and he was bleeding from a score of other injuries."

As he waited for the ambulances, Kiser kept trying to sit up. He wanted to see his leg.

A friend restrained him.

"It's all right, Earl," the friend said, "you have been hurt worse than this a number of times in the bicycle days."

But Kiser hadn't: doctors were forced to amputate his leg above the knee.

Still recovering from his own injuries, Oldfield was unable to compete in the main event on August 14, but during an exhibition run, he circled the track in his Green Dragon car—his head bandaged, his broken shoul-der still waiting to be set—in honor of Kiser.

Just four days later, another accident rocked the national champion-ship circuit.

The drivers were in Buffalo on August 18 when Webb Jay, whose popularity rivaled Oldfield's, disappeared in a cloud of dust on a backstretch turn. Spectators heard the distinctive sound of Whistling Billy, his steam-powered White Sewing Machine Company car—and then, the sound of a crash. Whistling Billy had hurtled through the air and come to rest in a pond at the bottom of an embankment. Jay was thrown into the water. The first people to reach him—a group of boys—saw only his coat and one arm on the surface. The rest of him was submerged.

The boys pulled Jay's bleeding body from the pond and an ambulance brought him to the hospital, where doctors treated him for a broken arm, broken leg, nine broken ribs, and a punctured lung. His career was over—but his machine emerged in better shape. Except for a bent brace and a crumpled hood, Whistling Billy had not sustained damage.

"Although Jay and I are rivals on the track," said Oldfield, "I admire him as a thorough gentleman and I cannot tell you how much I regret this accident. I shall try to find some way to be of assistance to him."

———————

THE THREE ACCIDENTS IN nine days jolted the automobile world. These were not local motorists making local headlines for accidents, but national celebrities in a sport that was challenging baseball, college football, and horse and bicycle racing for prominence.

Condemnation came swiftly.

On the day that Jay wrecked, William H. Hotchkiss, Buffalo lawyer and president of the influential New York State Automobile Association, said he would seek a state supreme court injunction against track racing in the state. He was concerned for race-car drivers' safety—and the impact track accidents might have on motoring in general.

"It is a little short of suicide for men to drive fast cars on circular tracks in clouds of dust and it is wrong to send men into such contests," Hotchkiss said. "The events of the last two or three weeks have convinced me that the game must be stopped, partly because the more accidents there are, the more prejudice will be aroused in the public mind against automobiles and the more restrictive legislation we shall encounter."

The *New York Times* predicted the end was near.

"Track racing is dying out," the paper wrote. "Manufacturers are realizing the fact that their benefits are not commensurate with the expense, while drivers of fast cars are looking to their own personal safety more than they did before accidents became so frequent."

Nevertheless, the National Championships went on, and Oldfield soon competed again. At Poughkeepsie on September 29, he won before a crowd of 20,000 and was crowned national champion. Before the race, Oldfield thumbed his nose at the critics: after a warm-up run, the *Times* reported, "He then diverted the crowd massed in the grandstand and field with a fence-breaking exhibition at high speed which was featured as a representation of the accidental episode in which he figured at Detroit."

Still, the outcry following August's crashes prompted mea culpas and vows of change from many motoring organizations.

In a filing from Manhattan, *Motor Age* in its August 24 issue said: "The sentiment of the press, trade and automobiledom in this city is practically unanimous that the track racing game is not worth the sacrifice of life and limb its promotion during the past two years has occasioned." A filing from Cleveland asserted: "If the daily newspapers are mirrors of public opinion, then truly the Cleveland public has had enough, for the editorials and still more telling cartoons of the past few days tell a story of disgust. . . . "

Under the headline, "Track Racing Condemned to Die: Prominent Motorists from all Parts of the Country Pass Sentence on a Man-killing Pastime," *Motor Age* devoted three pages to the single topic. Saying "the game is not worth the candle," the general secretary of the AAA threatened to stop sanctioning track races. The Morris Park Motor Club secretary proposed that the fastest cars be allowed to race only on straight roads and beaches. State legislators in several states talked of bills to ban or limit track racing. A Pittsburgh man who officiated at races in the city quit his post, citing the danger not just to drivers but also to spectators. The Chicago Automobile Club canceled a fall race, substituting a picnic and dance in its place.

And Windsor T. White, head of White Sewing Machine Company, expressed sympathy for Jay and his wife, and declared the company was done with track racing. Jay's machine might compete in road races, White said, but that was it: "The Whistler was not injured in the least, but it will never again be entered in a track event."

Winton announced it had no plans to repair Kiser's Bullet—and Kiser himself joined the ranks of those swearing off track competition.

"I have promised my mother that I will never race again, although I had planned at first to be the only one-legged driver in the business," he said. "I am out of it for good, and I shall keep that vow. There is nothing in the game for drivers—not a thing. It's a little advertising for that car that some foolhardy fellow drives. If a man reels off a mile in less than a minute, he is praised from coast to coast, but that is all it amounts to."

Smith did not add his voice to the public protest. Oldsmobile was not as deeply committed to track racing as some other carmakers, favoring instead hill climbs, reliability runs, endurance contests, and stunts, such as the 1,000-ruble bet it won when a Curved Dash climbed 193 steps in Odessa, Russia, that September. Huss was at the wheel.

But ALAM president Charles Clifton professed outrage. "I do not believe there is enough interest in the game to make it a lasting sport," he said. "This seems to me the logical time to quit it. Why not stop it before it dies."

And Henry Ford weighed in, though with his own racing background, so instrumental in building his brand, he did not join the call for banning track racing. "I am of the opinion that if the inside fences were removed and lighter cars used," Ford said, "racing on circular tracks would be reasonably safe."

Whatever the outcome, *Motor Age* wrote, it was wrong to blame the machine—on a street or on a racetrack—for the actions of its driver.

"The automobile is somewhat akin to a wife," the magazine wrote. "When a husband can find nobody else to blame for anything, he blames his wife; when an accident cannot be attributed to anything else, it is laid to the automobile. It is the automobile, seldom the operator."

In the long term, of course, manufacturers would not abandon racing, with its proven marketing value; nor would danger discourage drivers, who craved speed.

———

Joyously toying with death.

From *Motor Age.*

THE AUGUST WRECKS RAISED the temperature further on the already heated conflict in newspapers and trade journals between motorists and those less enthusiastic about motoring. For years now, the sides had battled in stories, editorials, opinion pieces, cartoons, and letters to the editor.

In a November 9, 1905, story, the *Automobile* estimated that fully one-third of the space devoted to cars in the weekly and daily general-circulation papers in 1905 involved accidents, arrests, suits, trials, and criminal prosecutions of motorists, the downside of the revolution that was transforming America.

Motorists were losing the press wars, the journal declared.

"Almost anyone keenly interested in automobiling would be staggered if he could have the opportunity to examine one week's accumulation of press comment on the subject and note the nature of the thousands of items published and the state of the public feeling they reveal," the magazine wrote. "The matter is a serious one, for the newspapers mold popular opinion, and also reflect it, and a continuance of such a state is almost certain to result in a crystallization of unfavorable sentiment that will bring about drastic action."

From their offices in Manhattan's Flatiron Building, the *Automobile* 's journalists considered the editorialists at the *New York Times*, now working from their new building in the square renamed for Adolph Ochs's paper, enemy number one.

These were the editorialists who had called Ford "a young speed maniac" after his Lake St. Clair record run and fretted that other "idiots" would "try similar exploits on public roads, in which case the least to be regretted of the resulting casualties will be the breaking of the chauffeur's neck." Their antagonism could be traced to at least early 1902, when they took issue with the Cocks speeding bill, calling its fines "wholly inadequate" and declaring that "owners of motor vehicle do not need the lesson of experience to teach them that they should not convert public highways into private speedways."

But in a June 14, 1905, editorial, the *Times* seemed to suggest a shift in policy. Writing about a case where a magistrate had released a doctor arrested for speeding as he responded to an emergency, the paper urged discretion in administering the law. And it went a step further, stating that "except in much-traveled city and village streets, there is or ought to be no real need for making an iron rule as to maximum speed."

A few days later, the *Automobile* pounced. Expressing surprise at what it called the *Times*'s "plea for the injection of a little common sense into the administration of the automobile speed laws of New York," the magazine taunted the occupants of the new building at Times Square. "Hitherto," it wrote, "the *Times* has been famous for its fanatical—it would be unfair to write 'ignorant' about that thirty-story temple of learning— opposition to anything and everything pertaining to automobiles."

What had changed policy, the *Automobile* claimed, was publisher Adolph Ochs's recent purchase of an automobile—"one of those smelly devils," the magazine wrote, with undisguised sarcasm. And what had happened next? With Ochs as passenger, his chauffeur had been arrested for speeding in Yonkers, the magazine claimed.

Not that the paper had written about *that*.

"Now, had it been any ordinary lawbreaker who had been arrested," the *Automobile* wrote, "no doubt it would have made a good local story to go with 'all the other news that's fit to print' in the next morning's issue and one of those thought molders in the *Times* editorial foundry would have cast a great big knocker for the editorial page to help make a noise. . . . As for newspaper publicity, [Ochs] can truthfully say, 'Never touched me!'"

On June 26, the *Times* responded. Chiding the *Automobile* for using the word "famous" and not "infamous"—a snippy bit of grammatical finger-wagging at the supposedly ill-schooled journalists in the Flatiron Building—an editorial excoriated what it described as the "not too important little paper published in this city" by a staff that was, to be blunt, stupid.

"*The Automobile* would have been much better employed in performing the not difficult task of learning what our policy is and has been—and in adopting that policy as its own," the editorialist wrote. Ouch.

A week later, the *Automobile* fired back, accusing its antagonist of betraying its own lofty principles for the sake of money.

"Not that it matters much to the well-informed what the *Times* thinks or says about automobiles, their construction, or use," it wrote, with pointed sarcasm, "but there are doubtless many persons who read the *Times* who know little or nothing practically about automobiling and who, reposing confidence in the information and fairness of that paper, are sure to be misled by its editorial utterances on the subject." And where was lofty principle, the *Automobile* wrote, with the *Times* apparently having softened its hostility now that carmakers were buying advertisements in its pages, providing revenue that helped pay editorialists' salaries and further enrich Adolph Ochs?

The *Automobile*'s two-part "Unfavorable Newspaper Influence and How to Counteract It," published in November, offered tips to motorists in the campaign against the naysayers.

Enthusiasts should remember "that newspapers are edited by human beings," and so the first step was to personally—and politely—help educate these human reporters and editors. The best means to that end was to invite a journalist on a ride—provided the driver was not trying to be Barney Oldfield but a reasonable man who "had the general good of automobiling at heart." The magazine urged understanding of the anxiety a man taking his first ride likely would experience, especially in traffic or near pedestrians, whose tragic tangles with cars the dailies played on the front page. The *Automobile* predicted that the first-time passenger would be amazed at the belligerence of horse-drawn vehicle drivers—and pleasantly surprised at how quickly an automobile could stop compared to an animal-powered wagon. With patience, the war could be won.

"Every successive ride will do more to convince him that a great deal of the adverse criticism arises from ignorance on the subject and unwarranted prejudice on the part of persons who have but one point of view—that of the pedestrian or the driver of horses," the magazine wrote. As evidence, the series included an excerpt of an editorial written by an editor at the Woodstock, Illinois, *Sentinel,* after a ride in a car through the countryside. Besides being pleasant, the trip apparently convinced the journalist that farmers were misguided in their automobile antipathy. "It would be well to cultivate a better feeling," the editor wrote. "Obey the law and by careful treatment, teach horses to become acquainted with the competition." And pay attention to what the machine seemed poised to bring: better roads, from which a farmer, too, would benefit.

PERIODICALLY, EACH SIDE TURNED to the medical profession to buttress their respective points of view.

Car critics found support in a *Pacific Medical Journal* editorial that claimed to have documented a multitude of disorders caused by the motor vehicle in San Francisco, where the journal was published. Among those listed were inflammations of the nose, throat, outer and middle ear, eye, larynx, pharynx, and bronchial passages. Automobiles caused burning pain in the face and elsewhere, the journal asserted. But the worst disorders, according to the editorial, were the "nerve tension" and "nerve waste"—anxiety, irritability, and fatigue, in other words—that resulted from the "mental intoxication" produced by fast driving.

The *Pacific Medical Journal* told the story of a prominent Bay area doctor who loved his auto-wagon but had to stop driving it when the nervous energy he had to devote behind the wheel began to interfere with the care he gave his patients: thoughts of his car kept him awake at night, the journal said, and the desire to drive faster than others consumed his attention during the day. One look at the doctor, like others obsessed with their machines, told the tale, the journal declared:

"The auto 'face' as we see it is a composite of anxiety showing mental strain, determination at the cost of much will power, and fear. . . . The auto 'face' is not a happy, healthy, contented face. There is too much of the acrobat's uncertainty mixed with fear about it to make it enjoyable to look at or pleasurable to feel."

Enthusiasts countered with testament from other purported medical experts.

The *Horseless Age* offered the testimony of a doctor from Lyons, France, who had been stricken by influenza, pleurisy, and finally tuberculosis, which cost him his livelihood for six months, during which he took open-air treatment, commonly prescribed as a treatment for the deadly disease before antibiotics. "When he took up his practice again," the weekly magazine reported, "he bought an automobile and made two trips of about 50 miles each day. Since then, the cough has ceased, he recovered his appetite and gained about ten pounds in weight."

Another of automobiling's "curative" effects on consumptives was a boost in lung power that speed induced, the magazine claimed. "Dr. Blanchet, for instance, reports that his chest capacity was greatly increased by his automobile rides. Other physicians are said to have had the same experience."

And then there was the oft-quoted Hugh Galt, professor of medicine at the University of Glasgow, whose ludicrous pronouncements—accepted by some as truth—were first published in the March 21, 1904, issue of the *Automotor Journal: A Record and Review of Applied Automatic Locomotion*, published weekly in London. The Scottish professor claimed that the changing temperatures experienced by a motorist imparted immunity to colds and chills, and that motoring soothed the nerves by a process involving an elevated heart rate, increased breathing, and more oxygen in the blood. But the greatest benefit of motoring, Professor Galt asserted, was its miraculous ability to purify the body and strengthen the mind.

"It is a recognised fact that long residence in the vitiated air of a city introduced poisonous secretions into the system which reacted upon the nerves in producing malaise, headaches, biliousness, a 'run down' condition and such like," Galt said. "A motor car run had the effect of stimulating the kidneys, liver, and to a less extent, the bowels, by which the poisons referred to were released and carried away. This not only affected the physical health, but invigorated the mind also."

The press battles did not lack a dose of humor. As early as 1899, the *Chicago Tribune* noted the arrival of a new ailment, which would variously be known as motor fever, chauffeur mania, and automobiliousness. The *Tribune* joked:

A Coming Disease.

DR. SQUILLS: "What was the matter with that cab driver you were called to see last night?"

DR. KALLOMELL: "As nearly as I can describe what ails him it is automobiliousness."—*Chicago Tribune*

A funnier article appeared in the February 1905 issue of the *Doctor's Factotum: A Periodical Presentation of Matters of Interest to the Physician, Both Scientific and Humorous*, a journal with offices in Yonkers. Originally published in *Medical Visitor*, the piece lampooned the vehicle that so many doctors had purchased for themselves.

"Authorities disagree as to the etiology of motor fever, but the exciting cause is generally believed to be the diplococcus financii, although some observers insist that the bacillus getthereus is the chief causative factor," the piece read. "Of the pathology of this disease, we also know little, but it is believed that there is a rapid hypertrophy of certain brain cells producing enlargement of the cranium, moral anaesthesia, and hypercussedness of the whole nervous mechanism. Gobbs reports one patient killed by an irate farmer whose brain exhibited extensive ecchymosis, but it is uncertain whether this was attributable to the disease or to the farmer's club."

It was, however, easy to spot a case, the magazine asserted.

"The symptoms are mainly those of intense mental excitement. The patient exhibits a morbid desire to annihilate time and space regardless of the consequences. . . . He becomes impatient, autocratic and unreasonable, and acquires a strong aversion to officers of the law. Anorexia and insomnia sometimes develop in the later stages of the malady, hallucinations supervene, and the patient exhibits strange tastes such, for example, as preferring the odor of gasoline. . . . The disease is slowly progressive and in time, the patient becomes a pitiable nervous wreck."

The *New York Times* published a shorter version of the spoof, and even the prestigious *Journal of the American Medical Association* got into the act, with a facetious letter to the editor from a reader in Columbus, Ohio.

"In the etiology of chauffeur mania," the reader wrote, "the automobile is the direct cause, and the sporty disposition, plus a large bank account, constitute the predisposing causes. The disease affects a large class of people. It is, indeed, pandemic."

## BACK ON THE STAND

In October 1905, the operators of the Gundlach-Manhattan Optical Company, a manufacturer of cameras, binoculars, and microscopes, closed off a section of their factory in Rochester, New York. Only a small number of mechanics and others with the need to know were allowed in. ALAM was beginning construction of Exhibit 89, the so-called 1877 gas buggy, an automobile—of a sort—based on George Selden's patent. The buggy, which required three months to complete, would use the motor Selden had stored at his house for decades. Its construction was intended to bolster the case against Ford and others.

But Ford knew nothing of this when, on the Wednesday before Thanksgiving, he was called back to the stand to testify in ALAM's suit against French manufacturer Panhard—a co-defendant in the Selden patent case. Attorney John P. Murray, of New York's Coudert Brothers law firm, which worked closely with Ralzemond Parker, represented Ford in his appearance in Detroit.

Ford's testimony was reminiscent of his first time on the stand, in July 1904. He spoke of technology: water jackets, mixing valves, the capacity of gas tanks, the size and composition of wheels, many of the other parts of a motor vehicle. He listed the trade publications that he read: *Horseless Age* and *American Machinist*. He described the Benz automobile he had seen at R. H. Macy & Co. in New York in 1895, the first cars that he built, his childhood interest in steam and gasoline machines.

"My people tell me I was trying to build an automobile when I was ten years old," he said, with some slight exaggeration.

During cross-examination, attorney Edward W. Vaill Jr., of ALAM's Betts, Betts, Sheffield & Betts firm, tried to rattle Ford—but Ford could not be rattled.

"If the Selden patent in suit is sustained as valid," Vaill asked, "either in the present suit or that against Ford Motor Company and injunction should issue against the Ford Motor Company, do you consider that it would be detrimental to your business?"

Murray objected, but Ford answered nonetheless.

"No," he said.

"You would rather see the Selden patent declared invalid than sustained, would you not?" Vaill continued.

"It would not affect me, as we do not infringe the Selden patent, in my mind," Ford said.

Again, Murray objected.

Vaill pressed on.

"Aside from your opinion of the question of infringement you had rather see the patent in suit invalidated than sustained, would you not?"

"I don't think it makes any difference to me," Ford responded. "In fact, I would rather see it sustained."

"Then you consider the Selden patent a benefit to your business, do you not?"

"It does not make any difference," Ford said.

On the Monday after Thanksgiving, Ransom Olds testified for the first time, in a deposition given in Lansing. Like Ford—though with greater flourish—he began by recounting his own experiences in making automobiles.

I commenced experimenting in automobiles in 1887, which was steam. . . . I commenced the experiments of my first combustion engines for automobiles in 1894; this vehicle was not completed until 1895. I have had the experience of acting as general manager for the Olds Company for 23 years; part of this time was devoted to the manufacture of steam engines.

I invented the Oldsmobile and took out a large number of patents, as well as the Olds gas engine; these two makes are very extensively used throughout the world. I was general manager of these companies up to January, 1904. In August 1904 the Reo Motor Car Company was organized. The people organizing the company made me a present of controlling interest in the company for my past experience as manufacturer of gas engines and automobiles. Since that date, the company has been doing a very satisfactory business.

Only a minute or two into his testimony, and it was clear that Olds was a formidable witness. And he was just warming up. His remaining testimony was a brutal refutation of Selden's claim to have invented anything, let alone a car. And as he took aim at Selden, Olds likely had Smith in his sights as well. Self-interest motivated Olds—his first priority was building his new company—but it certainly would be sweet revenge to vanquish the man who had ousted him from the firm he had founded and built to greatness.

Murray showed Olds two pages of drawings that Selden had submitted in applying for US Patent No. 549,160. Almost childlike in their lack of detail, they depicted a contraption that somewhat resembled an automobile—but lacked certain parts that an actual manufacturer of cars knew were essential. They looked exactly like what they were: an idea that almost certainly never could become a reality, let alone be called the invention of the automobile.

"Will you please look at the figures one and two of the Letters Patent and state whether you ever saw a self-propelled vehicle similar to or resembling the one illustrated here?" Murray said.

Vaill objected, on the grounds that Olds had not been qualified as an expert.

But Olds answered: "No, sir, I never have."

"Will you please state whether or not you ever saw a motor of the kind there illustrated used or tried on a self-propelled vehicle?"

Vaill objected.

"No, sir, I have not," Olds said.

"Will you please examine that figure and also the letters patent and state whether or not the same contains any suggestion or instruction as to how to start the motor?"

"No, sir, I see no starting device."

Vaill kept objecting, but Murray and Olds kept going, deeper and deeper into critical technical details.

"Could a motor of that type and of such weight be mounted on a reservoir as indicated in figures 1 and 2?" Murray asked.

"Not very well," Olds answered.

"What can you say as to whether or not an operative structure would result from an attempt to do so?"

"It would not."

"Do you know of any make of automobile now in use or ever in use into the cylinder of which liquid fuel was pumped?"

"No, I do not."

"Will you please look at figures 1, 2 and 3 and state whether or not you can see any way of placing a balance wheel on the structure described and illustrated?"

"No, sir, there is no way."

"Did you ever hear of a self-propelled vehicle known as the Selden vehicle?"

"No, sir, until the matter of this patent came up."

"What I refer to in my preceding question was a vehicle existing otherwise than on paper?" Murray said.

Vaill objected strenuously, calling the question "grossly leading and incompetent, irrelevant and immaterial."

In truth, it was the central question. The scramble to build Exhibit 89, the 1877 gas buggy, behind the closed doors of a factory in Rochester, New York—apparently unknown to Olds, as well as Ford and their attorneys—was only a scam, an impossible attempt to rewrite history.

"No, sir," Olds answered, "I never heard of the Selden vehicle."

Murray asked Olds to read the second paragraph of the four-page text that Selden submitted with his drawings. It stated: "The object of my invention is the production of a safe, simple, and cheap road-locomotive light in weight, easy to control, and possessed of sufficient power to overcome any ordinary inclination." It could climb hills, in other words.

Murray asked Olds if a machine built to Selden's specifications would actually be able to perform like that.

"No, sir, it would not," Olds said.

"Will you briefly give the reasons for your last answer?"

"There are many reasons why this plan would not work," Olds said. "I would hardly know where to begin to explain."

Had the case been decided on Olds's testimony alone, it almost certainly would have ended unfavorably for ALAM on that December 4, 1905. But more than two years into the legal proceedings, nothing could yet persuade ALAM to stop.

———

AFTER THE RACE TO PORTLAND, Huss went back to work showcasing Oldsmobiles.

Smith sent him overseas again, to Russia, where he won the stair-climbing event, and then France, where he drove the approximately 160 miles from Boulogne-sur-Mer to Paris in a fast seven hours, a run that Smith trumpeted in ads. Huss was the American star of the Paris auto show at the Grand Palais des Champs-Élysées, where Olds exhibited the Curved Dash of cross-continental fame along with other vehicles and nearly two dozen trophies that Olds drivers had won. "Mr. Huss, who was instrumental in securing much of this silverware, is, if not exactly on exhibition, at least on hand for the numerous visitors who gather around the Oldsmobile exhibit," wrote the *Automobile*.

Percy Megargel returned to New York. He had little interest in domestic life: He wanted more adventure, not more time with his wife and their toddler daughter.

He found what he wanted in a plan to complete history's first so-called double continental crossing: a drive from New York to the West Coast and back, a voyage that might total nearly 10,000 miles, the longest motorized journey ever conducted on the American continent. Smith was not interested in sponsoring Megargel—but Ransom Olds was. A small story tucked into *Motor Age*'s August 24 special "Track Racing Condemned to Die" report stated that Megargel, accompanied by Reo mechanic David F. Fassett, left Manhattan in a Reo car on August 19 and had reached Buffalo by press time. The hope was to be back in New York in January for the two 1906 auto shows, ALAM's and Ford's.

Like the Curved Dash, the $1,250, 16-horsepower, four-seat stock Touring Car—"Mountaineer," as Reo named the trip vehicle—had no roof, sides, or windshield. But it could serve as a bed. "By a very clever arrangement," *Cycle and Automobile Trade Journal* reported, "Mr. R.E. Olds, the designer of the Reo car, has arranged the tonneau so it can be changed into sleeping quarters when desired." Megargel also had secured backing from the Diamond Rubber company, an Ohio manufacturer of tires, and the Weed Chain Tire Grip Company, which would challenge magician Harry Houdini to escape padlocked Weed chains (in April 1908, Houdini accepted the challenge on a Broadway stage).

Making arrangements to chronicle this journey for the *Automobile* as well as for *Motor Way,* Megargel would broaden his audience. Other trade publications and general newspapers would follow his progress. The trip promised great risk along with the rewards: unless Megargel and Fassett

Megargel, left, with Fassett on their 1905–1906 trip.
Library of Congress, LC-DIG-det-4a21366.

had the most extraordinary luck, some of their return trip would occur during winter, along some roads that were barely passable in the best weather.

Megargel and Fassett did not have that kind of luck. They required almost two months to reach Idaho, a trip that had taken Megargel just thirty-six days the previous spring—and winter already was calling when the writer filed for the *Automobile* on October 19 from the small community of Hailey, Idaho. "It has snowed nearly every day for the past week, and the mountain trails are now covered to a depth of several inches, making the going very difficult," Megargel wrote. "We have been breaking through the ice every morning in order to secure water with which to wash and fill our radiator."

Writing for *Motor Way* from Portland, Oregon, on November 10, Megargel proclaimed himself, Fassett, and Mountaineer "weather-beaten but in good physical trim, and ready to start southward along the [Pacific] coast on our circuitous way to New York again, and home." But another omen of the difficulties ahead could be found in Megargel's account—comical on the surface—of a night on the road to Portland that they spent on a hill, sleeping in a haystack owned by an elderly Native American, who charged them a dollar. The temperature dropped to 18° F, and Megargel and Fassett had only a blanket apiece to warm them.

"To make matters worse," Megargel wrote, "the hay stack was shared by an animal announced by a rustling of the straw and then by a peculiar odor which told us where and what it was." Apparently, a skunk had crawled in with them. "For 36 hours in this vicinity we lived on coffee, crackers and canned salmon, from our grub box."

From Portland, Megargel drove south to California. He had company: California in 1905 had 8,020 registered motor vehicles, trailing only New York and Pennsylvania.

In Palo Alto, the men stopped at Stanford University, where they listened to a pipe organ in a chapel and saw some 230 automobiles "filled with pretty girls and college enthusiasts," Megargel wrote, parked for the Stanford–University of California game, which Stanford won, 12 to 5. They drove on to San Francisco, departing on November 21. On the road back to Palo Alto, Megargel's suitcase fell off the car, but he did not immediately discover it missing.

"No amount of telephoning has succeeded in locating it," he wrote. "Besides all my clean clothing and business suit, it contained a lot of papers, notes, maps, and my barometer, compass, film for the camera, revolver, and other necessities. So I feel much like the fellow that went in swimming and had his clothes stolen."

Heading south through California, Megargel drove on well-maintained roads with gentle climbs and descents through the mountains. He was pleased with what he had seen in the state so far.

"California has not harsh laws regarding the running of automobiles," he wrote, "and the surrounding country is not flooded with the glory-seeking town marshal, ever ready to assert his tin-badge authority. The roads admit of fast speeding, the farmer's horse is accustomed to it, and the farmer himself in many cases is the owner of a fast machine."

Megargel arrived in Los Angeles, which had a thriving motoring scene, on Tuesday, November 28, the day before Ford testified in Detroit. He spent Thanksgiving there, then headed east, reaching San Bernardino on December 6. Battling sandstorms, he and Fassett became the first drivers to cross the Mojave Desert—to the amazement of residents of the small oasis communities through which they passed.

"One man said he was proud to doff his hat to an automobile that could travel through the sand, as he never believed it possible," Megargel wrote on December 11 from Needles, on the Colorado River. "Everywhere we were asked our names, the name and power of our car, and requested to give our cards, as they wanted to always remember the first automobile to cross the desert."

When they left Williams, Arizona, at 9:00 p.m. on Saturday, December 16, Megargel and Fassett expected to reach Flagstaff, just thirty-four miles east, the next morning. Megargel wired ahead to the Commercial Hotel to alert the proprietor of their imminent arrival. But a blinding snowstorm trapped them, and days passed without word from the men.

A search party was organized. The newspapers and magazine waited to see if this chapter of the double crossing would end the story.

———

Buick production totaled 725 vehicles in 1905, an impressive number for any manufacturer—but a phenomenal number for Durant's company, considering that in 1904, it had made just thirty-seven cars.

Ford Motor Company business also continued to improve, with sales of 1,745 cars during the fiscal year that ended on September 30, 1905. Dollar sales totaled $1.9 million, an increase of nearly $1 million in a year, and net income was $289,232, up almost 20 percent. The company employed about three hundred workers and paid $200,000 in dividends during the year. Just two years old, Ford's third firm was clearly a success.

Smith must have envied it, given that Oldsmobile's numbers kept trending downward as 1905 drew to a close. The company would sell only about 2,500 vehicles during the year—ahead of Ford, but a decline from the 3,400 it sold in 1904 and more than one-third fewer than the record year of 1903.

The car Smith had bet heavily on, the $1,400 Heavy Touring, had been a catastrophic failure, with only about one hundred of the vehicles sold. The year would end with a loss of $340,000, first in the company's history. The cross-continent race had failed to deliver what Smith wanted.

Still, Smith maintained what apparently was the largest workforce in the industry, 612 workers, on his hope that the 1906 models would reverse his fortunes. The lineup would officially debut in January in New York, but Smith gave a preview in mid-November to approximately one hundred domestic and foreign dealers whom he invited to Lansing on a two-day junket. The Curved Dash would be offered again in 1906, still at the affordable price of $650. But the exciting news, in Smith's view, was the production of two new larger and more expensive vehicles: the $1,250 Model L "double action Oldsmobile" and the Model S, sold in two versions, the Gentleman's Roadster and the Palace Touring Vehicle. At $2,250, the Model S was far and away the most expensive car Oldsmobile had ever produced.

The dealers beheld the new cars during a dinner held on Friday, November 17, in one of Lansing's factory buildings. Chapin, secretly convinced now that he would leave Oldsmobile, joined Fred Smith in delivering a speech. The dealers were entertained by a vaudeville show that likely included a rendition of Gus Edward's "In My Merry Oldsmobile." The tune, sung by Billy Murray, had debuted at the top of the charts in October and would be the third-biggest hit of the year (behind "The Preacher and the Bear" and "Yankee Doodle Boy").

The next day, the dealers traveled to Ann Arbor, where Smith treated them to a football game at his alma mater. Michigan was playing Wisconsin. Since the hiring of head coach Fielding H. Yost for the 1901 season, Michigan had won four national championships; defeated Stanford to win the first Rose Bowl, in 1902; compiled a 55–0 record going into the November 18 game; and so astoundingly outscored opponents during Yost's tenure, 2,734 to 40 points, that the team had earned a new nickname, the "point-a-minute" Wolverines.

Nearly 18,000 spectators were on hand at Ann Arbor to watch the Michigan–Wisconsin contest that November 18. Perhaps Smith regaled the dealers with tales of his own college days—his wrestling championship, his quarterbacking the Wolverines during the 1888 season, which had ended in a loss, but which nonetheless was part of a glorious tradition. Perhaps he hoped the thrill of watching such a storied team would crown his sales pitch and the orders would begin flowing.

Michigan was on its way to defeating Wisconsin, 12 to 0, in a game that the *New York Times* described as "the hardest kind of football," when, amid the cheering for what the paper called "a sensational play," some 2,000 spectators crowded onto temporary wooden bleachers heard the sound of the lumber beneath them breaking. Pandemonium ensued.

"The cheering was suddenly turned to anguish as the bleachers began to give way," the *Times* wrote. The injured were rushed to the dressing room, where doctors attending the game, assisted by players and trainers, treated them. More than 1,000 people suffered scratches and bruises, though nothing more serious, according to the newspaper.

The Olds dealers and executives apparently escaped harm. But the accident cast a shadow on a year that was ending with disappointing numbers.

And though it may not have affected the dealers' interest in Smith's 1906 lineup, the agents placed just 1,500 orders during the junket, fewer than Smith had hoped. When manufacturers gathered in New York, Smith would be under incredible pressure. The very survival of Oldsmobile would be at stake.

# 10

## DOUBTS SUBSIDING

### TWO CAMPS

The American auto industry was more bitterly divided than ever by the Selden patent case as 1906 began. The rift was physically manifested by New York's two competing automobile shows: Smith's ALAM event, at Madison Square Garden, and Ford's new American Motor Car Manufacturers' Association exhibition, at the Sixty-Ninth Regiment Armory Building, less than a block away.

But whatever the motoring public thought of the Selden case, it did not dissuade people from flocking to Manhattan. Within minutes of both shows' opening at 8:00 p.m. the evening of Saturday, January 13, the Garden and Armory were filled to capacity. "Magnificent is the only word that aptly sums up the universal sentiment expressed last night by several thousand visitors to the two big automobile shows," the *New York Times* reported in its Sunday edition.

ALAM and AMCMA had both invested heavily in pageantry. Entering the Garden for the ALAM show, visitors beheld a massive arch supported by gold-trimmed Corinthian columns under which a female statue named Speed raised her arms in welcome. Two other figures—Chauffeur and Automobile Girl—stood watch, too, while six gold frogs spouted water into a pool that was bathed in changing green, red, and yellow light. Blue cloth decorated with thousands of twinkling electric bulbs hung from the ceiling, creating the impression of a star-filled sky. It was a far cry from the inaugural New York automobile show, in late 1900, as the *Motor Way*—which had assigned eight reporters, four artists, and several photographers to cover both shows—noted in "The Tale of Two Cities," its massive special January 18 edition.

"Looking out from the upper balcony," the magazine wrote, "the mind goes back to the first automobile show in America in this same garden, with its little track, its funny obstacle races and braking contests, the crowds that were eager to take their first ride in an automobile within the limits of the oval. Is it possible that the same men who were then building square ugly black boxes on wheels with a single cylinder are the same who stand today beside such cars as the Apperson, the Winton, the Peerless and the Packard; and is it five years ago or fifty?"

Visitors entering the Armory next door beheld a giant statue of Mercury, Roman god of commerce and speed. It anchored the center of the main floor, where Ford and Selden co-defendant Panhard displayed their vehicles. The Reo exhibit also commanded attention. Ransom displayed his $675 runabout and his $1,250 Touring Car, the model Megargel was driving back from California—along with a two-hundred-pound miniature car, "Baby Reo," which became one of the sensations of the show. The miniature Touring Car was not for sale, but the general public could see it later when it joined the Barnum & Bailey circus. Ransom knew how to get attention.

Airships hung from the Armory ceiling, and visitors interested in another technological revolution about to transform America could proceed to the gymnasium, to view the first-ever exhibit from the Aero Club of America, a national organization founded by Pope and Charles Glidden, of the 1904 St. Louis run fame. The club displayed photographs and an assortment of wings, rudders, propellers, and motors; flying machines seemed to float below the ceiling, among them the novel "ballo-plane," an electric-fan-propelled dirigible constructed of metal and silk that had been designed by a man from the exclusive enclave of Tuxedo Park, New York. The ballo-plane so fascinated a fellow balloonist, Aero club member

The Armory show of 1906 featured automobiles and blimps, two wonders of the age.
Courtesy of the AACA Library and Research Center, Hershey, PA.

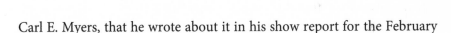

Carl E. Myers, that he wrote about it in his show report for the February 17 edition of *Scientific American.*

The *Times* was similarly impressed. "Never before in this country has so complete a collection of aeronautical material been brought together," the paper declared. "They illustrate some of the latest inventions of man toward solving the problem of aerial flight." Not only were Europeans and Americans building airships, but the Wright brothers had recently completed their longest powered flight: twenty-four and one-half miles in thirty-eight minutes, in the early fall of 1905, a trip that ended only when the fuel ran out.

But the airplane did not outshine the car. Added together, the number and makes of automobiles displayed at the Armory and the Garden represented the largest exhibit ever held in America.

The Garden show boasted more of the most-prominent names in the industry than its Armory counterpart, including Oldsmobile, Cadillac, Buick, Winton, Studebaker, and Packard. In all, thirty-five companies exhibited thirty-three commercial vehicles and 109 cars, of which eighty-three were gas-powered, twenty-six were electric, and none of them steam.

The Armory show, which AMCMA conducted in partnership with the Automobile Club of America, featured a greater total number of machines: fourteen commercial vehicles and 155 cars, of which 136 were powered by gas, ten by electricity, and nine by steam. Twelve motorcycles were also exhibited. Ford, Reo, Daimler, and White were the headline manufacturers. The remaining twenty-six companies included Frayer-Miller, Grout, Pungs-Finch, Acme, and Compound—a mix of smaller manufacturers that mostly were late to the game, and all destined for failure.

The *Times* only acknowledged and did not comment upon the contention that had led to competing shows, writing simply on the eve of the openings: "The manufacturers who will show complete cars in the Garden all recognize the basic rights of the Selden patent and pay royalties upon its use, while in the armory the majority of exhibitors are known in the trade as independents, as they have thus far refused to admit the sweeping provisions claimed for the Selden patent. . . . "

Trade publications, relying more than general-circulation newspapers on the goodwill of manufacturers for advertisements and reporters' access, also soft-pedaled ALAM's lawsuits and Ford's aggressive defense. No good could come from choosing sides in such a costly and bitter battle—one that would enter its fourth year in October and gave not the slightest indication of ending soon.

"The new line of demarcation which has been drawn, the mystic circle of the great Selden patent, has served to relieve the crowding which was one of the serious evils of the older shows, to give more space to the spectators, and to enable the fortunate exhibitors to display their cars to much better advantage," is about all the *Automobile* had to say. "Why there are two rival shows this year need not be told here," the *Motor Way* wrote in its introduction to its special edition. "The political side of the matter is of no immediate significance; the practical point is that those who visit both shows, as everyone is certain to, will see twice as many cars, and to far better advantage, than in recent years." This was sugar-coating of the highest degree.

The furthest the trade press went was to hint at the discussions, concerns, and backroom maneuvering taking place as ALAM and AMCMA neared the next critical stage of the suit: George Selden's upcoming testimony and the court-supervised introduction of Exhibit 89, the 1877 gas buggy built in secrecy in 1905 in Rochester.

"So far as the matter of independent shows in New York is concerned," the *Motor Way* reported in its January 25 post-show edition, "the outlook is uncertain and rather unpromising at this time. Considerable agitation is being stirred up against the leasing of the Sixty-ninth Regiment armory in the future." That same day, the *Automobile* reported that after the National Automobile Dealers Association's meeting at the Victoria Hotel, "rumors were afloat" that the organization considered seceding from ALAM because "the agreement to handle none but licensed cars worked a hardship to many of its members." The president of the national dealers' group denied the rumors but did admit that some of his members were upset at the prospect of being blacklisted if they sold nonlicensed cars, such as Fords and Reos.

ALAM itself kept a low profile during the shows, as did Smith, who had been reelected treasurer of the group at its annual meeting. The lawyers could handle the legal proceedings: Smith needed orders for Oldsmobiles, particularly for his new $2,250, three-speed, 28-horsepower Model S sedan, sold in similar Gentleman's Roadster and Palace Touring models. Olds plugged the car at the Garden and in a full-page ad that trumpeted Dwight Huss's cross-continent victory and his 202-mile run from Boulogne to Paris. "Good French roads helped," the ad declared, "but seven hours is as fast [a] time as that particular course is ever run by the most powerful European cars."

Once again, Smith was confronted with the dilemma inherent in his quest for profits: those who could afford more than $650 for a runabout had many models from which to choose in the midrange and upper markets. For the same price as the Palace Touring, a buyer could have a Premier; for $2,400, a buyer could have a Reo, or a Cadillac with two more horsepower; for $2,500, a Winton. Another $1,000 or so, and a motorist could buy a four-speed Peerless or a 40-horsepower Pope-Toledo. And the Palace Touring could never challenge the gold standard of luxury: the $7,500 American Mercedes.

———————

IN THEIR JANUARY COVERAGE, the industry publications gave the Palace Touring little more than the obligatory inclusion in their cataloguing of all 1906 cars by price, manufacturer, and technical specifications, and the $1,250 double-action Model L fared no better. In writing about the 16-horsepower truck that Olds displayed, the *Automobile* hinted at the larger problem confronting the company. The problem—not that they'd have used this term at the time—was one of branding: "The name Oldsmobile has become so thoroughly identified with the light and nimble curved dash runabout that it does not seem to fit the heavy delivery wagon," the magazine wrote.

Smith received few orders for his big Palace car—or any of his cars—while in New York: the approximately 1,500 vehicles that dealers had committed to during November's junket would account for nearly all of Oldsmobile's production in 1906, as it would happen. Like 1905's $1,400 Heavy Touring, the Palace model was a dud.

And the Heavy Touring remained a loser. The Times Square Automobile Company, on West Forty-Sixth Street, which billed itself as "the largest dealer in the world [carrying] in stock at all times from 200 to 300 machines of various makes," was selling the car for a fire-sale price of $775. The company was also trying to clear out its inventory of Oldsmobile's jazzed-up version of the Curved Dash. Ordinarily, the Dash sold for $750; Times Square Automobile offered it for $490.

But Times Square Automobile was not selling any marked-down Fords. The Ford Model N was receiving rave reviews.

With signature marketing flair, Ford had created excitement for the vehicle even before coming to New York. In a letter published in the January 11 issue of the *Automobile*, he explained the philosophy that had guided him in designing the car. It began with his belief that more

Americans could afford to buy some sort of car than consumers in any other nation—and that despite increases in production capacity, US manufacturers would be unable to meet the demand in 1906. As a result, he argued, carmakers saw no reason to drop prices or build cheaper cars. In essence, he identified the cornerstone of his rival Smith's business plan.

"The prospect of filling the demand is exceedingly slim," Ford wrote, "and for this reason, most of the factories building cars claim that prices should be maintained and to put out a low-price car is unjustifiable and suicidal."

But Ford begged to differ.

"The greatest need today is a light, low-priced car with an up-to-date engine of ample horsepower and built of the very best material," he wrote. "One that will go anywhere a car of double the horsepower will; that in every way is an automobile and not a toy; and most important of all, one that will not be a wrecker of tires and a spoiler of the owner's disposition." It must be a car that did not require a chauffeur to drive, or a mechanic riding along or on call, Ford maintained. It had to be a vehicle that could start at any time and travel anywhere. And it had to be simple to operate.

"We are today in a position to build and deliver 10,000 of our four-cylinder runabouts," Ford concluded. "I am now making arrangements whereby we can build and deliver 20,000 of these runabouts, and all within twelve months." It was a boast Ford would not make good on, but the bold pronouncement—no company had ever promised or delivered so many cars, of any kind—could not be ignored. This was Henry Ford, who had made good on his vow to set a world speed record on a frozen lake and was determined to slay the Selden dragon.

"THE SHOW'S SENSATION," the *Motor Way* hailed the Model N. "The Ford four-cylinder $500 runabout made its debut at the armory show Tuesday noon, one car being on exhibition and one outside for demonstrating purposes. It was eagerly awaited by many visitors who had made frequent trips to the Ford exhibit asking if this model had arrived."

What seemed to impress attendees and journalists were the many features the car shared with the costlier vehicles Ford also displayed in New York, the Model B and the Model F. Also on exhibit was his original

Quadricycle—a reminder of what a true pioneer, not a pretender like Smith or Selden, had actually accomplished.

Ford elaborated in a full-page, thirteen-paragraph ad in the Sunday, January 14, New York *Sun*. "Why Henry Ford Fought the Selden Patents" amounted to a manifesto—a fiery denunciation of what he considered ALAM's attempt to stifle free enterprise and denigrate, if not dismiss entirely, the efforts of the inventive "thousands of minds" that had collectively created the automobile. Ignoring for the moment the many others that ALAM had sued, Ford said that he and his company—and he and it alone—had shouldered the long and expensive burden of defense, in the courts and in the court of public opinion. And in truth, Ford had underwritten the lion's share of the legal costs.

Because he had done so, Ford declared, "hundreds of non-licensed factories started up all over the U.S., turning out thousands of cars and giving employment to hundreds of thousands of men, and in every way the automobile industry and the public at large have been benefited and every man of brain has been given an opportunity to develop his ideas and get the benefit therefrom."

The automobile industry, Ford asserted with patriotic flair, was a core part of an American economic revolution that was propelling the country to global dominance: "American genius and enterprise have brought about the time when automobiles are built in America by the same methods that are enabling American goods to surpass all others in the world's market. Who wants anything better than an American watch, an American sewing machine, an American yacht, an American bicycle or an American locomotive?"

Ford closed with a statement of resolve that Smith by now well understood.

"The Ford Motor Company started in business with this one great principle in view: to take the automobile out of the list of luxuries and put it in the class of necessities, and have not allowed any man or set of men to interfere or dictate to them as to how many cars they should build or what price they should set for them."

DIVIDED THOUGH THE MANUFACTURERS were, a decade after incorporation of Duryea, the first American car company, no one could credibly dispute that motoring was more a part of the fabric of American life than ever. The historic crowds at the January shows provided evidence. So did the voluminous press coverage.

"We believe that the auto business is here to stay as long as man," Jesse Draper, sales manager of the Wayne Automobile Company, wrote in a letter to the *Automobile*. As 1906 unfolded, the soundness of his observation was confirmed by many measures. For better and for worse, the motor vehicle really had arrived.

The federal government would report that 108,100 motor vehicles were registered in the United States in 1906, an increase of better than one-third from 1905; New York state accounted for 11,753 of those registrations, an increase of 3,128 over 1905 (7,667 licenses were issued, compared to 4,387 in 1905). Sales of passenger vehicles totaled 33,200, according to later calculations by the US Census Bureau, up from 24,500 in 1905—and a better than eightfold increase from 1900. The wholesale value of cars sold in 1906 was $61 million, compared to $38 million in 1905, and just $4 million in 1900.

But no government agency or industry organization in the early 1900s had the ability or inclination to thoroughly track an industry that had arisen so relatively quickly and was still rapidly evolving. Numbers told but part of the tale. More meaningful insights into the state of motoring in 1906 could be found in newspapers and periodicals such as the consumer-oriented *Motor*, William Randolph Hearst's first magazine, which he founded in 1903 after a honeymoon auto tour of Europe.

Readers of the popular *Motor* and similar magazines and the daily newspapers learned of the newest manufacturers in 1906, including Bay State, based in Boston; Imperial, of Williamsport, Pennsylvania; Jewel, of Cleveland; Page, of Providence, Rhode Island; Perfection, of South Bend, Indiana; Springer, of New York City; and Success, of St. Louis. They were less likely to read of the failures, including, in 1906, Walker, Wolverine, and Finch Limited, all based in Detroit; Cannon, of Kalamazoo, Michigan; Palmer, of Ashtabula, Ohio; Walworth, of Chicago; and Providence's Thompson, which opened and closed the same year, a graphic illustration of the industry's continuing volatility. The siren's call continued, although the time was approaching when only a handful of companies would have the resources and sales success needed to survive.

More exciting to autoists were the reports of the new dealerships, clubs, and driving schools; and the new auto shows, in New Orleans; Omaha, Nebraska; and Portland, Maine. In some places, consumers could now buy on credit. Buffalo's W. C. Jaynes, the dealer with the expensive 10,000 square-foot garage, was among the pioneers of "the installment plan"—and when he first offered automobile financing, in 1905, he had been rewarded.

"Only Oldsmobiles are disposed of in that way by the company so far," *Motor Age* reported, "but the announcement of the change in business methods was followed by a rush of business which may make the change desirable in regard to other cars." Like cars, car debt had arrived.

Dealers also offered an increasing selection of used cars—and, like Times Square Automobile, discounts on unsold new cars still on the lot when the latest models arrived.

Drivers could now buy automobile insurance. Founded in 1873 to provide marine insurance, the Boston Insurance Company claimed to have sold the first American automobile policy, in 1902. The company in 1906 advertised insurance that "covers car wherever it may be in U.S. or Canada, against fire from any cause, and lightning included; also marine and transportation risks, theft or pilferage," for an annual premium of 3 percent of the worth of a car, or $30 for every $1,000 valuation. Listing several brokers in New York City that were specializing in auto policies, *Motor* predicted that the business "is destined in the near future to become a profitable branch of the insurance industry."

And it wasn't even necessary to own an automobile to experience motoring: companies and individuals now could rent cars by the hour, day, week, or trip. The emergence of yet another new business was confirmed by the car-friendly lodging establishments that advertised themselves under the banner "Motor Hotels." Commercial and residential garages continued to proliferate. So did service stations, with ninety-one of them in New York City advertising in the March 1906 issue of *Motor* alone. Due in part to the continued influence of the Good Roads movement, more farmers switched to motor power. States and municipalities continued to purchase motor vehicles—and build and improve roads.

In Washington, Representative Marion E. Rhodes of Missouri introduced legislation to establish a national highway commission to build and maintain roads; from an appropriation of $50 million the first year, and $25 million annually thereafter, each state and territory would qualify for up to $500,000 a year in work. But the bill did not clear Congress. Rhodes shared the frustration of Tennessee representative Walter P. Brownlow, whose similar legislation, introduced in 1902 and again in 1903, did not make it to President Roosevelt's desk. It would be 1916 before the Federal Aid Road Act headed America toward an interstate highway system. Still, in 1906, that seemed less of a fantasy than ever.

———

THE US BUREAU OF Public Roads lacked the resources to complete an inventory of road mileage and maintenance expenditures for all states in 1906, but it did manage to compile select data from a few states for 1904. Pennsylvania reported 99,777 total miles, of which 2,129 miles, just 2.1 percent, had been improved with gravel or stone; in 1904, $4.8 million had been expended to maintain them. Maryland reported 16,773 miles, with 9 percent improved, and an expenditure of $873,470.50. Arizona, a state with 114,000 square miles of space, reported only 5,987 miles of roads, of which 217 were improved. Only $109,309.43 was spent on maintenance.

Road work anywhere was mostly financed with a hodgepodge of state, county, and local taxes and fees assessed on drivers. Whatever the formula for a community, many motorists reacted with anger. They found fresh meaning in Benjamin Franklin's axiom that nothing was certain except death and taxes.

New York state senator Irving L'Hommedieu had felt motorists' wrath. After failing to win passage of a motor-vehicle tax bill in 1905, he introduced new legislation in January 1906. As originally submitted, the bill called for a tax of $1 per vehicle, plus an additional 50 cents for every five hundred pounds weight (or fraction thereof) for vehicles weighing more than one-fourth of a ton. Based on an estimate of 24,000 cars in the state, approximately $400,000 would have been raised in the first full year, all earmarked to maintain and build a total of nearly 700 miles of state roads. (New York's counties used separate means to maintain the roughly 2,100 miles of roads under their jurisdiction.)

But the bill died in the Assembly on May 2, a victim of squabbling over language and the precise application of the earmarks. The Automobile Club of America, which along with other organizations supported some form of taxation to build and maintain roads, led the opposition. The National Association of Automobile Manufacturers joined it.

"Personally, I did not favor the bill from the beginning," NAAM president Charles T. Terry told the *New York Times*. "The taxation plan seemed particularly unfair, as it singles out the motor users for special, or class, taxation."

Some motorists protested more creatively. In Grand Rapids, Michigan, where assessors sent notice to some three hundred owners asking them to report the cost and present value of their machines, by which taxes would be calculated, drivers suddenly all owned junkers.

"The automobiles of Grand Rapids are in a very bad condition," the *Automobile* reported on March 8, 1906. "Their tires are punctured; their engines refuse to work; they are in the repair shop half the time. New cars must have a great deal of work done upon them; some have to be rebuilt entirely. The evidence tends to show that of the entire 300 machines in town, scarcely one is in condition to whiz along the streets and fill the heart of the owner with joy."

Like death and taxes, lying to the tax collector was another certainty.

## AUTOFLIRTATION

But the continuing advances in power, cooling, steering, suspension, shock absorption, transmission, ignition, batteries, braking, tires, tops, bodies, seating, and overall comfort did bring joy to motorists everywhere. They found joy, too, in the latest motoring fashions and the growing variety of horns, lamps, motor clocks, gasoline gauges, gasoline-test hydrometers, ignition-switch locks, tire repair kits, jacks, foot pumps, washers and cleaners, battery chargers, and "cigar lighters" that could jazz up a driving life.

A motorist also could buy many maps. Or a Warner Auto-Meter, to calculate distance and speed: "It goes on the dashboard, where it can be read from the seat, and fits any automobile," asserted its Wisconsin manufacturer. "It is actuated by the same *unchangeable magnetism* which makes the Mariner's Compass unfailing and certain forever." The company maintained that its odd-looking widget "always tells the truth" without explaining how. Nor did the makers of another seemingly magical device that was introduced to the American public in 1906 reveal its secret.

"A new automobile map has been brought out in Paris which will constantly indicate to the driver his position on the road and will roll out before him automatically in proportion to his speed," the *Automobile* reported on February 8. The device was nonsense, a GPS-like navigational aid in concept only, and it is unclear if it was ever produced in quantity:

> The apparatus consists of a glass top box about 8 inches long and 3 inches wide attached to the top of the dash. On the right hand side is exposed a strip map of the road supported on a roller at each extremity and made to unroll at a rate proportionate to the speed of the car but always in such a way that 5 miles of the road ahead can be seen. On the left hand side of the road map is a narrow strip giving an explanation of all the signs shown on the map.

> At a speed of 37 miles an hour, every obstacle or change in the nature of the road is known 8 minutes before it is reached. At 74 miles an hour, the same would be indicated 4 minutes in advance. The map is made to unroll by means of gearing on the front wheel of the car imparting motion to a gear on the chart box by means of a flexible cable exactly as is used for speedometers. When passing through towns, the map indicates left/right so that it is possible to go right through without stopping to ask directions.

---

AS 1906 PROGRESSED, MANUFACTURERS broadened their reach into the commercial market, building more and more taxis, trucks, ambulances, buses, fire trucks, mail vans, and trailers. They watched the development of military vehicles in Germany and other European countries and read with interest an editorial in the *Automobile* that urged the United States to follow suit, despite the magazine's optimistic assertion that America "may not be involved in any international complications for years to come, if ever." Cavalry would persist, the editorial predicted, "but an auto cavalcade consisting of armored cars equipped with the latest form of close hand gunnery and capable of covering distance quickly would prove equal in an emergency to thousands of infantry."

But the army was not immediately persuaded. Of the nearly $2 million that Congress appropriated for summer training in 1906, the army spent more than $16,000 to buy six different model touring cars. The experiment did not impress the brass. "It does not appear that the automobile has exactly covered itself with glory," wrote Captain F. P. Avery in the *Horseless Age*. "It is probably true that the roads in the West and South are not at all suited to such vehicles. It would seem rather doubtful, therefore, whether they will be found practicable for warlike operations in America. I am aware that this opinion is somewhat at variance with that advanced by European military observers, but it may be that the better roads all over Europe and the difference in the nature of the country accounts for this."

Other specialized vehicles debuted. One company introduced the Motor Potato Planter, and another in Fresno, California, announced what may have been the first powered hearse: the "auto morgue wagon," a vehicle with two seats on the right and a wooden compartment for a casket on the left, constructed atop a Rambler chassis. The firm, Stephens & Bean, completed its first hearse in November 1905. Since then, the *Automobile* wrote in March 1906, "many letters have been received by them inquiring concerning it and are coming in every day. It is, they say, making a decided hit in undertaking and they expect to hear of many such vehicles before long."

Unfortunate motorists might have use for the auto morgue wagon. They were learning of a new way their machines could kill them.

Henry Fischer, of Newark, New Jersey, was nearly one such fatality. A story in the *Automobile* during auto show week in New York reported that one day recently, Fischer had closed the windows and door to his garage but kept his car running. He became drowsy and thinking he was only tired, sat on the floor and gradually drifted off to what he thought was sleep.

"He probably would not have awakened again but for the timely appearance of his brother, who chanced to enter the garage and saw Fischer's prostrate form lying on the floor," the *Automobile* wrote.

The brother called a doctor, who needed an hour to revive him. Apprised of the case, "several scientific men" later concluded that asphyxiation was the culprit: the running engine had exhausted the oxygen in the garage, and Fischer, unable to get the right air, succumbed.

But the real cause was the accumulation of invisible, odorless carbon monoxide from automobile exhaust in an enclosed, unventilated space. Few, if any, motorists in 1906 understood this.

No less an authority than Charles Duryea, writing in *Cycle and Automobile Trade Journal*, erroneously claimed that carbon monoxide "has a very pungent odor," and he mentioned nothing of its toxic qualities. An editorial in *Power Wagon*, published in Cleveland, ridiculed individuals who believed that automobile exhaust was polluting the environment and endangering people.

"For weeks past, the columns of the daily press have teemed with cabled notices of the peril to the human race from the exhaust of gasoline engines in road vehicles," the editorial stated. "A titled professor of chemistry started the general apprehension by declaring that the emanations from gasoline motors is slowly but certainly poisoning the atmosphere we breathe."

"'Too much carbon dioxide,' he complains."

"'Too many automobiles,' shriek his admirers. . . . "

"'And there's carbon monoxide also to be reckoned with,' snaps the professor."

"Whereupon the multitude, which has heard that a whiff of carbon monoxide will waft a soul to paradise, proceeds to curse invention and the internal combustion engine."

But any ignoramus, the magazine implied, surely knew the multitudes and the professor were grossly misinformed—and interested only in assailing the evil auto. "One feels sorry for the 'eminent man of science,'" the editorial said. "The foremost medical authorities do not consider the carbonic acid and carbon monoxide emanations from a motor vehicle as in the least threatening to human life. The best known medical journal in the world dismisses the subject."

————

ALTHOUGH THERE REMAINED PUZZLEMENT in 1906 at the notion that ladies would want to drive cars, women motorists were less and less a novelty.

"It is not surprising to find that women are becoming victims of the automobile microbe and that they covet the seat behind the steering wheel, where their brothers and husbands and fathers find such absorbing pleasure," the *Automobile* wrote in its June 14 edition. "As usual, they have had their will, and on any fine day, the roads in the neighborhood of the larger cities are traversed by many automobiles of all types driven by women, and driven smartly, too."

Another story offered practical advice for the women who wished to experience what the author, a Mrs. A. Sherman Hitchcock, described as the exhilaration of motoring—a feeling unequaled by anything else, she asserted, a point on which motoring men could certainly agree.

To truly appreciate a car, Mrs. Hitchcock wrote, a lady should become acquainted with its mechanical operation, which began with overcoming what she described as a woman's natural disinclination to technology. She must learn to steer, control the throttle, shift the clutch, learn the rules of the road, and exercise caution in congested areas. She should learn to clean spark plugs with an old toothbrush and a few drops of gasoline and remember to carry extra plugs, should replacement be required on the road.

"A woman to be a successful driver should be possessed of cool nerves, a level head, courage and determination," Mrs. Hitchcock advised. "She must have perfect confidence in herself, be ever alert and calculative, and quick of application in case an emergency should arise where instant

This 1906 Automobile Calendar featured a stylish lady and her car.
Library of Congress, LC-USZC2-521.

action would be necessary. Practical experience is of far greater value than a theoretical study could ever be, and a break-down upon the road will be an effectual lesson."

But as many gentlemen had discovered to their delight, a woman needn't learn to drive to experience another sort of motoring exhilaration—romance, which Johnny Steele had offered his queen of his gas machine, the merry Oldsmobile, in the hit song. Real-life parking—of the sexual sort—had become so popular that a new term, "autoflirtation," had been coined to jokingly describe motor-car dalliances.

A writer for *Lippincott's Monthly Magazine* explained the new lingo in an article in 1906:

> The latest fad in high society is automobile flirtation. What such flirtation is and how it is conducted I have discovered at great personal danger while disguised as a chauffeur and accompanying a high society queen on one of her flirtatious expeditions. Here is the "language":
> "Dashing against stone wall—Meet me at the hospital tonight."
> "Letting your machine be run into—You've made a hit with me."
> "Running over dog—I think you're perfectly killing."
> "Dashing off bridge—You can send me your message by Dr. Blank."
> "Running into store window—Forgive me. I'm all broken up about it."
> "Violating speed ordinance—You can have me if you can catch me, but you'll have to go some!"

———————

THERE WAS POSSIBILITY EVEN for people with disabilities. A Holland, Michigan, man who lost his right arm to amputation but still "manages his automobile with the greatest dexterity, day or night, with his left hand," wrote the *Automobile*, was one of the pioneers.

The man, Samuel W. Miller, drove an 18-horsepower Wolverine and had experienced just one accident during his many years of one-arm motoring.

"He was driving down a steep country road one windy afternoon," the magazine wrote, "when his hat blew off. Unconsciously, he reached for it with his left hand, letting go of the lever. One of the forward wheels struck a small stone in the road, turning the machine off into a ditch. The auto was overturned but only slightly damaged and Mr. Miller escaped without injury. There has been considerable talk of Mr. Miller entering the derby races at Grand Rapids."

Such stories suggested to the *Automobile* that the days of "unjust auto-mobile antagonism" were numbered. As further evidence, in March it published brief accounts of recent favorable developments in Georgia, California, Illinois, Ohio, Boston, and Brooklyn, New York.

"Throughout the country accumulates evidence that serves to show how near is the dissolution of unavailing prejudice, and the farmer is succumbing—grudgingly, but still succumbing—to the influence of the automobile and what it will mean to country folk in general. The unjust persecution of the law-abiding automobilist is arousing spokesmen in his favor, and the universal trend is toward the appreciated acceptance of the great boon of the age."

That rosy view minimized the rising human cost. America in 1906 witnessed 338 traffic fatalities, a nearly 50 percent increase from 1905—and thirteen times greater than the twenty-six recorded in 1899, the first year the government began tracking deaths involving motor vehicles. The trend was indisputably sharply upward.

Many citizens saw this as anything but evidence of a great boon. Woodrow Wilson, then president of Princeton University, spoke for them when he said in a speech in New York on February 27:

> I think that of all the menaces of today the worst is the reckless driving of automobiles. In this, the rights of the people are set at naught. When a child is run over the automobilist doesn't stop but runs away. Does the father of that child consider him heartless? I don't blame him if he gets a gun. I am a Southerner and know how to shoot. Would you blame me if I did so under such circumstances? Nothing has spread Socialistic feeling in this country more than the use of automobiles. To the countryman they are a picture of arrogance of wealth with all its independence and carelessness.

---

INGENIOUS WITH MECHANICS AND with marketing, Ford showed further ingenuity in resolving his dispute with investor and nominal treasurer

Malcomson, who against Ford's strong wishes still wanted to build more cars like the six-cylinder $2,500 Model K, by far the most expensive automobile the company sold in its early days. With the support of Couzens and other allies, Ford cleaved the company in half.

Once split, Ford and his inner circle retained control of production—and thus their destiny—with the establishment of the new Ford Manufacturing Company. Malcomson stayed with the original Ford Motor Company, primarily a sales operation now that production was separate. Ford was elected president of Ford Manufacturing Company, and Couzens, secretary; they and a handful of loyalists received all of the stock, with Malcomson getting none.

Angered at having been emasculated, Malcomson in December 1905 announced formation of his own firm: the Aerocar Company, which hurriedly introduced a 24-horsepower, one-ton, $2,800 touring car. Still a stockholder and treasurer in name of Ford Motor Company, Malcomson had backed himself into a corner. He threatened lawsuits but knew only surrender would let him out. So he waved the white flag: He had a new company, after all, in which he reportedly had invested $90,000 of his own money. After weeks of discussion with Couzens, Malcomson on July 12 sold his 255 shares to Ford for $175,000. The death of another of Ford Motor's original stockholders and pressure on others to sell eventually returned full control of Ford Motor to Henry and Couzens, leaving them unchallenged to build on the success of the cheap Model N. In 1907, Ford Manufacturing Company and Ford Motor would be merged, creating a unified company.

Smith had no such ingenious solution to his own management problem at Oldsmobile. He apparently didn't even know he had one until sales chief Chapin, who had stayed in New York after the 1906 Garden auto show closed, sent him a telegram: Effective March 1, he was resigning.

Back in Lansing, Chapin met with brilliant young chief engineer Howard E. Coffin and two other Olds employees to discuss establishing a new company. On February 28, the men signed papers of incorporation, from which grew the E.R. Thomas-Detroit Company, predecessor to Chapin's Hudson Motor Car Company, one of the most successful manufacturers of the first half of the twentieth century.

Smith gave no public indication of the considerable impact the loss of such talent would have on Oldsmobile. He replaced Chapin and busied himself with the upcoming selling season. In addition to the usual advertising, he needed a major marketing opportunity, something to rival the 1905 cross-continent race—and, he hoped, something with better return to the bottom line.

The AAA handed him one on April 9, when its Racing Board, meeting in New York, set the dates and rules for the 1906 Vanderbilt Cup.

———

FROM ITS FIRST RUNNING, on Long Island in October 1904, the Cup was America's premier road race, watched by hordes of spectators and covered fanatically by the press—not only in the United States but overseas, where audiences in France, Germany, and Italy followed racers from their countries who competed against the Americans. The race was so popular that a play based on it had opened at New York's Broadway Theatre during auto show week in January 1906 and was booked to run through the first of June. Starring teenage actress Elsie Janis, who was destined to become a Hollywood film actress and screenwriter, *The Vanderbilt Cup* featured real automobiles "racing" each other on roller treadmills that had been constructed on stage. In some performances, Oldfield drove his famous Green Dragon race car against the dashing Tom Cooper, who had helped Ford build his twin 999 and Arrow race cars and gone on to his own racing fame. Oldfield earned $1,000 a week for his appearances in New York and, later, London.

The AAA set October 6 as the date of the Cup and September 22 for the US elimination trials. A maximum of twenty-five American cars could compete in the trials, with the top five finishers advancing to the final. The Racing Board did not immediately announce that the Cup would be run again on Long Island, where some residents objected to the crowds, the noise, and the danger, but the AAA ultimately settled on it, establishing an almost thirty-mile course through Jericho, East Norwich, Greenvale, Old Westbury, Roslyn, and Mineola, all on public roads. Ten laps would be run, for a total of 297 miles.

Smith had not entered a race car in the 1904 or 1905 Vanderbilt Cup races, but shortly after the AAA's April 9 meeting, he announced that Oldsmobile would devote "every mechanical and financial facility," as the *Automobile* phrased it, to building a six-cylinder race car for Cup competition. His driver would be Olds engineer Ernest D. Keeler, a handsome young man originally from California. Keeler caught the attention of the *New York Times,* which confirmed on April 20 that he had already begun training, in a stock model Olds, for the September qualifying race. "He has made several runs over the proposed Long Island course in a touring car, and by the time the racer is ready, he will be thoroughly familiar with the roads for fast work," the paper wrote.

From then on, Smith used Keeler as his marketing ace. Keeler appeared on Broadway in *The Vanderbilt Cup* when Oldfield had stepped away from the stage. Smith sent him to the nation's first open-air car show, at Yonkers's Empire City track in late May, where, driving a Model S, he placed first in the braking test and first in the vibration contest—spilling just three-eighths of an inch of water from the full pail he carried two hundred yards at speed from a standing start. A week later, Keeler drove New York mayor George B. McClellan Jr. and Police Commissioner Theodore A. Bingham in an Oldsmobile in a police parade that passed by Madison Square.

Smith also scored a major publicity coup when Mark Twain agreed to let Keeler drive him around in a new double-action Model L. Smith turned a photo of Twain in the backseat into a postcard—and a writer for *Motor* who witnessed Twain riding with Keeler presented what he said were the humorist's views on speeding and scofflaws:

"While Mr. Clemens delights in speeding, he wants to do it all on a country road, where there will be no danger to life or limb," the *Motor* scribe wrote. "The carelessness of chauffeurs and the way they break the laws in not having the car numbers displayed led Mr. Clemens to write an article not long ago, which appeared in one of the monthlies. He was further prompted to do it, owing to the fact that a member of his family had come very near being killed by a reckless driver, and Twain himself also had several close shaves.

"He suggested a punishment to fit the crime for those who knock people down and do not bother to stop and have such small indistinct numbers that they cannot be read even at a short distance. He recommends that offenders should be forced to carry numbers on the rear of their machines, two, three and four feet in height for the first few offences; larger numbers for chronic cases. This awful disgrace would cure them, he thinks."

For Smith, the stars finally seemed to be realigning.

## HEATED EXCHANGES

By the time George Selden took the stand for the first time, in New York City on May 2, 1906, the patent case had become a hydra, with five major interrelated suits against domestic and foreign industry firms in multiple jurisdictions, and numerous smaller actions against smaller parties. ALAM was feeling the financial strain and paying a price in bad publicity. It needed a command performance by its marquee witness.

Selden, about to turn sixty, had come to consider himself as exalted— and to ALAM, he was, "the patron saint of the Association of Licensed Automobile Manufacturers," as the *Automobile* described him. He was called "the father of the automobile" by some residents of Rochester, where he still lived and where once he had been mocked.

But Selden was bitter, and his long fight for respect had turned him bullheaded and irritable. He quarreled internally with ALAM's lawyers, who themselves were at odds. When Selden went about in public, he presented a defiant posture—literally. He had paid a jeweler to fashion a stickpin miniature of the vehicle depicted in US Patent No. 549,160: its headlights and hubcaps were small diamonds, the body all sapphires. He wore it on his cravat, beneath his perpetually clenched jaw, gray moustache and hair, and cold, steely eyes. His testimony—and what he expected to be a final verdict in his favor—would be long-overdue vindication. Selden's belittling father was long dead, but Ford and his lawyer, Parker, were not. Selden was ready for them.

He began his testimony on that spring day by recounting his early experiments and the construction of his engine, which he first fired up in May 1878, nearly three decades before, presenting letters and notebooks to support his recollections. Parker occasionally objected, but Selden told a compelling tale. Someone hearing only that might really believe that he was the father of the automobile.

When Selden had finished that part of his testimony, Parker went for the jugular.

Making little effort to hide his contempt for this man who wore a diamond-studded miniature replica of a car he had never built—and which could never have been built, the lawyer maintained—Parker drilled in on Selden's scant mechanical background before 1878. He wrestled Selden into admitting that most of the parts used to build Exhibit 89, the 1877 gas buggy—and the parts used by ALAM in constructing a similar vehicle, Exhibit 157—had not existed until just a few years before. When Selden refused to name all of the supposedly original parts of his engine, instead going off on a long tangent about how he had been able to reduce weight, Parker growled: "Answer objected to as not responsive. Mr. Selden, I will cross-examine you all summer if you don't answer that question."

But Selden could not be cowed. He accused Parker of asking unnecessary and repetitive questions—and dragging out the trial to give Ford time to sell more cars. He accused Ford's lawyer of attempting to bully him.

"You have tried several times to dictate my answer to me," Selden said at one point, "and as far as I know, you have not yet succeeded and I really doubt whether you will."

At another point, Parker tried to force Selden to admit that he had begun work on his car after four other gas engines had already been built: the Belgian Lenoir, the American Brayton, the German Otto, and its successor, the Otto-Langen.

"I fail to see how it is material," Selden said.

"You have adroitly dodged the point," Parker said.

"I am not aware that I have dodged your question adroitly or in any other manner whatsoever," Selden replied.

And in another exchange, Parker asked Selden to reveal details of the private contract with ALAM that provided him with his cut of the royalties. Selden at first said that no effort had been made to hide the details, but after conferring with his attorneys, he refused to say more.

"Did you intend to tell the truth?" Parker asked.

"You question is an insult, sir," Selden said, "and I refuse to answer it."

Selden was not the only witness Parker attempted to skewer, but all were not so effective with counterattack—notably British engineer Hugo C. Gibson, hired by ALAM to help manage mechanical exhibits, including Exhibit 89, the conspicuously labeled 1877, but in fact built less than a year before. Purportedly an expert in flame ignition, Gibson sounded like a fool, if not a bumbling liar, under the heat of Parker's cross-examination.

"I have no knowledge in my present capacity of flame ignition," Gibson said.

"What do you mean by 'in my present capacity?'" Parker asked.

"I mean that as an ordinary individual without special knowledge I have no knowledge of pure flame ignition."

"Have you any knowledge of 'purely flame ignition' as used in this case as an expert?"

"I cannot say what I know as an expert."

Parker referred Gibson to the motor in Exhibit 89.

"As a matter of fact," he said, "do you know what flame ignition is as applied to that engine?"

"As an ordinary individual, I do not, nor could I possibly," Gibson said.

"Do you know as an expert?"

"I cannot tell what I know as an expert."

"You mean you can't or won't?"

"I mean I can't, as I say."

"Why can't you?"

"I don't know."

Judge Emile H. Lacombe ordered the British engineer to answer. When Gibson responded evasively, the judge said:

"Do you know what a fact question is?"

"No, I do not," Gibson said.

———

WHEN LAWYERS FOR ALAM agreed to let Parker and his technical experts observe a test of Exhibit 89 at noon on May 19 at a garage on Broadway and West Fifty-Sixth, they promised Ford's team that the session would be confidential.

They lied.

A throng of journalists who showed up not only were allowed to write about and photograph the vehicle—they were treated to rides, inside the garage, where the vehicle made a few unimpressive circles.

Parker had been blindsided.

"I cannot imagine how they found out that we were going to examine the car," he told a reporter for the *Horseless Age*. "I surely did not send them word, and if the licensed association people did so without saying anything about it to me, I regard it as a personal affront. Our proceedings were so greatly embarrassed that we shall have to get at it another time."

An ALAM representative minimized Parker's concerns but did not deny lying.

"I am in turn surprised that Judge Parker should feel that way," the official told the *Horseless Age*, "and I see no very good reason for it. I cannot believe the newspaper men interfered with his examination. We did not mean any affront to him. Naturally, the various automobile journals have taken a great interest in this machine and we thought it was a good opportunity to let them learn something about it when technical men were examining it."

Parker did not take well to being duped, and he did not need a courtroom to respond. In a published statement in early June, he discredited the gas buggy as a laughable attempt to substantiate Selden's alleged inventive genius. How ALAM could have spent an exorbitant sum to build it defied his belief.

"I am surprised that an attempt should have been made to offer this car in evidence," he said. "With only a few of the original parts, the carriage bore a misleading plate marked '1877.' It seems a pity that almost a million dollars should have been paid on what was seen the other day." Selden used a technical critique worthy of his professional experts to explain why the buggy's ignition was of contemporary design and not included in the patent, and why only a handful of other parts could have existed in the late 1870s. "Everything else was new and does not date back earlier than about last October," he said. Even as fraudulently constructed, Parker contended,

George Selden and sons with the buggy in New York.
Courtesy of the Rochester Public Library, Local History
and Genealogy Division, Rochester, NY.

the buggy would generate no more than one-half horsepower, insufficient for a practical automobile—and a further indication of disingenuousness.

All in all, Parker implied, George Selden was a pretender: "It is doubtful from the patent specifications, together with what was known in the art before 1879, if an operative engine and car could have been made without instructions which are not found in the specifications."

A few days later, Ford chimed in.

"The Selden people," as Ford dismissed them, had committed yet more fraud by bringing smaller lawsuits against purportedly "belligerent" people who had bought unlicensed vehicles and, after a "lame" legal defense, admitted wrongdoing. In other words, the defendants were plants. ALAM was using their phony confessions to further intimidate the public.

These were also evasive actions, Ford maintained.

"If there is any basis for the claims of Selden," he said, "the owners of that patent, the A.L.A.M., have a good chance to demonstrate it in the pending suit with the Ford Motor Company. Why do they not vigorously press that suit instead of taking advantage of every technicality to secure delays and otherwise impede the progress of the litigation in the very evident attempt to put the day of final decision afar off?"

———————

PERCY MEGARGEL COMPLETED HIS double cross-continent voyage on Saturday, June 9, when he crossed Central Bridge from the Bronx into Manhattan. Nine months and twenty-one days had elapsed since he left. The odometer on his Reo car read 11,784 miles, confirming his adventure as the longest continuous road trip yet in America.

As his readers already knew, the search party sent during the late-December blizzard from Flagstaff, Arizona, had found the drivers safe, although at least seven other people had died in the storm. "Possibly it was because their matches gave out," Megargel wrote in the *Automobile,* "but more likely because they did not have a little gasoline to start campfires with, for the wood was so wet and damp that without gasoline we never could have started a fire, and had we not kept a bright blaze all night, we should certainly have shared the fate of the frozen ones. . . . Although the newspapers throughout the country have been printing, under terrifying headlines, accounts of the frozen New Yorkers, I can assure my friends that we are in excellent health."

Continuing east, Megargel was soon tortured again. In New Mexico in January, the Reo crashed through ice and was sucked into quicksand below, where it was stuck for three nights and two days. Arriving in Denver on March 24, the car was a battered mess, and in April, the Nebraska roads beat up Mountaineer more.

"In the hollows, deep mud and sometimes deep water still exist," Megargel wrote, "while the higher points along the road where the ruts have become hardened are so infernally rough that tires, axles, machinery and, in fact, the entire automobile are subjected to such a shaking up that almost anything is liable to happen unless the speed is reduced to that of a farm wagon." Approaching Des Moines, Iowa, the car went into a ditch and broke a transmission gear, which forced cancellation of a celebration at an agency that the dealer had advertised in the local papers. Megargel and Fassett reached Chicago on May 19, but they had only traveled two miles out of the city on their way east when the Reo broke down and they had to return for repairs. The men were in Ohio when Megargel learned of his father's death in Scranton. He put the trip on hold and took a train to his native city for the funeral.

"A little late, but here to tell the story," Megargel told reporters in New York on June 9. "I never gave up hope of riding down Broadway once more, even when the newspapers of the country had us buried for good in the snowdrifts of Arizona during Christmas week."

The Reo 16-horsepower Touring Car had completed a historic journey, but the final weeks, along well-traveled Eastern routes, had been anticlimactic and reporters' interest had waned. The return of Megargel rated a story only on a back page of the June 14 edition of the *Automobile*, which had once headlined his exploits.

## A BRIGHT NEW STAR

The cover story in that same issue of the *Automobile* conveyed bigger news: arrangements had been finalized for the 1906 Glidden tour. Here was the next great automobiling adventure, and journalists were all over it. Before it even started, the *New York Times* alone would publish no fewer than forty-five stories that featured or mentioned the adventure.

The Glidden tour was the third annual national parade sponsored by the AAA, whose first, the 1904 run to St. Louis, had been such a success. For two years now, it had borne the name of Charles J. Glidden, the millionaire auto excursionist. Participants could drive in a noncompetitive division or compete separately for the prestigious Glidden trophy, awarded according to a scoring system that rewarded punctuality, with drivers losing a point for every minute they arrived past the set time for each day's destination, and losing two points for each minute they arrived early. Like golf, the lowest scorer would win.

The AAA had decided that the 1906 tour would start on July 12 in Buffalo, continue east to Saratoga Springs, head north along Lake Champlain to Montreal and on to Quebec City, then to Jackman and Waterville in Maine. It would end on July 28 at Bretton Woods, New Hampshire, at the base of Mount Washington. The total distance would be 1,105 miles.

Megargel did not enter; perhaps he needed time with his wife and daughter. But Smith put his bright new star Keeler in competition with drivers of more than four dozen cars, among them Packards, Pierce-Arrows, Popes, a Reo, and three Buicks, one of them driven by Durant himself, though he dropped out after six days. Driving an Olds Model S, Keeler finished with a perfect score. He rested one night and then set off on a virtually nonstop run to New York, arriving after twenty-six hours and eighteen minutes. "Even at brief stops made for refreshments for the inner man and the inner automobile, the engine was kept turning over," the *Automobile* reported, "Keeler was so exhausted when the end of the journey was reached that he instantly fell asleep." But he had captured big headlines for himself and Olds once again.

Smith had invested nearly $4,000 on the Glidden tour and had gotten a rich return. He expected the same from the blizzard of ads he bought in the Sunday editions of major newspapers that summer.

"Sold and represented in every civilized country in the world," the ad proclaimed, Oldsmobiles were the best cars on the planet, giving superior performance anywhere a driver went: "High speed up hill, brakes on down hill—hell for action on the level." The ads featured the Palace Touring and the Curved Dash and emphasized the theme of winner: medals and prizes in London, Paris, Berlin, Milan, Calcutta, Japan, and St. Louis and many other US cities; and fabulous finishes in endurance runs originating in New York, Pittsburgh, Chicago, Detroit, Cincinnati, Toronto, and elsewhere. Oldsmobiles had climbed stairs in Russia and before the US Capitol, and mountains in America and abroad.

---

As THE SUMMER PROGRESSED and Smith's engineers completed the new Olds racer, the American Vanderbilt Cup field was settled.

Fifteen cars in addition to Keeler's were entered: a Pope-Toledo, a Matheson, three identical Thomas cars, three identical Frayer-Millers, a Christie, a Locomobile, a Haynes, two Maxwells, an Apperson, and a B.L. & M. (Breese, Lawrence and Moulton) machine. Buick, Reo, and Ford skipped the event, although Ford had not abandoned racing: In 1905, he built a new fourteen-foot, 105-horsepower race car and drove it himself that August 25 on the Cape May, New Jersey, beach. Competing against Louis Chevrolet and others, with a crowd of 10,000 watching, he failed to set any record. He had a similarly disappointing result on January 21, 1906, at Ormond.

The description of the Olds race car that the *Automobile* published on the eve of the September 22 Vanderbilt elimination trials suggested that Smith's spring vow to invest "every mechanical and financial facility" in building a six-cylinder race car for Keeler to drive had been more bluster than truth. The engine had four cylinders, not six, with a rating of from 40 to 45 horsepower—a small output compared to other race cars that sought to represent the United States in the Cup final, such as the 90-horsepower Locomobile and the 110-horsepower Frayer-Miller. Some of the foreign cars that would compete in the Cup final were even mightier: the two 120-horsepower Fiats and the two equally monstrous Mercedes machines, for example. The Italians and Germans did not mess around.

Nonetheless, Smith highlighted the Olds race car in his marketing.

"It is the boast of the Olds Motor Works that the Oldsmobile racer entered as a competitor in the elimination trials for the Vanderbilt Cup race is in all its main features a regular stock model," the *Automobile* wrote, "and that any honor that may accrue to the racer will be rightfully shared by every touring car of this model sold. Naturally, there are some changes from the touring car design, but these are of a minor nature and are only such as are necessary to fit the car to run at the highest speed the engine will drive it and to make it readily controllable at top speed."

Put kindly, the boast was poetic license. Built of steel, the car had no body and only two seats: one for the driver, the second for his mechanic, a customary arrangement for many race cars of the time. The engine was exposed. A massive twenty-five-gallon gas tank was mounted directly behind the driver, close enough to touch. A second, smaller tank contained oil that the mechanic fed by hand pump to the crankcase as the motor at high revolution devoured lubricant. Keeler's car bore more resemblance to Ford's 999 and Arrow than a stock Oldsmobile.

But being relatively light, it went exceedingly fast. Keeler had a chance of winning, in a field that had narrowed even before the start of practice when three contestants withdrew—one blew a cylinder driving from New York City to Long Island, another damaged a crankcase, and a third could not complete testing in time to compete—and was winnowed further at pre-race practices. The Apperson struck a tree and then a telegraph pole, destroying the car. Walter Christie wrecked his car in a similar accident and was forced to continue with a stock model. Keeler himself crashed, but the Olds crew repaired his machine, putting Keeler back into the zone. On the day before the trial, he completed the 29.1-mile course in thirty-four minutes, the fastest run of any car during the days of practice. Yes, Smith could believe, the stars really were realigning.

A huge crowd—by one estimate, as many as 200,000 people—gathered along the Vanderbilt course on September 22. Gone, at least in the trade journals, was the anti-racing backlash of the year before, when Oldfield, Kiser, and Jay had been injured during competition. Excitement was running so high that it had sent Hugh Dolnar, a writer for *Automobile Trade Journal*, into a frenzy of purple prose.

"The human desire to go fast and far," Dolnar wrote, "and go where and when one wills and wishes, unfettered by time tables and the rules and regulations and acts of others was one of the deep compelling forces which drove many thousands of the dwellers and sojourners in the city of New York out of their beds in the first hours of the twenty four that made up the day of the Elimination trials, and thronged the dark streets and crowded the Long Island City ferryboats with touring cars filled with men and women who end most days with the small dark hours in which they began this gray Saturday of the early autumn."

And Dolnar was just warming up in his account, which ran twenty-four pages long with illustrations:

> The automobile racer combines the possible excitations of the yacht, the gladiatorial arena, the race course and the gaming table, and sates the elementary human lusts for display of wealth, exhibition of creative power

and skill in designing and construction, life-scorning courage in driving, quickness of action that rivals the swordsman's flashing blade, brute courage of the prizefighter's kind, of breathless speed, reckless throwing away of money, and the risk of limb and life, as no other one thing ever combined these elemental lust appeasements before. Honor, fame, vanity, daring hazard of wealth, speed and the final and most piercing culmination of life matched against life in reckless grasping for the desire of the moment, all of these thrills of the human heart and quickenings of human emotion are combined in their highest potentials in the racing automobile and automobile racing.

———

HAVING EARNED THE NUMBER one spot in a drawing, Keeler was first from the tape at the 6:00 a.m. start of the trials. A minute later, the next car, a Pope-Toledo, was on its way. So it went, minute by minute, until all twelve contestants were off.

The first lap brutalized more than half the field.

When Richard Belden fired up his Frayer-Miller, white flame shot from the exhaust and the car lurched along foot by foot, refusing to accelerate for some long while.

The Number 7 starter, a Thomas driven by Montague Roberts, had gone only a few hundred feet when a rocker arm broke. Roberts trudged on until he reached a garage—but by then, his transmission was damaged and required replacement. He lost three hours before even completing a single lap.

Lee Frayer, at the wheel of another of the Frayer-Miller cars, broke a radius rod near Roslyn, and that was his day. Sharing his disappointment was his mechanic: the fifteen-year-old Eddie Rickenbacker, who would become one of America's foremost race-car drivers, World War I flying ace, and head of Eastern Airlines.

The bad luck continued.

Ralph Mongini, driving the Number 3 Matheson, blew a tire, crashed into a telegraph pole, and was thrown from the car; dazed in the accident, he wanted to continue, but the car owner and the team manager, Tom

Cooper, decided they'd lost too much time to have any chance of winning, and that was that.

Joe Tracy, driving the Locomobile, had a tire go flat in Old Westbury.

At the fifteen-mile mark, a cylinder broke on Gustave Callois's Number 4 Thomas.

But Keeler was doomed, too: his carburetor failed, and then his front axle broke. He managed to complete the first lap—in two hours and twenty-four minutes, nearly two hours slower than the first-lap leader. He did not attempt a second lap. His car was too badly damaged.

———————

KEELER REDEEMED HIMSELF IN a one-hundred-mile race at Empire City on October 27, when he placed second, behind the winning Buick—but ahead of a Mercedes, two Cadillacs, a Peerless, a Packard, and a Matheson driven by Cooper.

He did even better on November 6 in a race at Waverly Park in Newark, New Jersey. Before an estimated 25,000 or more spectators—the largest crowd ever at an American track meet, the *Automobile* claimed—Keeler, driving a 40-horsepower machine, set a new track record in the day's main event, the ten-mile free-for-all. On November 12, he distinguished himself again. Competing for the fifty-mile Philadelphia Inquirer Cup, at Point Breeze Park racetrack in South Philadelphia, Keeler took a quick lead from the starting gun—fired by Elsie Janis, who was on stage at the Philadelphia production of *The Vanderbilt Cup*. A Darracq won, but Keeler placed second. Buick also fared well, winning two of the nine other nonchampionship races.

Eight days later, tragedy struck the racing world again.

This time, it was Cooper.

Capping an evening of fun with a friend and two young ladies, the thirty-two-year-old was racing a Thomas automobile through New York's Central Park shortly after midnight on November 20 when the cars collided. The other car continued on—but Cooper lost control, throwing him and his passengers, a Wall Street broker and the two young women, into the air.

Police found Cooper dead, his chest crushed and his head mangled by his steering wheel. The broker, a "Mr. Barlow," the papers said, suffered a fractured skull and was not expected to live; Helen Hall, one of the women, sustained a similar injury and also was believed headed for the grave. Only Virginia Vernon, who suffered cuts, bruises, and a broken leg, was conscious when officers reached the scene.

In a front-page story in the *New York Times*, Vernon, of Jersey City, New Jersey, recounted what had happened. She said that Cooper—who had "made vast sums of money" in automobiling and as a champion bicycle racer previously, according to the paper—was hot-dogging through the park when the car reached a terrifying speed.

"When the Thomas car shot ahead," she said, "we told Cooper not to mind them, as we were tired of the speed. I remember my friend saying to Cooper that it was no use trying to catch them."

Cooper took that as a challenge. As the cars approached Seventy-Seventh Street, he had caught up. He was trying to smoke the Thomas when the cars tangled.

"When I woke up after the collision, I found my friend insensible on the grass," Vernon said. Dazed though she was, she tried to help.

"Miss Vernon, a plucky young woman," the *Times* reported, "limped around, rendering her companions what assistance she could give, and telling the police in a disconnected manner all she knew of the matter. She did not go to the hospital until all the others had been seen. At the Roosevelt Hospital Mr. Barlow, it was found, had $405 in his pockets."

———

THREE DAYS AFTER COOPER died, Keeler did, too.

He was practicing for the fifty-mile Philadelphia Press trophy at Point Breeze Park in the waning light of November 23 when he told his mechanic he wanted "just one more mile." Keeler sped off, alone in his car.

As he roared down the home stretch into a tricky turn, a work wagon suddenly appeared. Keeler went left—into a Fiat. The Fiat crashed into the wagon, injuring its driver and its horse, which later had to be put down. Keeler went airborne.

"The Olds went over and over like a chipped bowling ball, throwing Keeler many feet ahead," wrote the *Automobile*. He was still alive when rescuers brought him to St. Agnes Hospital, but he soon expired, his skull and collarbone fractured.

"Injuries accdly rec'd while driving automobile, machine falling on him," his death certificate read. Keeler, twenty-seven, had celebrated his second wedding anniversary less than three weeks before. He left behind his wife, Mabel, and their infant son, Edward, born in August.

———

THE "SENSATION" OF THE January show, Ford's Model N, remained sensational after the crowds departed the Armory—so sensational that the company could not meet demand for the vehicle. By May, Couzens was returning money to dissatisfied dealers who were not being shipped the cars they had ordered. The pace of production was short of the 10,000 to 20,000 vehicles a year Ford had promised in January.

Large-scale engine manufacture, he was learning, was extraordinarily vexing. Ford cam shafts frequently broke, and measures to harden the steel were not completely successful until 1907. Another challenge was precision machining of parts that could fit interchangeably into different models—standardization, a potentially time- and cost-saving innovation that most other companies, with their preference for making this part for this car and that part for that, were not adopting. But Ford was unflinchingly demanding. He knew well the fate of vehicles built by slipshod means: buyers believed they had been cheated, word spread, and companies went out of business, still at a frightful rate in the new industry. Ford would not intentionally sell a flimsy car. No one buying one would ever come back, or have a good word to say. That would prove deadly.

Ironing out the kinks slowed production and reduced revenues. Total vehicle sales for the Ford fiscal year ending on September 30 fell by 146, to 1,599 cars, and net income decreased, by more than half, to $116,084. The company paid a dividend to investors of just $10,000, one-tenth of the year before—and the lowest since 1903, when the company was founded.

But this was the next-to-last year Ford would see his numbers tumble so precipitously.

Buick, meanwhile, was taking off, with production rising from 725 cars in 1905 to 1,400 in 1906, most of them the two-cylinder Model F.

But Olds was tanking. If one believed in omens, the death of Keeler was a very bad one.

Smith had little encouraging to say at the Olds Motor Works board meeting of December 29. The company had produced just 1,700 vehicles in 1906, one-third fewer than in 1905: most were the two versions of the Model S, which had sold reasonably well despite the lackluster start to the year. Only about one hundred double-action Model Ls had been produced, an unadulterated failure. And America's love affair with the Curved Dash had soured as rivals such as Ford's Model N charmed consumers.

Not so long before, Olds had been the industry leader. Its market share was now less than 5 percent.

Other indicators confirmed the company was in free fall. Cash reserves were disappearing and the company had made a profit of only $45,000 for the year. More alarmingly, at least for the Smiths—brothers Fred and Angus and their father, Samuel, now seventy-six years old—was the fact that the family was putting some $100,000 of its own money every month into the company to keep it afloat.

At the December 29 meeting, Smith confided that a prominent competitor in the industry had recently paid him a late-night call.

Billy Durant, ever restless, wanted to sound him out about the possibility of combining Buick and Olds Motor Works. Smith gave him a tour of the after-hours factory, and then they returned to his office, where they reached what Smith later described as "a provisional understanding" that the companies some day would marry.

For the time being, the relationship went no further.

# 11

## "EQUAL TO HIS WEIGHT IN WILDCATS"

### BUGGY BLUES

The prime 1907 selling season was winding down when residents of New York had the opportunity to witness what surely ranked among the strangest motoring events thus far in the city. On two days in mid-September, the Selden 1877 buggy was given its first street demonstrations. The result was an embarrassing disaster for ALAM.

The first test began on the afternoon of Thursday, September 12, when lawyers and technical experts for both sides gathered in the midtown-Manhattan garage where the buggy was stored. A mechanic nicknamed "Cranky Louis" for his talent in starting automobiles, furiously cranked the buggy's motor, but it would not catch; the gas intake had been shut off. The valve was then opened and Cranky Louis got it going.

It died after ten seconds.

Cranky Louis cranked another forty-seven seconds and it started again—and immediately misfired and died. Men pushed the buggy into an elevator and brought it down to the ground floor, where the use of electric ignition started it.

Fifty seconds later, the engine stalled. The car had traveled just twenty-five feet on the floor.

At 3:47 p.m., the engine was started again and the driver made it outside and took a short spin. After a stop for adjustments, the buggy headed off again.

The engine choked after two minutes and forty-seven seconds.

Shortly before 4:00 p.m., ALAM's people got Exhibit 89 running again. The buggy went east on West Forty-Seventh Street, crossed Broadway and Seventh Avenue, and was turning for the short trip back to the garage when it stalled. After a minute, the men succeeded in firing the engine. The buggy moved slowly—and then the engine died once more, after coasting about fifty feet. By now, the motor had overheated and was smoking badly. Hugo C. Gibson, who had been overseeing the test for ALAM, called for a stop to let the engine cool down.

While it did, Cranky Louis poured more oil into the crankcase. He then poured water, which sent a geyser of steam nine feet into the air and caused oil to drip from a drain cock. Finally, at 4:26 p.m., the vehicle was started again. It stalled after forty-four seconds. By now, the clutch was failing, and both sides agreed to try again on Monday, September 16.

That second test was worse.

Two attempts were required to get the buggy running inside the garage, but it finally made it to the street, where it was stopped for adjustments. Started again, it ran six feet and died. A succession of starts and stops followed—but now, the crankcase was leaking. Covered in oil and water, Gibson pushed the buggy down a slight grade toward Broadway. With the pull of gravity, the car started—and traveled just seventy yards or so in the next forty-five seconds.

And this was downhill.

Meanwhile, another leak had developed in the crankcase, sending steam some twelve feet into the air.

The buggy was towed back to the garage.

———

THE VEHICLE'S EMBARRASSING PERFORMANCE was all the more confounding in view of the untold hours and dollars that had been invested in building and testing it. The car's feeble run inside a New York garage in May 1906 had portended trouble, and when the vehicle finally had been brought to New York in June 1907 for the court-ordered tests Parker had been demanding, ALAM's lawyers had balked. Arguing that city ordinances forbade testing on city streets—a ridiculous claim that the court nonetheless upheld—the tests were moved to a racetrack near Guttenberg, New Jersey.

There, on June 14 and June 15, Parker had watched those tests of the buggy (and another car ALAM had built, the so-called Hartford-Selden Vehicle, Exhibit 157) with two of his expert witnesses: Charles E. Duryea and Rolla C. Carpenter, a professor of engineering at Cornell University. The buggy ran falteringly, requiring frequent cranking and changing of spark plugs, and the crankcase oil boiled "furiously," according to Carpenter's notes. At one point, the engine overheated so badly that the test had to be stopped.

Parker then demanded that the tests be conducted in New York, as specified in the original court order. ALAM relented. In late June, the buggy was fired up inside a Manhattan garage. Again, the machine embarrassed, spewing flames and smoke, its exhaust pipe turning red from the excessive heat.

Three months had passed, and the thing remained a caricature of a real automobile.

"How long this litigation will last it is of course impossible to say," a reporter for the *Horseless Age* wrote after watching the September tests, "but what it is proving, except the general incapacity of Exhibit 89 to perform the tests witnesses said it made in Rochester and the lack of desire on the part of the complainants to end the suits, is more than uncertain."

———

OTHER DEVELOPMENTS IN 1907 also bode poorly for ALAM.

In May, the organization filed motions in the US District Court for the Southern District of New York that would have made any decision against

Ford binding against others named in separate suits, including Rambler, Premier, and Reo—but the filings had only succeeded in strengthening Ford's hand. Angered by them, Ransom Olds and leaders of other companies had traveled with their lawyers to Detroit to meet with Parker, who boosted their morale by outlining Ford's defense. Many of the men then offered financial support. Ford declined, but a more united front had resulted.

In another setback for ALAM, president George H. Day died in 1907. The organization suffered a further blow when the Electric Vehicle Company, which had served as a straw man for the Selden patent, went into receivership on December 10 after being unable to borrow money to meet $2.5 million it owed in bonds. Trade publications favorable to Ford seized on it as additional evidence of ALAM's hollow purpose.

Under the headline "The Trail of the Serpent," the *Horseless Age* excoriated ALAM's leaders, without naming them, for using Electric Vehicle as a foil. "It has been current report for some time that the company has never made a dollar from the manufacture of automobiles and that its mainstay has been the revenue derived from the licenses under the Selden patent," the editorial stated. "So far as manufacturing automobiles is concerned, it is hardly probable that the original promoters ever contemplated making more than were sufficient to carry through the stupendous bluff they had undertaken. They cared little what became of the company after it had served their speculative purposes."

That Electric Vehicle was permitted to operate—with its principals enriching themselves for doing little but file lawsuits and cash royalty checks—was indicative of a larger problem, the editorial said: namely, unregulated banks and Wall Street schemers who saw in the new industry not opportunity to support a wondrous advance in civilization but opportunity to reap obscene profits at the expense of others, the many aspiring carmakers and their workers who lost their jobs when companies went under.

"The automobile was seized upon as a godsend by the manipulators of Wall Street," the *Horseless Age* said:

> It was the very thing which these "devourers of widows' houses" needed to dazzle the imaginations and stimulate the cupidity of their victims. The

automobile was a novelty. Its practical uses were not known, and its possibilities were therefore capable of as vast [an] extension as the stock of the companies they formed to "exploit" it. This was the Wall Street serpent's favorite lure.

A servile press was easily enlisted in the work of hypnotizing the public while the serpent gorged itself on its prey, returning to its lair to lie in wait for other prey. Safe and secure from harm under our present laws, the wily serpent of Wall Street lives and plots in his gilded den, creeping stealthily forth into every industrial garden of promise, squeezing, crushing, blighting and destroying, extending its scaly folds even into the remotest corners of the land to bring idleness, suffering, want and suicide to millions unconscious of his power. When will we scotch this snake and save our national honor from stain and our infant industries from spoilation?

Worse than damning words was an action by a carmaking giant.

Buick had belonged to ALAM since its 1904 incorporation, but by the end of 1907, Durant had joined Ford and had stopped paying royalties, which by virtue of Buick's prodigious production had been the highest of any member. A captain of his industry now, Durant had tired of ALAM's heavy-handed antics. He had better use for the money than lining the pockets of the guardians of a bogus patent.

ALAM responded with a suit seeking back royalties from Buick. But Durant stood firm.

"We are not paying any license fee," Buick attorney John J. Carton said in response. "We have concluded that the Selden patent does not mean anything."

---

ALAM WAS PREPARING ITS flimflam of a car for its New York tests when Ford raced for the final time. It happened in September 1907 at the Michigan State Fair, in Detroit, when he and driver Frank Kulick took turns driving Ford's newest racer: a six-cylinder car that he named the 666, which of course was 999, upside down. Like the car he raced on frozen Lake St. Clair, this machine was mostly engine.

Kulick, a longtime Ford employee, had established a reputation as a daredevil in the Oldfield style, and like Oldfield, he won races: at Grosse Pointe in 1903 and 1904, and in California, New York, Rhode Island, and other places in subsequent years. His greatest success was on June 21 and 22, when he and rookie L. B. Lorimer won a twenty-four-hour race at Detroit Fairgrounds, where the state fair was held, beating a Buick, among other vehicles. The rules permitted substitution of cars and drivers, and Kulick and Lorimer drove two Ford Model Ks a total of 1,135 miles—a new record, besting the previous twenty-four-hour distance of 1,094 and 3-16ths mile set on November 11, 1905, at Indianapolis.

At the Michigan State Fair, Kulick, another mechanic, and Ford alternated driving the 666 during a warm-up. Bringing it to full speed, Kulick lost control as it circled the track. The 666 plowed through a fence, shot into the air, and somersaulted twice, throwing Kulick. Someone telephoned a Detroit hospital, but when it refused to send an ambulance—the track was outside city limits—Ford himself drove Kulick there. Kulick had suffered a broken leg, and he walked with a limp after that, but he raced again.

Ford, however, was done. The members of his inner circle, who needed him to build a company, not risk his life racing, welcomed his decision. Ford drivers continued to race, but as Parker continued the patent fight, Ford could now devote all his time, safely, to business.

———

IN HIS ADS, FORD continued to emphasize his cars' quality and reliability, made possible thanks to comparatively long experience and quality control at the plant. "Ford cars are manufactured—have been made in immense quantities and by modern American methods from the first," read one ad. "And the first Ford ever made is still giving excellent service—what of the 'cut and try' contraptions made in that same year?"

Ford could produce such vehicles in large volume only by adopting economies of scale at the factory. Many competitors used a separately designed and built chassis for each of its models, an expensive proposition that contributed to many firms' bankruptcies—but Ford had decided to build just one chassis that could be used on more than one model.

A chance discovery had led to another innovation. Watching a race at Palm Beach one day in 1905, Ford happened to pick up a small part of a French automobile that had wrecked. It was lighter than the one he used in his own cars. Curious, he learned that it was made of vanadium steel—not only lighter, but stronger than the nickel steel he used. Finding no company in America that produced it, he tracked down a man in England who knew the process, which Ford conveyed to a small Ohio company that agreed to make it. The result was a material that not only reduced weight—it better withstood the punishment of bad roads, an enticement to consumers fed up with cars that easily broke.

As they aimed higher and higher, Ford and Couzens realized they needed an exceptional factory manager to implement better worker efficiencies, inventory control, buying practices, and the myriad other details of mass production. Such men were in short supply, but in 1906, they had succeeded in hiring Walter E. Flanders, a salesman and manager whose reputation in the machine-tool industry was without equal, to run the Bellevue and Piquette plants.

The result was a phenomenon: Model N sales took off in 1907, contributing to overall Ford sales of 8,423 vehicles in the fiscal year ending September 30, better than a 500 percent increase over 1906. Dollar sales rose to $5.7 million, nearly a fourfold increase. Net income was $1.1 million—more than ten times the prior year. Ford paid $100,000 in dividends.

But Ford was still only setting the stage for the car he would produce in unprecedented quantity; the car that the average Joe would feel he must have, and could afford.

With Spider Huff and a handful of others, Ford began designing the Model T in an experimental room he had created in a back corner on the third floor of his Piquette plant. There, in that small locked space with its drafting equipment, tools, and chalkboard, and his late mother's rocking chair, the car began to take shape. Ford's son, Edsel, a teenager now—and the future president of Ford Motor Company—often came by after school to spend evenings there with his dad.

The "experimental room" where the T was born.
Courtesy of The Ford Piquette Avenue Plant National Historic Landmark.

By the spring of 1908, a prototypical T had been built. Ford rode in it through downtown Detroit, making sure to drive past the office of Malcomson, whose insistence on the big, costly Model K had spelled his doom with his former partner.

Ford was ebullient.

"Well, I guess we've got started," he said.

In late October 1907, the Automobile Club of America partnered with the American Motor Car Manufacturers' Association to stage the club's eighth annual fall show at Grand Central Palace in New York. Before departing Detroit, Ford allowed a reporter a look at the Model N, Model S, and a $1,000 landaulet/taxicab version of the Model S that he would be exhibiting. Apparently flattered that Ford would find time for him, the reporter repaid him handsomely with a theatrical account.

> When the cab, clean-cut and eye-pleasing, beautifully finished and upholstered, was revealed by Mr. Ford and the approximate price named, the Motor World man was moved to protest. But the Henry Ford characteristic at once asserted itself.

"That's all it's worth," he snapped.

It was suggested that double that price easily could be obtained for every one produced—a suggestion which merely served to bring out more of the Ford philosophy in quick-fire epigrammatic reply.

"You can never sell many of anything for more than it's worth," he responded.

"That's what it's worth," he went on. "It's the price we set for it in the first place and it's the lowest price at which it can be made and sold in the largest quantities. By at once setting the price at that figure, competition is eliminated before it starts."

"Look here," Ford continued rapidly. "Look what we saved yesterday on one contract alone! On one part, the cost of dies was $1,400. To build one hundred machines would be $14 each. On the 10,000 we will build it will be 14 cents each. Work that same thing through the whole car and you can get some idea of how we are able to do it. There's vanadium wherever there is stress, the cab weighs only 1,600 pounds, and it will wear better and be far cheaper to maintain than anything of its kind in the world."

Ford teased the reporter with a hint of something much, much bigger on the horizon. "If there are those who lulled themselves with the notion that Henry Ford and the Ford Motor Co. was resting on the laurels gained by reason of their popular priced four-cylinder runabout and six-cylinder touring car, they will have reason for a startling awakening," the reporter wrote. "For far from resting on laurels or anything else, Ford and his associates have quietly been preparing another series of sensations, one of which at least will prove in the nature of forked lightning."

## GENERAL MOTORS

On the day that Ford showed the *Motor World* reporter his models, Otto Heinze, brother of banker and United Copper mining magnate Fritz A. Heinze, began buying shares of United Copper company as part of a financial manipulation scheme he believed would make a fortune. Instead, the ploy collapsed, the price of United Copper shares plummeted, fear spread, and the Panic of 1907 was underway. Wall Street was ravaged and banks and trust companies failed as depositors made runs on their money. The chaos rippled into the larger economy, which was already experiencing a period of contraction that had resulted in bankruptcies, decreased industrial output, and high unemployment throughout the country.

The battered economy punished the automobile industry, already so volatile. Among the companies that went bankrupt were St. Clair, Huber, Marvel, Detroit Auto Vehicle Company, and Malcomson's Aerocar—and these were just the Detroit-based firms. Even Ford experienced difficulties during that fall: more than once, payday had to be postponed.

But Ford had the resources to weather the panic. Olds Motor Works, already on the ropes, was pushed to the brink.

The Smiths' debt continued to mount as the year 1907 ended with still more dire numbers. Olds was phasing the Curved Dash out of production, in favor of the bigger cars that obsessed Smith, but in 1907, Smith's obsession was poisoning the company more gravely than ever. Olds's new Model A—essentially, a Model S Palace Touring, only $500 more expensive—sold poorly, as did the Model H Flying Roadster, another minimal advance over the Gentleman's Roadster that also upped its $2,750 price by an additional $500. A limousine model, the company's first enclosed vehicle, went for $3,800. But Oldsmobile sold just 1,200 total vehicles in 1907, some 30 percent fewer than 1906. The stunning decline that began with Smith's first year as Olds chief was accelerating.

So one had to wonder if Smith had lost command of his faculties with his decision to introduce the Olds Model Z. The seven-passenger Z did offer an unprecedented 48 horsepower from its massive six-cylinder, 543-cdi engine—and embodied other technical advances as well. These made for an appealing sales pitch—until it came to price. At $4,200, excluding an optional top, the Model Z was Olds's costliest car yet. For that kind of money, a buyer could purchase any number of fine automobiles at equal or better value, by such marquee companies as Packard and Pierce-Arrow.

Smith's folly was now nearly complete. One could almost feel pity for this man who had ousted Ransom Olds—now king of Reo, one of America's largest car companies.

DURANT WAS HOME ONE night in late 1907 or early 1908 when he got a call from Benjamin Briscoe of Maxwell-Briscoe, a charter member of the American Motor Car Manufacturers' Association. Briscoe, one of the investors in the tiny Buick Company that Durant had propelled to market leader, had founded Maxwell-Briscoe with Jonathan Maxwell, a former Olds employee who had been instrumental in designing the Curved Dash. (Maxwell-Briscoe was the progenitor of the Chrysler Corporation.)

Would Durant be interested in discussing a merger, not just of Buick and his own company, but possibly many others? Briscoe wanted to know.

Durant was naturally intrigued.

The men talked the next day over breakfast at a Flint hotel, and then at Durant's Buick office. Briscoe wanted to involve nearly two dozen companies, but Durant saw a better chance of success with a less unwieldy group. He suggested reaching out to Reo and Ford, which both made cars sold in the same low- and medium-price range as Buick.

When Durant and Briscoe contacted Ransom Olds, he was interested. And Ford was at least willing to hear the pitch. A meeting of the four men was arranged in Detroit, with a follow-up meeting involving lawyers and investors in New York. Members of J.P. Morgan & Co. agreed to provide some financing. Ford demanded $3 million in cash to continue the negotiation—whereupon Olds demanded an equivalent payment. Salesman though he was, Durant did not believe he could raise $6 million, and the talks ended.

With Ford and Reo out, Durant and Briscoe decided to merge just their two companies—a merger that still would create the largest US automobile manufacturer. The J.P. Morgan & Co. principals were interested in underwriting the combine. Discussions continued in secrecy, but somehow the *New York Times* got wind. It published its scoop on July 31, in a story with a bold headline and three subheads at the top of a business page.

"The first big combination in the automobile world is now in the making," the paper wrote, "the plans calling for a company to be known as the International Motor Company, with $25,000,000 capital, $11,000,000 common and $14,000,000 preferred stock. Among the underwriters of the $900,000 of preferred stock which will be first put out, it is understood, [are] several members of the banking house of J.P. Morgan & Co., although the banking house does not figure in the transaction. If the negotiations now under way are successful, the company will be ready for operations by Sept. 1."

The *Times* sources were good. The story correctly identified the two major firms to be joined, Buick and Maxwell-Briscoe. It correctly named the attorneys involved in the transaction and some of the more detailed exchanges of stock among Buick, Maxwell-Briscoe, and the proposed new International Motor Company. It speculated, fairly, that the new company could produce 15,000 cars in 1908, a remarkable output. And it hinted at more consolidation to come as Durant and Briscoe achieved unprecedented clout.

But the *Times* story did not sit well with the J.P. Morgan financiers.

From New York, Briscoe wrote to Durant in Michigan that the publicity had left the financiers "in something of a chaotic state" and "very upset," though their reaction perplexed him. "Why they should feel it as deeply as they do I can't quite fathom myself," he wrote.

Whether they had already soured on the deal or really were spooked by the unwanted look behind their closed doors was never clear to Briscoe or Durant, but the deal collapsed.

Having glimpsed greater things, Durant wasn't ready to quit. Under his leadership, Buick had prospered, producing 4,641 cars in 1907, up from 1,400 the year before—and it was on track to build 8,820 vehicles in 1908. In the month of June, it had set an industry record: a total of 1,654 vehicles from its two main plants in Flint and Jackson. As impressive as that was, it was unlikely Durant could soon reach the numbers promised by International Motor Company in his two factories alone. So he went to Plan B.

Samuel Smith and sons Angus and Fred were Plan B.

———

THIS YEAR FOR Olds Motor Works was unfolding even more abysmally than 1907.

The company would build just fifty-five Model Zs in 1908, and total vehicle output would fall to 1,055, barely one-fourth the glorious year of

1903. By the summer of 1908, Smith family debt had risen to about $1 million and was still climbing. Having already discussed possibilities with Fred, Durant now urged him to ask whether his brother and father would be receptive to a way stop their unchecked bleeding. He was not being charitable: he saw potential in the Olds brand. After all, it was not so long ago that "In My Merry Oldsmobile" had been a hit song of the land.

"While that company was not a financial success, I believed it had possibilities," Durant later said.

By early September, Durant and the Smiths had agreed to a complicated stock swap worth just over $3 million that would not only relieve the Smiths of their debt but would give them a stake in the new company. Fred Smith would get a seat on its executive board. Durant would get Oldsmobile's assets and the Olds brand, tarnished but ready for a good repolishing.

With "International Motor Company" no longer feasible for a name, Durant ran other possibilities past his New York lawyers. For tax purposes, the company would be incorporated in New Jersey—but the lawyers found that one name Durant liked, "United Motors Company," was too close to an existing "United Motor Car Company" already registered in the state.

On September 10, the lawyers wrote to Durant: "We suggest the name 'General Motors Company,' which we have ascertained can be used."

Six days later, papers of incorporation were filed with New Jersey's secretary of state.

Olds Motor Works already had its 1909 line planned when General Motors was formed, and Smith's stamp was all over it: among the offerings were a new $3,500 coupe and a Model Z with a bigger engine that developed 60 horsepower. Durant needed no Ouija Board to see how that would end. Moving swiftly, he instructed his managers to conduct a makeover of the popular Buick Model 10, which sold for $1,000, and to put the Olds name on it.

The resulting car, the Olds Model 20, was essentially no different than its Buick counterpart—but with its Olds radiator and hood, it looked sufficiently new, at least to an ordinary consumer, that Durant believed he could charge $200 more for it, a tidy profit for little work.

He was right. At $1,200, General Motors's Olds Model 20 moved by the hundreds.

## THE AMAZING T

Ford followed his tease to the *Motor World* reporter with another in the February 3, 1908, *Detroit News*. Regarding the Piquette factory, the paper wrote: "There are now 500 men working at this plant, which number, it is expected, will be materially increased in the near future. Since January 15, about 150 men were put to work, and a night shift is also working." On March 19, Ford alerted dealers in the first circular the company sent mentioning the Model T. The response was explosive.

"It is without doubt the greatest creation in automobiles ever placed before a people," a Pennsylvania dealer wrote to Ford, "and it means that this circular alone will flood your factory with orders." Wrote a Detroit dealer: "We have rubbed our eyes several times to make sure we are not dreaming." An agent in Rockville, Illinois, wrote that the circular had been locked in a drawer, lest the secret get out. Inevitably, it did, not that Ford protested.

Less than two weeks had passed when the *Horseless Age* published a story.

"The leader of the Ford line for 1908 will be what will be known as Model T," the magazine wrote, "a four-passenger, 20 horse power touring car to sell for $850. Nothing has yet been given to the press regarding this model, but some confidential information has been given to dealers, and as is often the case, has been allowed to leak out."

The article described the car's one-hundred-inch wheelbase, light weight, vanadium steel, magneto ignition, multiple disc clutch, easily shifted planetary transmission, pedal-operated brakes, and other inviting features. It also noted a novelty that would soon become US industry standard: "The control levers and steering post are on the left hand side of the car, contrary to ordinary practice."

Following the tradition of horse-drawn carriages, most automobiles before the Model T that did not use tillers had the steering wheel on the right. Ford saw advantages in moving to the left. The rationale was spelled out in a Ford catalog:

> The control is located on the left side, the logical place, for the following reasons: Travelling along the right side of the road the steering wheel on the right side of the car made it necessary to get out on the street side and walk around the car. This is awkward and especially inconvenient if there is a lady to be considered. The control on the left allows you to step out of the car on to the curbing without having had to turn the car around. In the matter of steering with the control on the right, the driver is farthest away from the vehicle he is passing, going in opposite direction; with it on the left side he is able to see even the wheels of the other car and easily avoids danger.

---

BUT THE PLACEMENT OF the steering wheel was only the beginning. The revolutionary nature of the Model T was not its appearance: on style alone, it was somewhere between ugly and ho-hum, although its utilitarian look would become as uniquely branded as its name (despite other companies, including Cadillac, having already produced cars they called "Model T"). Its genius was utility. The four-cylinder engine produced 20 horsepower, sufficient for any hill or road condition given its weight, just 1,200 pounds, thanks to the vanadium steel. The sixteen-and-one-half-gallon gas tank for the runabout model promised long trips without re-gassing, and the ten-gallon tank for the touring was generous, too. The sturdy springs, suspension, and wheels promised toughness. The engine, transmission, and drive shaft were enclosed—a further protection of the guts of the vehicle from ruts, rocks, and other enemies. Replacing the familiar but ornery dry battery was a magneto, one of Huff's contributions, that generated spark with every revolution of the flywheel. And all for $825 and up, depending on model—a bargain that no competitor could beat.

Ford could profit at those price points because he had not started from scratch. In his 1922 memoir, Ford chronicled the evolution of his Models

A, B, C, F, N, R, S, and K, listing successive improvements in the stroke, horsepower, and cylinders of their engines, and the similar innovations in clutch, transmission, drive, ignition, and more—all reaching crescendo with the car he would introduce on October 1, 1908.

"The Model T had practically no features which were not contained in some one or other of the previous models," Ford wrote. "Every detail had been fully tested in practice. There was no guessing as to whether or not it would be a successful model. It had to be. There was no way it could escape being so, for it had not been made in a day."

---

IN PHASING OUT PRODUCTION of the Model N to prepare for the October debut of the Model T, Ford set new industry records—building, on June 4, in a ten-hour day, 101 automobiles. Workers completed and tested one of them in just fourteen minutes. This extraordinary pace was made possible in the cramped Piquette plant in part by the use of a monorail, cranes, hoists, and other innovations that were a precursor to Ford's moving assembly and overhead conveyor lines that soon would revolutionize automobile manufacturing.

Ford reached a steady daily production of one hundred cars by the middle of summer. That would seem inconsequential when the new Highland Avenue plant, which the leading architectural firm of Albert Kahn Associates had begun designing, opened.

"The time is only measured by months when this hundred-car figure will be multiplied by five," Ford predicted.

---

ON OCTOBER 1, 1908, Ford Motor Company began deliveries of the Model T.

Like all cars of the era, it was flawed. Starting it in winter was difficult; the rear-axle bearings did not take bumps well, necessitating replacement; and the riveting was of inferior quality, among other problems. Ford had designed the car with different size wheels: three inches wide in the

front, three and a half in the rear, which meant drivers had to carry separate sets of inner tubes and tires as spares, an inconvenience that prompted
complaints.

But the virtues greatly outweighed the drawbacks.

"The biggest value ever announced in automobiles," read an ad published in the Joliet, Illinois, *Evening Herald* in early spring 1909. "A car
designed by Henry Ford, who never designed a failure. . . . It has speed if
you want speed, forty or fifty miles an hour if you need it. It has power:
There isn't a hill in this country that this car with its load will not climb. If
you want endurance [and] long life, the Model T's useful life, with ordinary care, will exceed five or six years. If you desire economy of maintenance, this car will travel more miles, more days, for less money than any
other. . . . "

Consumers across America responded to the Model T with a frenzied
enthusiasm that the motoring world had never seen.

"We are building and shipping more cars than at any similar business,
but the orders have already reached a total in excess of any previous entire
season's business," *Ford Times*, the company's new publication, reported
on May 1, 1909.

Not content with advertisements and word of mouth alone, Ford called
on the old racing formula again. Two Model Ts were among the cars that
left New York on June 1 in a race to Seattle sponsored by the Automobile
Club of America, with a $2,000 prize and trophy donated by Robert Gug-
genheim. Arriving in downtown Seattle at 12:55 p.m. on June 23, one of
Ford's new cars won. Here was proof positive of the company's claims of
reliability and endurance. The fact that the crew of the winning Model T
had changed engines mid-race, against rules, did not figure in the promotion. In November, the ACA stripped the Ford of its title, awarding first
place to the second-place car, built by Shawmut of Stoneham, Massachusetts. It was small consolation to Shawmut, which had gone out of business
by then, and of little concern to Ford, who was moving every Model T he
could build.

When the books closed for the fiscal year on September 30, 1909, the
phenomenon had helped boost overall Ford sales to 10,607 vehicles, 4,209
more than 1908. Dollar sales more than doubled, to $9.04 million. During

Henry Ford with his Model T.
From the Collections of The Henry Ford.

the 1909 year, the company made eleven dividend payments amounting to $1.3 million. Thanks to the Model T, many more fabulous years lay just ahead.

PERCY MEGARGEL'S DREAMS OF writing and adventure ended at 1:23 a.m. on May 2, 1909, when he died in his New York City apartment, a victim of cancer that had spread through his body, slowly wasting him away. He was thirty-four years old.

After returning to Manhattan in June 1906 from his double continental crossing, Megargel had sought new excitement in flying. He joined the Aero Club of America and solicited advice from pioneering long-distance balloonist George L. Tomlinson on how to build an airship of his own. But motoring and writing remained his passions.

When he learned that the *New York Times* was sponsoring a New York–to–Paris automobile race in 1908, a more outrageous proposition than the 1905 Oldsmobile contest—and an irrefutable sign that the paper now fully endorsed motoring—he endeavored to find a car and a sponsor for the historic odyssey, which included passage by ship from the West Coast across the Pacific Ocean to Asia. The *Times* itself reported his efforts, and for a few weeks in early 1908 cited him as an authority in long-distance contests. But Megargel had failed to find a sponsor. Six contestants left Times Square on February 12, and when they reached Rochester, Megargel played the smallest of parts, leading the automobiles to Batavia, halfway to Buffalo.

Megargel did have one last hurrah. Collaborating with Grace Sartwell Mason, a popular novelist and short-story writer, he finished his novel, *The Car and the Lady*, a fictionalized account of his 1905 race against Huss—with a pitch for better roads and a torrid love affair thrown in. "It is a romance seen through the log-book of an actual journey," Megargel and Mason wrote in the book's foreword. "The authors hope that, with the progress of good highways across this fascinating continent of ours, more motorists may feel the lure of the American road."

Publisher Baker and Taylor felt so strongly about the book that its publicists were flogging the title months before its August 1908 publication, prompting the *San Francisco Call* on March 29 to hail it as "the first purely American automobile romance, the first to deal with difficulties encountered by motorists in touring the great unknown west, where quicksands abound and the road becomes a trail." The reviews were favorable when the book appeared. "Exciting events in plenty, and the story moves with appropriate swiftness," wrote the *New York Times*. "There can be no doubt of the breathless interest of the story," declared the Washington, DC, *Evening Star*.

Megargel's new fame was short-lived. His obituary in the *Scranton Times*, published in the city where he had been born and raised, laid blame for his death on the blizzard that trapped him near Flagstaff, Arizona, in late 1905.

"Coming across the continent, he encountered a terrible snowstorm in the southwest, his car became snowbound, and for several days no trace of him could be found," the obituary said. "When he was finally discovered, it was found that he had suffered terribly from the cold and exposure. This experience, it is said, greatly impaired his former robust health and his death is believed to be the outcome of the thrilling trip he made."

## VERDICTS RENDERED

On Friday, May 28, shortly after Megargel was buried, lawyers for Ford and ALAM assembled in Judge Charles M. Hough's courtroom in the Old Post Office Building in Manhattan. Finally, closing arguments in the Selden case were about to begin. Ford himself was present for the occasion.

Parker was concerned with Hough's assignment to the case: the judge's expertise was in admiralty law, not automobile patents. And Parker feared he would be impatient hearing the many minute technical details that he intended to argue in making his case, inclining the judge to be more receptive to ALAM's lawyers, who planned to present a broader and more easily digested interpretation of automobile patent law.

"Hough is said to be cranky & I *know* he is *not* a patent judge," Parker had written to Ford earlier in the year. But there Hough was, wielding the gavel.

Parker's fears were realized early in the proceedings. During a discussion of engine compression, Hough admitted that he did not comprehend technical fine points.

"All the discussion as to differences of type of the various engines, if they are a liquid hydrocarbon gas engine of the compression type, would seem to me at present to be beside the issue," he said. "Refined arguments on differences of machines seem to obscure the main issue."

And Hough indeed was receptive to the ALAM lawyers' broader argument that technical details mattered less than George Selden's broader stature as a visionary whose basic ideas, if not specific blueprints and drawings, made him the legitimate father of the automobile.

"It was not the work for a mechanic," argued Frederick P. Fish. "A poet might have done it."

On June 1, Hough appeared to signal what his decision would be. "If a man can see plainly what the future will bring forth," he said, "and indicates the lines along which development is going to take place, and suggests, not a perfect, but a feasible line of bringing that result to pass, is not such a person entitled to a combination patent?"

Hough was not without humor. When Ford left the courtroom to watch Mayor McClellan fire a gold-plated revolver to start the New York–to–Seattle race that one of his two Model Ts won, the judge watched with attorneys through the Old Post Office windows.

A lawyer on Ford's side said, "Your Honor, there is something that puzzles me. I don't see a Selden car. I see a Ford car, two Ford cars, but I see no Selden car!"

Hough laughed, along with the others.

---

THE FINAL ARGUMENTS WERE concluded after six days. Hough left for his vacation home in Rhode Island. He arranged for the massive case record to be shipped to him there, and he spent much of the summer studying it.

Back in New York on September 15, he rendered his verdict.

"Success is never anticipated by any number of failures, and when it is clearly kept in mind that what Selden claims is a combination, and not any one of its elements, the defendants' references to prior patents and publications may thus be finally disposed of so far as this court is concerned," he ruled.

The patent was upheld. ALAM could continue to collect royalties—and sue nonlicensed manufacturers.

Flush with cash from his Model T, and more resolute than ever after six years of war with ALAM, Ford vowed another battle. He would appeal Hough's decision.

"Selden suit decision has no effect on Ford policy," he said in a telegram to one of his dealers the day after Hough ruled. "We will fight to a finish." He later told the *Detroit News* that he would not stop until Hough's decision was overturned, even if it took all of his company's assets. "There will be no let-up in the legal fight, and I expect that ultimately the Supreme Court of the United States will hold that the Selden basic patent is not valid," he said.

Ford's vow drew high praise.

A March 1, 1910, Detroit *Free Press* editorial began "Ford, the fighter, salute!" and declared him "equal to his weight in wildcats. . . . As a human being he presents a spectacle to win the applause of all men with red blood; for this world dearly loves the fighting man, and needs him too, if we are to go forward."

ALAM, however, was jubilant.

Some nonlicensed manufacturers began paying royalties.

––––––––––

GENERAL MOTORS PROSPERED WILDLY in 1909, with production increasing and Durant, never satisfied, buying more companies. One prize was Cadillac, which he purchased for $4.75 million from Wilfred C. Leland and his father Henry M. Leland. General Motors in 1909 made a profit of more than $9 million, on net sales of $29 million. Another company Durant wanted, but did not get, was Ford Motor Company. Durant offered $8 million, but Ford was not interested.

Durant began 1910 with his typical energy and ambition. GM had already bought, or was about to, more than twenty-four companies, including Champion Ignition, Novelty Incandescent Lamp Company, Oak Park Power Company, and several more automobile firms, notably Oakland, Reliance, Rapid, Rainier, Elmore, and Welch. GM produced some 20 percent of all cars made in the United States in 1910, achieving sales of nearly $50 million.

But Durant had expanded too rapidly and recklessly, and the house he'd built on debt began to creak and moan. The banks and suppliers wanted their money—and it was a lot of money. Meeting in New York in August, GM's creditors learned that Buick's debt alone totaled from $6.7 to $7.7 million.

"My bankers, up to that time, had been more than generous, but there is nothing more sensitive, more sought after, more god-like, if I can use the term, in the minds of the great majority of men, than money," Durant later recalled. He felt betrayed, but also responsible.

"We sometimes pay dearly for overconfidence," he said, "and in this case, I did pay plenty."

Durant walked the streets of Flint alone after dark, lost in thought, but he could devise no way out of the worsening mess that would not threaten his control of GM, the company he later described as "'my baby,' born and raised by me, the result of hectic years of night and day work and diligent applications." On September 26, 1910, Durant agreed to a bailout that was as complex as many of his acquisition deals. And it carried an exorbitant price, both in real dollars and the personal cost to Durant.

In return for an infusion of $15 million into General Motors, the bankers received a commission of more than $6 million in GM stock and a mortgage to all of GM's properties in Michigan. More grievously for Durant, they assumed control of the company for at least the five-year term of the loan. The founder remained vice president, but it was now a powerless position.

The loan agreed to on September 26 was issued in November. General Motors's new banker bosses quickly sold or consolidated some GM subsidiaries and took other measures—few, if any, Durant believed, that were in the best interests of making cars.

"Many of the new men, friends of the parties in control—splendid men, no doubt, in lines in which they were familiar—never having had experience in, or with, automobile design and production, with ideas of their own as to how business should be run, trained in banking rather than practical lines, made my position a difficult one," Durant said.

> I had been given a title and a position, but the support, the cooperation, the spirit, the unselfishness that is needed in every successful undertaking, was not there. In a way, it was the same old story, "too many cooks": a board of directors comprised of bankers, actions by committees, and the lack of knowledge that comes only from experience.
>
> I saw some of my cherished ideas laid aside for future action, never to be revived. Opportunities that should have been taken care of with quickness and decision were not considered. The things that counted so much

in the past, which gave General Motors its unique and powerful position, were subordinated to "liquidate and pay."

————

ON NOVEMBER 22, 1910, the parties to the Selden suit gathered again at the Old Post Office Building to begin arguments and submit written briefs in Ford's appeal. More than forty lawyers were present. A panel of three justices with the US Circuit Court of Appeals for the Second Circuit was hearing the case.

Having decided that other lawyers more familiar with the court could better argue the case, Parker had deferred to the well-respected New York attorneys Edmund S. Wetmore and Livingston Gifford to handle Ford's appearance. Parker took an advisory role. He deemed the three judges more favorable than Hough; one, Walter C. Noyes, had deep experience with patent cases. On Friday, November 25, the oral arguments ended. Gifford had taken all but a few minutes of the Ford side's allotted four and one-half hours. The lawyer for Panhard, fellow defendant, took the rest.

On January 9, 1911, the parties returned to court. Noyes read the three judges' decision.

They ruled decisively, completely, for Ford and Panhard.

Selden, Noyes said, deserved nothing. "These defendants . . . ," he declared, "neither legally nor morally owe him anything."

More stingingly, Noyes said, in an echo of Henry Ford's own dismissal of George Selden, US Patent Number 549,160 was worse than useless: it had proven harmful.

"From the point of view of public interest, it were better even that the patent had never been granted," the judge said.

After seven years, two months, and seventeen days, after hundreds of individuals had been sued or called as witnesses, and millions spent on legal fees and public relations, after a case record of more than 14,000 pages and 5 million words had been written—the scarecrow was dead.

————

WORD OF THE DECISION, which came on the eve of auto show week in New York, prompted an outpouring of congratulatory letters and telegrams to Ford, and a flurry of flattering newspaper stories. "I hope the great American public will awake to the result and not fail to appreciate the champion of their rights against trust methods," wrote Charles Duryea. The *Detroit Journal* hailed the outcome as "a declaration of liberty and equality of opportunity." Calling it "the great sensation of the decade," *Automobile Topics* reprinted the entire decision, eleven pages long.

ALAM did not even hint at an appeal. Rather, the organization seemed relieved to be rid of a case that had been intended as a weapon against competitors but had wound up a noose around members' necks. If his memoir of a decade later is to be believed, even Fred Smith agreed too much had been wasted on what he, with the benefit of hindsight, at least, held as a dubious proposition.

"By what miracle that flimsy patent was ever sustained in the lower court, I know not," he wrote. But Smith did not show remorse.

Once more, George Selden felt the pain of rejection. *Engineering News* was among those to excoriate him. "As a means of levying blackmail," the publication wrote, "the Selden automobile patent is doubtless the most remarkable."

Whatever his true feelings, Selden—who had profited greatly financially but who at last had been confirmed a fool—publicly shrugged the decision off. "I have succeeded much better than I expected," he said, "and as my patent has but a year or two to run, the decision has no severe significance."

Ford did not join in the public condemnation. "He was a decent old fellow," he later said of Selden. "But when others began to make automobiles, he got into the hands of those who wanted to exploit the industry by claiming tribute from every motor car manufacturer."

———

ON JANUARY 11, AS he was about to leave by train for New York, Ford declined a Detroit *Free Press* reporter's request for a comment. "Whatever

I'd say now might sound like boasting," Ford said. "I think the decision speaks for itself."

Ford was hailed when he reached Manhattan—and not just by his supporters. ALAM officials invited him, Couzens, and lawyer Benton Crisp to their annual banquet, held at the Hotel Astor on January 12. They wanted, in their way, to thank the victors.

"The presence of the erstwhile enemies who had fought so long, so violently and so successfully to establish the fact that they had not infringed the Selden patent was whispered of in the lobby, where the diners gathered before going into the banqueting room," *Automobile Topics* wrote in a story headlined, "A.L.A.M Banquet Is a Love-Feast."

When Ford and his men entered, the magazine wrote, "They were warmly welcomed, and on every side one heard remarks to the effect that it was a happy thought to invite these special guests and a gracious and courageous act to accept."

Ford declined to speak, but he received thunderous applause when he rose and waved a pipe in a peace offering to ALAM president Charles Clifton. In his talk, Clifton praised the decision, which, he said, had unified the industry. "He went on to say that in defeat, the ALAM found its victory and that the old order was ended and it gave him pleasure to usher in the new," *Automobile Topics* wrote.

An industry that had been at war with itself for nearly eight years had, for the moment, reached a truce.

———

DURING THE FISCAL YEAR that ended on September 30, 1911, Ford sold 34,528 cars, nearly double sales of the year before, and more than twenty times its first full year, 1904. Dollar sales reached $24.56 million, almost 175 times the first year, an astonishing increase. Net income was $7.33 million—nearly thirty times that of 1904. Ford employed an average of 3,976 workers in 1911. In 1904, the workforce had averaged just three hundred.

Ford's growth was extraordinary, but it had not happened in a vacuum. American manufacturers produced almost 200,000 passenger cars in 1911, nearly fifty times the output in 1900. Motor vehicle registrations totaled 639,000, almost 8,000 percent of 1900. Two years later, they would pass the million mark.

"A new motor carriage . . . if the preliminary tests prove successful as expected, will revolutionize the mode of travel on highways, and do away with the horse as a means of transportation," a reporter with the Massachusetts *Springfield Evening Union* wrote in September 1893 as Frank Duryea was about to test a prototype of the car he and his brother would sell.

The reporter's assessment had come true, and then some. And with the ascension of the new machine, American life had been fundamentally changed, forever.

# EPILOGUE


The federal appeals court decision that handed Ford his unqualified victory in the Selden patent case unleashed the American automobile industry.

Five years later, manufacturers' production passed the 1 million mark, reaching a remarkable 1.52 million automobiles. American motor-vehicle registrations during the five-year period jumped to 3.6 million, an increase of better than 500 percent.

The Ford Motor Company produced 735,020 vehicles in the US in the firm's fiscal year ending September 30, 1916. In 1921, Ford US production reached the million mark. In 1923, the firm produced 1.8 million Ford cars in the US—2.1 million total vehicles, when trucks, tractors, and Lincoln cars were counted. Canadian and foreign production brought the 1923 total to 2.2 million vehicles. Ford bought Lincoln in 1922, when the firm, founded by former Cadillac head Henry Leland and his son, went bankrupt. With its Model T leading the way, Ford Motor Company had won the race for the mass market.

After strokes and a cerebral hemorrhage, Henry Ford died at the age of eighty-three on April 7, 1947, at Fair Lane, his estate in Dearborn, Michigan, where Ford Motor Company is headquartered today. Ford's vision of the automobile as a fixture of everyday life for most Americans had long since come true. His obituary led the front page of the *New York Times* on April 8, and on April 9, an estimated 75,000 people, some having waited in a line a mile long, paid their respects as he lay in state in Greenfield Village, the living museum he had built. At 2:30 p.m. on April 11, when his funeral began at St. Paul's Episcopal Church in Detroit, drivers across Michigan stopped their vehicles. "Literally, the whole state stood still," the *Times* reported.

Ford was remembered as the most successful of the American automobile pioneers and one of the wealthiest people on the planet, a man whose "career was one of the most astonishing in industrial history," the *Times* said. But his reputation was tarnished by his 1920s sponsorship of the anti-Semitic the *Dearborn Independent*, source of articles reprinted in the four-volume *The International Jew: The World's Foremost Problem*. Ford later was sued for libel and apologized, but the harm had been done.

Fred Smith died in Beverly Hills, California, on August 6, 1954, at the age of eighty-four, leaving only his wife, Norah. He had played no major role in the auto industry after Durant brought Oldsmobile into General Motors, but he did leave insights in his 1928 memoir, *Motoring Down a Quarter of a Century*. Part autobiography, part history, Smith's slim book contained no mention of Ransom Olds but instead entirely credited himself and his father with making Oldsmobile such a fabulous success through 1903. It did not mention how he then ruined the company. And Smith was ludicrous in writing that ALAM "had served a useful purpose with a minimum of damage to the individual by bringing order into the business in the critical days when chaos threatened."

Cast from General Motors, Durant returned to automobile manufacturing on November 3, 1911, when he co-founded Chevrolet with Louis Chevrolet, who had once raced Durant's Buicks. In 1916, he bought sufficient shares in GM to control it again; he served as president until 1920, bringing Chevrolet into the corporation. Durant lost a fortune estimated at $120 million in the crash of 1929 and passed the rest of his life basically penniless. He told someone who visited him in 1940 in Flint, where at the age of seventy-eight he was running a bowling alley and planning to build a chain of them: "I haven't a dollar. But I'm happy and I'm carrying on because I can't stop. There's much more to life than money." Durant died on March 18, 1947. He was eighty-five.

After wearying of internal management friction, Ransom Olds gave up the title of general manager of Reo in 1915 and of president in 1923, when he became chairman of the board. The Great Depression crippled Reo, and Olds's effort in 1934 to restructure the company failed. Done with passenger cars, Reo made trucks until 1954, when it sold its production facilities. After a period of bad health that left him in a coma, Olds, eighty-six, died on August 26, 1950, at his mansion in Lansing.

Barney Oldfield died at age sixty-eight at his Beverly Hills home on October 4, 1946, of an apparent heart attack. He was one of the few prominent racers from the early era to die of natural causes. His *New York Times* obituary listed race cars he had driven: the 999, Green Dragon, Bullet, Golden Submarine, Big Ben, Blitzen Benz, and 120 Benz. Oldfield lost all his money during the 1929 crash, after which he took a job with Plymouth as, ironically, a highway safety adviser. He last made speed headlines in 1932, when he vowed to be the first man to drive three hundred miles an hour, but his plans ended when British racer Sir Malcolm Campbell hit 301.3 miles per hour on September 3, 1935, on Utah's Bonneville Salt Flats. Oldfield was married four times.

Selden died on January 17, 1922, after suffering a stroke and was buried in Rochester's Mt. Hope Cemetery. He went to his grave, at the age of seventy-five, still claiming to be the father of the automobile: his tombstone contains an engraving of the 1877 buggy and the inscription, "Inventor of the Gasoline Automobile." At last, no one could question him.

––––––––

THE FINAL OLDSMOBILE LEFT the assembly line at a GM factory in Lansing, Michigan, on April 29, 2004. Despite an effort begun in the late 1980s to rebrand it as new and exciting—"Not your father's Oldsmobile" was the mantra—the line had become tired, unappealing, and unprofitable. But the Buick and Cadillac brands have remained mainstays of the company Durant founded. The Chevrolet division, named for race-car driver Louis Chevrolet, has kept the spirit of racing alive with its Corvette. The 2015 model Z06 generates 650 horsepower—nearly one hundred times the power of a 1905 Curved Dash Olds.

The last decade has brought more changes at General Motors and in the industry. GM went bankrupt in 2009 during the global recession, was saved by a government bailout, and returned to profitability; Mary T. Barra, who became CEO in January 2014, is the first woman to head a major global car manufacturer. Chrysler, founded by former GM executive Walter P. Chrysler in 1925 from what was left of Maxwell-Briscoe, also experienced difficulties during the last decade: having been merged into Daimler-Benz AG in 1998 and then sold to an equity firm nine years later, it also went bankrupt in 2009 and was eventually acquired by Fiat. But Ford weathered the recession, requiring no bailout, and through their ownership of a special class of stock, the descendants of Henry Ford still control the company— and remain committed to innovation and excellence. Great-grandson William C. Ford Jr., who served several years as company CEO, president, and COO and is today executive chairman, has steered the company toward greater fuel efficiencies and hybrid and electric cars.

By 2015, the "Big Three" were the only major US carmakers left, with all of the other big manufacturers from the first three-fourths of the twentieth century—Packard, Hudson, Studebaker, and American Motors among them—having long since gone out of business. Vehicles from firms in Japan, which had only a primitive auto industry in the early 1900s, entered the US market in 1957, when Toyota began selling its Toyopet Crown; Korea, which had no car industry at all until the 1950s, also sold with great success in the American market starting when Hyundai began exporting its Excel model in 1986. German cars remain big sellers. Most automobiles still are gasoline-powered, but hybrids are selling in increasing numbers and the electric market is growing. Steam disappeared decades ago, and it is impossible to imagine how it could ever return.

The manufacture and assembly of automobiles in America today are concentrated in the Midwest, but US and foreign carmakers operate factories in states with little or no industry in the early 1900s, notably South Carolina, Alabama, and Texas. Manufacturers, suppliers, and dealers nationwide provide more than 7 million jobs that pay some $500 billion a year.

In 2012, the last year for which complete data are available, 265.6 million motor vehicles were registered in America—nearly one for every woman, man, and child. There were 211.8 million licensed drivers, who drove a total of 2.9 trillion miles.

And horses?

The predictions of Olds and Ford came true. The US Department of Agriculture calculates that the American horse population peaked at 19.8 million in 1910, the second full year of Model T production; when donkeys, mules, and burros are added, the total equine population was 24 million. Today, the horse population is less than half that of 1910, and the majority of the animals are engaged in recreation, showing, and racing.

———————

IN 1956, A CENTURY and a half after President Thomas Jefferson authorized construction of a national road, and three-fourths of a century after the League of American Wheelmen was organized, President Dwight Eisenhower signed the National Interstate and Defense Highways Act into law. Construction of the Interstate Highway System began. In 2012, the system included 47,432 miles of highway; those and another 175,514 miles of key roads together form the National Highway System. They are but a fraction of the nation's total 4.09 million miles of road, 2.98 million miles of those roads being in rural regions. Approximately 2.65 million miles are paved, but their conditions vary widely. In many areas of the country, the infrastructure is decaying.

Twenty-six motor vehicle fatalities were recorded in America in 1899. With some exceptions, notably during the Great Depression, the toll rose annually until reaching a peak of 54,589 deaths in 1972; with improvements in technology and other factors, the trend then began to reverse. In 2012, 33,561 people died in 5.6 million motor vehicle crashes, including 4,743 pedestrians and 726 bicyclists; 2.3 million people were injured. The federal government estimated the economic cost of this at $277 billion.

Another cost is the toll that motor vehicles have exacted on the environment, through seepage of fluids into soil and water and emissions released into the air, a significant factor in climate change. Improved technology and the advent of green cars have lessened the impact, but the appetite for carbon-based fuels remains huge: Americans used 168.3 billion gallons of motor-vehicle fuel in 2012. Thanks to increased engine efficiencies, that was down from the peak year of 2007, when 176.2 billion gallons were used.

Climate change has not been the only global cost of the motor vehicle. Many battles and wars have been caused, directly or indirectly, by mankind's insatiable thirst for oil.

------

As ANYONE EVER STUCK in rush-hour traffic or trying to cross a busy city street can attest, the rosy prediction that automobiles would ease or eliminate horse-drawn congestion was way off the mark. But the car did transform America, in ways more profound.

Along with commercial air travel, the automobile nearly killed intercity passenger rail service, and in some urban areas, it stifled the development of public transit. Conversely, the automobile was a major force in the well-documented expansion of suburbia. Vehicle manufacture was the foundation on which many related major industries rose: the fuel, repair, maintenance, accessories, rental, loan and finance, insurance, and motor-travel industries, among others.

The car has also profoundly influenced the culture, of course. Pioneered by Percy Megargel at the dawn of the American Century, the road trip became a favorite narrative form in literature, with John Steinbeck's *The Grapes of Wrath* and *Travels with Charley*, Jack Kerouac's *On the Road*, Tom Wolfe's *The Electric Kool-Aid Acid Test* and, more recently, Bill Bryson's *The Lost Continent: Travels in Small-Town America* and Michael Paterniti's *Driving Mr. Albert: A Trip Across America with Einstein's Brain* typifying the form. In film, think: *Easy Rider, Badlands,* and *Thelma & Louise,* and, within the last few years, *Little Miss Sunshine* and *Nebraska.* And does any action-adventure movie or TV episode not include a car race or chase? Starting with the 1905 hit "In My Merry Oldsmobile," music has been strongly influenced by cars, too: Kanye West, Taylor Swift, The Beatles, Bruce Springsteen, and Woody Guthrie are among the many musicians to write songs about driving. In the sporting world, NASCAR, Formula One, and IndyCar are among the many leagues that keep the speed traditions of Henry Ford and the early racers alive. Getting a license to drive remains a rite of passage, the first purchase a celebration of full independence. Cars can be symbols of power or status, a public image of self, or simply a means of transportation.

Whether driving a sedan, a pickup, a minivan, or a sports car, or just riding in a taxi or on a bus, most Americans cannot live without motor vehicles. Some side with Megargel, who agreed with fans who wrote him in 1905: "It's great to be crazy and ride around in an automobile." Others agree with Dwight Huss, who told *Life* magazine in a fiftieth-anniversary story about the 1904 parade to St. Louis: "The truth is, we'd all be better off if we'd never had any danged automobiles at all."

Fifteen years into the twenty-first century, some demographic groups—a percentage of Millennials and urban residents, for example—do not want or need a car, or cannot afford one. For them, public transportation, the bicycle, and the foot suffice.

As technology continues to advance, others feel excitement that the visionaries of the early twentieth century would surely share: Detroit having met Silicon Valley, the possibilities seem limitless. GPS navigation, rear-mounted radar, night vision with pedestrian detection, and onboard Internet, among other wonders, already are here. Biometric technologies that monitor a driver's condition—sobriety and attention to the road, for example—are in development. Battery improvements are making the electric car a more practical reality. Google is developing a driverless car. Solar-powered vehicles have achieved speeds of greater than fifty miles per hour.

"So get your minds fermenting; give your imagination free play; and invent the real limit of human daring. Show us how to fly to the moon," said Mademoiselle Mauricia de Tiers of Paris, the "aerial automobilist," 110 years ago.

Her words, too, ring true today.

# Acknowledgments

During the long gestation of this book, many people helped in many ways. My thanks to you all. Your research, observations, encouragement, and edits are deeply appreciated.

At The Henry Ford's Benson Ford Research Center in Dearborn, Michigan—the repository of all things Ford—my gratitude to Stephanie Lucas, Linda Skolarus, Rebecca Bizonet, Bart Bealmear, CarolAnn Missant, Lauren Stamm, Jim Orr, and former archivist Carol Whittaker. My hours spent in the Ford museum were invaluable, too.

The Detroit Public Library has a treasure of automotive history materials, and they proved invaluable. Thanks to Mark Bowden, coordinator for special collections, Burton Historical Collection; and Carrie Pruitt and Robert Tate of the National Automotive History Collection. Former NAHC assistant manager Paige Plant was also helpful.

At Michigan State University Archives and Historical Collections, where I found a rich vein of material about Ransom Olds, Fred Smith, Oldsmobile, and early motoring in general, thanks to Jennie Russell, assistant records archivist; Portio Vescio, assistant director; and Lisa M. Schmidt, electronic records archivist.

Christo Datini, lead archivist, GM Media Archive/GM Heritage Center, Sterling Heights, Michigan, helped me, as did Kathy Adelson, researcher, GM Media Archive; and Bill Van Luven and Dave Hederich, formerly with GM Heritage. I relied on the Antique Automobile Club of America for much, and my thanks to Steve Moskowitz, executive director; Chris Ritter, librarian, and Kim Miller, former librarian, AACA Library and Research Center; and Wes Peterson, editor in chief and art director, *Antique Automobile*, the AACA's publication.

William Adcock, executive director, R.E. Olds Museum in Lansing, Michigan, provided help, as did David C. White, archivist, Kettering University Archives, where William C. Durant's papers reside.

Gratitude to the many librarians and historians who gave of their time, including Linda Henderson; Gail Stein, archivist, Historical Collection, Beverly Hills Public Library; Karen L. Jania, reference archivist, Margaret A. Leary, volunteer reference librarian, and Emma E. Hawker, former project archivist, Bentley Historical Library, University of Michigan; Sandra P. Mundy, former director, and Linda Rivet, reference head, Jesse M. Smith Memorial Library, Harrisville, Rhode Island; Jim Davies, local history and reference librarian, Albany (New York) Public Library; Elizabeth Spring, metadata librarian at Rochester (New York) Public Library; Christine L. Ridarsky, city historian and historical services consultant, Rochester (New York) Public Library; William Keeler, librarian and archivist, Rochester (New York) Historical Society; Joan Gosnell, Terre Heydari, and Anne E. Peterson of the DeGolyer Library at Southern Methodist University; Nancy Darga, of the Ford Piquette Avenue Plant in Detroit; Jaime Bourassa, with the Missouri History Museum Library and Research Center; and the New Baltimore (Michigan) Historical Society. Thanks also to Doug R. Hecox and Richard F. Weingroff of the Federal Highway Administration; Geoff Sundstrom, former director of national publications for AAA; and Carol Lee (Berk) Boyce of Isla Vista, California, for information about Ernest Keeler.

Several antique car owners and experts assisted me. My thanks to Curved Dash Olds owners Gary Hoonsbeen, Wes Anderson, and John Masters, who published an Oldsmobile maintenance manual. These Model T Ford Club of America members and Model T owners assisted me greatly: Jerry Van, Thomas Mullin, and Arrdeen Vaughan. A special thanks to Bruce Balough, whose grandfather, Charles Balough Sr.—lured by the 1904 St. Louis Fair—emigrated from his native Hungary to America. He became an engineer for Ford. Balough worked first on the Model N and then the Model T, in the Piquette Avenue experimental room. And a tremendous thanks to Royce Peterson, Model T restorer and expert extraordinaire.

During the early research, I was kindly assisted by Tony Farqué, archaeologist at the Sweet Home Ranger Station, Sweet Home, Oregon; Bruce E. Seely, a technology historian at Michigan Technological University; Palmer Nebraska Public Library director Cara Kuhl; Amy Bowman, archivist, Oregon Historical Society; Laura Wilt, Oregon Department of Transportation Library; Peter Joffre Nye, author, *The Six-Day Bicycle Races*; Rhonda Lorenz, Reference Librarian, Rochester Minnesota Public Library; Mary Devine, reference librarian, Social Sciences Department, Boston Public Library; and the reference staff of the Worcester Massachusetts Public Library, which has a substantial automotive history collection.

The Megargel and Huss stories came together with the assistance of many. Deep gratitude to John W. Huss, son of Dwight, and John's daughter Judy Wier, for the many documents, photographs, and other materials that helped bring Dwight to life. Thanks also to Laura Carnahan, formerly public and electronic information services librarian, Perry T. Ford Memorial Library, Trine University; Kristina Brewer, director, Library and Information Services, Sponsel Library, Trine University; the late Diane Moule, senior lecturer at Bentley University; James Longhurst, associate professor and coordinator of public and policy history, Department of History, University of Wisconsin–La Crosse; Edward Megargee; Laura Schiefer, assistant librarian, Buffalo and Erie County Historical Society, Buffalo, New York; Mary Dwight, Laura Eberly, and Jill McCullough of the Ohio Public Library Information Network Reference Desk; Sandy Groth, librarian, Aurora Free Library, Aurora, New York; Sheila Edmunds, former village historian, Aurora, New York; Judy Andrews; Kendra B. Ferries; Ronald Pollock, former reference librarian, Albany, New York Public Library; and Betsy Caldwell, collections assistant, Reference Services, Indiana Historical Society.

Assisting in the Wyoming passages were Teresa Martinez, clerk of the town of Diamondville, Wyoming; Patricia LaBounty, outreach and collections manager, Union Pacific Railroad Museum, Council Bluffs, Iowa; Judy Julian, museum director, Fossil Country Museum, Kemmerer, Wyoming; Larry K. Brown, volunteer researcher, Wyoming State Archives, Cheyenne, Wyoming; Susan Havers, general manager, The Historic Elk

Mountain Hotel, Elk Mountain, Wyoming; and Larry K. Brown, volunteer researcher, Wyoming State Archives.

Although I did not begin writing until many years later, the roots of this book date to 2000 and 2001, when I was first introduced to real speed. That was the period I was embedded with Jack Roush's Ford team, now Roush Fenway Racing, following drivers Mark Martin, Matt Kenseth, Jeff Burton, Kurt Busch, and Greg Biffle. I was present at the Daytona 500 on February 18, 2001, when Dale Earnhardt, the Barney Oldfield of the modern era, died. So I owe a debt to Jack and his drivers and crews, and to my dear friend Jamie Rodway and a multitude of others from those fondly remembered years. Also a debt to Jon Karp, now publisher of Simon and Schuster, who in his editor days helped steer me to the world of speed, old and contemporary, and who began this book-writing journey with me many years ago.

At the *Providence Journal*, I thank Janet Hasson, Karen Bordeleau, Sue Areson, John Kostrzewa, Bill Reynolds, and Paul Parker. A special thanks to Tom Mooney for reading some early passages and providing his usual spot-on suggestions.

At Salve Regina University, thanks to Sisters Jane Gerety and M. Therese Antone, and Kristine Hendrickson; and to Jim Ludes and Teresa Haas of the Pell Center for International Relations and Public Policy. A tip of the hat to Robert B. Hackey, Pell fellow, Providence College professor, and NASCAR fan.

This is my third book with PublicAffairs and I cannot say enough good things about the house. Gratitude to founder and editor-at-large Peter Osnos, publisher Clive Priddle, associate publisher and director of publicity Jaime Leifer, marketing director Lindsay Fradkoff, managing editor Melissa Raymond, senior project editors Melissa Veronesi and Michelle Welsh-Horst, marketing coordinator Nicole Counts, publicist Tony Forde, publicity assistant Kristina Fazzalaro, copy editor Michele Wynn, editorial assistant Maria Goldverg, book designer Trish Wilkinson, indexer Catherine Bowman, and Pete Garceau, who designed the great cover of *Car Crazy*.

Lisa Kaufman, who handled the marketing for *Men and Speed* and edited *The Xeno Chronicles,* was the brilliant editor of *Car Crazy*. I thank her deeply for her smart and deft work, which greatly improved this book—and also for her grace and humor, and friendship over many years. I know of no better book editor anywhere.

A huge thanks to Jim Donovan, my wonderful literary agent; Michael Prevett of Rain Management Group, my longtime and loyal friend who represents me in the screen world; and Drew Smith, my screenwriting partner. Thanks to the good folk of Angry Child Productions for their commitment to this book and another of mine, *Toy Wars*: Ida Darvish, Josh Gad, and Ryan Dixon. Ryan read an early draft of a passage in *Car Crazy* and his insights helped me.

Finally, my dearest Yolanda. Thanks once again for your patience and understanding during the countless hours it took to research and write *Car Crazy*, and your insightful critiques of some early drafts. Also, for listening to endless car stories. And, finally, for your belief in me. I love you!

# Notes

~~~~~

## GENERAL NOTES

The research for *Car Crazy* brought me to many physical and online archives. I relied extensively on The Henry Ford's Benson Ford Research Center in Dearborn, Michigan; the GM Media Archive/GM Heritage Center, Sterling Heights, Michigan; the Detroit Public Library; The Worcester, Massachusetts, Public Library; and the Michigan State University Archives and Historical Collections. The Henry Ford museum, which has Ford's Quadricycle, the 999, and so many other vehicles and machines, informed and inspired me during the hours I spent there.

The online archives of the *New York Times* were invaluable, as was Chronicling America, http://chroniclingamerica.loc.gov/, the online repository of historic newspapers maintained by the Library of Congress and the National Endowment for the Humanities. Archives for newspapers in some states through which Megargel and Huss passed were also useful, including New York (http://nyshistoricnewspapers.org/) and Wyoming (http://newspapers.wyo .gov/). The genealogy site ancestry.com was helpful in finding Census Bureau and vital statistics records. Newspaper Archive.com (http://newspaperarchive .com) was a good resource.

Thanks to Google Books, many automobile, bicycle, and transportation trade journals from the late 1800s and early 1900s are online, and I spent untold hours reading issues of *Automobile Topics*, the *Automobile*, the *Automotor Journal*, *Cycle and Automobile Trade Journal*, the *Motor Way*, the *Motor World*, *Motor Age*, *Motor Talk*, *Motor*, the *Horseless Age*, the *Power Wagon*, *L.A.W. Bulletin and Good Roads*, *Paving and Municipal Engineering*, and other publications (and some of these, as well, in hard-copy editions in libraries).

Antique car and racing enthusiasts maintain comprehensive online sites where I found—or confirmed—many pertinent facts, photographs, and statistics. Auto Racing Records, www.autoracingrecords.com, maintained by Will White, has international listings of race-car drivers, tracks, and series dating back to the earliest days. Another useful site, www.firstsuperspeedway.com, maintained by Mark Dill Enterprises, describes itself as "the largest on-line archive of primary research about pre-1920 auto racing history in the world," and having spent hours on the site, I could not dispute the claim. Royal Feltner's *History of the Early American Automobile Industry: 1861–1903,* www.early americanautomobiles.com, has a wealth of information and more than 7,000 photographs. Driver Data Base, www.driverdb.com, has valuable archives. And there is nothing like The Henry Ford's Online Collections, http://collections .thehenryford.org/Index.aspx.

A wealth of wisdom and information is found on two leading antique-car forums, and I often went there to get members' expertise: The Model T Ford Club of America, www.mtfca.com/discus/index.html; and the Antique Auto Club of America, http://forums.aaca.org/.

Definitive biographies of four of the leading characters in *Car Crazy* proved helpful: Allan Nevins's 1954 *Ford,* George S. May's 1977 *R. E. Olds,* Lawrence R. Gustin's 1973 *Billy Durant,* and J. C. Long's 1945 *Roy D. Chapin.* For some of the early Oldsmobile history—along with designations, prices, and sales and production figures for early Olds cars—I relied on Earley and Walkinshaw's *Setting the Pace,* the definitive book on the brand, according to Christo Datini, lead archivist, GM Media Archive/GM Heritage Center. Despite an exhaustive effort, I was unable to locate Frederic L. Smith's papers—if in fact he left any. I did find correspondence, reports, and other material in various places, but for deeper insights into his thinking, I had only *Motoring Down a Quarter of a Century,* his 1928 memoir (he does not come across as an endearing character). I also failed to find Megargel's papers, if they exist, despite a similarly time-consuming search. I was provided with copies of Huss's papers by his son, John W. Huss, and John's daughter, Judy Wier.

Regarding automotive data: wherever possible, I have cited authoritative sources, such as trade organizations and government agencies. But the automobile industry took birth at a time when much of the data was not collected or was collected imprecisely or incompletely. Many companies came and went in the blink of an eye, their balance sheets and reports, if they kept them, gone with them. Writing in the *Munsey* magazine in January 1906 (and reprinted in the *Automobile* on February 1, 1906, p. 3131), publisher Frank A. Munsey said it well: "Facts and figures about the beginning and progress of the automobile industry are so conflicting and there is such a dearth of accurate knowledge on the subject that I cannot show year by year our growth in the manufacture of automobiles."

## CHAPTER NOTES

I have not included some citations here for stories that are named by publication source and date in the main text.

### Chapter One: Fastest Man on Earth

Ford built two virtually identical race cars: the 999 and Arrow. Many writers and others—and even Ford himself—sometimes used the names interchangeably. Harry W. Edmunds, in his March 29, 1971, Benson Ford Research Center memo titled "Arrow/999" describes the interchangeability. "Ford's '999' and Cooper's 'Arrow,'" by George DeAngelis, published in the November–December 1993 issue of *Antique Automobile*; "On the Streets of Detroit's Yesteryear: How Henry Ford Sped Toward Fortune in the Fastest Car in the World," by Hans Tanner, Detroit *Free Press*, January 26, 1969; and "Auto Racing Was Chilly When Ford Drove 25 Years Ago," by Theodore Delavigne, Detroit *Free Press,* December 11, 1927, also provided useful details.

"The Chesterfield," a brochure about the hotel published when it opened in 1900, found in the New Baltimore Historical Society archives, gave me a description of the hotel. Known for its mineral baths, opera house, saloons, and bathing, fishing, and sailing on Anchor Bay, the Chesterfield was just an hour from Detroit via Rapid Railway Co.

Noteworthy dates in the history of the American Automobile Association, AAA, are found in "AAA Timelines," http://exchange.aaa.com/about-aaa/aaa -timeline/.

The *Automobile* admonition for motorists to carry fire extinguishers: "Attachments Galore," July 20, 1905, p. 89.

According to my count of the 640-page *The Complete Encyclopedia of Motorcars, 1885 to the Present,* at least 194 American companies were manufacturing cars in 1905; by then, at least 220 other US firms had opened and then gone out of business. Charles Duryea's calculation of car companies from 1900 to 1908 was reprinted in Nevins's *Ford: The Times, the Man and the Company,* p. 234.

The $850 Model A was the first of two Ford models to be labeled "A."

Ford records show 658 cars sold from July 1903 through the end of March 1904, with net revenue of $354,190 and a profit of $98,851; an average 125 employees were recorded for 1903. These and all other data on production and financials of Ford—along with model designations, descriptions, and prices, and size of labor force—are contained in the appendices of Nevins's *Ford: The Times, the Man and the Company*, and Nevins and Hill's *Ford: Decline and Rebirth, 1933–1962,* the definitive two-volume Ford study. As noted, the Ford fiscal year in the early days was from October 1 to September 30.

I learned about Fred Smith's background from the biographies published in *Xi Chapter of the Zeta Psi Fraternity at the University of Michigan, Ann Arbor, Michigan: 1858–1897*, published by the chapter in New York, 1897.

## Chapter Two: Native Sons

In addition to other sources, listed in the bibliography, the GM Heritage Center entry on Olds, "Olds, Ransom Eli," written by James R. Walkinshaw, was useful: https://history.gmheritagecenter.com/wiki/index.php/Olds,_Ransom_Eli.

"Probably the most successful vehicle": Detroit *Free Press,* quoted in the *Hub,* vol. 38, October 1896. "Said to work to perfection": the *Grand Rapids Democrat,* August 14, 1896. Both from the footnotes of *R.E. Olds,* p. 420. I judge May's 458-page *R.E. Olds* to be the authoritative biography of Ransom Olds. Similarly, I deem Nevins's 688-page 1954 *Ford: The Times, the Man and the Company,* Gustin's 304-page 1973 *Billy Durant,* and Long's 269-page 1945 *Roy D. Chapin* as the authoritative, though hardly only, biographies of those men.

A more detailed account of the Thanksgiving Day 1895 race appears in *Carriages Without Horses,* pp. 101–117.

For much of Ford's early years, I relied on his 1922 memoir, *My Life and Work.*

The Detroit *News-Tribune* 1900 account of a ride in Ford's delivery wagon— so representative of the wonderfully flowery journalism of the time—is from Nevins's *Ford: The Times, the Man and the Company,* pp. 180–183.

*Ladies Home Journal:* "Ladies' Home Journal to Cease Monthly Publication," Marco Santana, *Des Moines Register,* April 24, 2014, www.desmoines register.com/story/money/business/2014/04/24/meredith-earnings-fall-37 -percent/8089633/.

I found letters by Smith and Olds and other materials related to Olds leaving the company—and Oldsmobile matters in general—at the Michigan State University Archives and Historical Collections.

## Chapter Three: The Selden Patent

The cozy relationship between manufacturers and the press is described in the account of a junket: "Scribes Entertained," *Motor Age,* January 14, 1904, p. 6. Winton Motor Carriage Company brought thirty journalists from the *New York Times,* the *Boston Herald,* and other newspapers to its Cleveland factory. Some traveled "in a special Pullman car," wrote *Motor Age.* "Once in a while, men find in their business the material for much pleasant friendship," the magazine wrote. "Many of the acquaintances formed primarily for the promulgation of commercial interests prove of much more lasting value. There is a certain satisfaction in feeling that one's business acquaintances are also friends."

Test drives at the 1904 New York show: "Biggest Show of Automobiles," *New York Times,* January 17, 1904.

The roots of the Automobile Club of America are chronicled in "Automobile Club Formed," *New York Times,* October 17, 1899, p. 3. The paper wrote about the ACA's 1904 banquet in "Auto Enthusiasts Demand Good Roads," January 24, 1904, p. 2. The photograph of the car that went up in flames in the Manhattan-to-Pittsburgh run is at www.kcstudio.com/colnypbcl.html. The 1904 American Motor League convention: "Anxious for Good Roads," *New York Times,* January 20, 1904. Although it maintained its independence, the ACA was one of the nine clubs to join AAA; it withdrew after a dispute over dues in early 1908, according to "A.C.A. Leaves A.A.A. Ranks," *Cycle and Automobile Trade Journal,* April 1, 1908, p. 42.

The Ford-Oldfield feud: "High Automobile Speed," *New York Times,* January 18, p. 10; and "Automobiles to Race," *New York Times,* January 24, 1904, p. 11.

ALAM's organization and royalty arrangements: Greenleaf's *Monopoly on Wheels,* p. 98. The exchange between Ford and Couzens and Smith: McManus and Beasley's *Men, Money and Motors,* p. 56.

Brief Couzens biography: "Couzens, James (1872–1936), Biographical Directory of the United States Congress, http://bioguide.congress.gov/scripts /biodisplay.pl?index=C000812.

Background on Parker: "Ralzemond A. Parker Papers," Clarke Historical Library, Central Michigan University, http://quod.lib.umich.edu/c/clarke/ehll -parkerr?view=text.

The first deposition of Henry Ford: The Selden case record, on file at Benson Ford Research Center. Ford's second deposition and the deposition of Ransom Olds in 1905 (Chapter 8) were also found at Benson.

## Chapter Four: Meet Me in St. Louis

Percy F. Megargel, born January 4, 1875, was the oldest of the three sons of Gertrude (Jones) Megargel and Isaac F. Megargel, a wealthy grocer, banker, and investor in lumber, forging, and other businesses: from *History of Scranton, Penn.,* published in 1891 by United Brethren Publishing House of Dayton, Ohio. Details of Megargel's years at Cayuga Lake Military Academy were found in two school catalogs: 1893–1894 and 1894–1895. A description of Cayuga, "Cayuga Lake Military Academy," was published in the *Auburn Daily Advertiser– Semi-Centennial Number,* 1895, p. 27.

Megargel's appearance at the January 1896 bicycle manufacturers' show at Madison Square Garden: "A Big Crowd of Cyclists," *New York Times,* January 23, 1896, p. 6. His employment at Novelty Bicycle Works: *Rochester Democrat and Chronicle,* February 29, 1896. The story of Patrick Collins: "Oswego Man

Robbed," *Oswego Daily Times,* November 20, 1900, p. 4. *Sidepaths*: advertisement in *American Newspaper Directory,* vol. 32, no. 1, p. 756. Census Bureau
and other information on Megargel was posted at http://boards.ancestry.com
/thread.aspx?mv=flat&m=7143&p=localities.northam.usa.states.newyork
.counties.monroe; more on Megargel also at www.fultonhistory.com.

All of Megargel's accounts on his preview run to St. Louis and the run itself
were published in the *Automobile.*

Huss, born September 10, 1873, near Clyde, Ohio, was the younger of the
two children of Maurice Lemmon Huss and Henrietta Alta Storer. Maurice
farmed fruit and ran a farm-equipment and carriage business in Clyde; by 1907,
according to the *Clyde Directory: 1907–1908,* "M. L. Huss & Co.," dealer of
"Buggies, Harness, Wagons and Farm Machinery: Rubber Tires a specialty,"
also sold the "Hoover Potato Digger" and Reo automobiles and supplies. Huss
attended Tri-State Normal School (now Trine University), a technical school in
Angola, Indiana. He married Maud McCartney, the first of his three wives, in
1896, after the first of his three children was born, according to "Christian Huss
Family Tree," compiled by Fae Elaine Scott and published in 1972 by Bodie
Printing Company of Angola, Indiana. Huss began work at Olds on September
18, 1899, according to his obituary: "Dwight Huss, Clyde Native and Early Auto
Driver, Dead at 90," *Clyde Enterprise,* September 3, 1964, p. 3.

John W. Huss, son of Dwight, and John's daughter, Judy Wier, provided
a wealth of material that helped in depicting Huss. Among the materials:
"Dwight B. Huss Scrapbook: Volume # 1, 1900 to 1931," Huss's scrapbook, a
compendium of photographs and newspaper clippings; "Early Memories of My
Dad," "Memories of My Father Dwight B. Huss," "Memories of Huss Relatives,"
and "Memories of John Wilson Huss," all by John W. Huss; "Dwight B. Huss'
Automobile Lifetime Keepsakes," an inventory of memorabilia; and "Letter from
Russia 1" and "Letter from Russia 2," transcriptions of what he wrote from Eu-
rope to his Michigan friend Clyde Wilson, apparently a fellow Olds employee.

Huss and the 1903 English Reliability Trials: www.gracesguide.co.uk/1903
_Reliability_Trial.

Huss recounted his drive into the Kremlin for the December 29, 1959, Detroit *Free Press*: "It was a stunt" staged during a visit to two brothers who owned
an Olds dealership, Huss recalled. The dealers talked in Russian to sentries and
Huss handed them each a ten-ruble bribe. "They let us in and I stood on one of
the brothers' shoulders and wrote my name on the Czar bell."

Huss at the 1903 Paris Salon: https://archive.org/stream/TheAutomotor
Journal1stHalf1903/automotorjournal1903a_djvu.txt.

The White Sewing Machine Company ad: www.earlyamericanautomobiles
.com/americanautomobiles7.htm.

Roy G. Megargel resurrects Pepsi-Cola Company from bankruptcy in 1923:
Tristan Donovan, *Fizz: How Soda Shook Up the World,* p. 103 (Chicago: Chicago Review Press, 2014). The Megargel story is told in many other places as

well, including the company's own history, *The Pepsi-Cola Story: Over 100 Years of Fun and Refreshment, 2005,* www.pepsi.com/PepsiLegacy_Book.pdf.

Background on Webb Jay: www.firstsuperspeedway.com/articles/webb-jay -oldfield.

The 1904 Louisiana Exposition was originally planned for 1903, the centennial of the Louisiana Purchase, but was delayed a year. In addition to *Inside the World's Fair of 1904: Exploring the Louisiana Purchase Expedition of 1904,* Volumes One and Two, I gleaned details of the fair at the Missouri Historical Society Web page: http://mohistory.org/exhibits/Fair/WF/HTML/Overview/page3 .html. Population figures for the United States, 1900 to 1999, from "Historical National Population Estimates: July 1, 1900 to July 1, 1999," *U.S. Census Bureau,* www.census.gov/population/estimates/nation/popclockest.txt. The Jack Daniel's story is on the distiller's site: www2.jackdaniels.com/TennesseeWhiskey/The Bottle.aspx.

Megargel on carnage to dogs: "Motoring from St. Louis to New York," Part 1, *Automobile Review,* May 11, 1905, p. 468. On ammonia: "Motoring from St. Louis to New York," Part 2, *Automobile Review,* May 18, 1905, p. 493.

Oldfield's race car Green Dragon II: www.firstsuperspeedway.com/sites /default/files/B_Oldfield_Green_Dragon.pdf.

The "Lucky Lansing" description in the Detroit *Free Press* was cited in May's *R.E. Olds,* p. 253.

It is unclear why ALAM waited until 1907 to sue Reo.

Marr's remarks to the *Flint Journal* in a July 13 story are cited in Gustin's *Billy Durant,* p. 63.

The story of Hardy is related in William Pelfrey's 2006 book, *Billy, Alfred, and General Motors: The Story of Two Unique Men, a Legendary Company, and a Remarkable Time in American History.*

Durant's initial skepticism about "annoying" automobiles is expressed in his papers, cited in Gustin's *Billy Durant.*

## Chapter Five: Sensation

The floor plan for the 1905 auto show at Madison Square Garden was published in the *Motor Way,* January 14, 1905, pp. 34–35.

The story of bicycle policeman Sherry's chase of Henri Fournier: "Henri Fournier Overspeeds," *New York Times,* January 17, 1905, p. 2. The Bruen chase: "Police and Chauffeur in Long, Wild Chase," *New York Times,* January 17, 1905, p. 1. Magistrate Ommen's chastisement of Bruen: "Magistrate Is Severe with Wild Chauffeur," *New York Times,* January 18, 1905, p. 16. The *Times* story below Bruen's tale was another one of mayhem: "Run Down in Maze of Autos: Man Who Tried to Dodge Plaza Machines Is Badly Hurt."

Mrs. John Jacob Astor's annual ball: "Mrs. John Jacob Astor Gives Her Annual Ball: Two Fifth Avenue Houses Thrown Together for Event," *New York*

*Times*, January 17, 1905, p. 9. McClellan's talk to the AAA annual dinner: "Mc-Clellan at Auto Dinner," *New York Times*, January 17, 1905, p. 2. Scarritt's comments at the Automobile Club of America annual banquet: "Auto Club's Dinner," *New York Times*, January 22, 1905, p. 16. Details on the ALAM patent sleuths are described in Greenleaf's *Monopoly on Wheels*, pp. 176–182. The story of Smith's group securing an exclusive lease on Madison Square Garden: "Licensed Association gets Control," *Automobile Review*, January 21, 1905, p. 68. The *Motor Age* tongue-in-cheek story, including the comments by Clifton, Gash, Jeffery, and Couzens: "A.L.A.M. Would Be Boss," January 19, 1905, p. 134. The AMCMA's articles of organization and Hedges's comments: "Independents Up," *Motor World*, March 2, 1905, pp. 1107–1108.

Couzens's "blood" quote: Greenleaf's *Monopoly on Wheels*, p. 171. The *New York Times* description of the Sixty-ninth Regiment Armory: "Two Automobile Shows Will Open This Weekend," January 7, 1906, p. 9.

Olds's full-page ad: *Motor Age*, January 19, 1905, p. 144. Praise for Reo as "a new star": *Automobile Review*, January 21, 1905, p. 60.

Taylor's cannon quote: "Over Falls and Lives," *Boston Daily Globe*, October 25, 1901, p. 1.

Whitman's seventy-two-day trip from San Francisco to Manhattan is elapsed time, not running time.

According to a report in the June 29 Princeville, Oregon, *Crook County Journal*, Oldsmobile invested "in the neighborhood of $14,000" in the race, according to a statement Megargel gave to the paper.

*Motor World's* story on Ford's plans for new factory: "Ford to Set New Figures," March 30, 1905, p. 19.

Olds ad in the April 20, 1905, the *Motor World*: p. 190. *Omaha Daily Bee* on the race: May 7, 1905, p. 7. "[C]hances of a lifetime": "Olds Offers Lifetime Chance: Wants Two Men to Cross Continent and Outlines Inducements That Should Cause a Rush," *Motor World*, April 27, 1905, p. 205. The *Automobile's* estimates of applicants: May 13, 1905, p. 594. The *Motor World*, on "deluge of applications: May 4, 1905, p. 249. Sartori crash: "Vanderbilt's Auto Wrecked: Paul Sartori Has Miraculous Escape at Brighton Beach," *New York Times*, May 6, 1905, p. 1. Stanchfield and Wigle competition: "Start of Olds Transcontinental Race to Lewis and Clark Centennial Exposition," *Automobile*, May 13, 1905, p. 594. The *New York Times* on racers in Cascade Mountains: "Autos Start To-Day for Pacific Coast," May 8, 1905, p. 11.

All of the major trade publications that I have cited in *Car Crazy* covered the race. It would be impossible to compile a complete list of every local and regional general-circulation newspaper that also wrote about it. I have mentioned many of them in the main text. These are among the major general-circulation papers where I found coverage: *Boston Daily Globe, Baltimore Morning Herald, Philadelphia Evening Telegraph, Washington Post, Evening Star* (Washington, DC), *St. Louis Republic, Chicago Evening Post, Chicago Record-Herald,* Detroit

*Free Press, Detroit News, San Francisco Call, Los Angeles Herald, Los Angeles Examiner, Daily Californian* (Bakersfield), *Minneapolis Journal, Daily American* (Nashville, Tennessee), *Omaha Daily Bee, Evening Bulletin of Honolulu, Salt Lake Tribune, Albuquerque Morning Journal, Iowa City Daily Press, Galveston* (Texas) *Daily News, Winnipeg Free Press, Buffalo News,* and *Buffalo Morning Express.* Published in New York: *New York Times, Sun, New York Daily Tribune, Evening World, New York Evening Mail,* and *New York Herald.*

The *Motor World's* account of the 9:58 a.m. departure: "The Oldsmobiles Are Off for Portland," May 11, 1905, p. 299.

## Chapter Six: Bad Behaviors, Bad Roads

Megargel's first dispatch, from Albany: "First Day's Run: Driver of 'Old Steady' Writes of Fast Trip Despite Mishaps," *Automobile,* May 13, 1905, p. 595. Except for instances where it is specifically warranted, I did not include citations for all of Megargel's stories in the *Automobile.* After the first, they ran, always with the title "Diary of the Transcontinental Race," in the editions of May 18 (p. 622), May 25 (p. 643), June 1 (p. 674), June 15 (p. 725), June 29 (p. 780), and July 13 (p. 46), 1905. Abbott wrote about the race in a three-part series for the *Automobile* that ran on August 10 (p. 150), August 24 (p. 210), and September 7 (p. 258), 1905.

Populations of New York cities: *Statistical Abstract of the United States: 2003,* table H5–7, Population of the Largest 75 Cities: 1900 to 2000. US Census Bureau.

The motor-vehicle accident firsts I include are widely accepted as authentic, but it is possible that earlier such accidents went unreported. Mary Ward's fate was recounted in "Famous Offaly People, a series of short biographies: Mary Ward, 1827–1869," Offaly Historical and Archaeological Society, Tullamore, Ireland, www.offalyhistory.com/reading-resources/history/famous-offaly -people/mary-ward-1827-1869. The Manhattan-to-Irvington-on-the-Hudson race: *Carriages Without Horses,* pp. 121–122. Henry Wells account in the *New-York Daily Tribune*: "The Car That Crashed into History," *New York Times,* May 26, 1996, www.nytimes.com/1996/05/26/nyregion/soapbox-the-car-that -crashed-into-history.html.

Motor vehicle fatality statistics: "Motor Vehicle Traffic Fatalities and Fatality rate: 1899–2003," *Advocates for Highway and Auto Safety,* Washington. Based on National Highway Transportation Safety Administration and Federal Highway Administration data, www.saferoads.org/federal/2004/TrafficFatalities 1899-2003.pdf.

Thomas and "White Ghost": "Fatal Automobile Ride," *New York Times,* February 13, 1902, p. 1. Gotshall car stoned: "Hits Woman in Auto," *New York Times,* May 23, 1904, p. 1. Schmittbergers attired as wealthy motorists: "Inspector's Wife in Auto Traps Hoodlums," *New York Times,* June 6, 1904, p. 1.

Clergyman defending stonings: "New Turn in Hoodlumism," *Automobile,* July 2, 1904, p. 27.

Howard Gibb: "Mr. Gibb's Chauffeur Held," *New York Times,* January 1, 1905, p. 12. The Mrs. Emerson story: "Auto Case Angers Emerson," *New York Times,* January 22, 1905, p. 1. Kate McGowan: "Auto Killed Old Woman," *New York Times,* January 12, 1905, p. 1. Seiler and Woodbury: "Mayor's Chauffeur Exceeds Speed Limit," *New York Times,* May 28, 1904, p. 1. Jerome on reckless drivers: "Jerome Denounces Autos," *New York Times,* January 5, 1905, p. 8.

Miss Tinns: "Auto Seriously Hurts Girl," *New York Times,* August 1, 1904, p. 1. Death of unidentified woman: "Crowd Sees Woman Die, Crushed by Auto," *New York Times,* November 11, 1904, p. 1. Magistrate Crane: "Increase in Auto Fines," *New York Times,* April 18, 1904, p. 3. Hill's 1904 bill introduced: "New Automobile Bill," *New York Times,* January 19, 1904, p. 7.

Henri de Dailloux: "Chased Vanderbilt's Auto," *New York Times,* May 9, 1905, p. 1 (the *Times* has three different spellings for Henri de Dailloux). Details of Vanderbilt's 90-horsepower race car and his Ormond-Daytona record: "110 years ago: William Vanderbilt sets new speed record for a land vehicle in a Mercedes 90 hp racing car," *Daimler.com,* January 16, 2014, http://media.daimler .com/dcmedia/0-921-614318-1-1665014-1-0-1-0-0-1-0-0-0-1-0-0-0-0-0.html.

Retired Army captain Treadwell: "Stepped in Front of Auto," *New York Times,* May 23, 1905, p. 1 (beneath "Chiefs in Auto Smash," about the chiefs of police of Omaha, Cincinnati, and Elmira, New York, injured in a car crash in Washington, DC).

All of the trade publications covered deliberations leading to the myriad laws in municipalities and states (and abroad). *Motor Age* ran a regular feature, "Legal Sense and Nonsense."

Cocks's 1902 bill: "To Punish Automobilists," *New York Times,* January 10, 1902, p. 1. The Anxious Mother's letter: "Dangers of the Automobile," *New York Times,* February 16, 1902, p. 14. John Jacob Astor IV's protest of Bailey Bill: "Automobile Bill Succeeds," *New York Times,* April 23, 1903, p. 3. The May 6 hearing set by Odell: "Arguments Heard on the Automobile Bill," *New York Times,* May 7, 1903, p. 3.

The New York State Automobile Association was organized on November 29, 1903: "Automobile Clubs Unite," *New York Times,* December 1, 1903, p. 10. Dislike of the Bailey Bill, and the bill reprinted in full: "New York's Automobile Bill," *Motor Age,* January 28, 1904, pp. 10–11. Bailey bill signed into law: "New York Bill Is Signed," *Motor Age,* May 12, 1904, p. 12.

Scarritt at the February 28, 1905, contentious hearing: "Automobilists Rally to Fight Saxe Bill," *New York Times,* March 1, 1905, p. 9. Scarritt on motorphobes: "Scarritt Has Remedy," *Motor Age,* February 16, 1905, p. 21. "Loud-mouthed cranks": "Successful Opposition," *Motor Way,* March 18, 1905, p. 300.

The suggestion that autoists carry revolvers for defense against constables was made by the Automobile Club of America: "Armed Automobiles," *New*

*York Times,* August 14, 1904, p. 8. Like many other *Times* anti-car editorials, this one hoped for bodily harm against miscreant motorists. A driver shooting a deputy sheriff, the editorial declared, would soon be avenged: "The man who should venture to sound his irritating 'honk' on one of its highways would find, like Roderick Dhu, that 'one blast upon his bugle horn were worth a thousand men'—not in the shape of allies and defenders, but as armed farmers who would take particular pleasure in making his journey pleasant in the way the Minute men entertained the British on their retreat from Lexington."

In crossing upstate New York, Megargel and Huss followed a route that had been blazed by Native Americans, used by colonialists, and chosen for the construction of the Erie Canal, one of the engineering marvels of the early republic. In 1905, rail linked the main cities: Albany, Schenectady, Utica, Syracuse, Rochester, and Buffalo. This was the same route motorists had traveled on the 1904 parade to St. Louis. It is now roughly the New York portion of Interstate Highway 90 (longest interstate highway today, linking Boston with Seattle).

The bicyclists' late-nineteenth-century campaign for good roads was comprehensively documented by James Longhurst, associate professor of history at the University of Wisconsin–La Crosse, in "The Sidepath Not Taken: Bicycles, Taxes and the Rhetoric of the Public Good in the 1890s," *Journal of Public Policy,* vol. 25, no. 4, 2013, pp. 557–586.

The first Survey of American Roads: Rickie Longfellow, "The Object Lesson Road," Federal Highway Administration Highway History, www.fhwa.dot.gov /infrastructure/back0607.cfm.

The National Road: Richard F. Weingroff, "A Noteworthy Year: The Golden Anniversary of the Eisenhower Interstate System Was Just One of Several Significant Anniversaries in Highway History in 2006," *Public Roads, Federal Highway Administration,* vol. 70, no. 3, www.fhwa.dot.gov/publications/publicroads /06nov/02.cfm.

The Cumberland Road: Searight, Thomas B. *The Old Pike: A History of the National Road, with Incidents, Accidents, and Anecdotes Thereon* (Richmond, IN: M. Cullaton, 1894 [Jefferson's March 29, 1806, authorization is on pp. 25–27 of the Project Gutenberg edition: www.gutenberg.org/files/41799/41799-h /41799-h.htm]). Also, Thomas, James Walter, and Thomas John Chew Williams, *History of Allegany County, Maryland, Vol. 1* (Baltimore: Regional Publication Co., 1923).

League of American Wheelmen organized in Newport, Rhode Island: "Bicycle Riders at Newport," *New York Times,* May 31, 1880. Pope's role in the bicycling movement: "Inductee: Albert Augustus Pope," *U.S. Bicycling Hall of Fame,* www.usbhof.org/inductee-by-year/20-albert-augustus-pope. Columbia history: www.columbiamfginc.com/columbia_history.html.

Potter's "Yes, my loyal friend" message to farmers: *The Gospel of Good Roads,* pp. 58–59. Pope's declaration that public roads are "of the first and highest importance": his *The Movement for Better Roads,* p. 3. The National League for Good Roads: "The League of American Wheelmen and Hartford's Albert Pope Champion the Good Roads Movement," by Richard DeLuca, *Connecticut History.org*, http://connecticuthistory.org/the-league-of-american-wheelmen -and-the-good-roads-movement-how-popes-bicycles-led-to-good-roads/.

More background on the Good Roads movement is contained in "Roads, Highways and Ecosystems," by John Stilgoe for the National Humanities Center's "The Use of the Land Essays": http://nationalhumanitiescenter.org/tserve /nattrans/ntuseland/essays/roads.htm.

Stone's background: Richard F. Weingroff, "Portrait of a General: General Roy Stone," *Federal Highway Administration Highway History*, www.fhwa.dot .gov/infrastructure/stone.cfm. Stone's Tennessee convention address: "The Great Road of America," *L.A.W. Bulletin and Good Roads*, November 12, 1897, p. 605. Stone on demonstration roads: "Portrait of a General: General Roy Stone," *Federal Highway Administration Highway History*. Pope's opinion piece: "Automobiles and Good Roads: One of the Captains of Industry Writes of the Increasing Public Interest in a Movement of Which He Has Long Been a Leader—Our Highways Are Not Always to Remain a Reproach to Civilization," *Munsey's Magazine*, April–September 1903, pp. 167–170.

A useful time line for federal involvement in the auto-era Good Roads movement: "Milestones for U.S. Highway Transportation and the Federal Highway Administration," www.fhwa.dot.gov/publications/publicroads/96spring/p96 sp44.cfm. More detail at: "30.2 Records of the Office of Road Inquiry and the Office of Public Road Inquiries," www.archives.gov/research/guide-fed-records /groups/030.html.

Ford's denigration of Selden: advertisement in the New York *Herald*, May 24, 1905.

W. C. Jaynes's new garage: *Motor Age*, January 14, 1904, p. 21; also, *Motor Age*, February 18, 1904, p. 13. Megargel's comment that the race thus far had been a breeze: *Buffalo Express*, May 11, 1905.

I spent untold hours in many places researching Megargel's background but learned of his wife and daughter only from his obituary and genealogical records: He indeed kept those circumstances private. Public accounts of Megargel included his early bicycling activities; his time with the Rochester News Bureau and *Sidepaths*; his promotion of the 1904 Rochester automobile show; his 1904 drives to St. Louis; his job as advertising manager for Buffalo's E.R. Thomas Motor Company, manufacturer of motorized bikes and cars; and his invention of a card game called "Race." The game featured what the April 1, 1905, *Automobile Review*, "Manufacturer and Dealer," pp. 342–343, described as two cards each of "twenty-six of the best known automobiles." Card games were a footnote to Megargel's grand ambition, which was being influenced by a new form of popular literature that the *Automobile* on May 25, 1905, "Automobile Novels," p. 646, predictably endorsed. The non-bylined piece, conceivably written by Megargel himself, declared: "The automobile, not being content with finding its way on wheels throughout the country, is finding its way into modern fiction in ever-increasing numbers, and no wonder, for it is of the greatest assistance to authors in complicated plots and straightening out desperate situations at the last minute when no other earthly power could do the trick. Very few plots were ever much more complicated than that of 'Lady Penelope' . . . The story of how a girl with strong ideas of her own handled a whole flock of lovers, and finally fell victim to her own theories regarding their management, is intensely amusing, and the author's use of the automobile in extricating the characters from the tangle into which he has got them is exceedingly skillful." *Lady Penelope* sounded much like *The Car and the Lady*, Megargel's first and only novel, published to critical acclaim in 1908, a year before he died, and co-written with the free-spirited Grace Sartwell Mason—with whom it was rumored that Megargel had an affair.

The Clyde weekly on Huss's arrival: The story was published on May 18, 1905, in either of the two Clyde weeklies, the *Clyde Reporter* or the *Clyde Democrat*. The clip sent to me does not indicate which.

Copies of the telegrams sent during the race, along with the many photographs taken, were provided by the GM Media Archive/GM Heritage Center.

Megargel on being escorted into cities by autoists: this is found in a forty-six-page document compiled by Edd Whitaker in his "From Hellgate to Portland: An Oregon-Produced Television Documentary," a 1997 documentary he produced for the Oregon Department of Transportation. Whitaker compiled unpublished reports believed to be from Megargel and transcriptions of newspaper accounts that he found in the Oldsmobile History Center, created by *Setting the Pace* authors Helen Jones Earley and James R. Walkinshaw (the center is now part of GM Heritage Center). Whitaker does not include headlines or page notations in his newspaper transcriptions, only name of paper and date of publication.

### Chapter Seven: The Horse Loses Power

"[T]hree and a half hours to cover a distance of one half mile": *New York World*, May 26, 1905. "[W]onder of all spectators": *Davenport Democrat*, May 19, 1905.

Olds's remarks to *Horseless Carriage* that barns with odors would disappear: Walkinshaw's GM Heritage Center entry.

The *Ladies Home Journal* ad "Good Bye, Horse": May's *R.E. Olds*, pp. 171–172.

"Humoring the Motor": The Autocar ad for its $900 runabout: *Motor World*, June 1, 1905, p. 465. "Horse Sense": *Motor World*, April 27, 1905, p. 218. The ALAM event when a horse panics: "With the Engineers on Their 'Observation Run,'" *Motor World*, May 11, 1905, pp. 301–302. Mules and Horses in American cities: "Motors as Sanitary Measures: How Their Displacement of the Horse Will Assist Public Health," *Motor World*, December 15, 1910, pp. 695–696.

Adams Express's fleet: "In the Service of the Adams Express Company," *Motor World*, May 18, 1905, pp. 347–348. The firm's motor vehicles included three different model electrics, a Knox gasoline, and two imported Daimlers. New York City municipal automobiles: "New York Owns Eleven Cars: Extent of City's Use of Automobiles Not Generally Known," *Motor World,* April 13, 1905, pp. 125–126. Woodbury's photograph was on p. 198 of the February 13, 1904, *Automobile.*

Five pages of motor-wagon trials: "Success of Motor Wagon Trials," *Automobile,* April 16, 1904, pp. 417–421. Garford ad: *Motor World,* July 13, 1905, p. 708. Packard ad: *Motor World,* June 1, 1905, p. 460. Braking tests at Crystal Palace: "Tests of Braking Power: Results Showing Relative Quickness in Stopping Motor Cars and Horse Drawn Vehicles," *Motor World,* June 22, 1905, p. 571. French tests: "Stops in Its Own Length," *Motor World,* May 25, 1905, p. 395.

Many accounts (particularly on the Internet) of the Farmers Anti-Automobile Association of Pennsylvania have presented the group as real, but I conclude it was farcical. "From the Four Winds: Glimpses at the World of Motordom," *Motor Age,* March 6, 1919, seems to confirm my assessment. Regarding the group, the article states, "Some joker is at work in Maryland . . . " and refers to "the wag" as author of the code of ethics.

The St. Louis businessman: "Held up in Missouri: Extortion by a Local Official Followed by a Brutal Assault," *Motor World,* August 24, 1905, p. 964.

Deere history: "John Deere Timeline," www.deere.com/en_US/corporate /our_company/about_us/history/timeline/timeline.page?.

Potter and farmers' stubbornness: *The Gospel of Good Roads,* pp. 6–7.

Horse fights back: "How the Horse Overturned the Automobile," *Motor World,* May 25, 1905, p. 388. New York Supreme Court decision: "Road Rights Equal: So the Supreme Court Declares, but Favors the Horse Drivers All the Same," *Motor World,* May 25, 1905, p. 392. Illinois indictment: "Auto Owner Indicted for Frightening Team," *Horseless Age,* October 24, 1906, p. 507. Supreme Court of Indiana: "Equal Road Rights Defined: Why a Horse's Fright Should Be Heeded," *Motor World,* June 15, 1905, p. 519.

Duluth Automobile Club: "Rules for Safe Driving," *Motor World,* May 11, 1905, p. 311. The American Society for the Prevention of Cruelty to Animals expressed concern for the effect of bad roads on horses, as reflected in a letter to the editor of the *New York Times*: "Bad Street Hard on Horses," *New York Times,* August 14, 1904, p. 8. "The President of the A.S.C.P.A. informs me that he has issued a warning," the writer stated. "Nevertheless, a great deal of suffering is still imposed."

Olds ad after reaching Chicago: *Motor World,* May 18, 1905, p. 365. Olds ad after reaching Omaha: *Motor World,* May 25, 1905, p. 409.

Omaha population: *Statistical Abstract of the United States: 2003*, table HS-7, Population of the Largest 75 Cities: 1900 to 2000. US Census Bureau, www .census.gov/statab/hist/HS-07.pdf.

The Honolulu *Evening Bulletin*: "Cross Country Autos," June 7, 1905, p. 6, datelined May 24.

The *Omaha Daily Bee* had been following the race religiously, with its latest update published the day before, in its Sunday, May 21 edition: "Automobile News Items," *Omaha Illustrated Bee* (the *Bee's* Sunday "magazine"), p. 7. An Olds ad in the main body of that Sunday edition noted "the wonderful records of the two Oldsmobile Runabouts now racing from New York to Portland, Oregon," p. 9.

## Chapter Eight: The West, Still Wild

Some newspaper citations in this chapter are from Whitaker's forty-six-page transcriptions used for "From Hellgate to Portland: An Oregon-Produced Television Documentary."

The coast-to-coast Lincoln Highway, brainchild of Indianapolis auto enthusiast and entrepreneur Carl G. Fisher, would later follow some of the same route Megargel and Huss drove across Nebraska (as does Interstate 80 today): Richard F. Weingroff, "The Lincoln Highway," *Federal Highway Administration Highway History*, www.fhwa.dot.gov/infrastructure/lincoln.cfm.

Several of the papers available at Wyoming Newspapers, a service of the Wyoming State Library, were very helpful in writing Chapter 7: http://newspapers.wyo.gov/.

Narrow escape from drowning: "Huss Shakes Off Megargel: His Cross Continent Rival Now a Day Behind—Nebraska Roads a Wallow of Mud," *Motor World*, June 2, 1905, p. 432.

Nebraska data: David Drozd and Jerry Deichert, "Nebraska Historical Report," *The Center for Public Affairs Research, University of Nebraska at Omaha*, 2007: http://nlcs1.nlc.state.ne.us/epubs/U8220/B090-2007.pdf. Iowa data: A. H. Davison, "The Census of Iowa for the Year 1905," *American Statistical Association*, June 1906, www.jstor.org/stable/2276476. National statistics on motor vehicle sales and registrations for this chapter and elsewhere are found in "Motor-Vehicle Factory Sales and Registrations, and Motor-Fuel Usage: 1900 to 1970," Series Q, 148–162, from *Bicentennial Edition: Historical Statistics of the United States, Colonial Times to 1970, Part 1* (Washington: US Census Bureau, 1975).

State-by-state registrations for this chapter and elsewhere: "Highway Statistics Summary to 1995: Motor Vehicle Registrations by States, 1900–1995," *Federal Highway Administration*, www.fhwa.dot.gov/ohim/summary95/section2.html.

Megargel on Old Steady mended: "Old Steady Finishes Race," *Portland* (Oregon) *Evening Telegram*, June 29, 1905, p. 10.

Buffalo Bill background: Paul Fees, "Wild West Shows: Buffalo Bill's Wild West," *Buffalo Bill Center of the West*, http://centerofthewest.org/learn/western-essays/wild-west-shows/. On a visit to Sheridan, Wyoming, in 1894, at the height of his success, Buffalo Bill Cody was brought into the Bighorn Mountains to experience the view. He was so enchanted with the area—its beauty, abundant fish and game, and proximity to Yellowstone National Park—that the next year, he joined other investors in founding a town on the Shoshone River. They named the town Cody, after the Wild West performer. Lynn Johnson Houze, "Cody, Wyoming," *WyoHistory.org, a Project of the Wyoming State Historical Society*, www.wyohistory.org/encyclopedia/cody-wyoming.

"Coughing like a cigarette fiend": "'Old Scout' Drives In," *Cheyenne Daily Leader*, June 1, 1905, p. 8.

"Automobile Stage Line for Wyoming": *Motor World*, May 4, 1905, p. 265.

"Sorely injured": "Old Steady Reaches City," *Cheyenne Daily Leader*, June 2, 1905, p. 8.

Roosevelt's visit to Laramie: "The President in Cheyenne: Rides to Speaker's Stand and Speaks in Slouch Hat, Boots, Spurs and Gauntlets," *New York Times*, June 1, 1903, p. 3.

McKinley first to ride in an automobile: "Presidential Key events: William McKinley," *Miller Center, University of Virginia*, http://millercenter.org/president /mckinley/key-events. Roosevelt first to ride publicly in a car: "Aug. 22, 1902: Theodore Roosevelt Becomes First President to Ride in an Automobile," Learning Network, *New York Times*, http://learning.blogs.nytimes.com/2011 /08/22/aug-22-1902-theodore-roosevelt-becomes-first-president-to-ride-in -an-automobile/. Roosevelt on dislike of cars: The Shapell Manuscript Foundation, www.shapell.org/manuscript.aspx?theodore-roosevelt-did-not-like-cars.

Hanna tragedy of 1903: "234 Lives Lost in Mine Disaster," *New York Times*, July 1, 1903, p. 1.

The George Parrott story really is one of the more bizarre incidents in US history. His shoes and other items are on permanent display at the Carbon County Museum in Rawlins, Wyoming, which posts this description on its web site, http://carboncountymuseum.org: "Dr. Osborne made a plaster death mask, then took the skin from Parrot's chest and thighs. He had it tanned and made into a pair of shoes and other personal items. See the death mask, a cast of George's skull, Dr. Osborne's shoes, and other fascinating parts of the story when you visit."

*The Car and the Lady*: pp. 81–82.

Bridgeport, Connecticut, *Post*: Whitaker's forty-six-page transcriptions.

Huss suffers from malaise: "Huss Six days Ahead: Despite Cloudbursts, Precipices and Deserts, His Rival Persists in Forlorn Chase," *Motor World*, June 19, 1905, p. 521.

Smith ran his Olds ads in several publications. These are the citations for their publication in the *Motor World*: "Everyone interested," May 11, 1905, p. 303; "From New York to Chicago," May 18, 1905, p. 365; "well-known authority," June 8, 1905, p. 497.

The Six Shooter: "Motor Boat Carnival Produces Fast Races," *New York Times*, September 15, 1905, p. 7.

Ford ad: *Motor World*, May 18, 1905, p. 367.

Background on the Wyoming coal industry: Chamois L. Anderson, "The Coal Business in Wyoming," *WyoHistory.org, a Project of the Wyoming State Historical Society*, www.wyohistory.org/encyclopedia/coal-business-wyoming.

Rock Springs massacre: "The Massacre of the Chinese," *New York Times*, September 5, 1885, p. 5. The "Sodom and Gomorrah" editorial: "Mob Law in Wyoming," *New York Times*, September 19, 1885, p. 4. In addition to condemning the miners, the editorial rebuked the local press, writing, "The newspapers of Rock Springs recounted these atrocities with a cynical and ghastly joy."

More on Diamondville mine disasters and details of miners' life: "Coal Camp Photos: Diamondville," *Wyoming Tales and Trails*, www.wyomingtale sandtrails.com/coal3a.html.

Diamondville, Kemmerer, and related Lincoln County, Wyoming, history: "History," *Wyoming: The 75th Year, Wyoming 75th Anniversary Commission*, www.lincolncountywy.org/History_Doc_Text.html. History of Diamondville: "Historic Diamondville," *The Town of Diamondville*, www.diamondvillewyo .com/history.htm.

The 1899 strike: "Women Use Guns and Clubs," *New York Times*, December 5, 1899, p. 2.

The 1901 Diamondville disaster: "Diamondville, WY, Mine Fire, Feb 1901," *GenDisasters.com, Events That Touched Our Ancestors' Lives*, www3.gendisasters .com/wyoming/1886/diamondville,-wy-mine-fire,-feb-1901. The *New York Times* report: "Thirty-Five Lost in a Mine," February 27, 1901, p. 2.

Wiley L. Brown: "Body Found by Hunters," (Evanston) *Wyoming Press*, November 25, 1905. Daly Hotel bankrupt: "Additional Local," (Evanston) *Wyoming Press*, December 27, 1902. Harvey Rogers accident: "Horribly Scalded," *Wyoming Tribune*, December 26, 1904.

The August 14, 1923, Kemmerer mine explosion: "Blast Entombs 138; Only 37 Are Saved," *New York Times*, August 15, 1923, p. 1.

## Chapter Nine: Victories and Defeats

Huss and Wigle's Wyoming, Idaho, and Oregon crossings and Huss's quotes: from a twenty-five-page chronology that Huss later compiled, passed on to John W. Huss and Judy Wier.

"[M]ud splattered, battered, worn": "Old Scout Passes Through City," *Crook County Journal*, Prineville, Oregon, June 22, 1905, p. 1.

Santiam Pass quotes: the twenty-five-page Huss chronology. Background on Santiam Pass: "Santiam Wagon Road, 1865–1939," *Oregon Historic Trails Report, Oregon Trails Coordinating Council*, May 1998, pp. 233–240. Michele Morseth, "Santiam Wagon Road: Overview," *Sisters County Historical Society*, 2006, www.sisterscountryhistoricalsociety.org/OV-WagonRoad.htm.

Megargel and Stanchfield racing until the very last: "Old Steady Finishes Race," *Portland* (Oregon) *Evening Telegram*, June 29, 1905, p. 10.

Olds ad after Huss wins: *Motor World*, June 22, 1905, p. 585.

The forty-six-page booklet: Abbott, Huss, and Megargel's *From Hellgate to Portland*.

"King Speed": "King Speed Is Rampant," *Motor Age*, June 15, 1905, p. 11.

Worcester hill climb: "Up Dead Horse Hill," *Automobile Review*, June 1, 1905, p. 534.

Cincinnati Reo performance: "Up Paddock Hill," *Automobile Review*, June 1, 1905, p. 513.

Morris Park spectators adore Chevrolet: "Many Close Finishes at Morris Park," *Automobile Review*, June 15, 1905, p. 576.

The AAA tournament: "AAA National Championship 1905 Standings," Driver Data Base, www.driverdb.com/championships/standings/aaa-national -championship/1905/.

Oldfield's August 9 accident: "Oldfield Faces Death Again in Auto Race," *New York Times*, August 9, 1905, p. 4.

Kiser crashes on August 12: "National Circuit Meet at Cleveland: Rain Causes Day's Postponement—Kiser's Serious Accident Mars Day's Sport—Unusual Attendance," *Automobile*, August 17, 1905, p. 189.

A full account of Jay's accident is in (among many other places) "Jay Victim of Dust," *Motor World*, August 24, 1905, p. 961. "His head was fast in the mud at the bottom" of the pond, the magazine reported, and in addition to broken bones, Jay suffered "from concussion of the brain and shock," internal injuries, and "severe cuts and abrasions about the head and shoulders." More on Jay: "Accident Ends Webb Jay's Career," *The First Super Speedway*, www.first superspeedway.com/articles/webb-jay-oldfield.

Comments by Hotchkiss, White, Kiser, Clifton, and Ford: "Track Racing Condemned to Die: Prominent Motorists from all Parts of the Country Pass Sentence on a Man-Killing Pastime," *Motor Age*, August 24, 1905, pp. 1–3.

"Track racing is dying": "Racing Autos Too Fast for Track Contests," *New York Times*, September 3, 1905, p. 11. Oldfield thumbs nose: "Autos Driven Fast," *New York Times*, September 30, 1905, p. 10.

Akin to a wife: "Don't Blame the Automobile," *Motor Age*, August 24, 1905, p. 8.

Bad motoring press: "Unfavorable Newspaper Influence and How to Counteract It," *Automobile*, November 9, 1905, p. 526. The *Times* on the 1902 Cocks speeding bill: "Speed Regulation for Automobiles," *New York Times*, March 29, 1902, p. 8.

The paper's 1905 policy shift: "Automobiles and the Speed Laws," *New York Times*, June 14, 1905, p. 8. The *Automobile* pounces: "Depends on Whose Ox Is Gored," *Automobile*, June 15, 1905, p. 735. *Times* chides for grammar: "Our

'Hostility' to the Automobile," *New York Times,* June 26, 1905, p. 6. The *Automobile* returns fire: "The Same Old 'Times,'" *The Automobile,* July 6, 1905, p. 22.

Tips to motorists to change anti-car sentiments: "Unfavorable Newspaper Influence and How to Counteract It," *Automobile,* November 9, 1905, p. 526.

Disorders alleged to be caused by motoring: "The 'Auto' Face," *Pacific Medical Journal,* January 1904, pp. 31–33. Dr. Blanchet: "Automobile Rides as a Consumptive Cure," *Horseless Age,* May 18, 1904, p. 522. Hugh Galt: "Scottish Automobile Club (Western Section)," *Automotor Journal: A Record and Review of Applied Automatic Locomotion,* published weekly in London, March 21, 1904, p. 321.

Motor fever and Dr. Squills: *Literary Digest,* July 1, 1899, p. 28, reprinted from undated *Chicago Tribune.* Etiology of motor fever: "Motor Fever," *Doctor's Factotum: A Periodical Presentation of Matters of Interest to the Physician, Both Scientific and Humorous,* February 1905, pp. 43–44. The *Times* version of the spoof: "Automobiliousness," *New York Times,* January 21, 1906, p. 37. *Journal of the American Medical Association* letter: "Automania: The New Disease," J. W. Clemmer, pp. 1543–1544.

"Nerve tension" and "nerve waste" are described in detail in H. C. Sawyer, *Practical Information Concerning Nervous Impairment and Nervous Exhaustion in Modern Life: Their Causes, Phases and Remedies, with Advice on the Hygiene of the Nervous Constitution* (San Francisco: Bancroft, 1888).

Testimony by Ford and Olds in November 1905: The Benson Ford Research Center. I found hard copies of the full Selden patent at Benson Ford Research Center and the Detroit Public Library. It is also available online (along with photos of several ceramics and other curios with the image of the 1877 buggy) at www.kcstudio.com/selden2.html.

Huss at Grand Palais des Champs-Élysées: "Opening of the Paris Automobile Salon," *Automobile,* December 21, 1905, p. 680.

Megargel leaves Manhattan: "Megargel Gets Away," *Motor Age,* August 24, 1905, p. 11. Mountaineer serves as a bed: "The 'Reo Mountaineer,'" *Cycle and Automobile Trade Journal,* September 1, 1905, p. 63. Haystack smells: "Reo Mountaineer's Task Half-Done," *Motor Way,* November 16, 1905, p. 9. Palo Alto, lost suitcase, glory-seeking marshal: "Reo Strikes Eastward from Coast," *Motor Way,* December 7, 1905, p. 13. Doff of hat in Needles: "Crossing the Great American Desert," *Automobile,* December 21, 1905, p. 688.

Top hits of 1905: "Top Songs of 1905," *MusicVF.com,* www.musicvf.com /top_songs_of_1905, from *Billboard* data.

## Chapter Ten: Doubts Subsiding

The "magnificent" shows: "Rival Shows Vie for patronage," *New York Times,* January 14, 1906, p. 10. "The Tale of Two Cities: Great Shows of a Great Industry,"

*The Motor Way,* January 18, 1906. Myers and the ballo-plane: Carl E. Myers, "A Visit to the First Show of the Aero Club of America," *Scientific American,* Supplement No. 1572, February 17, 1906, pp. 25,193–25,194. *Times* impressed: "Balloons the Feature of Armory Auto Show," *New York Times,* January 14, 1906, p. 10.

Numbers and types of cars at the shows: "General Trend in Construction: Table of Comparative Data," *Motor Way,* January 18, 1906, p. 15. The *Times* only acknowledging: "Two Automobile Shows Will Open This Week," *New York Times,* January 7, 1906, p. 9. "The new line of demarcation": "Garden Show a Beautiful Spectacle," *Automobile,* January 18, 1906, p. 144. "[T]wo rival shows": Introduction to show issue, *Motor Way,* January 18, 1906, p. 4. "[I]ndependent shows": "End of Two Unsurpassed Shows," *Motor Way,* January 25, 1906, p. 5. "[R]umors were afloat": "Dealers Deny Rumors," *Automobile,* January 25, 1906, p. 260.

Olds ad trumpeting Huss's French run: *Motor Way,* January 25, 1906, p. 30. Olds rebranding problem: "Olds Motor Works," *Automobile,* January 18, 1906, p. 156. The Times Square Automobile Company ad: *Motor,* March 1906, p. 10.

Ford letter to editor: "Arranging to Build 20,000 Runabouts," *Automobile,* January 11, 1906, p. 107. Model N hailed as sensation: "The Show's Sensation," *Motor Way,* January 18, 1906, p. 14. "Why Henry Ford Fought the Selden Patents," New York *Sun,* January 14, 1906, section 3, p. 13.

"Auto Business Here to Stay," J. S. Draper, *Automobile,* January 11, 1906, p. 105.

Motor Vehicle sales and registrations: "Motor-Vehicle Factory Sales and Registrations, and Motor-Fuel Usage: 1900 to 1970," Series Q, 148–162, from *Bicentennial Edition: Historical Statistics of the United States, Colonial Times to 1970, Part 1* (Washington: US Census Bureau, 1975). New York's increase from 1905 to 1906: "11,753 Autos in New York," *New York Times,* January 1, 1907, p. 1.

State-by-state data on the year motor vehicles were first registered, annual registrations from 1900 to 1995, and registration by state from 1900 to 1995: "Highway Statistics Summary," *Federal Highway Administration,* www.fhwa .dot.gov/ohim/summary95/section2.html.

Jaynes's installment plan: "Sells in Installments," *Motor Age,* June 15, 1905, p. 29. Boston Insurance Company claim as first: *Marine and Fire Insurance in Boston: An Illustrated Epitome of Its Origin and Growth Together with the Story of the Boston Insurance Company* (Boston: Boston Insurance Company, 1914), pp. 37–39. The company's 1906 ad: *Motor,* March 1906, p. 12. Ninety-one service stations in New York City; *Motor,* March 1906, p. 13.

Legislation by Tennessee Representative Walter Brownlow that preceded the bill by Marion Rhodes: *A Vast System of Interconnected Highways: Before the Interstates,* by Richard F. Weingroff, Federal Highway Administration, www.fhwa.dot.gov/highwayhistory/vast.pdf.

Select data for roads in states in 1904: Logan Waller Page, *Report of the Director of the Office of Public Roads for 1906* (Washington: US Department of Agriculture, 1906), p. 18.

L'Hommedieu's tax bill: "New York Tax Bill," *Automobile,* February 15, 1906, p. 408. Terry objects to bill: "Auto Club Will Fight Objectionable Bill," *New York Times,* April 17, 1906, p. 7. Grand Rapid autos: "Surprising State of Michigan Cars," *Automobile,* March 8, 1906, p. 487.

Warner Auto-Meter ad: *Motor,* July 1906, p. 75. Auto map from Paris: "Novel Auto Map," *Automobile,* February 8, 1906, p. 359. The *Automobile* editorial on military use: "The Automobile for Military Purposes," June 14, 1906, p. 942. Cars fail to impress army: "Automobiles in the Army Manoeuvres," *Horseless Age,* October 24, 1906, pp. 503–504.

Stephens & Bean hearse: "An Auto Morgue Wagon," *Automobile,* March 1, 1906, p. 456. Henry Fischer: "Asphyxiation in a Garage," *Automobile,* January 18, 1906, p. 187.

Duryea's claims on carbon monoxide made in a letter dated December 15, 1906, published in *Cycle and Automobile Trade Journal,* March 1, 1907, p. 145. The *Power Wagon* editorial was published in the September 1906 edition, p. 8.

Women and auto "microbe": "Instructing a Woman to Drive," *Automobile,* June 14, 1906, p. 935. Mrs. Hitchcock's advice: "Women as Drivers of Automobiles," *Automobile,* April 19, 1906, p. 674. I found the Lippincott's autoflirtation piece reprinted in the *Cambridge* (Massachusetts) *Chronicle,* November 17, 1906, p. 19. The Holland, Michigan, man: "One-armed Driver of Holland," *Automobile,* April 26, 1906, p. 694.

"Unjust" antagonism toward motorists ending: "The Turn of the Road in Sight: Evidence Accumulates That Around the Bend, Unjust Automobile Antagonism Will Not Be Found," *Automobile,* March 29, 1906, p. 570. Wilson's New York speech: *Auto Mania,* p. 12, which cites *The Papers of Woodrow Wilson* (Princeton: Princeton University Press, 1973), vol. 16, p. 320. Wilson spoke at the North Carolina Society of New York City.

Smith enters Vanderbilt Cup: "Vanderbilt Cup Entries," *Automobile,* April 19, 1906, p. 688. Keeler starts training: "Automobile Notes of Interest," *New York Times,* April 20, 1996, p. 15. Driving Pirate, Keeler steps in for Oldfield on Broadway: "New and Trade Miscellany," *Automobile,* May 10, 1906, p. 788 (also on this page: a report that William Randolph Hearst bought a Thomas "Flyer" in New York). Keeler wins vibration contest: "New York City Has an Open-Air Show," *Automobile,* May 31, 1906, pp. 853–856.

The *Motor* account of Twain was published in the May 1906 issue, p. 45; I found it reprinted in *Motor Talk*: "Mark Twain as a Motorist: What the Famous Humorist Thinks of Motoring," T. Quiller Wright, pp. 27–28, May 1906. I believe "T. Quiller Wright" was a pseudonym (and bad pun), which casts doubt on aspects of Wright's story; the postcards produced from photographs of Twain with Keeler, however, appear authentic.

Selden as "patron saint" of ALAM: "Selden Homestead in Connecticut," *Automobile*, cover story September 7, 1905, p. 253.

For some of the courtroom scenes in the Selden case, I relied on Nevins's *Ford: The Times, the Man and the Company* and Greenleaf's *Monopoly on Wheels*, which in turn relied on transcripts in the extensive case records on file at Benson Ford Research Center and the Detroit Public Library.

Parker on being blindsided: "Reproduction of Selden Car Examined by Judge Parker and Experts," *Horseless Age*, May 23, 1906, p. 739. Parker on the exorbitant cost of the buggy: "Views of Anti-Selden Counsel," *Automobile*, June 14, 1906, p. 947.

Megargel on the Arizona blizzard: "Megargel and His Companions Very Much Alive in the Mountainous Southwest," *Automobile*, December 18, 1905, p. 716. More details on Megargel and Fassett's trip back to Manhattan were found in the *Automobile* and the *Motor Way*, among numerous other publications. Bad Nebraska roads: "The Trip of the 'Mountaineer,'" *Automobile*, April 26, 1906, p. 697. Megargel talks to reporters on arriving in New York: "Auto Tourists Home from Continental Trip: Megargel and Fassett End Long Run to Pacific and Back; Once Given Up for Lost; Christmas Spent in Hauling Machine out of Arizona Canyon—Receive Ovations from New York Autoists," *New York Times*, June 10, 1906, p. 7.

The deed of gift for the Charles J. Glidden trophy is published in the *Automobile*, July 6, 1905, p. 13. The participants in the 1906 Glidden tour and their performances: "The Score of the Great Tour," *Automobile*, August 2, 1906, p. 131. Keeler's run from Bretton Woods to New York: "A Non-Stop Run," *Automobile*, August 2, 1906, p. 136.

Two Olds racers were built in 1906, including a six-cylinder car.

Ford races Chevrolet at Cape May: Robert W. Ellwell Sr., "Racing to Success," *CapeMay.com*, Cape May, New Jersey, www.capemay.com/blog/2013/03 /racing-to-success/.

The comprehensive site *Vanderbilt Cup Races*, www.vanderbiltcupraces .com, by Howard and Dana Kroplick, was a treasure trove of information and photographs. So, too, was the content on "The Vanderbilt Cup" pages of *The First Super Speedway*, www.firstsuperspeedway.com/articles/category/83. The trade publications and many general-circulation newspapers, especially in New York City, covered the Vanderbilt contest. Particularly helpful were the many details, photographs, and charts in "How the Great Race Was Won," *Motor Way*, September 27, 1906, pp. 1–7; and "America's Five for the Vanderbilt," *Automobile*, September 27, 1906, pp. 389–404.

Description of Olds racer and Olds's boast: "Oldsmobile Vanderbilt Cup Racer," *Automobile*, September 20, 1906, p. 363. The field narrows before the start: "The Elimination Trials," *Motor Talk*, October 1906, p. 28. Cars that entered but did not start, and the starting lineup: "Starting Lineup: The 1906 American Elimination Trial," www.vanderbiltcupraces.com/blog/article/saturday november_21_2009. Dolnar's exuberant prose: Hugh Dolnar, "The Race in Detail," *Cycle and Automobile Trade Journal,* October 1, 1906, pp. 76–77.

The size of the Newark crowd: "Keeler Lowers Record at Newark Meet," *Automobile,* November 8, 1906, p. 597. "Undoubtedly the largest crowd that ever attended an automobile track meet in this country" is how the magazine described it.

Account of Cooper's death: "'Tom' Cooper Killed in Park Auto Race: Noted Cyclist and Driver Breaks His Neck in Collision, Two Others May Die," *New York Times,* November 20, 1906, p. 1. "[L]ike a chipped bowling ball": "Ernest Keeler's Fatal Final Practice Mile," *Automobile,* November 29, 1906, p. 736. The *Times* story on Keeler's death: "An Auto Racer Killed," *New York Times,* November 24, 1906, p. 1.

## Chapter Eleven: "Equal to His Weight in Wildcats"

The two September tests of the buggy: "The Selden '1877' Buggy Again Tested," *Horseless Age,* pp. 371–373. The June Guttenberg tests: "Views Differ on Selden Tests," *Motor World,* June 27, 1907, p. 561.

Ford also entered a demonstration car into evidence: The Ford-Lenoir vehicle, built according to specifications in a patent granted in 1860 to Belgian inventor Jean Joseph Étienne Lenoir, who constructed one of the earliest practical internal-combustion engines. It was presented to refute Selden's claim that his engine had been first.

"The Trail of the Serpent," *Horseless Age,* December 18, 1907, pp. 859–861.

Buick disregards Selden patent: "Only One American Concern Seeks Tariff Reduction," *Automobile,* December 24, 1908, p. 903.

Kulick and Lorimer's record 1,135 run: "Over 1,100 Miles in 24 Hours," *Motor World,* June 27, 1907, pp. 569–570. Kulick's background: "Frank Kulick: Inducted into the Michigan Motor Sports Hall of Fame in 1992," *Michigan Motor Sports Hall of Fame,* www.mmshof.org/inductees/frank-kulick/. Ford built the 999 II, also called the Super T, a more powerful cousin of his original 999, and Kulick raced it across frozen Lake St. Clair on February 17, 1912: Nevins's *Ford: The Times, the Man and the Company,* p. 350.

A description and photograph of the experimental room are posted by the *Model T Automotive Heritage Complex,* Piquette Avenue Plant, Detroit: http://fordpiquetteavenueplant.org/?page_id=21#building. Ford shows reporter cars: "Ford's Triple Surprise," *Motor World,* October 17, 1907, pp. 105–106, 112.

Despite the common perception that the first Model Ts were sold only in black, none at first actually were sold in that color, according to T expert and restorer Royce Peterson, who writes (personal correspondence to author, March 10, 2015): "Model T colors in 1909 were red for tourings, grey for runabouts, and green for all cars later in the 1909 year. Dark green continued as the only color in 1910. Dark blue became the standard color for 1911, 1912, and 1913. Ford standardized the black finish from 1914 through 1925. In 1926 and 1927, a variety of colors were offered."

"[F]orked lightning": "Ford's Triple Surprise: Detroit Maker Discloses Three New Models at Startling Prices," *Motor World,* October 17, 1907, pp. 105–106.

I have been unable to pin down the precise chronology of the Smith, Durant, Briscoe, and Ford discussions, but the general dates are accurate, according to my reading of press accounts and Earley and Walkinshaw's *Setting the Pace;* Nevins's *Ford: The Times, the Man and the Company;* May's *R.E. Olds;* and Gustin's *Billy Durant.*

The *Times* scoop of International Motor Company: "Plan a $25,000,000 Merger: Group of Manufacturers in Process of Organization into a Large Corporation, Morgan's Relatives in It," *New York Times,* July 31, 1908, p. 9.

Dealers' responses to the Model T: Nevins's *Ford: The Times, the Man and the Company,* p. 387. Less than two weeks had passed when the *Horseless Age* published a story: "Ford 1908 Features," April 1, 1908, p. 391.

Steering wheel on left: Brian Lucas, "Which Side of the Road Do They Drive On?" *TSM Resources, Technology to Secondary/College Mathematics,* Oundle, England, www.tsm-resources.com/left/Which%20side%20of%20the%20 road%20do%20they%20drive%20on.htm. Lucas cites a Ford catalog published in 1908 for the 1909 Model T on file at the Benson Ford Research Center; T expert Royce Peterson confirms this.

Joliet, Illinois, ad: *Evening Herald,* March 31, 1909. The cross-continent race with two Model Ts: "Automobile Race," *When the World Came to Campus, AYPE 1909* (Alaska Yukon Pacific Exposition), University Libraries, University of Washington, https://content.lib.washington.edu/exhibits/aype/race.html.

Megargel's visit with long-distance Tomlinson: "Aeronaut Seeks World's Record," *Post-Standard* (Syracuse, New York), May 27, 1907, p. 6.

*New York Times* sees Megargel as cross-continent expert: "Megargel Will Start: He Already Has Made Three Transcontinental Motor Trips," January 2, 1908, p. 4; "Auto Clubs Will Assist Polar Run," January 8, 1908, p. 7; "Four Weeks' Time to San Francisco: Montague Roberts Says It Will Require That Long for Cars to Cross the Country, Some Will Take Longer, Megargel Hopes to Enter Car in Race from New York to Paris Before the End of the Week," January 15, 1908, p. 2; "In Nevada Mining District: Son of Brooklyn Divine Wants to enter Race to Paris," January 19, 1908, p. 1; "An Autoist's Winter Trip over the Rockies: Lessons from the Experience of Percy Megargel Which Should Be of Benefit to Contestants in the New York-to-Paris Race," January 19, 1908, p. 42; "New York to Paris Is Not Easy," January 24, 1908, p. 4; "Believe American Will Win Race," January 26, 1908, p. 29; "Naudin Broke Differential," February 14, 1908, p. 2; "Escorts for the Cars," February 16, 1908, p. 2.

The *Times* review of *The Car and the Lady*: "Romance and Instruction," September 5, 1908, p. 27. The *Evening Star* review was published on August 22, 1908.

Megargel's wife remarried after his death (Herbert W. Fitzgerald), and their only child, Gertrude, led a sad and troubled life until she died in 1980 at the Veterans Home of California-Yountville. Gertrude made headlines in May 1932, when she walked into a hospital in Brooklyn, New York, and announced that she had tried to kill herself with poison; her husband, she said, had left her, and her young son (and only child) was living with her mother. According to Associated Press accounts ("Binghamton Heiress Tries Poison Death," *Syracuse Herald*, May 2, 1932, p. 1; and "Woman Sorry Suicide Failed," *Poughkeepsie Eagle-News,* May 2, 1932, p. 2), Gertrude B. DeWitt, her married name, then collapsed and when she regained consciousness, claimed that her only friend was New York Yankees star first baseman Lou Gehrig. "At Washington, Gehrig said he had seen Mrs. DeWitt a few times, but their acquaintance was casual," the AP wrote. The AP further reported that Gertrude "became a taxi driver when a fortune willed by her father vanished." Gertrude served in England with the Women's Army Corps in World War II. In "Lady Taxi Driver Has Good Advice," *Pittsburgh Post-Gazette*, October 20, 1965, p. 21, Gertrude told the writer that she had been a driving instructor in England and "Queen Elizabeth II was in one of her classes and changed a tire with the best of them." Her appearance in Pittsburgh was a stop on a sponsored 3,000-mile tour that Gertrude, who had resumed driving a taxi in New York City, was taking to promote car-winterization products.

"The lady 'hackie' comes by her love of cars naturally," the *Post-Gazette* wrote. "Her dad drove an old Reo roundtrip from Manhattan to Reno, Nev., in 1906–7. She heard so much about it that she fell in love with driving. . . . Mrs. DeWitt prefers the 4 p.m. to 4 a.m. shift . . . and she's seen her share of celebrities. She had Jacqueline Kennedy in her cab when President Kennedy was still a senator. And she had all the Gabors in one day." And she had recently completed a cross-country drive her father would have appreciated, she said. "She had no trouble at all on a 20,000 mile cover-the-nation drive-it-herself vacation she took last year accompanied only by her Welsh terrier friend Llewellyn (Louie for short)."

Nevins's *Ford: The Times, the Man and the Company* casts doubt on whether Ford seriously considered Durant's $8 million offer.

Durant's observations on losing GM are from his papers, cited in Gustin's *Billy Durant.*

The *Detroit Journal* hails outcome: January 11, 1911. *Automobile Topics* reprints entire decision: "Selden Patent Decision: U.S. Circuit Court of Appeals Unanimously Reverses Judge Hough, Says Patent Is Valid But That It Has Not Advanced the Art and Ford and Other Defendants Did Not Infringe," *Automobile Topics*, January 14, 1911, pp. 969–980.

Smith on "flimsy" patent: *Motoring Down a Quarter of a Century,* p. 36.

Clifton praises decision: "A.L.A.M. Banquet Is a Love-Feast," *Automobile Topics,* January 21, 1911, p. 1031.

## Epilogue

National statistics: "Motor-Vehicle Factory Sales and Registrations, and Motor-Fuel Usage: 1900 to 1970," Series Q, 148–162. Ford Motor Company statistics: appendices, Nevins's *Ford: The Times, the Man and the Company* and Nevins and Hill's *Ford: Decline and Rebirth.*

Ford obituary: "Henry Ford Is Dead at 83 in Dearborn," *New York Times,* April 8, 1947. Ford lies in state: "75,000 Pay Homage at Bier of Ford," *New York Times,* April 10, 1947, p. 21. Drivers stop their vehicles: "Thousands Honor Ford at Last Rites: Throng Stands in Rain Outside Cathedral, Body Buried Near Graves of Parents," *New York Times,* April 11, 1947, p. 6.

Oldfield obituary: "Barney Oldfield, Ex-Racer, Is Dead: Pioneer Auto Driver Was First to Drive a Mile a Minute," *New York Times,* October 5, 1946, p. 17.

GM announced it would retire the Olds line in 2004 in a media statement issued on September 7, 2001.

Toyota enters US market: "History of Toyota (1950–1959)," Toyota Motor Corporation, www.toyota-global.com/company/history_of_toyota/1950-1959 .html.

Hyundai enters US market: "History," Hyundai Motor, http://worldwide .hyundai.com/WW/Corporate/CorporateInformation/History/index.html.

Car manufacture in the South: BMW in South Carolina, "BMWs Made in America Surging as Biggest Auto Export," *Bloomberg Business,* July 11, 2014, www.bloomberg.com/news/articles/2014-07-10/bmws-made-in-america -surging-as-biggest-auto-export-cars; Texas car-making, "The Texas Automobile Manufacturing Industry," *Texas Wide Open for Business,* 2014, https:// texaswideopenforbusiness.com/sites/default/files/01/13/15/2014_automotive _report_final.pdf; and Alabama, "Automotive Hub of the South," *Amazing Alabama,* July 21, 2014, www.amazingalabama.com/key-industry-targets -automotive.html.

More on manufacturing cars in the United States: "Born in the U.S.A.: The Cars and Trucks That Are Currently Built in the United States," *New York Times,* February 27, 2011, www.nytimes.com/interactive/2009/06/19/automobiles /20090619-auto-plants-4.html?_r=0.

More than 7 million jobs: "Contribution of the Automotive Industry to the Economies of All Fifty States and the United States," *Center for Automotive Research,* January 2015, www.autoalliance.org/files/dmfile/2015-Auto-Industry -Jobs-Report.pdf.

Horse population in 1910: "Equine 2005: Part II: Changes in the U.S. Equine Industry, 1998–2005," *USDA's National Animal Health Monitoring System,* March 2007, www.aphis.usda.gov/animal_health/nahms/equine/downloads /equine05/Equine05_dr_PartII.pdf. Horse population today: the 2006 Global Horse Population report from the United Nations' Food and Agriculture Organization, as cited in "U.S. Has 9.5 Million Horses, Most in World, Report Says," *DVM360 Magazine,* the veterinary publication, October 1, 2007, http:// veterinarynews.dvm360.com/us-has-95-million-horses-most-world-report -says?rel=canonical; and "National Economic Impact of the U.S. Horse Industry," *American Horse Council,* www.horsecouncil.org/national-economic -impact-us-horse-industry.

Latest data on registrations, drivers, and miles driven: "Traffic Safety Facts 2012," *National Highway Traffic Safety Administration, U.S. Department of Transportation,* www-nrd.nhtsa.dot.gov/Pubs/812032.pdf.

Miles of roads in America: "Transportation FAQs," *American Road and Transportation Builders Association,* Washington, DC, from FHWA data (Highway Statistics 2012, Tables HM-20, HM-10, HM-12, HM-15), www.artba .org/about/transportation-faqs.

Data on fatalities, injuries, and economic costs: "Traffic Safety Facts 2012," *National Highway Traffic Safety Administration, U.S. Department of Transportation,* www-nrd.nhtsa.dot.gov/Pubs/812032.pdf.

Motor-vehicle fuel usage: "Table 4–9: Motor Vehicle Fuel Consumption and Travel," U.S. Bureau of Transportation Statistics, www.rita.dot.gov/bts/sites /rita.dot.gov.bts/files/publications/national_transportation_statistics/html/table _04_09.html.

The American Automobile Association, now known simply as AAA, had fewer than 1,500 members when it was founded in 1902; today, the organization claims 54 million members. No longer directly involved in racing or other motoring competitions, it offers its members roadside assistance, bail bonds, loans, credit cards, travel and trip-planning services, and more: http://news room.aaa.com/about-aaa/aaa-fact-sheet/.

Huss lost his job at Olds when Durant acquired the company in 1908 but then found employment as a purchasing agent at Huppmobile, founded by former Olds employee Robert C. Hupp. He was unemployed during some of the Great Depression. He ended his career at Ford's River Rouge plant in 1952, at the age of almost eighty. He died on August 14, 1964, in Detroit: he was ninety years old and left three children. The *Life* story was a recollection of the 1904 parade to St. Louis: Robert Wallace, "Meet Me (Pop!) in (Crash!) St. Louis, (Squawk!) Louis: The First Great Automobile Tour 50 Years Ago Was a Hilariously Haphazard Trek over Roads Coated with Mud, Dust and Chickens," *Life,* July 12, 1954, pp. 100–108.

# Bibliography

Abbott, James W., Dwight B. Huss, and Percy F. Megargel. *From Hellgate to Portland: The Story of the Race Across the American Continent in Oldsmobile Runabouts, Told by the Men Who Rode and the Man Who Looked On. Profusely Illustrated by Photographs Taken En Route.* Detroit: Olds Motor Works, 1905.

Ambrose, Stephen. *Undaunted Courage: Meriwether Lewis, Thomas Jefferson, and the Opening of the American West.* New York: Simon and Schuster, 1996.

Black, Edwin. *Internal Combustion: How Corporations and Governments Addicted the World to Oil and Derailed the Alternatives.* New York: St. Martin's, 2006.

Bliss, Carey S. *Autos Across America: A Bibliography of Transcontinental Auto Travel, 1903–1940.* Austin, TX: Jenkins and Reese, 1982.

Casey, Bob, and John and Horace Dodge. *Racing in America.* Dearborn, MI: The Henry Ford, 2011. Available at www.thehenryford.org/education/erb/RacinginAmerica.pdf.

Curcio, Vincent. *Chrysler: The Life and Times of an Automotive Genius.* New York: Oxford University Press, 2000.

Earley, Helen Jones, and James R. Walkinshaw. *Setting the Pace: Oldsmobile's First 100 Years.* Lansing, MI: Public Relations Department, Oldsmobile Division of General Motors Corporation, 1996.

Eckermann, Erik. *World History of the Automobile.* Warrendale, PA: Society of Automotive Engineers, 2001.

Fenster, Julie M. *Race of the Century: The Heroic True Story of the 1908 New York to Paris Auto Race.* New York: Crown, 2005.

Flink, James J. *America Adopts the Automobile, 1895–1910.* Cambridge: MIT Press, 1970.

Ford, Henry, in collaboration with Samuel Crowther. *My Life and Work.* New York: Doubleday, Page, 1922.

Fox, Elana V. *Inside the World's Fair of 1904: Exploring the Louisiana Purchase Expedition of 1904, Volumes One and Two.* Bloomington, IN: 1st Books, 2003.

Gardner, A. Dudley, and Verla R. Flores. *Forgotten Frontier: A History of Wyoming Coal Mining*. Boulder: Westview Press, 1989.

Georgano, G. N., ed. *The Complete Encyclopedia of Motorcars, 1885 to the Present*. New York: Dutton, 1968.

Goddard, Stephen B. *Colonel Albert Pope and his American Dream Machines: The Life and Times of a Bicycle Tycoon Turned Automotive Pioneer*. Jefferson, NC: McFarland, 2000.

Greenleaf, William. *Monopoly on Wheels: Henry Ford and the Selden Automobile Patent*. Detroit: Wayne State University Press, 1961.

Gustin, Lawrence R. *Billy Durant: Creator of General Motors*. Ann Arbor: University of Michigan Press, 1973.

Hammond II, John S. *From Sea to Sea in 1903 in a Curved Dash Oldsmobile: The Authentic Story of the Whitman-Hammond Horseless-Carriage Expedition from San Francisco to New York, Boston and Portland, Maine*. Egg Harbor City, NJ: Laureate Press, 1985.

Kimes, Beverly Rae. *Pioneers, Engineers and Scoundrels: The Dawn of the Automobile in America*. Warrendale, PA: SAE International, 2005.

Kirsch, David A. *The Electric Vehicle and the Burden of History*. Brunswick, NJ: Rutgers University Press, 2000.

Long, J. C. *Roy D. Chapin: The Man Behind the Hudson Motor Car Company*. Detroit: Wayne State University Press, 2004. Originally privately published in 1945 by J. C. Long.

Masters, John F. *1901–1905 Curved Dash Oldsmobile: A Service and Repair Manual*. East Wichita, KS: John F. Masters, 1999.

May, George S. *R.E. Olds: Auto Industry Pioneer*. Grand Rapids, MI: William B. Eerdmans, 1977.

McCarthy, Tom. *Auto Mania: Cars, Consumers, and the Environment*. New Haven: Yale University Press, 2007.

McConnell, Curt. *Coast-to-Coast Auto Races of the Early 1900s: Three Contests That Changed the World*. Warrendale, PA: Society of Automotive Engineers, 2000.

———. *Coast to Coast by Automobile: The Pioneering Trips, 1899–1908*. Stanford: Stanford University Press, 2000.

McManus, Theodore F., and Normal Beasley. *Men, Money and Motors: The Drama of the Automobile*. New York: Harper and Brothers, 1929.

McShane, Clay. *Down the Asphalt Path: The Automobile and the American City*. New York: Columbia University Press, 1994.

Megargel, Percy F., and Grace Sartwell Mason. *The Car and the Lady*. New York: Baker and Taylor, 1908.

Nevins, Allan. *Ford: The Times, the Man and the Company*. New York: Scribner's, 1954.

———, and Frank Ernest Hill. *Ford: Decline and Rebirth, 1933–1962*. New York: Scribner's, 1962.

Nolan, William F. *Barney Oldfield: The Life and Times of America's Legendary Speed King.* New York: Putnam's, 1961.

Nye, Peter Joffre, with Jeff Groman and Mark Tyson. *The Six-Day Bicycle Races: America's Jazz-Age Sport.* San Francisco: Van der Plas Publications/Cycle Publishing, 2006.

Pope, Colonel Albert A. *The Movement for Better Roads: An Open Letter to the People of the United States.* Boston: Pope Manufacturing, 1892.

Potter, Isaac B. *The Gospel of Good Roads: A Letter to the American Farmer.* New York: League of American Wheelmen, 1891.

Scharchburg, Richard P. *Carriages Without Horses: J. Frank Duryea and the Birth of the American Automobile Industry.* Warrendale, PA: Society of Automotive Engineers, 1993.

Shedlen, Michael. *Mark Twain: Man in White, the Grand Adventure of His Final Years.* New York: Random House, 2010.

Simonds, William A. *Henry Ford: Motor Genius.* New York: Doubleday, 1929.

Smith, Fredric L. *Motoring Down a Quarter of a Century.* Detroit: Detroit Saturday Night, 1928.

Stern, Jane, and Michael Stern. *Auto Ads.* New York: Random House, 1978.

Yarnell, Duane. *Auto Pioneering: A Remarkable Story of Ransom E. Olds, Father of Oldsmobile and Reo.* Lansing, MI: Franklin DeKleine Company, 1949.

# Index

G. Wayne Miller is a staff writer at the  *Providence Journal*; a documentary film-maker; and the author of eight books of nonfiction, four novels, and three short-story collections. He has been honored for his work many times, including with the 2013 Roger Williams Independent Voice Award from the Rhode Island International Film Festival and the 2015 Bell of Hope: Mental Health Hero award from the Mental Health Association of Rhode Island, and he was a member of the *Providence Journal* team that was a finalist for the 2004 Pulitzer Prize in Public Service. Three documentaries he wrote and coproduced have been broadcast on PBS: *On The Lake,* about the tuberculosis epidemic in America in the early 1900s and globally today; *Behind the Hedgerow,* about Newport, Rhode Island, high society; and *The Providence Journal's Coming Home,* about veterans of the wars in Iraq and Afghanistan. *Coming Home* was nominated in 2012 for a New England Emmy and won a regional Edward R. Murrow Award. Miller is a visiting fellow at Salve Regina University's Pell Center for International Relations and Public Policy in Newport, Rhode Island, where he is co-founder and director of the Story in the Public Square program, www.publicstory.org, and former chairman of the board of trustees and now trustee emeritus of the Jesse M. Smith Memorial Library in Harrisville, Rhode Island. With his wife, Yolanda Gabrielle, he enjoys travel and time by the ocean. Visit him at www.gwaynemiller.com.

PublicAffairs is a publishing house founded in 1997. It is a tribute to the standards, values, and flair of three persons who have served as mentors to countless reporters, writers, editors, and book people of all kinds, including me.

I. F. STONE, proprietor of *I. F. Stone's Weekly*, combined a commitment to the First Amendment with entrepreneurial zeal and reporting skill and became one of the great independent journalists in American history. At the age of eighty, Izzy published *The Trial of Socrates*, which was a national bestseller. He wrote the book after he taught himself ancient Greek.

BENJAMIN C. BRADLEE was for nearly thirty years the charismatic editorial leader of *The Washington Post*. It was Ben who gave the *Post* the range and courage to pursue such historic issues as Watergate. He supported his reporters with a tenacity that made them fearless and it is no accident that so many became authors of influential, best-selling books.

ROBERT L. BERNSTEIN, the chief executive of Random House for more than a quarter century, guided one of the nation's premier publishing houses. Bob was personally responsible for many books of political dissent and argument that challenged tyranny around the globe. He is also the founder and longtime chair of Human Rights Watch, one of the most respected human rights organizations in the world.

•　　•　　•

For fifty years, the banner of Public Affairs Press was carried by its owner Morris B. Schnapper, who published Gandhi, Nasser, Toynbee, Truman, and about 1,500 other authors. In 1983, Schnapper was described by *The Washington Post* as "a redoubtable gadfly." His legacy will endure in the books to come.

Peter Osnos, *Founder and Editor-at-Large*